Sand Chronicles

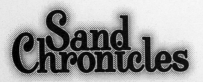

Shojo Beat

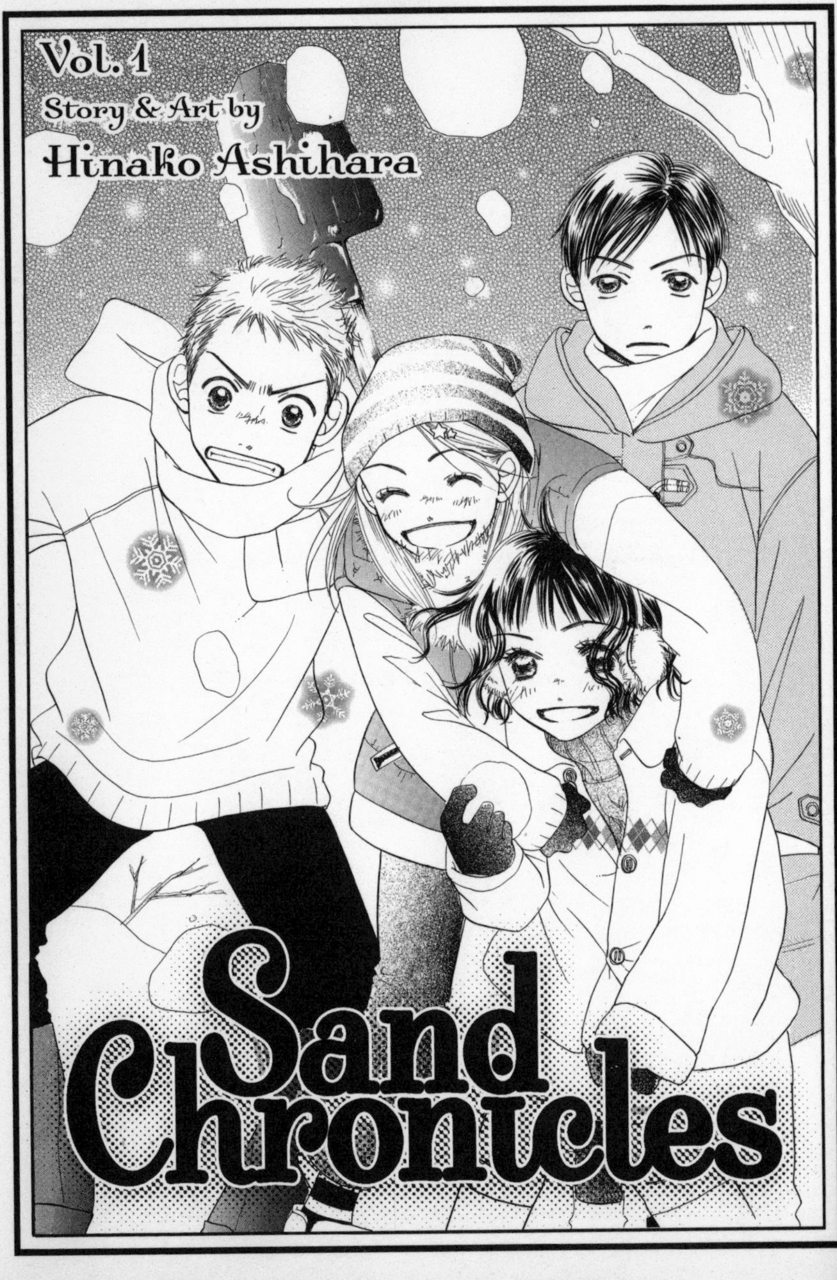
Vol. 1
Story & Art by
Hinako Ashihara
Sand Chronicles

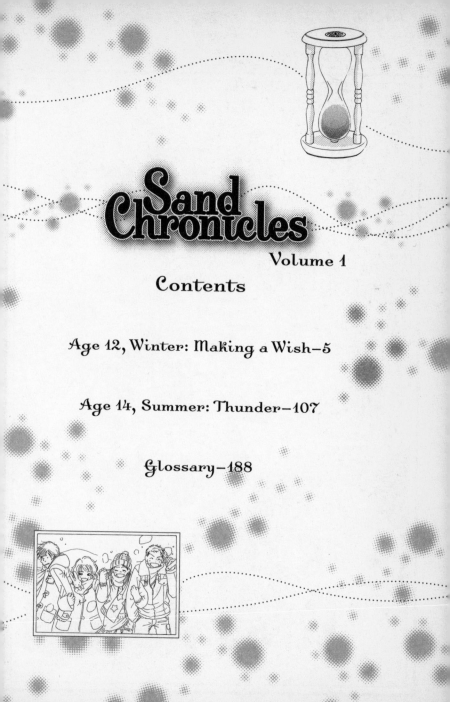

Sand Chronicles

Volume 1

Contents

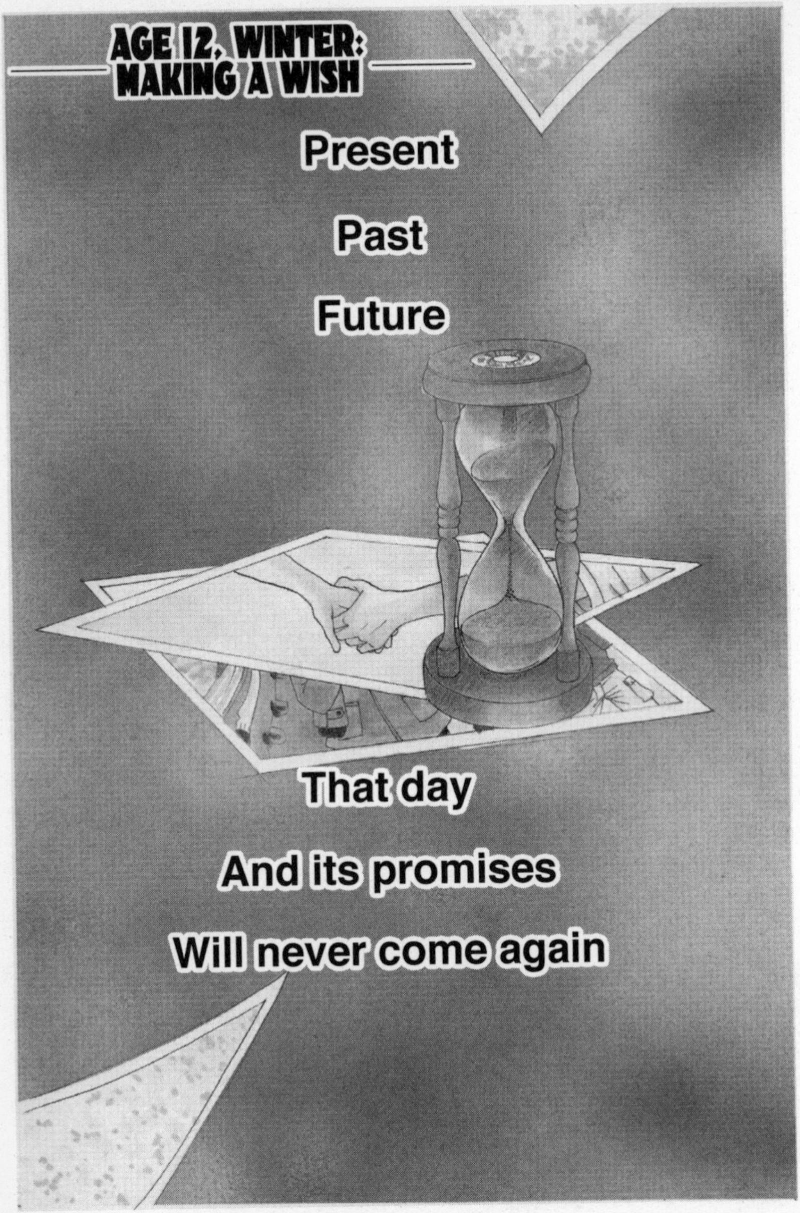
AGE 12, WINTER:
MAKING A WISH
Present
Past
Future
That day
And its promises
Will never come again

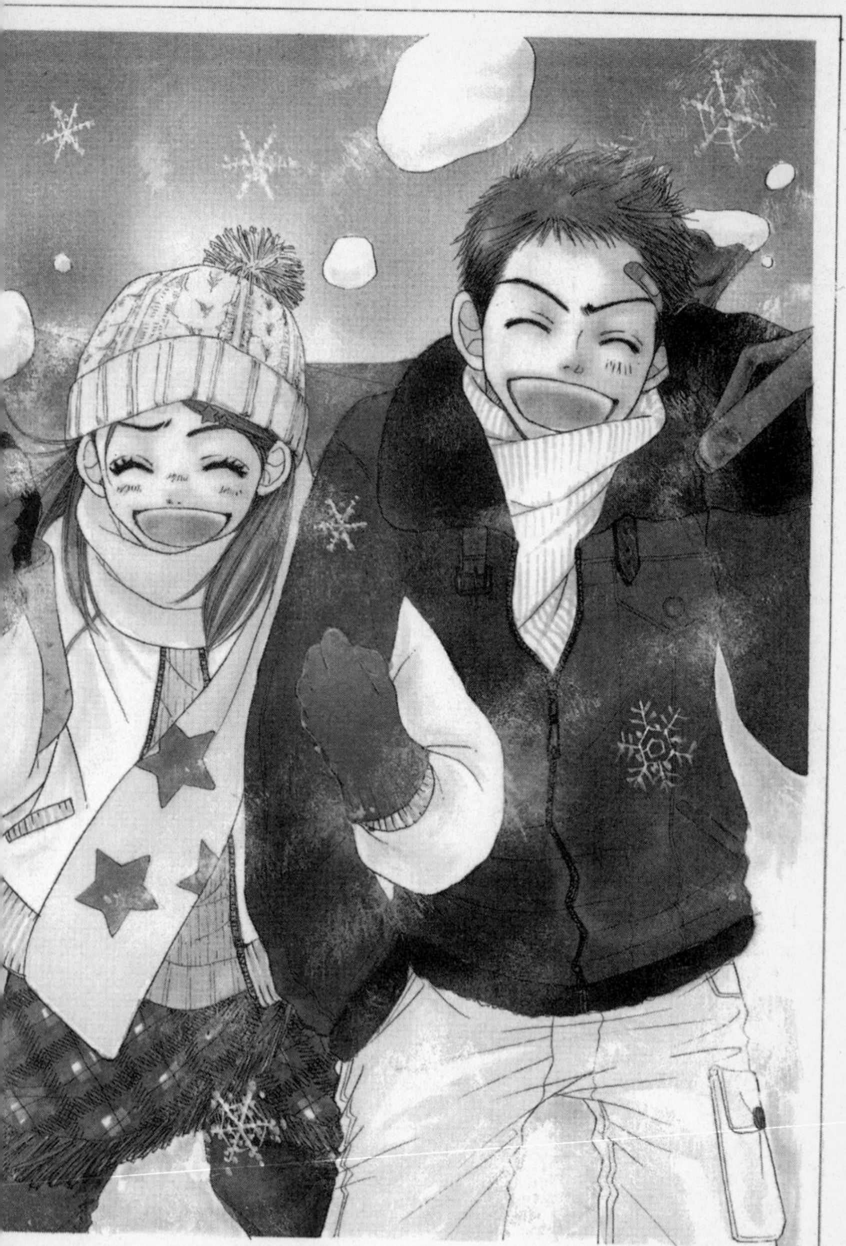

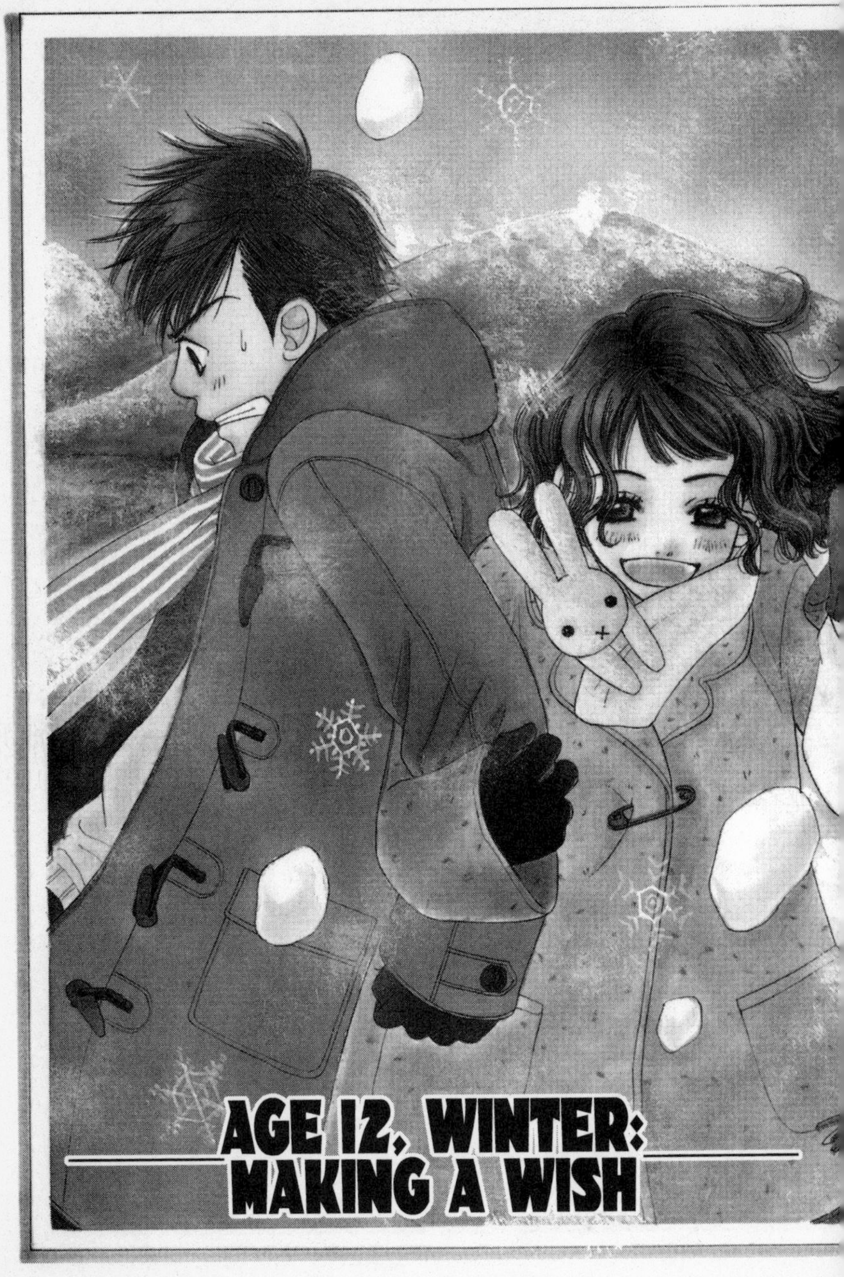
AGE 12, WINTER:
MAKING A WISH

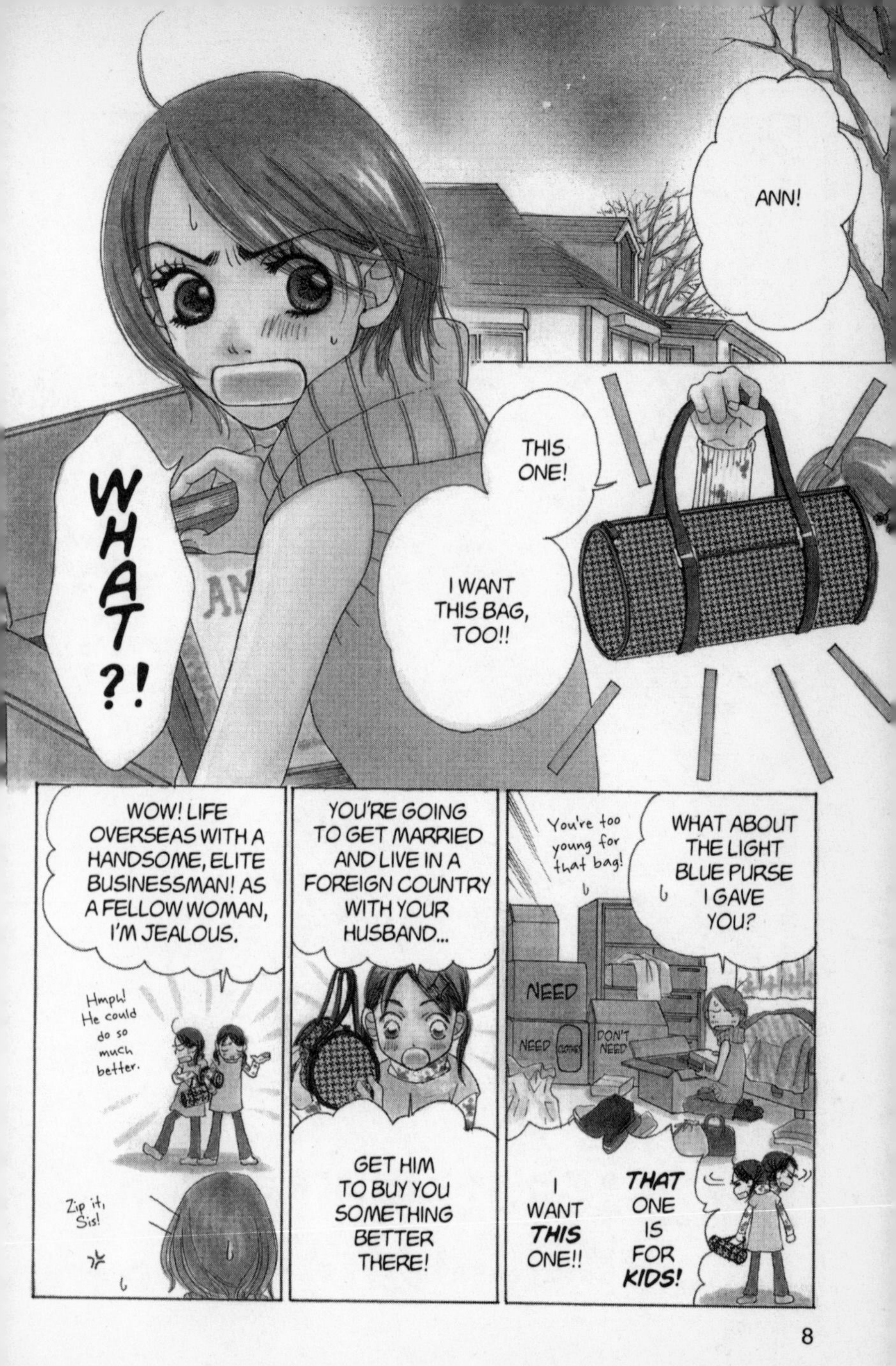
ANN!
THIS ONE!
I WANT THIS BAG, TOO!!
WHAT?!
WHAT ABOUT THE LIGHT BLUE PURSE I GAVE YOU?
You're too young for that bag!
NEED
NEED
CLOTHES
DON'T NEED
THAT ONE IS FOR KIDS!
I WANT THIS ONE!!
YOU'RE GOING TO GET MARRIED AND LIVE IN A FOREIGN COUNTRY WITH YOUR HUSBAND...
GET HIM TO BUY YOU SOMETHING BETTER THERE!
WOW! LIFE OVERSEAS WITH A HANDSOME, ELITE BUSINESSMAN! AS A FELLOW WOMAN, I'M JEALOUS.
Hmph! He could do so much better.
Zip it, Sis!

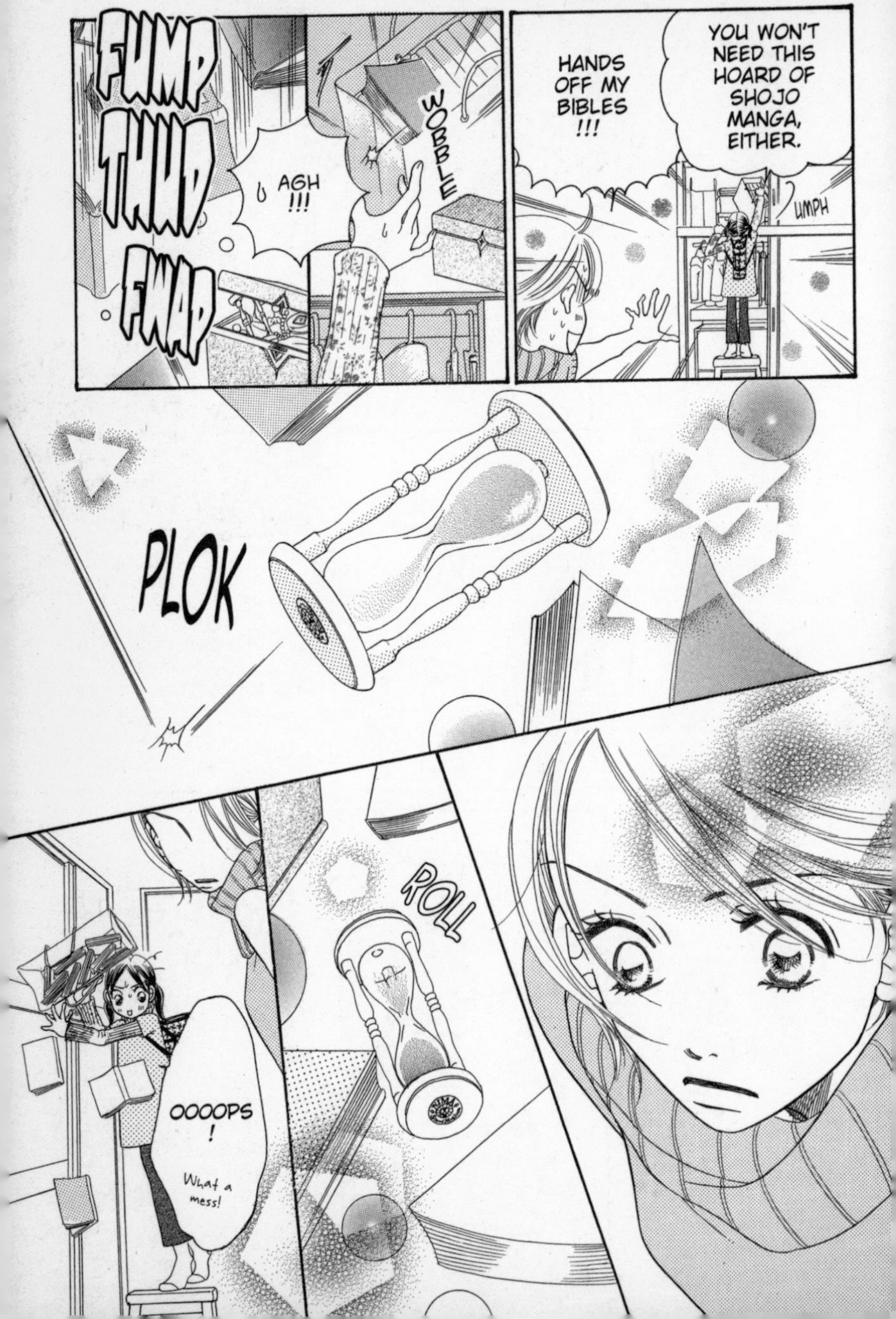
YOU WON'T NEED THIS HOARD OF SHOJO MANGA, EITHER.
HANDS OFF MY BIBLES !!!
UMPH
WOBBLE
AGH !!!
FUMP
THUD
FWAP
PLOK
ROLL
OOOOPS !
What a mess!

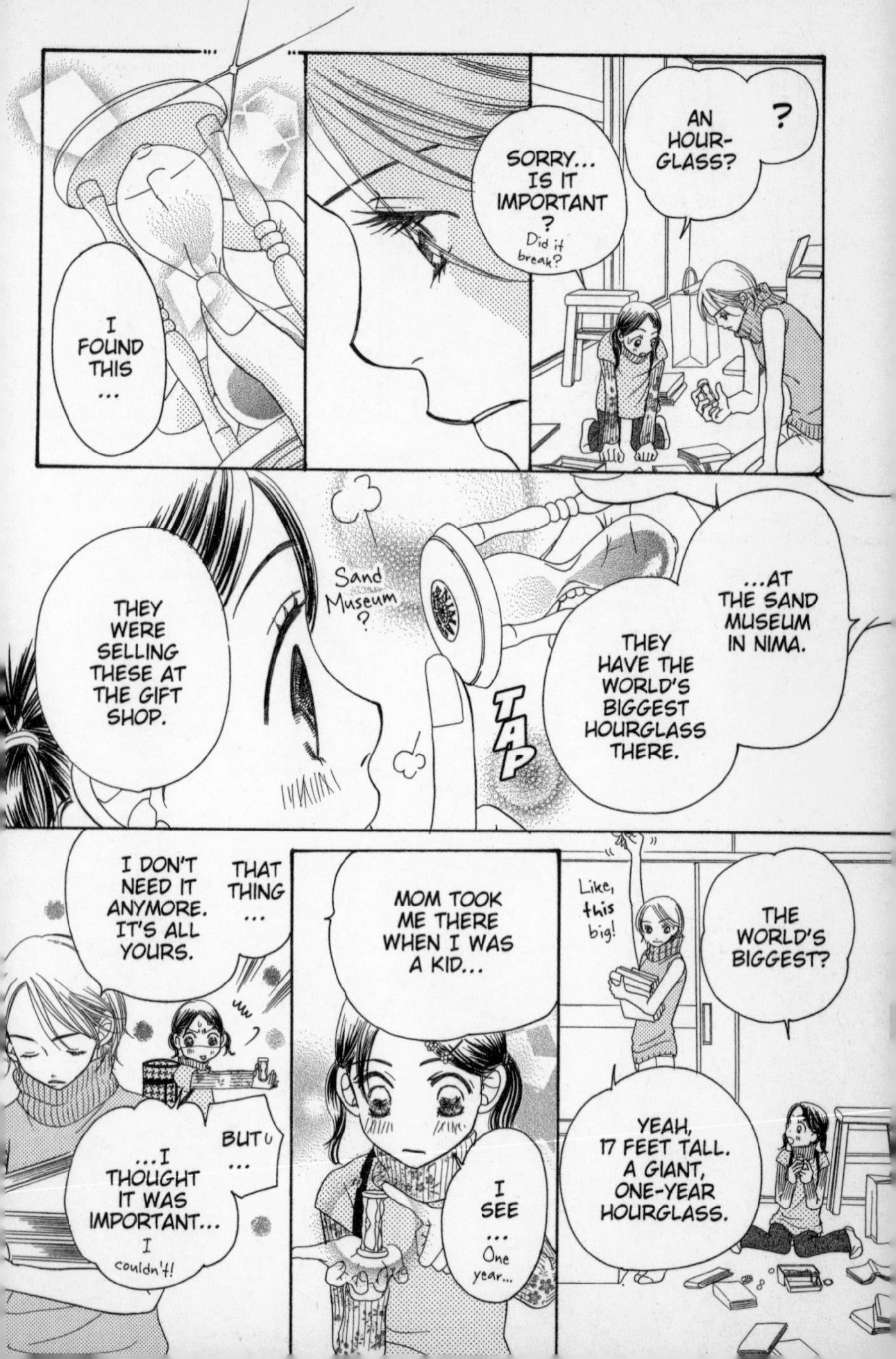
?
AN HOUR-GLASS?
SORRY... IS IT IMPORTANT?
Did it break?
I FOUND THIS ...
...AT THE SAND MUSEUM IN NIMA.
THEY HAVE THE WORLD'S BIGGEST HOURGLASS THERE.
TAP
Sand Museum?
THEY WERE SELLING THESE AT THE GIFT SHOP.
THE WORLD'S BIGGEST?
Like, this big!
YEAH, 17 FEET TALL. A GIANT, ONE-YEAR HOURGLASS.
MOM TOOK ME THERE WHEN I WAS A KID...
I SEE...
One year...
THAT THING...
I DON'T NEED IT ANYMORE. IT'S ALL YOURS.
BUT...
...I THOUGHT IT WAS IMPORTANT...
I couldn't!

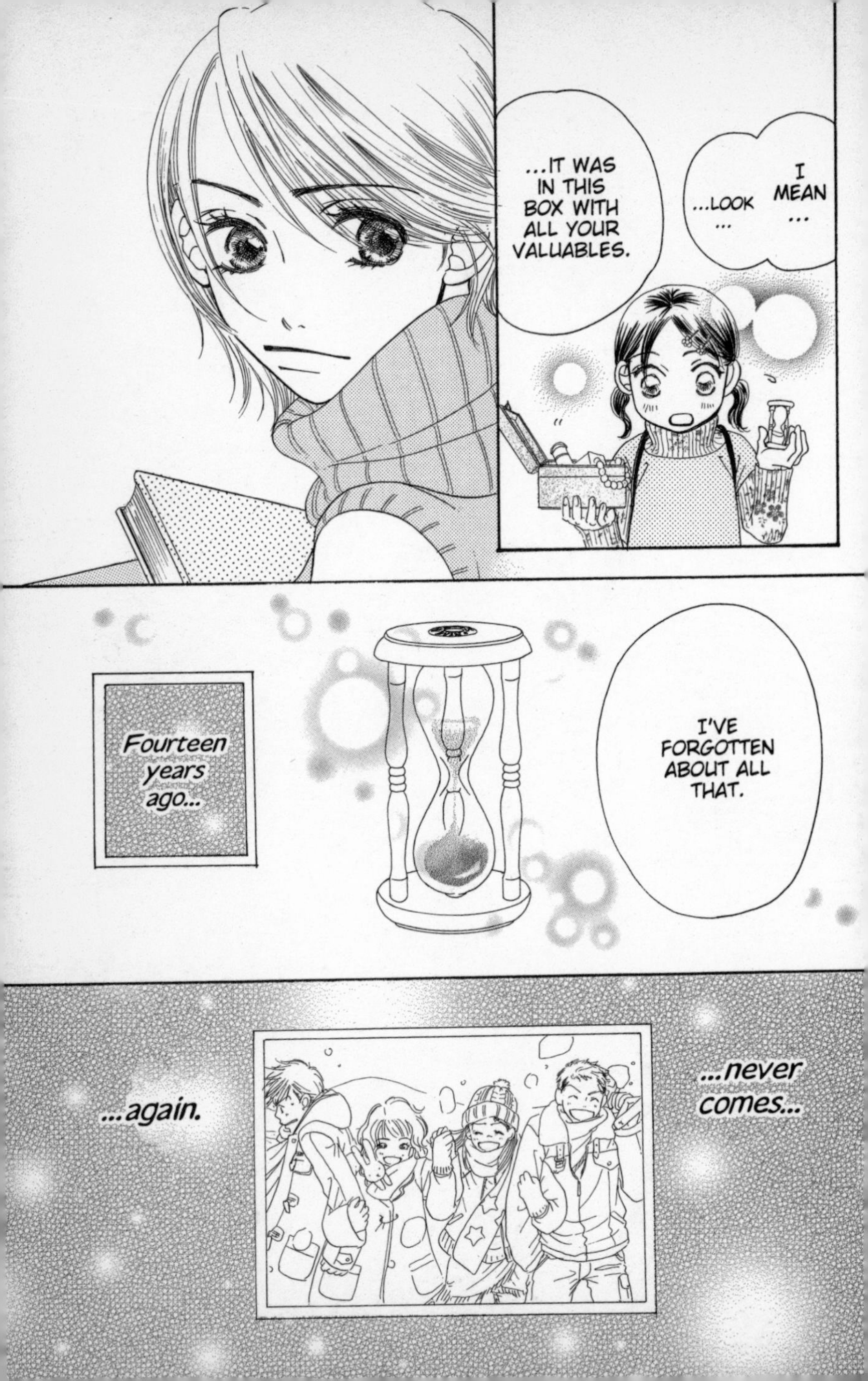
I MEAN ...
...LOOK ...
...IT WAS IN THIS BOX WITH ALL YOUR VALUABLES.
I'VE FORGOTTEN ABOUT ALL THAT.
Fourteen years ago...
...never comes...
...again.

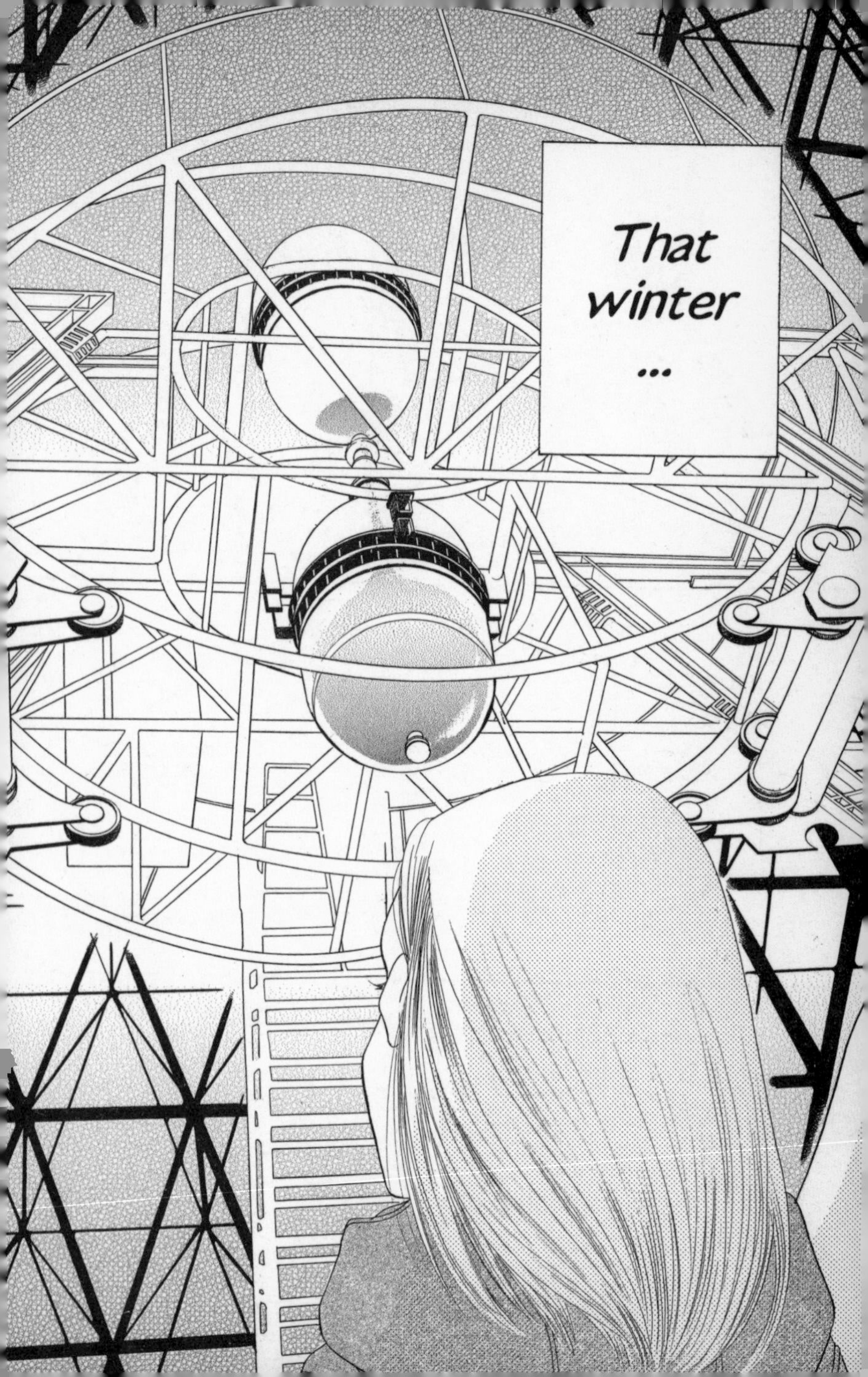
That winter ...

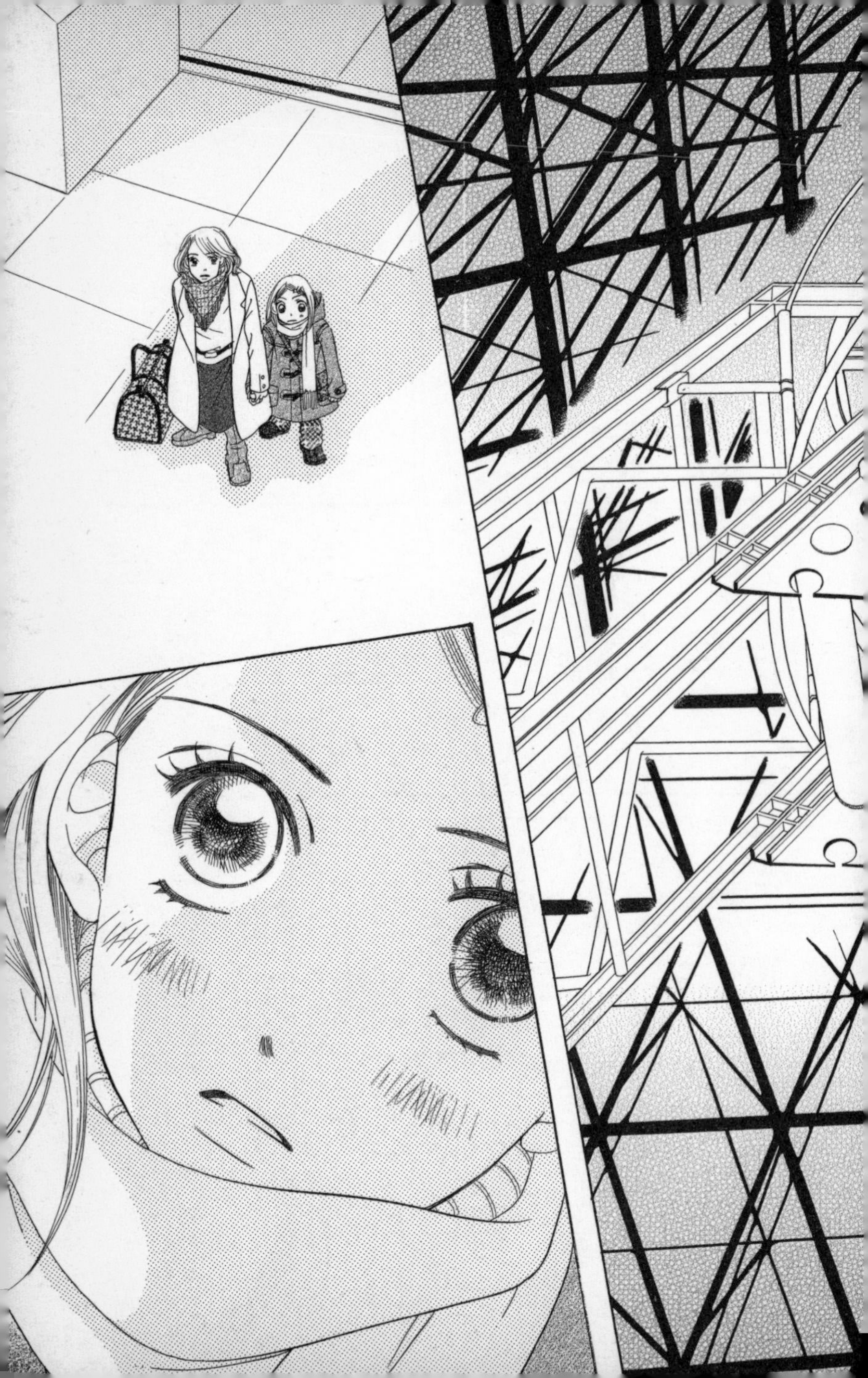

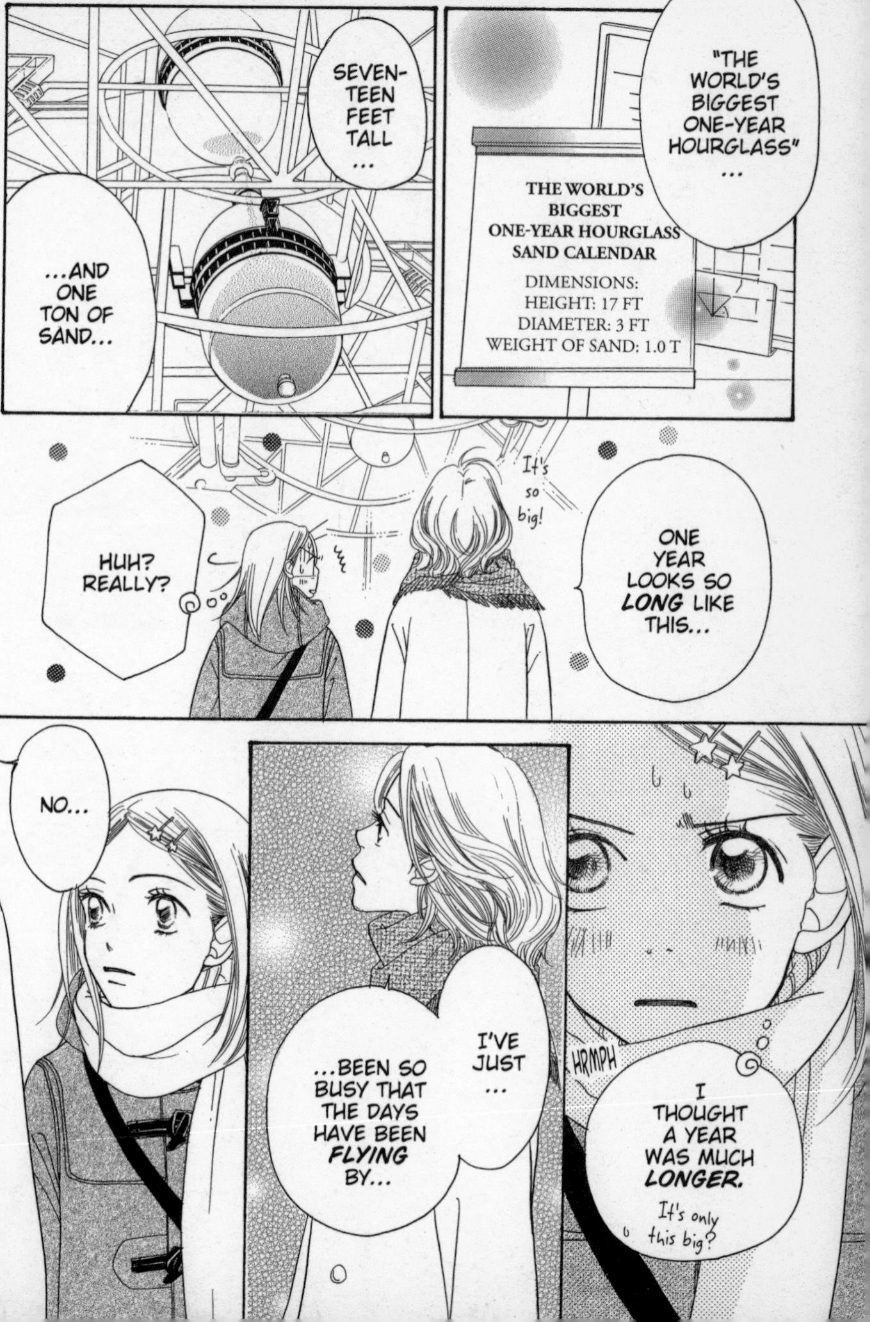
"THE WORLD'S BIGGEST ONE-YEAR HOURGLASS" ...
THE WORLD'S BIGGEST ONE-YEAR HOURGLASS SAND CALENDAR
DIMENSIONS: HEIGHT: 17 FT DIAMETER: 3 FT WEIGHT OF SAND: 1.0 T
SEVEN-TEEN FEET TALL ...
...AND ONE TON OF SAND...
It's so big!
ONE YEAR LOOKS SO LONG LIKE THIS...
HUH? REALLY?
HRMPH
I THOUGHT A YEAR WAS MUCH LONGER.
It's only this big?
I'VE JUST ...
...BEEN SO BUSY THAT THE DAYS HAVE BEEN FLYING BY...
NO...

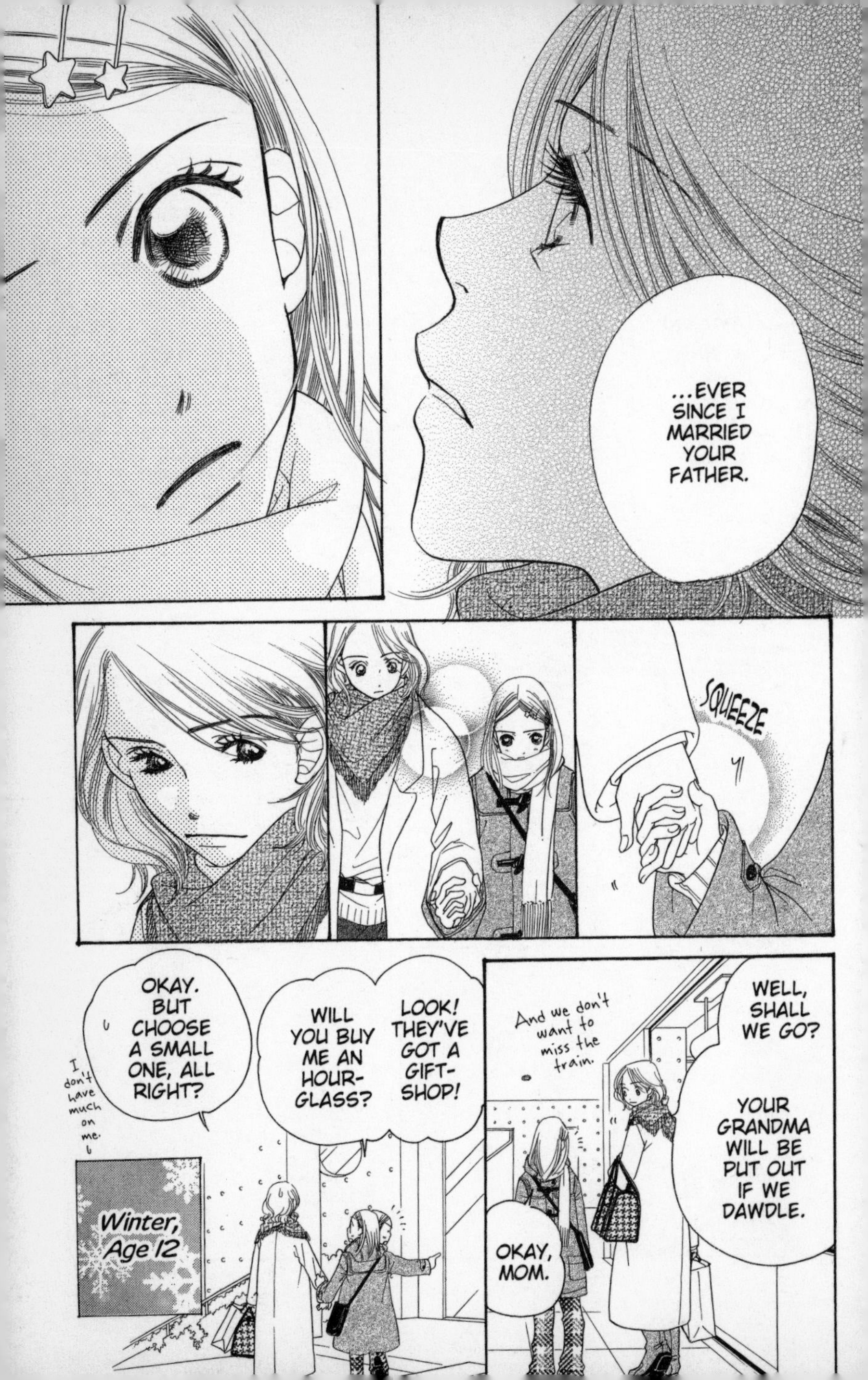
...EVER SINCE I MARRIED YOUR FATHER.
SQUEEZE
WELL, SHALL WE GO?
YOUR GRANDMA WILL BE PUT OUT IF WE DAWDLE.
And we don't want to miss the train.
OKAY, MOM.
LOOK! THEY'VE GOT A GIFT-SHOP!
WILL YOU BUY ME AN HOUR-GLASS?
OKAY. BUT CHOOSE A SMALL ONE, ALL RIGHT?
I don't have much on me.
Winter, Age 12

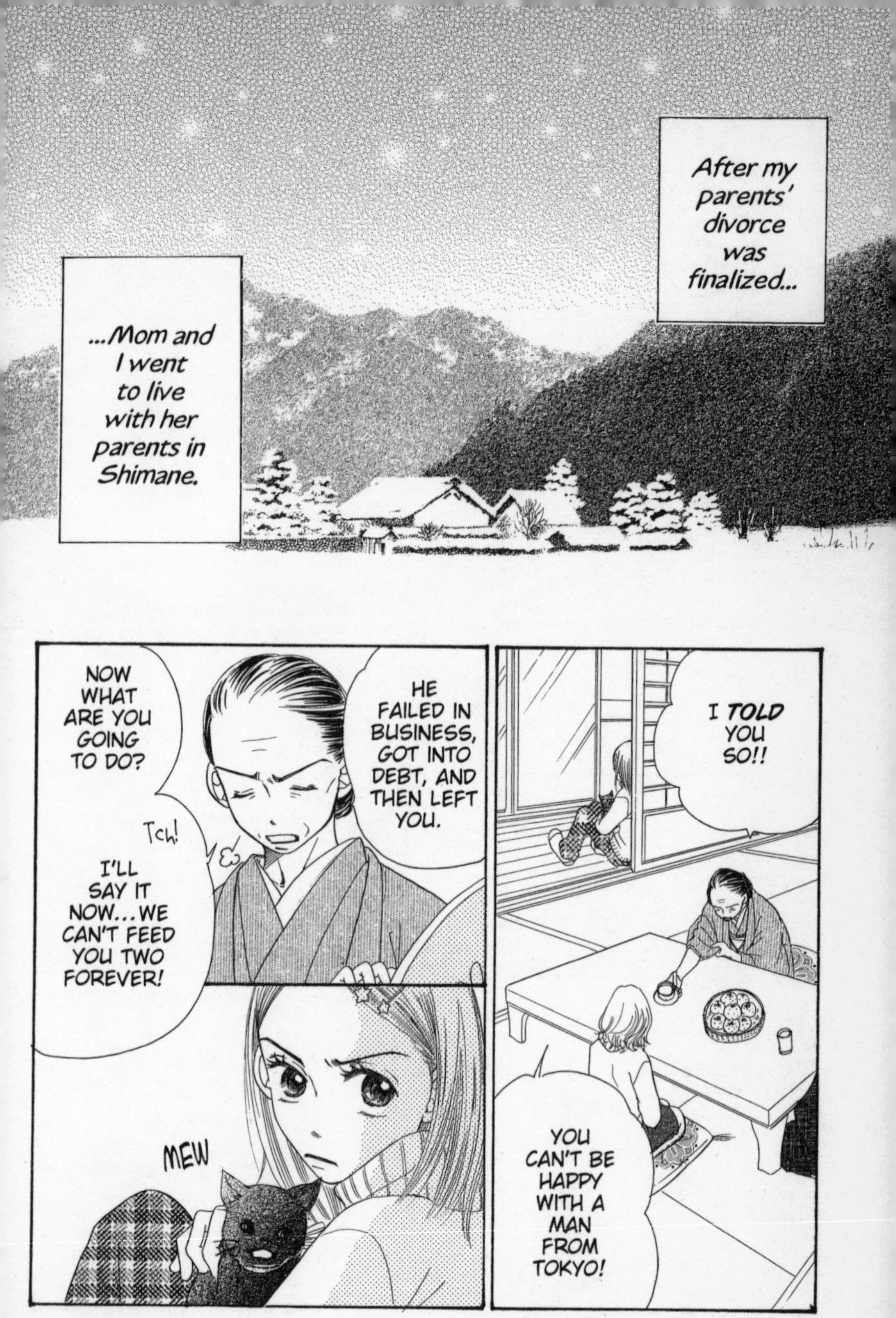
After my parents' divorce was finalized...
...Mom and I went to live with her parents in Shimane.
I *TOLD* YOU SO!!
YOU CAN'T BE HAPPY WITH A MAN FROM TOKYO!
HE FAILED IN BUSINESS, GOT INTO DEBT, AND THEN LEFT YOU.
NOW WHAT ARE YOU GOING TO DO?
Tch!
I'LL SAY IT NOW...WE CAN'T FEED YOU TWO FOREVER!
MEW

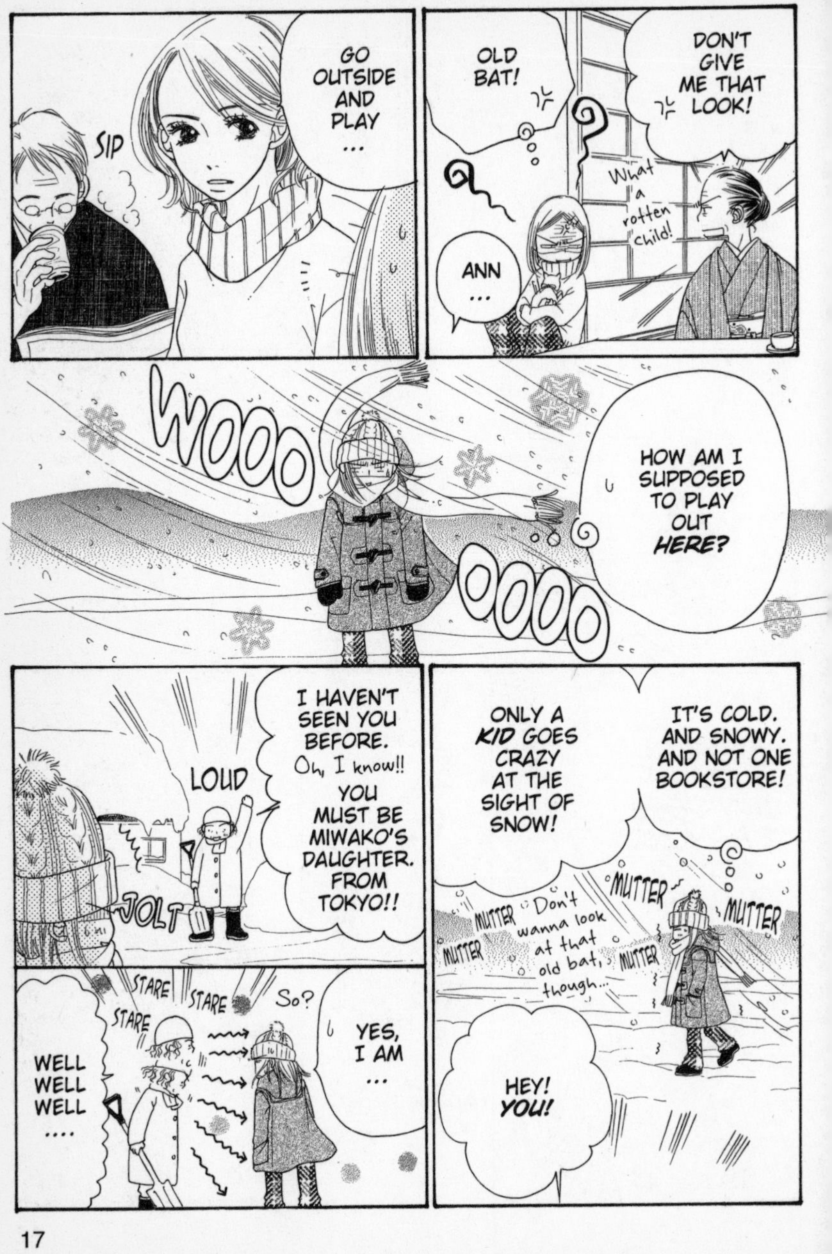
DON'T GIVE ME THAT LOOK!
OLD BAT!
What a rotten child!
ANN ...
GO OUTSIDE AND PLAY ...
SIP
HOW AM I SUPPOSED TO PLAY OUT HERE?
WOOO
OOOO
IT'S COLD. AND SNOWY. AND NOT ONE BOOKSTORE!
ONLY A KID GOES CRAZY AT THE SIGHT OF SNOW!
MUTTER
MUTTER
Don't wanna look at that old bat, though...
MUTTER
MUTTER
MUTTER
HEY! YOU!
I HAVEN'T SEEN YOU BEFORE. Oh, I know!! YOU MUST BE MIWAKO'S DAUGHTER. FROM TOKYO!!
LOUD
JOLT
YES, I AM ...
So?
STARE
STARE
STARE
WELL WELL WELL ....

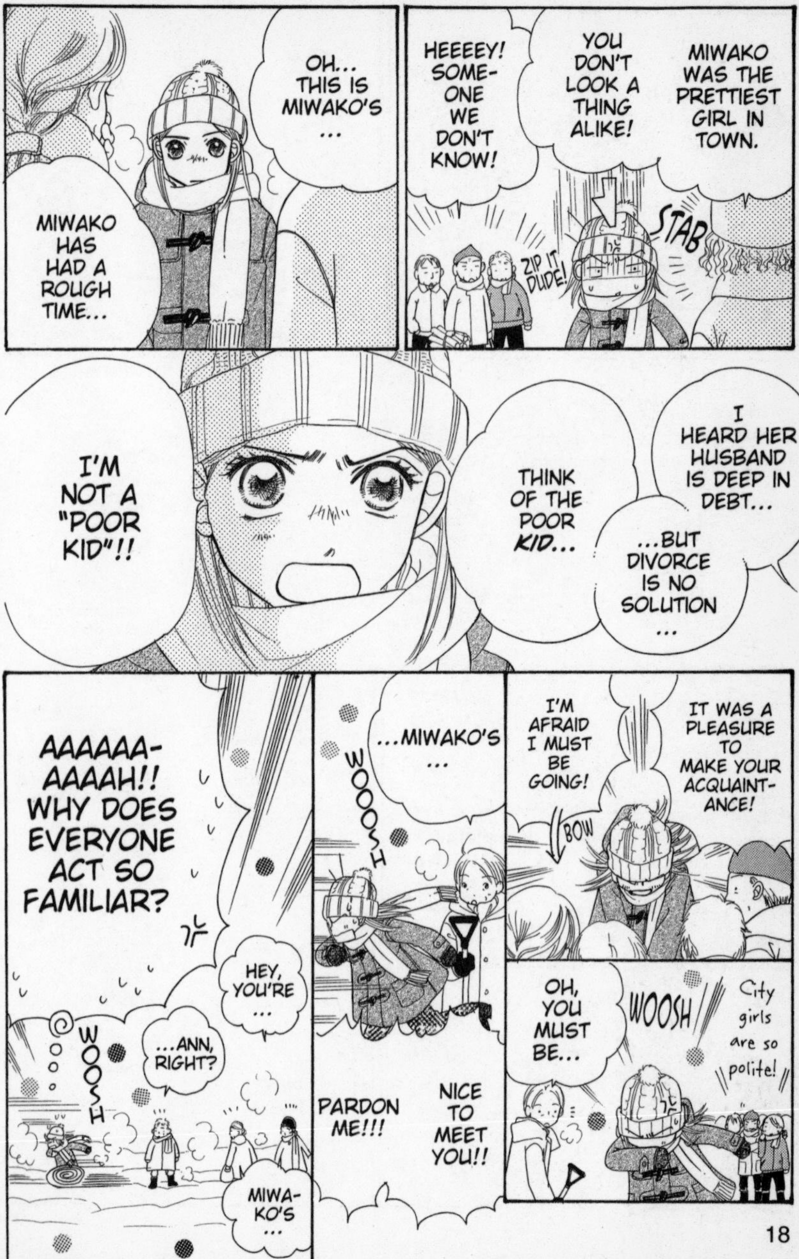
MIWAKO WAS THE PRETTIEST GIRL IN TOWN.
YOU DON'T LOOK A THING ALIKE!
HEEEEY! SOME-ONE WE DON'T KNOW!
STAB
ZIP IT DUDE!
OH... THIS IS MIWAKO'S ...
MIWAKO HAS HAD A ROUGH TIME...
I HEARD HER HUSBAND IS DEEP IN DEBT...
...BUT DIVORCE IS NO SOLUTION ...
THINK OF THE POOR KID...
I'M NOT A "POOR KID"!!
IT WAS A PLEASURE TO MAKE YOUR ACQUAINT-ANCE!
I'M AFRAID I MUST BE GOING!
BOW
City girls are so polite!
WOOSH
OH, YOU MUST BE...
...MIWAKO'S ...
WOOOSH
NICE TO MEET YOU!!
PARDON ME!!!
AAAAAA-AAAAH!! WHY DOES EVERYONE ACT SO FAMILIAR?
HEY, YOU'RE ...
...ANN, RIGHT?
WOOSH
MIWA-KO'S ...

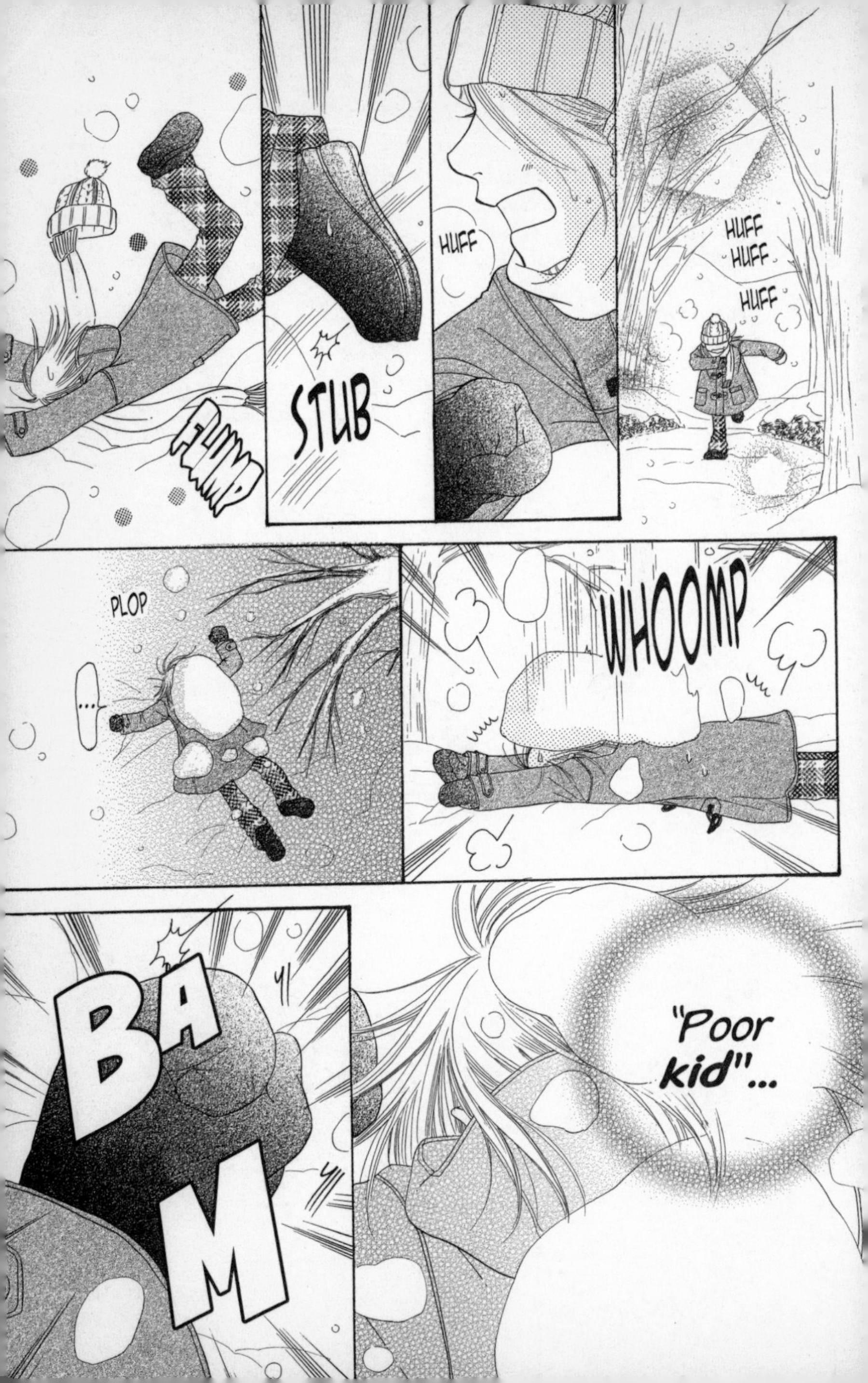
HUFF
HUFF
HUFF
HUFF
STUB
FLUMP
WHOOMP
PLOP
...
"Poor kid"...
BAM

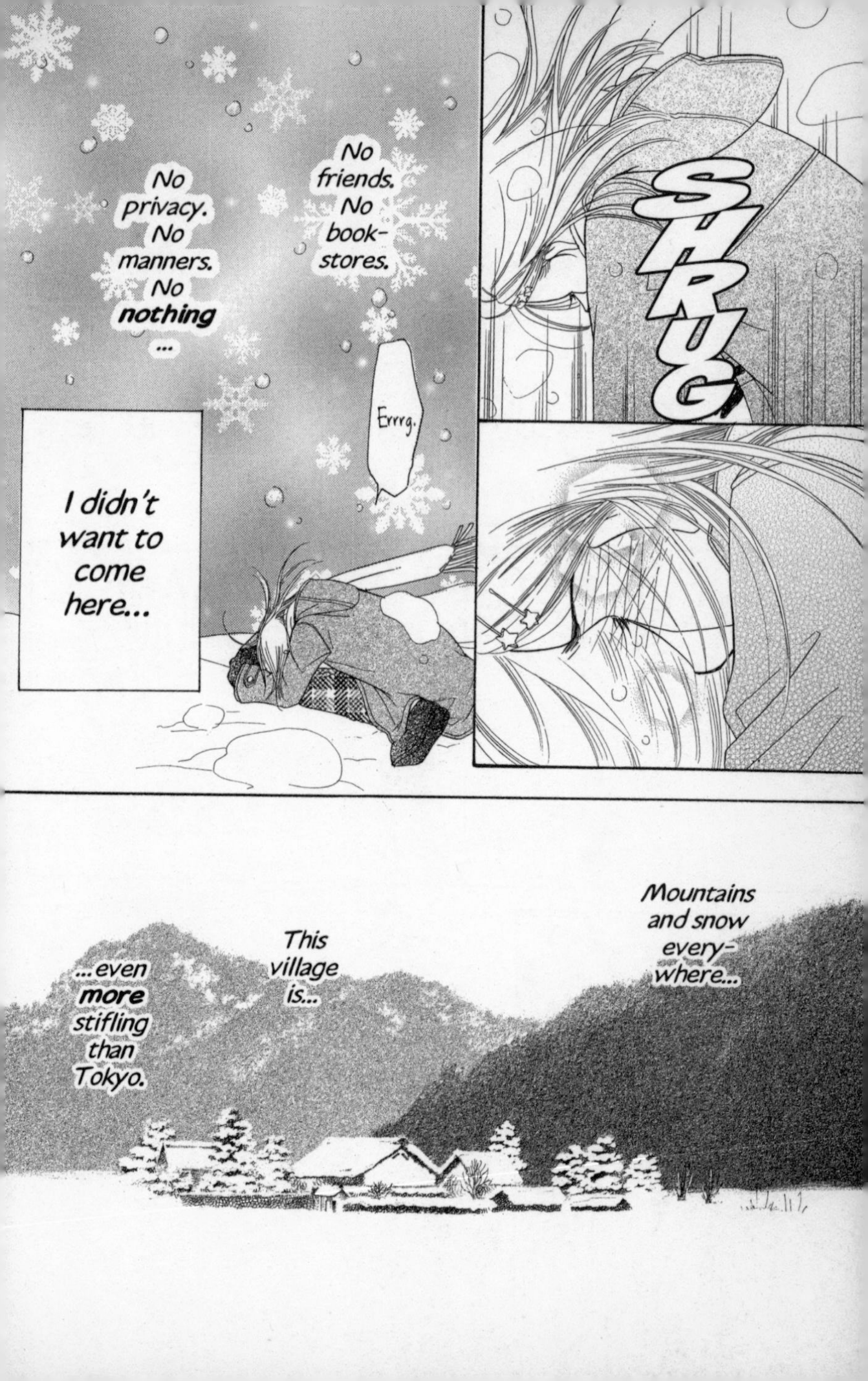
SHRUG
No friends. No book-stores.
No privacy. No manners. No **nothing** ...
Errrg.
I didn't want to come here...
Mountains and snow every-where...
This village is...
...even **more** stifling than Tokyo.

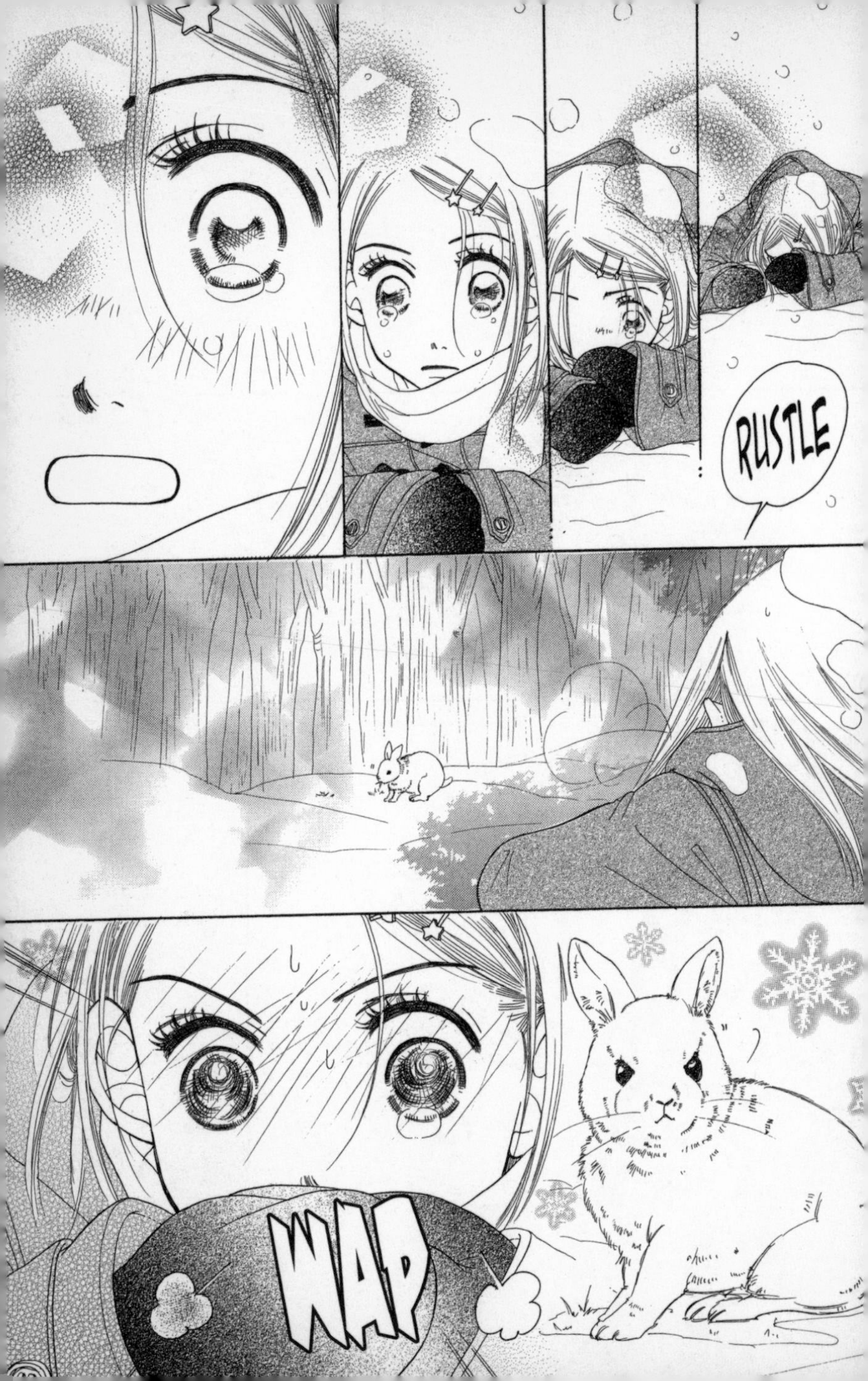
RUSTLE
WAP

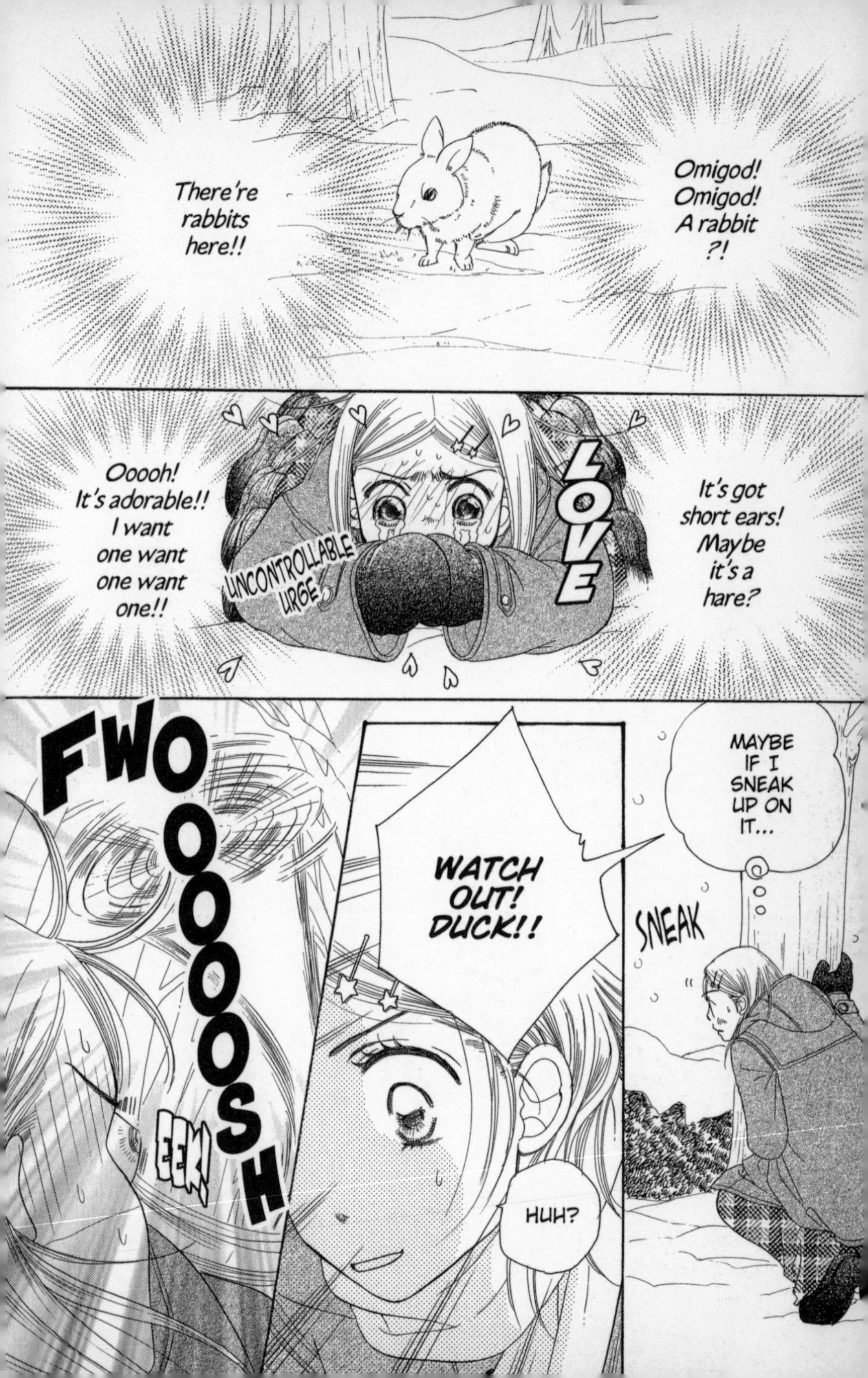
Omigod! Omigod! A rabbit ?!
There're rabbits here!!
It's got short ears! Maybe it's a hare?
LOVE
UNCONTROLLABLE URGE
Ooooh! It's adorable!! I want one want one want one!!
MAYBE IF I SNEAK UP ON IT...
SNEAK
WATCH OUT! DUCK!!
HUH?
FWOOOOOSH
EEK!

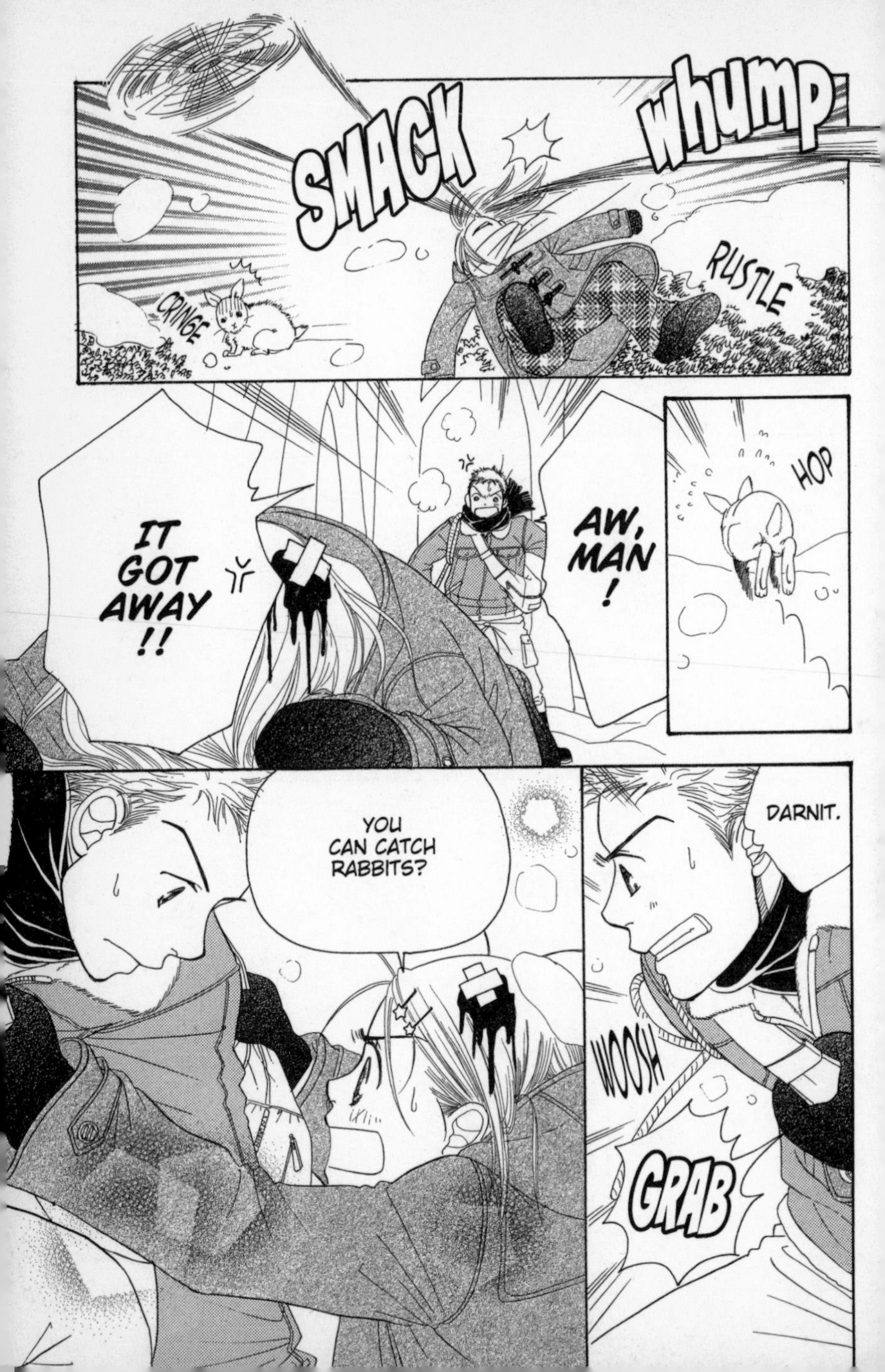
whump
SMACK
RUSTLE
CRINGE
HOP
AW, MAN!
IT GOT AWAY!!
DARNIT.
WOOSH
GRAB
YOU CAN CATCH RABBITS?

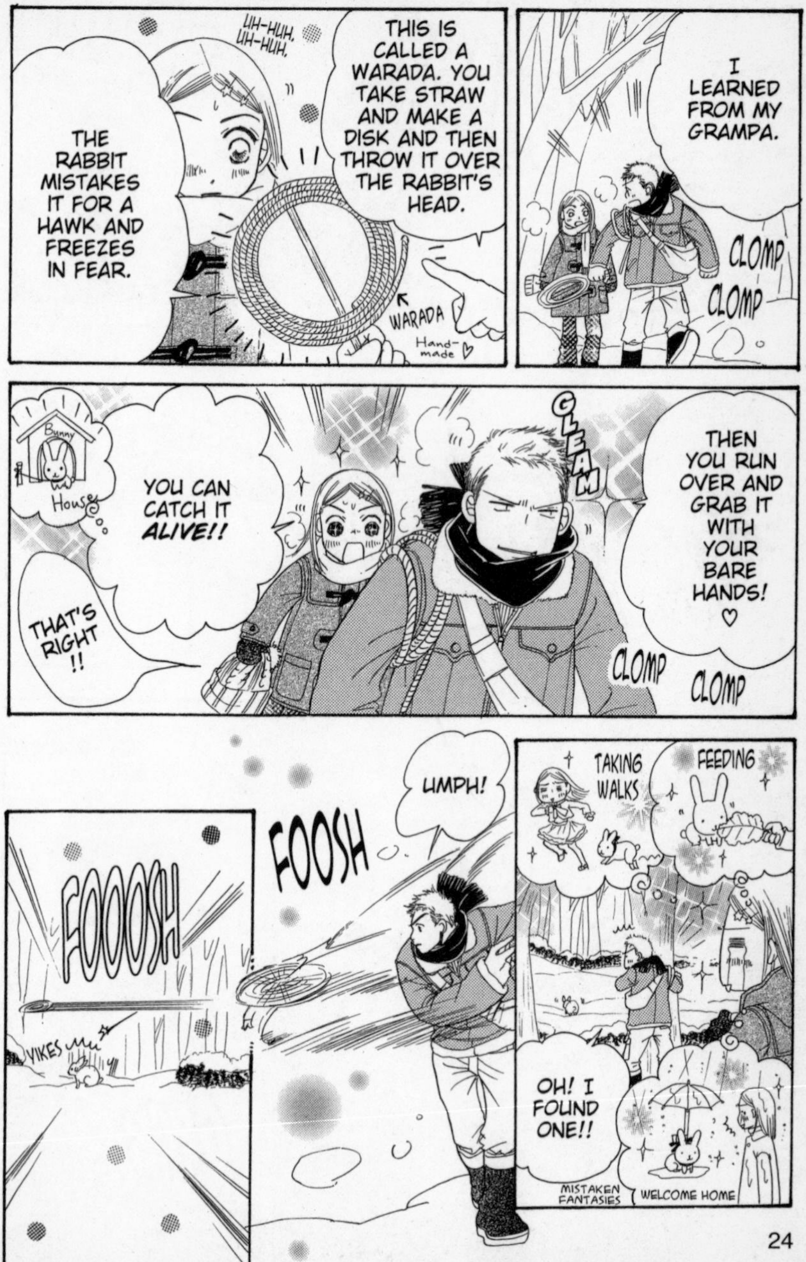
I LEARNED FROM MY GRAMPA.
CLOMP
CLOMP
THIS IS CALLED A WARADA. YOU TAKE STRAW AND MAKE A DISK AND THEN THROW IT OVER THE RABBIT'S HEAD.
UH-HUH, UH-HUH.
THE RABBIT MISTAKES IT FOR A HAWK AND FREEZES IN FEAR.
WARADA
Hand-made ♡
THEN YOU RUN OVER AND GRAB IT WITH YOUR BARE HANDS! ♡
CLOMP
CLOMP
GLEAM
YOU CAN CATCH IT ALIVE!!
Bunny
House
THAT'S RIGHT!!
FEEDING
TAKING WALKS
OH! I FOUND ONE!!
WELCOME HOME
MISTAKEN FANTASIES
UMPH!
FOOSH
FOOOSH
YIKES

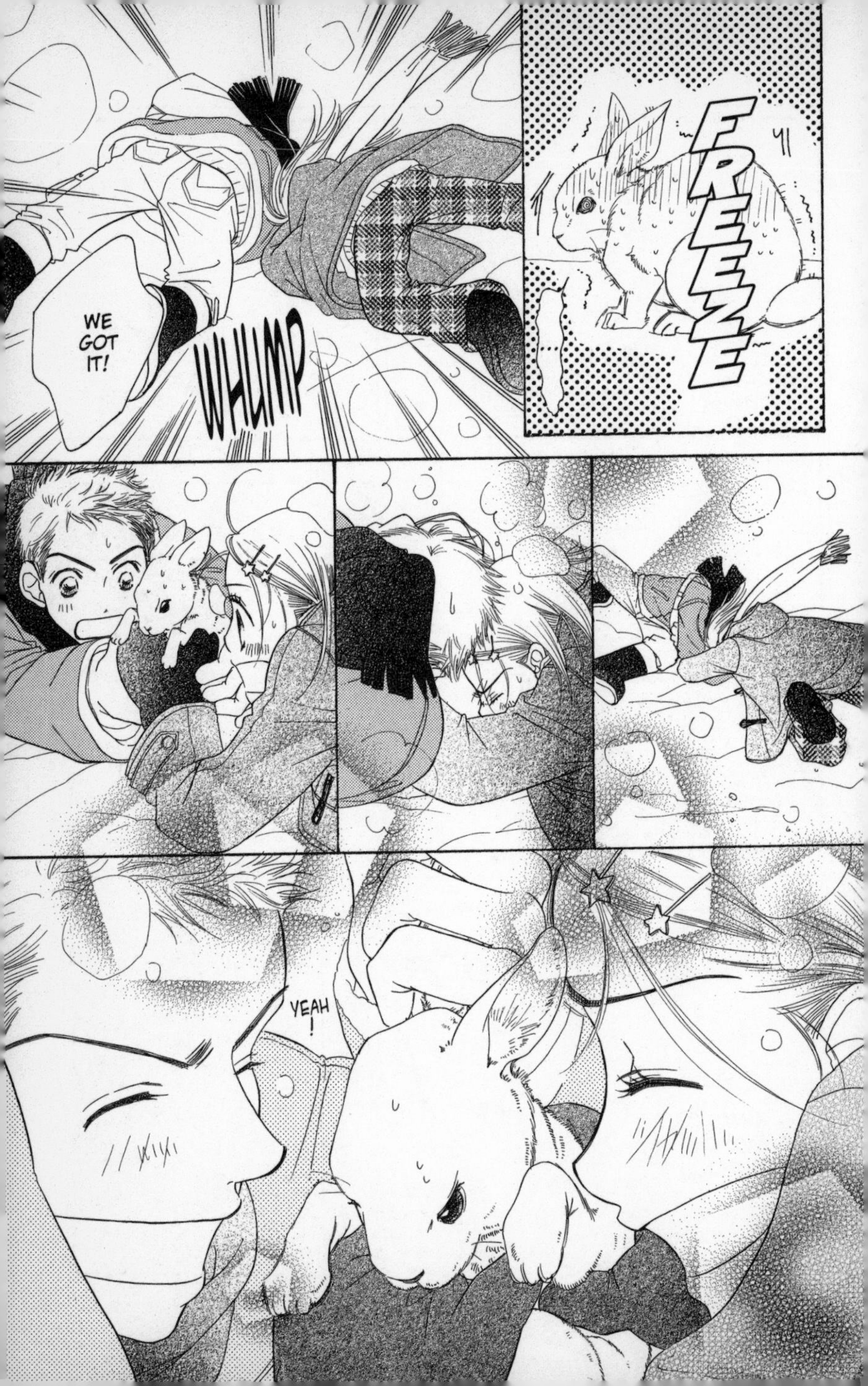
FREEZE
WE GOT IT!
WHUMP
YEAH!

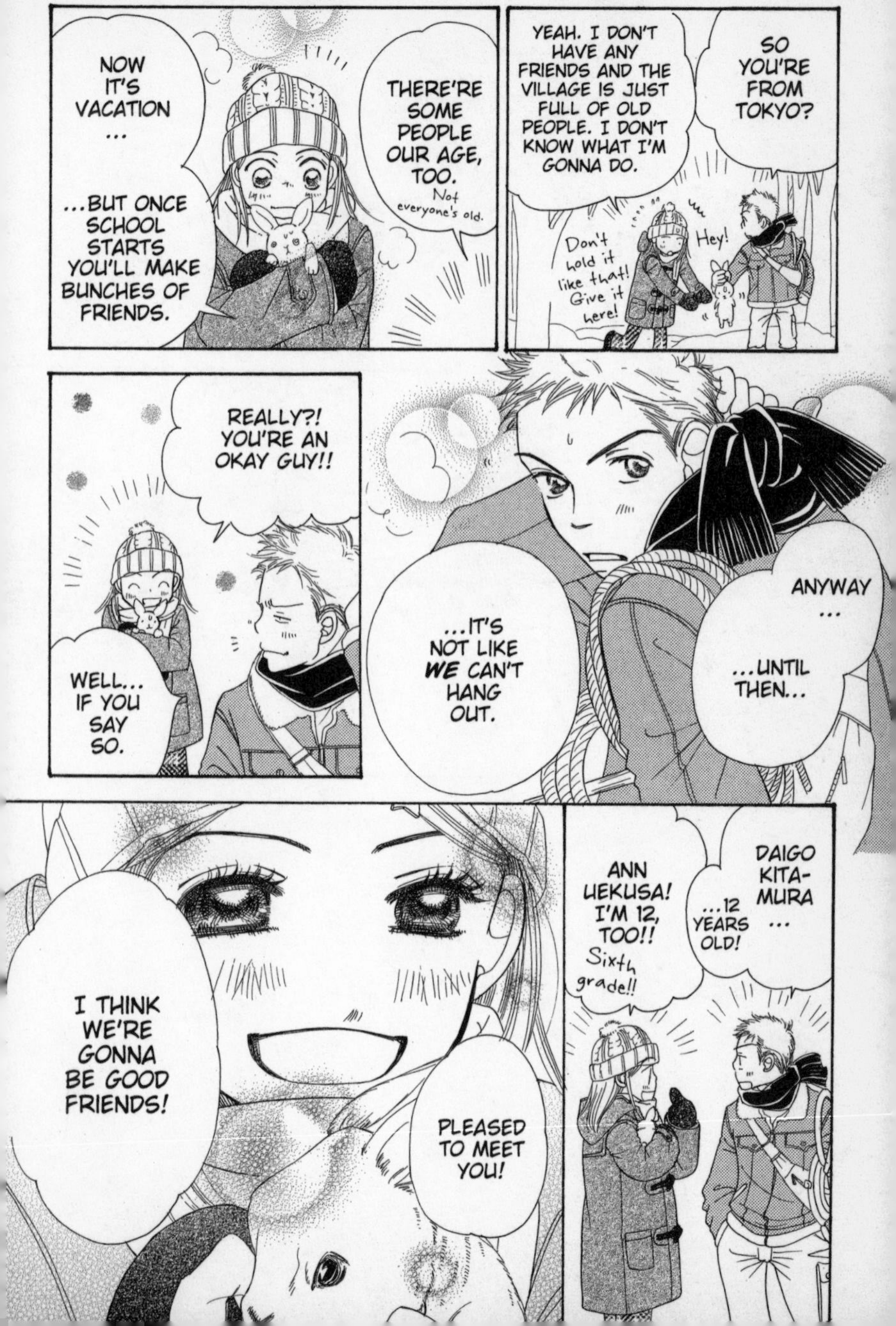
SO YOU'RE FROM TOKYO?
YEAH. I DON'T HAVE ANY FRIENDS AND THE VILLAGE IS JUST FULL OF OLD PEOPLE. I DON'T KNOW WHAT I'M GONNA DO.
Hey!
Don't hold it like that! Give it here!
THERE'RE SOME PEOPLE OUR AGE, TOO.
Not everyone's old.
NOW IT'S VACATION...
...BUT ONCE SCHOOL STARTS YOU'LL MAKE BUNCHES OF FRIENDS.
ANYWAY...
...UNTIL THEN...
...IT'S NOT LIKE *WE* CAN'T HANG OUT.
REALLY?! YOU'RE AN OKAY GUY!!
WELL... IF YOU SAY SO.
DAIGO KITAMURA...
...12 YEARS OLD!
ANN UEKUSA! I'M 12, TOO!!
Sixth grade!!
I THINK WE'RE GONNA BE GOOD FRIENDS!
PLEASED TO MEET YOU!

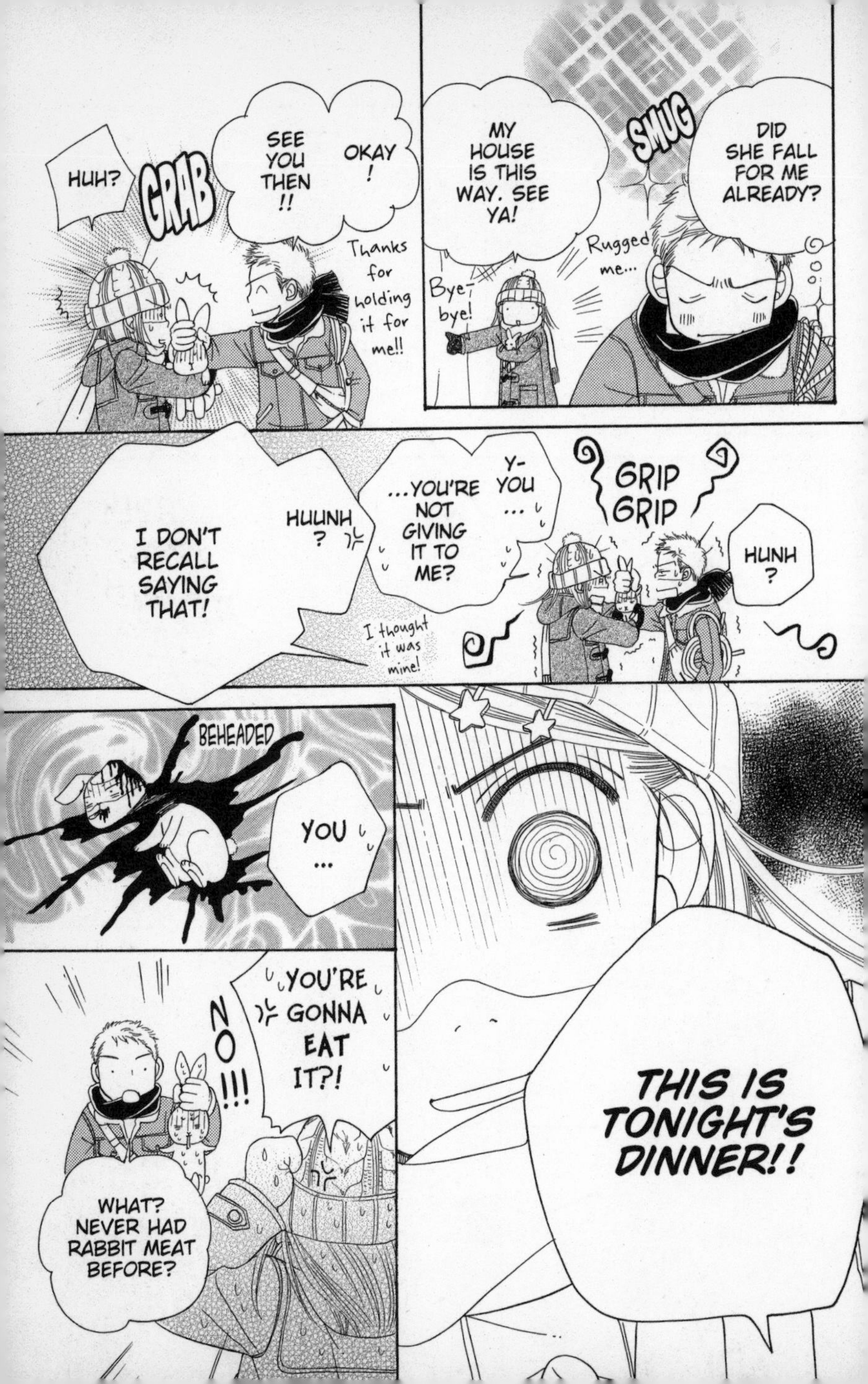
DID SHE FALL FOR ME ALREADY?
SMUG
Rugged me...
MY HOUSE IS THIS WAY. SEE YA!
Bye-bye!
OKAY!
SEE YOU THEN!!
Thanks for holding it for me!!
GRAB
HUH?
HUNH?
GRIP GRIP
Y-YOU...
...YOU'RE NOT GIVING IT TO ME?
I thought it was mine!
HUUNH?
I DON'T RECALL SAYING THAT!
THIS IS TONIGHT'S DINNER!!
BEHEADED
YOU...
YOU'RE GONNA EAT IT?!
NO!!!
WHAT? NEVER HAD RABBIT MEAT BEFORE?

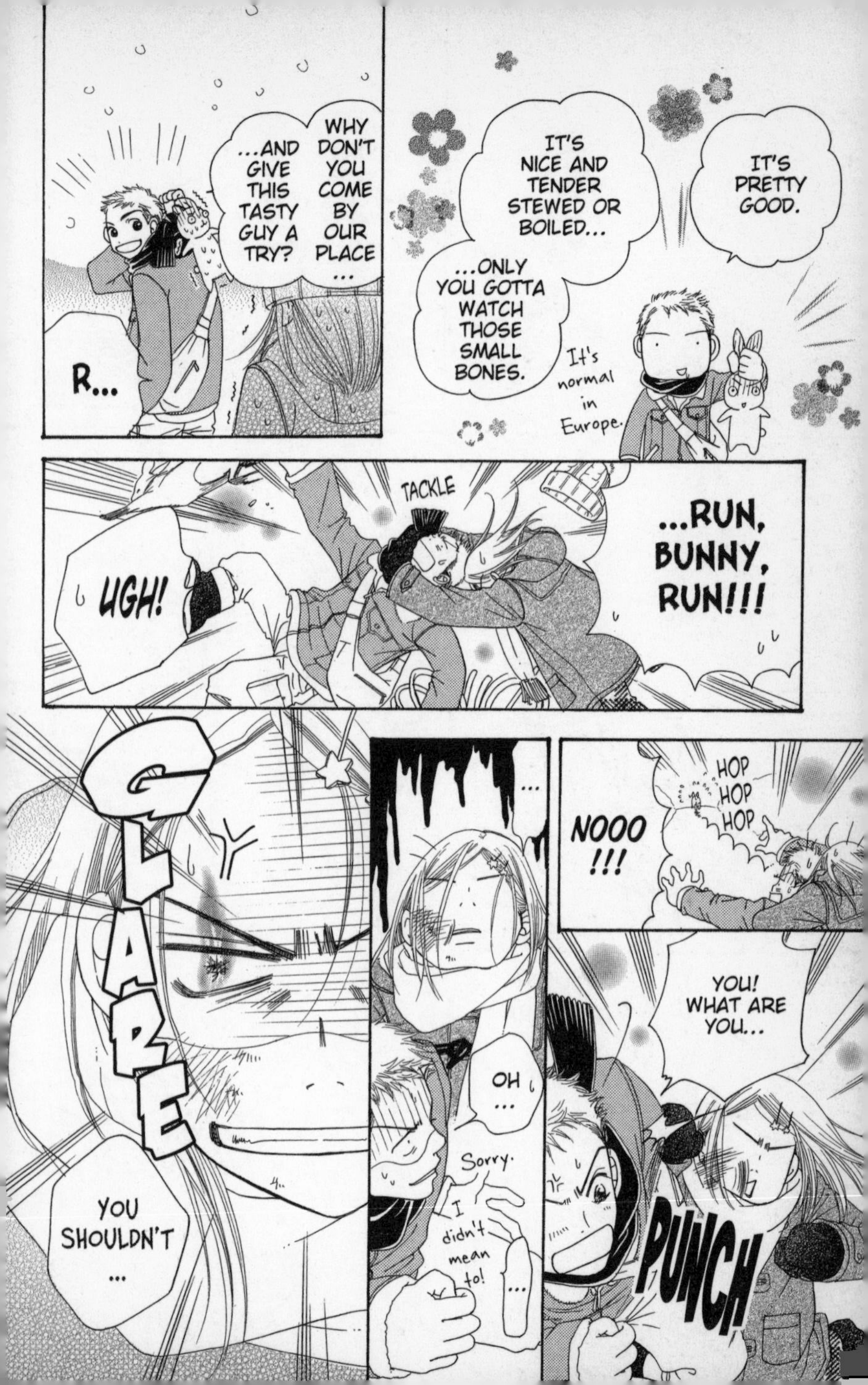
IT'S PRETTY GOOD.
IT'S NICE AND TENDER STEWED OR BOILED...
...ONLY YOU GOTTA WATCH THOSE SMALL BONES.
It's normal in Europe.
WHY DON'T YOU COME BY OUR PLACE...
...AND GIVE THIS TASTY GUY A TRY?
R...
...RUN, BUNNY, RUN!!!
TACKLE
UGH!
HOP HOP HOP
NOOO!!!
YOU! WHAT ARE YOU...
PUNCH
...
OH...
Sorry.
I didn't mean to!
...
GLARE
YOU SHOULDN'T...

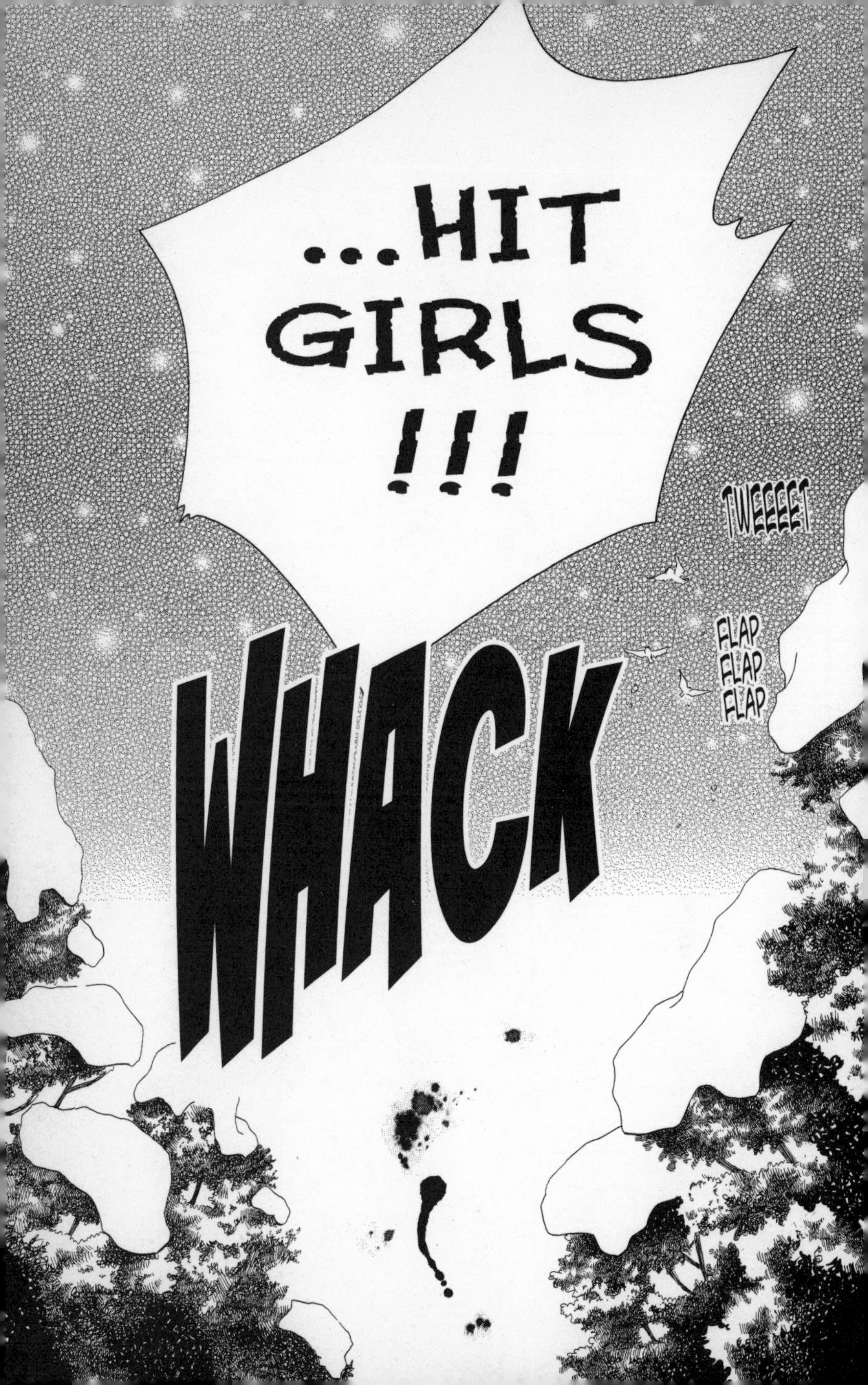
...HIT GIRLS !!!
TWEEEEET
FLAP FLAP FLAP
WHACK

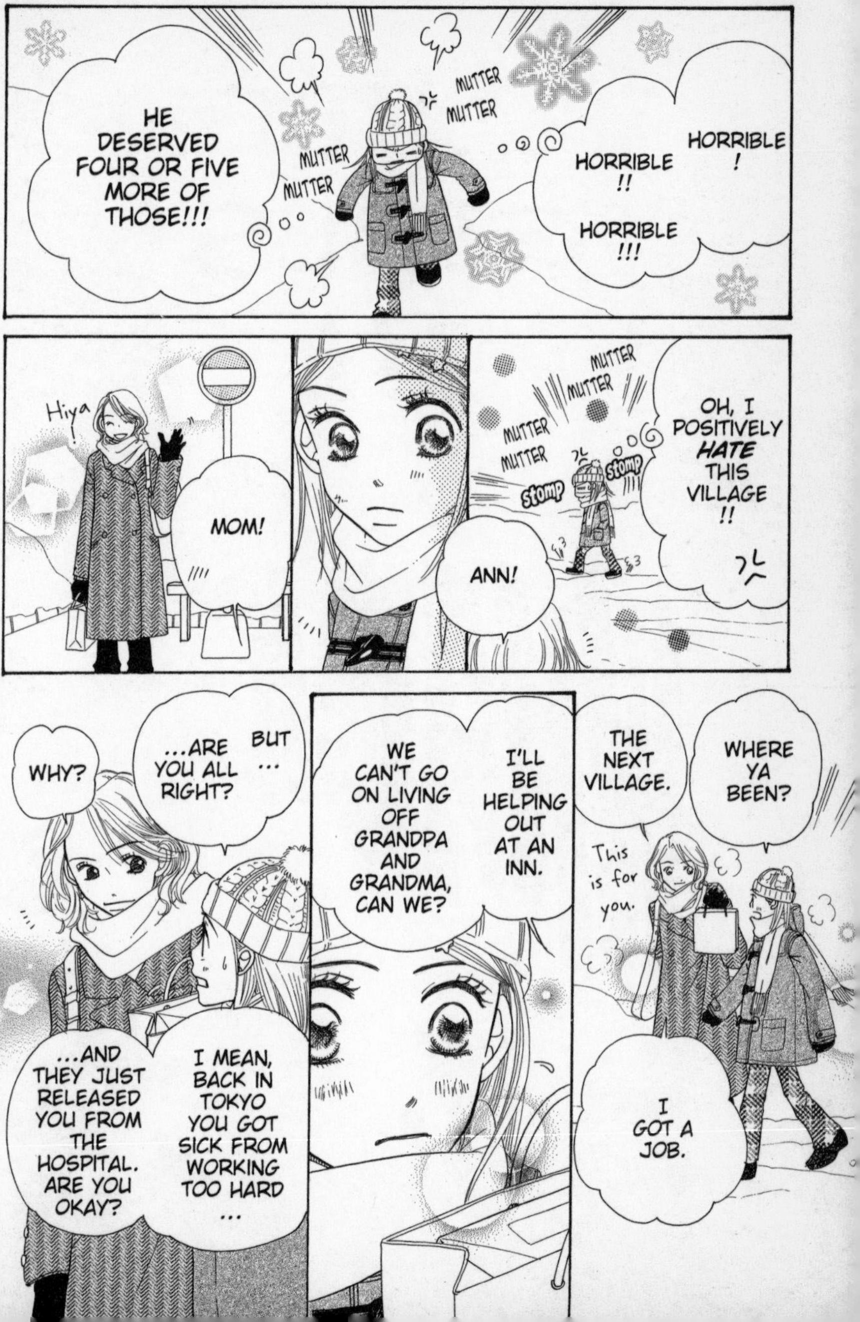
HORRIBLE!
HORRIBLE!!
HORRIBLE!!!
MUTTER MUTTER
MUTTER MUTTER
HE DESERVED FOUR OR FIVE MORE OF THOSE!!!
OH, I POSITIVELY HATE THIS VILLAGE!!
MUTTER MUTTER
MUTTER MUTTER
stomp stomp
ANN!
MOM!
Hiya!
WHERE YA BEEN?
THE NEXT VILLAGE.
This is for you.
I GOT A JOB.
I'LL BE HELPING OUT AT AN INN.
WE CAN'T GO ON LIVING OFF GRANDPA AND GRANDMA, CAN WE?
BUT ...
...ARE YOU ALL RIGHT?
WHY?
I MEAN, BACK IN TOKYO YOU GOT SICK FROM WORKING TOO HARD ...
...AND THEY JUST RELEASED YOU FROM THE HOSPITAL. ARE YOU OKAY?

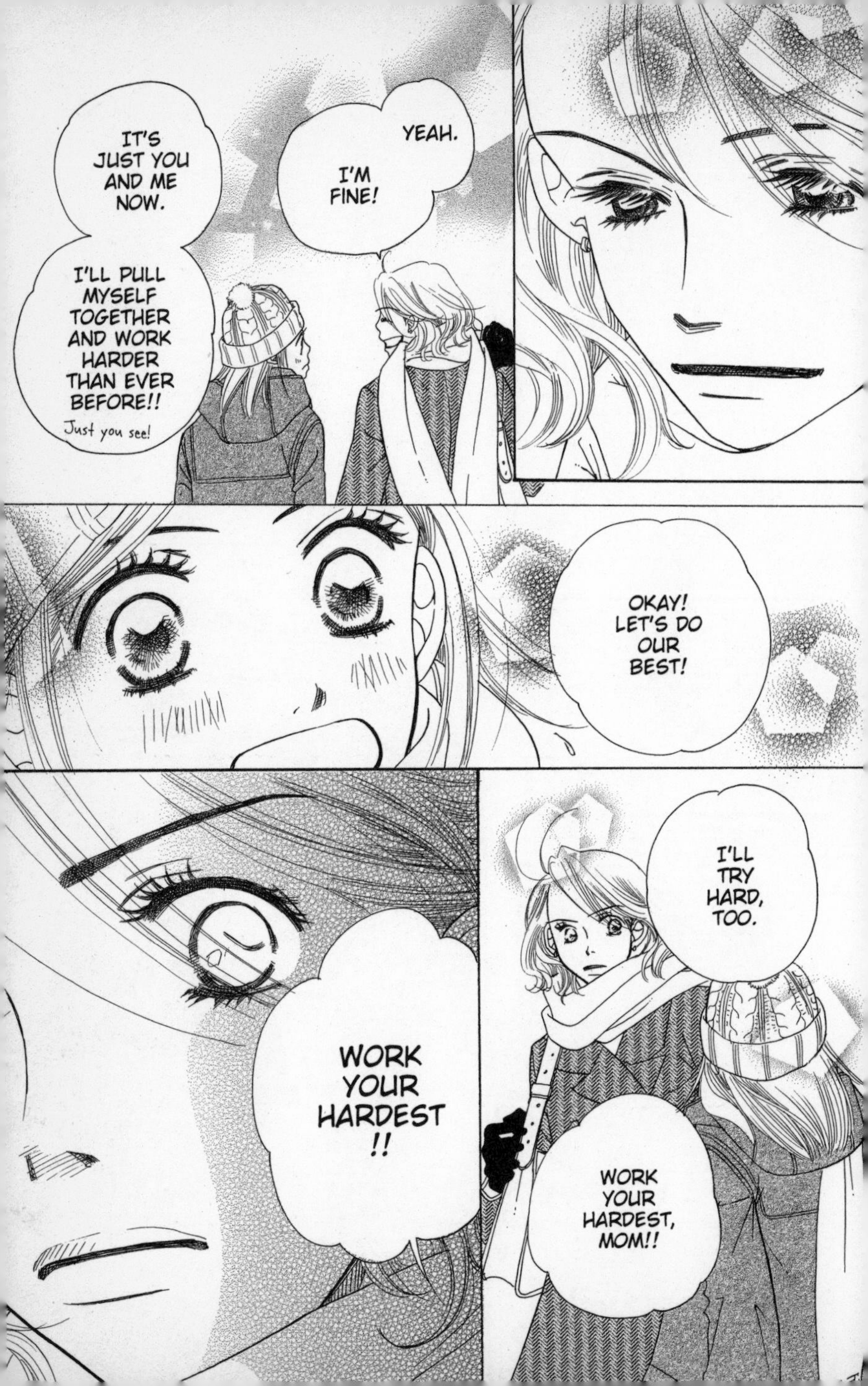
YEAH. I'M FINE!
IT'S JUST YOU AND ME NOW.
I'LL PULL MYSELF TOGETHER AND WORK HARDER THAN EVER BEFORE!!
Just you see!
OKAY! LET'S DO OUR BEST!
I'LL TRY HARD, TOO.
WORK YOUR HARDEST, MOM!!
WORK YOUR HARDEST!!

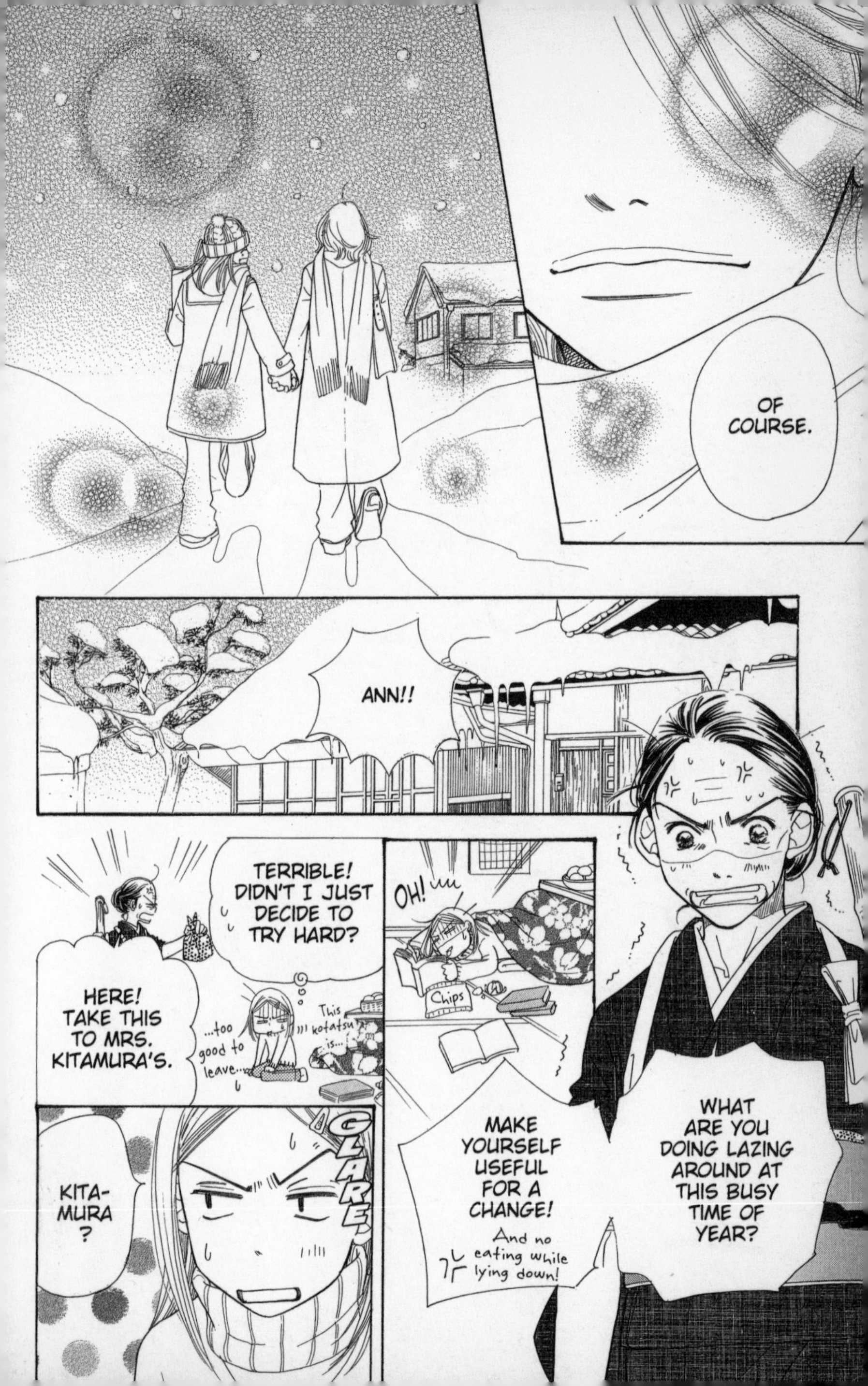
OF COURSE.
ANN!!
WHAT ARE YOU DOING LAZING AROUND AT THIS BUSY TIME OF YEAR?
MAKE YOURSELF USEFUL FOR A CHANGE!
And no eating while lying down!
OH!
Chips
TERRIBLE! DIDN'T I JUST DECIDE TO TRY HARD?
HERE! TAKE THIS TO MRS. KITAMURA'S.
This kotatsu is...
...too good to leave...
GLARE
KITA-MURA?

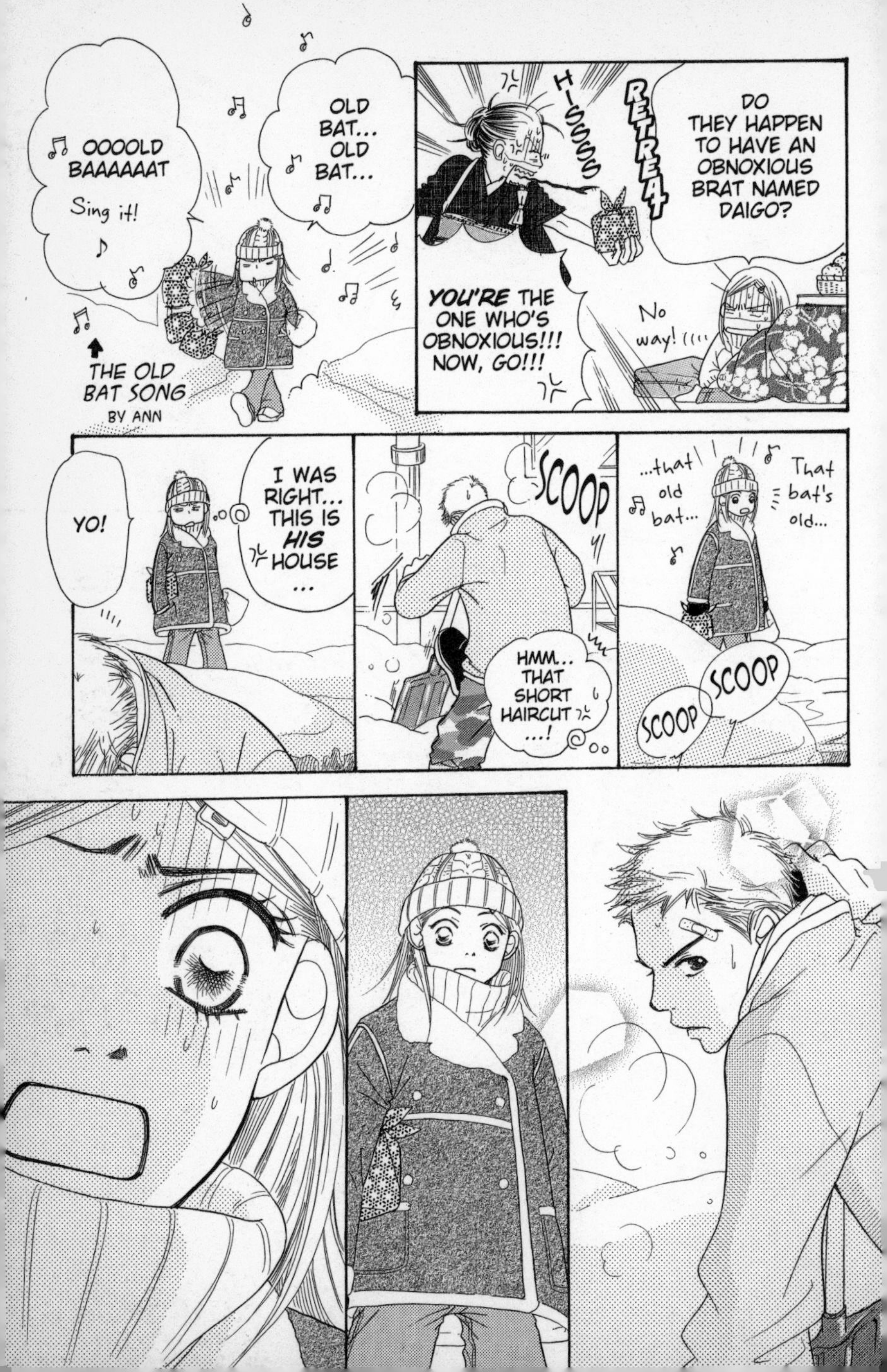
DO THEY HAPPEN TO HAVE AN OBNOXIOUS BRAT NAMED DAIGO?
RETREAT
HISSSS
No way!
YOU'RE THE ONE WHO'S OBNOXIOUS!!! NOW, GO!!!
OLD BAT... OLD BAT...
OOOOLD BAAAAAAT
Sing it!
THE OLD BAT SONG
BY ANN
...that old bat...
That bat's old...
SCOOP
SCOOP
SCOOP
HMM... THAT SHORT HAIRCUT ...!
I WAS RIGHT... THIS IS HIS HOUSE ...
YO!

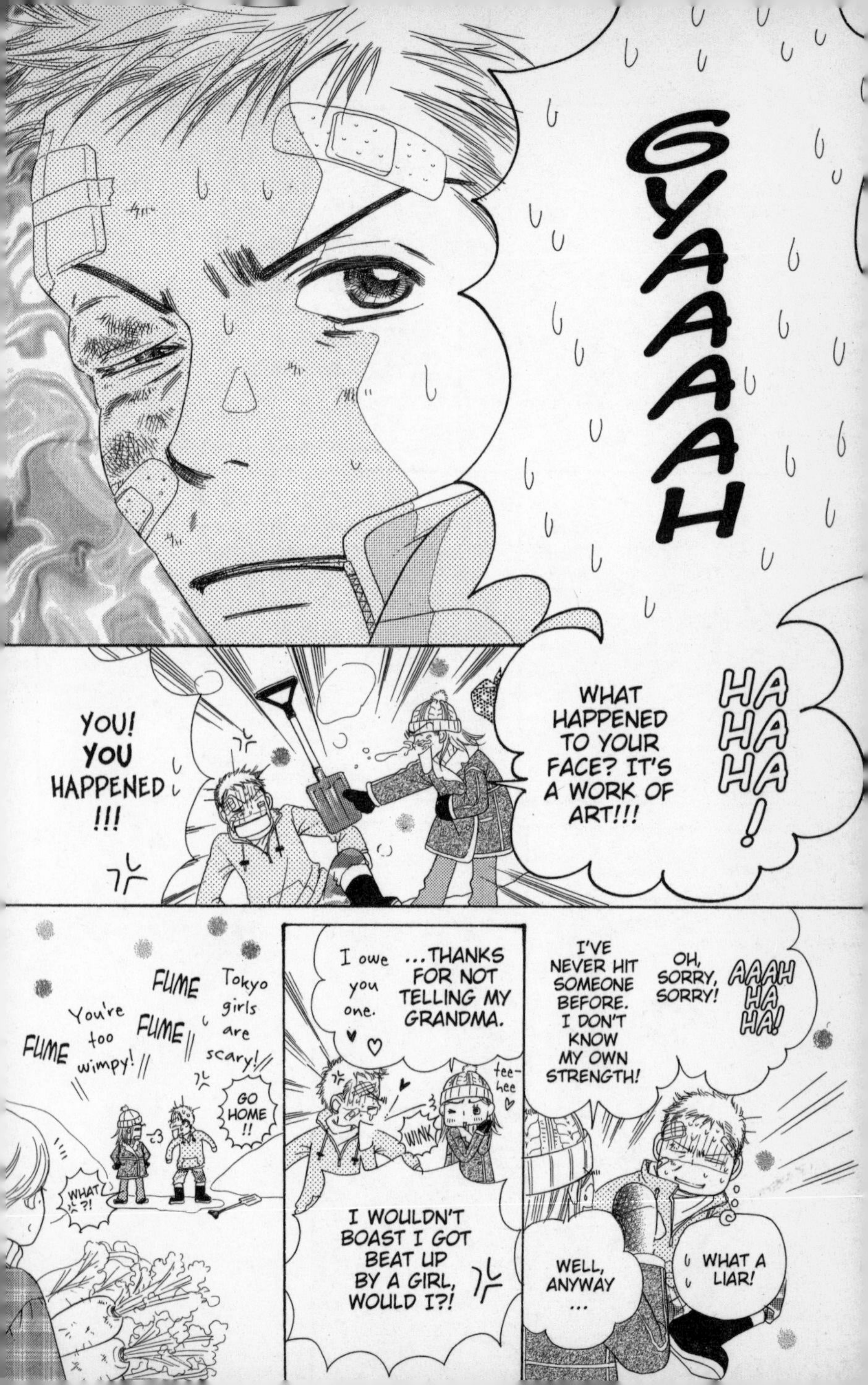
GYAAAAH
HA HA HA HA HA HA!
WHAT HAPPENED TO YOUR FACE? IT'S A WORK OF ART!!!
YOU! YOU HAPPENED!!!
AAAH HA HA!
OH, SORRY, SORRY!
I'VE NEVER HIT SOMEONE BEFORE. I DON'T KNOW MY OWN STRENGTH!
WHAT A LIAR!
WELL, ANYWAY...
...THANKS FOR NOT TELLING MY GRANDMA.
I owe you one.
tee-hee
WINK
I WOULDN'T BOAST I GOT BEAT UP BY A GIRL, WOULD I?!
Tokyo girls are scary!
FUME
FUME
You're too wimpy!
FUME
GO HOME!!
WHAT?!

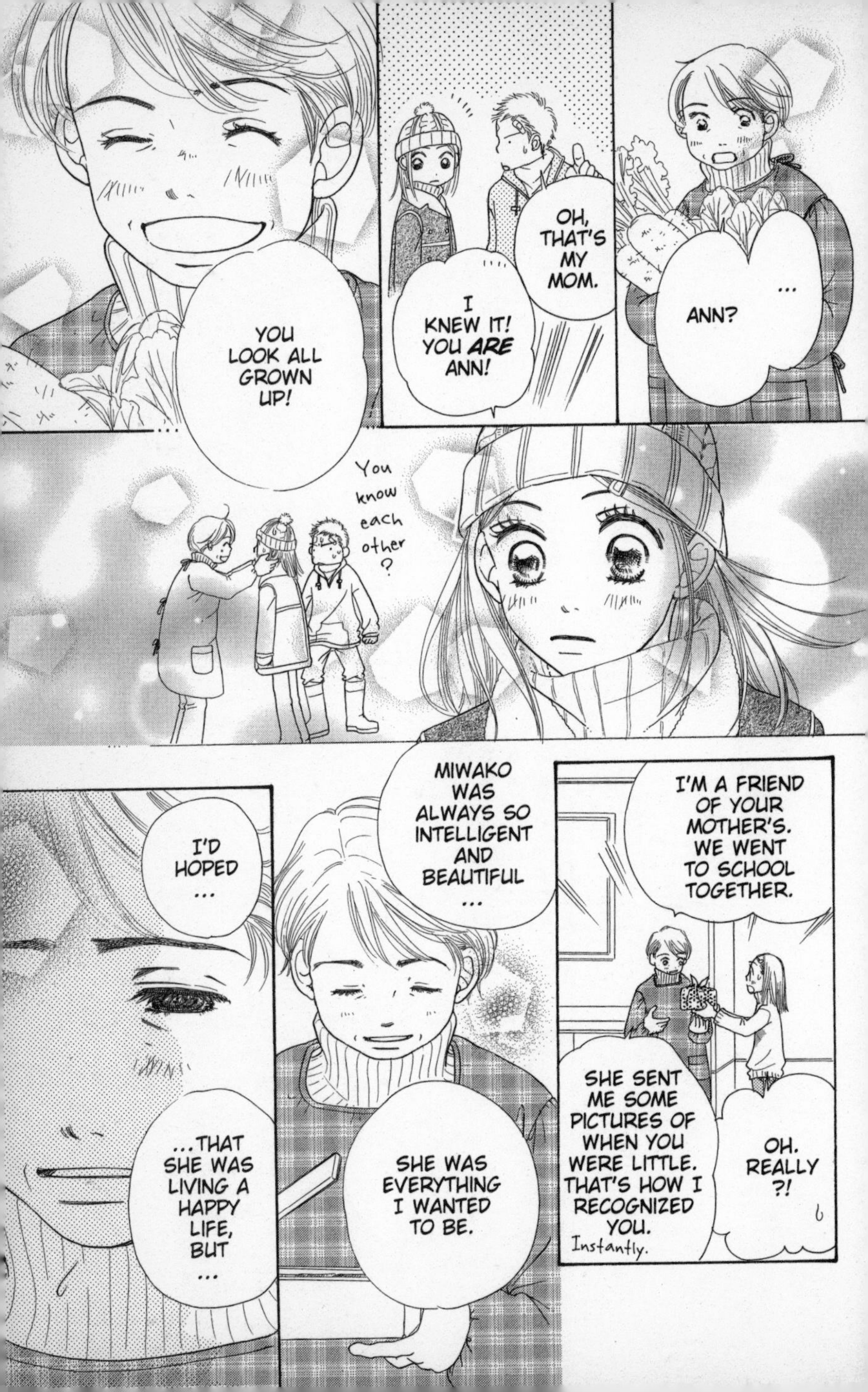
...
ANN?
OH, THAT'S MY MOM.
I KNEW IT! YOU ARE ANN!
YOU LOOK ALL GROWN UP!
You know each other?
I'M A FRIEND OF YOUR MOTHER'S. WE WENT TO SCHOOL TOGETHER.
OH. REALLY?!
SHE SENT ME SOME PICTURES OF WHEN YOU WERE LITTLE. THAT'S HOW I RECOGNIZED YOU.
Instantly.
MIWAKO WAS ALWAYS SO INTELLIGENT AND BEAUTIFUL...
SHE WAS EVERYTHING I WANTED TO BE.
I'D HOPED...
...THAT SHE WAS LIVING A HAPPY LIFE, BUT...

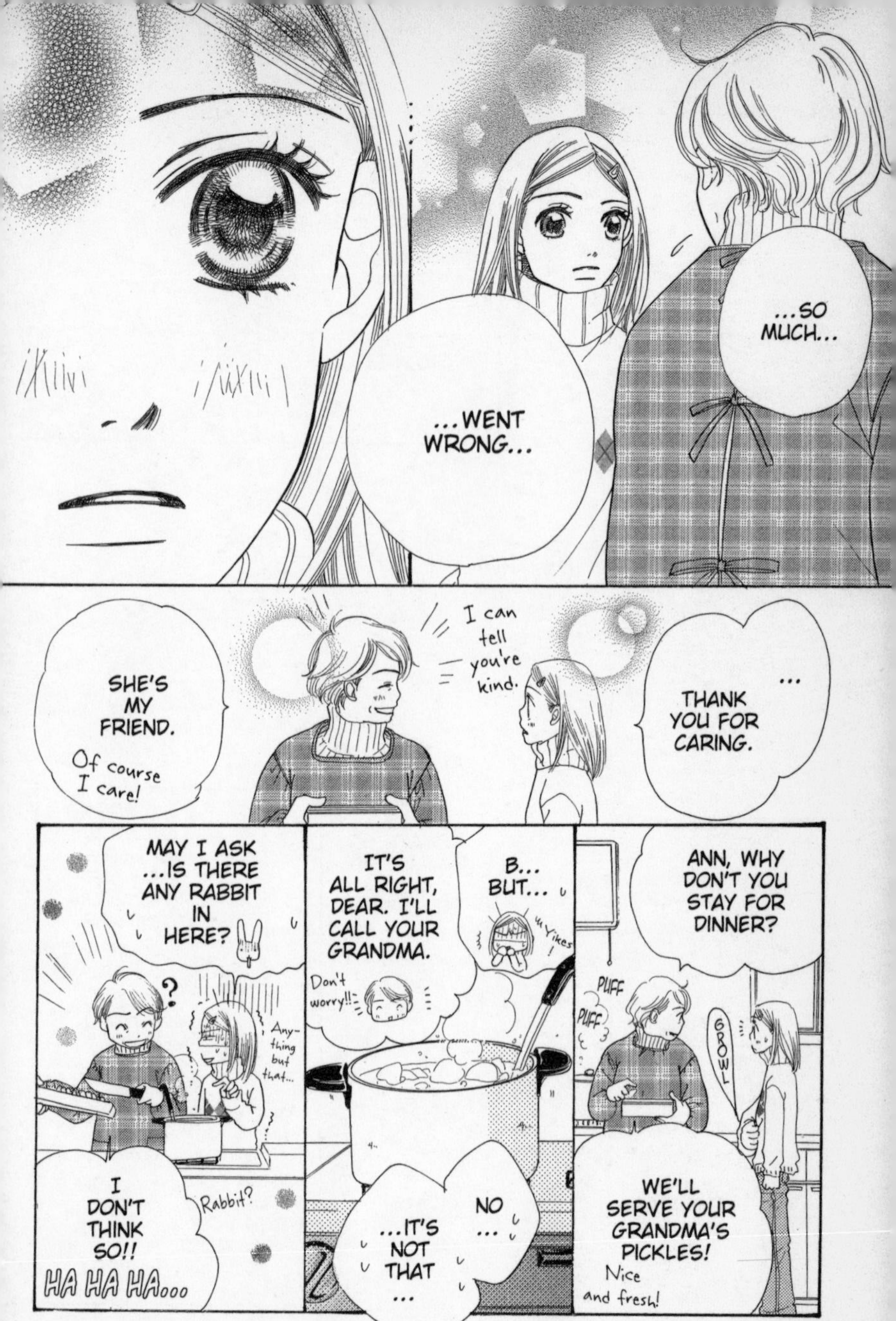
...SO MUCH...
...WENT WRONG...
...
THANK YOU FOR CARING.
I can tell you're kind.
SHE'S MY FRIEND.
Of course I care!
ANN, WHY DON'T YOU STAY FOR DINNER?
PUFF
PUFF
GROWL
WE'LL SERVE YOUR GRANDMA'S PICKLES!
Nice and fresh!
B... BUT...
Yikes!
IT'S ALL RIGHT, DEAR. I'LL CALL YOUR GRANDMA.
Don't worry!!
NO...
...IT'S NOT THAT...
MAY I ASK ...IS THERE ANY RABBIT IN HERE?
Anything but that...
I DON'T THINK SO!!
Rabbit?
HA HA HA...

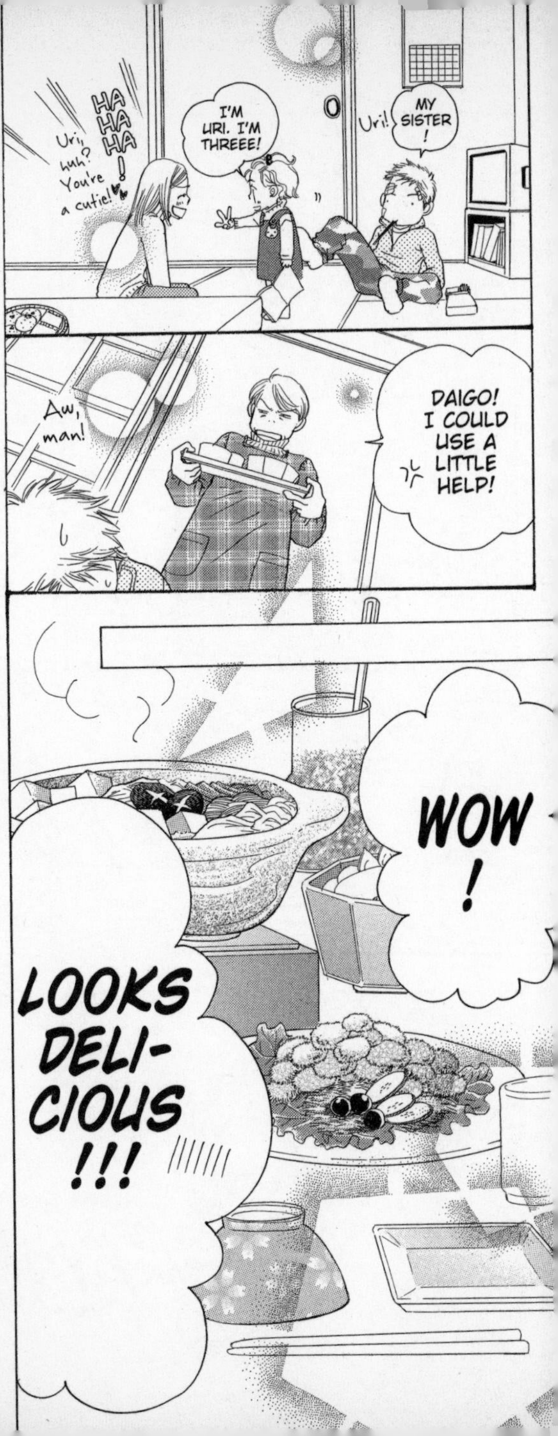
MY SISTER!
Uri!
I'M URI. I'M THREEE!
HA HA HA!
Uri, huh? You're a cutie!
DAIGO! I COULD USE A LITTLE HELP!
Aw, man!
WOW!
LOOKS DELICIOUS!!!

About Sand Chronicles

Thank you so much for reading Sand Chronicles. The story begins in winter when the main characters are 12 years old and shows in detail how they change over the course of the seasons. It's been quite a while since I've done a continuing story, so I guess I'm a bit nervous while at the same time enjoying it.

I like hourglasses. I like sitting and staring at them absently as well as telling time with them. I was considering the word "sunadokei*" for the title of this series for some time when I learned about the world's biggest one-year hourglass in Shimane...I was like...one year...One **year**? I went to see it right away. I'll tell you more about it later...

*SUNADOKEI IS THE JAPANESE TITLE.

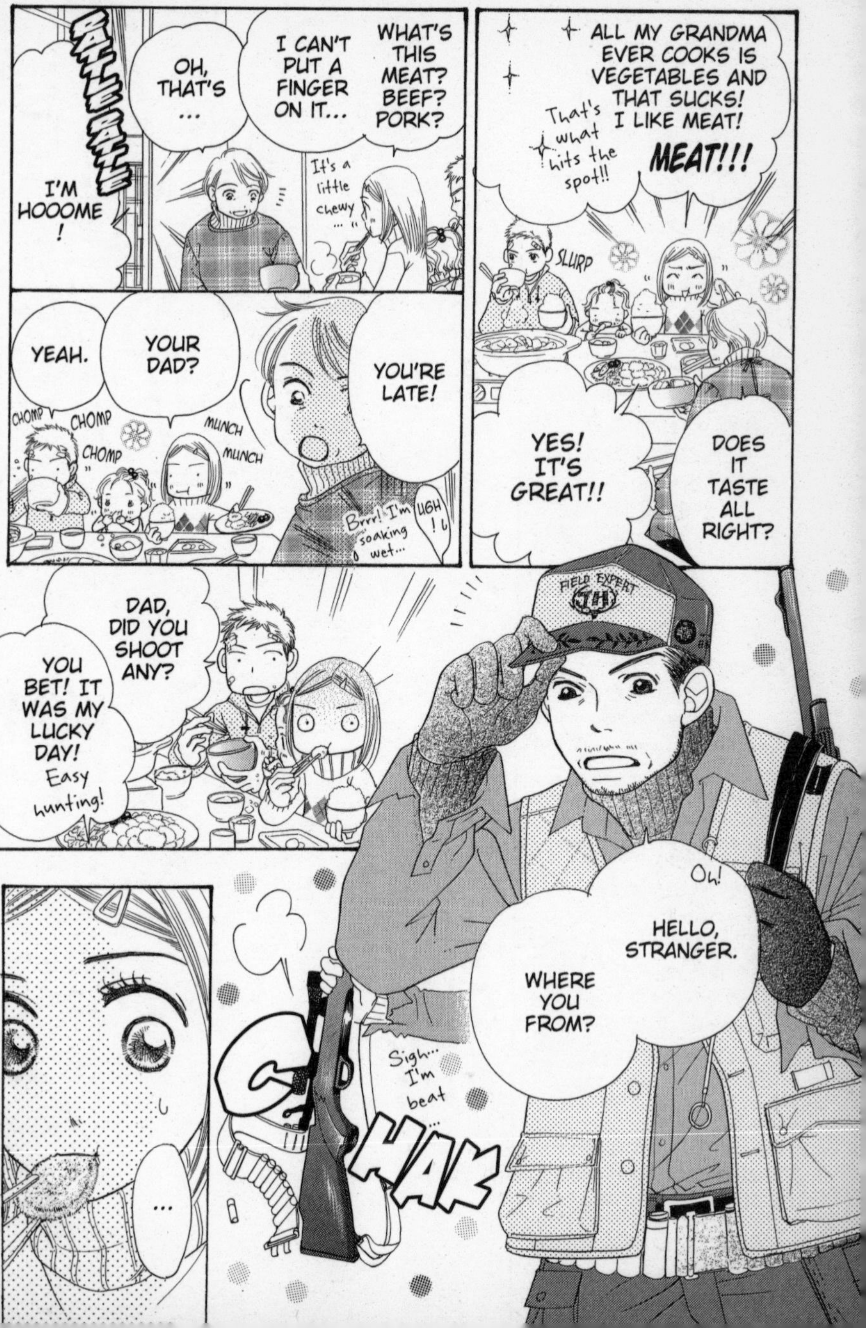
ALL MY GRANDMA EVER COOKS IS VEGETABLES AND THAT SUCKS! I LIKE MEAT!
That's what hits the spot!!
MEAT!!!
SLURP
DOES IT TASTE ALL RIGHT?
YES! IT'S GREAT!!
WHAT'S THIS MEAT? BEEF? PORK?
I CAN'T PUT A FINGER ON IT...
It's a little chewy...
OH, THAT'S...
RATTLE RATTLE
I'M HOOOME!
YOU'RE LATE!
UGH!
Brrr! I'm soaking wet...
YOUR DAD?
YEAH.
MUNCH MUNCH
CHOMP CHOMP CHOMP
FIELD EXPERT
Oh!
HELLO, STRANGER.
WHERE YOU FROM?
Sigh... I'm beat...
CHAK
DAD, DID YOU SHOOT ANY?
YOU BET! IT WAS MY LUCKY DAY!
Easy hunting!
...

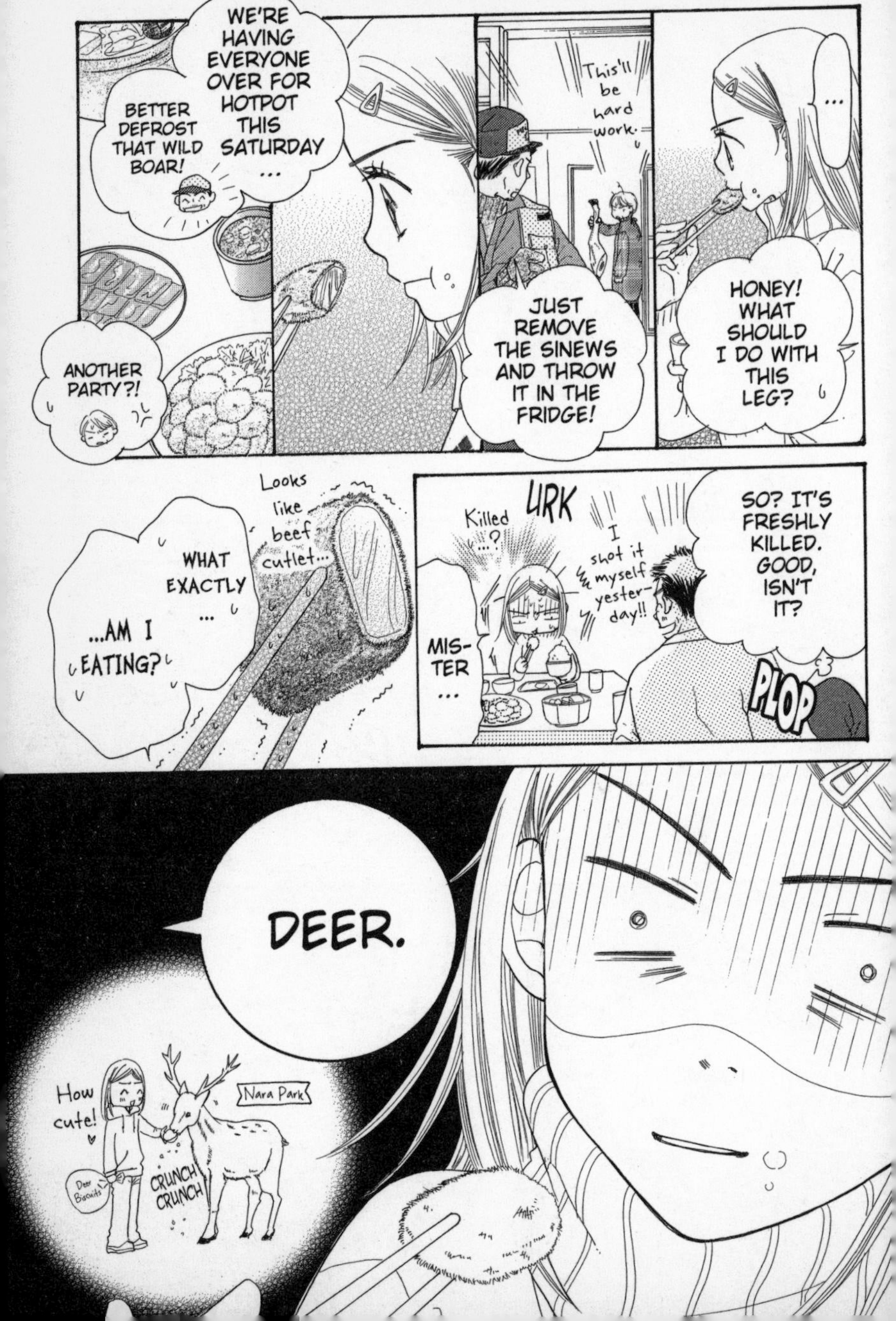
...
HONEY! WHAT SHOULD I DO WITH THIS LEG?
This'll be hard work.
JUST REMOVE THE SINEWS AND THROW IT IN THE FRIDGE!
WE'RE HAVING EVERYONE OVER FOR HOTPOT THIS SATURDAY ...
BETTER DEFROST THAT WILD BOAR!
ANOTHER PARTY?!
SO? IT'S FRESHLY KILLED. GOOD, ISN'T IT?
PLOP
I shot it myself yester-day!!
URK
Killed ...?
MIS-TER ...
Looks like beef cutlet...
WHAT EXACTLY ...
...AM I EATING?
DEER.
Nara Park
How cute!
Deer Biscuits
CRUNCH CRUNCH

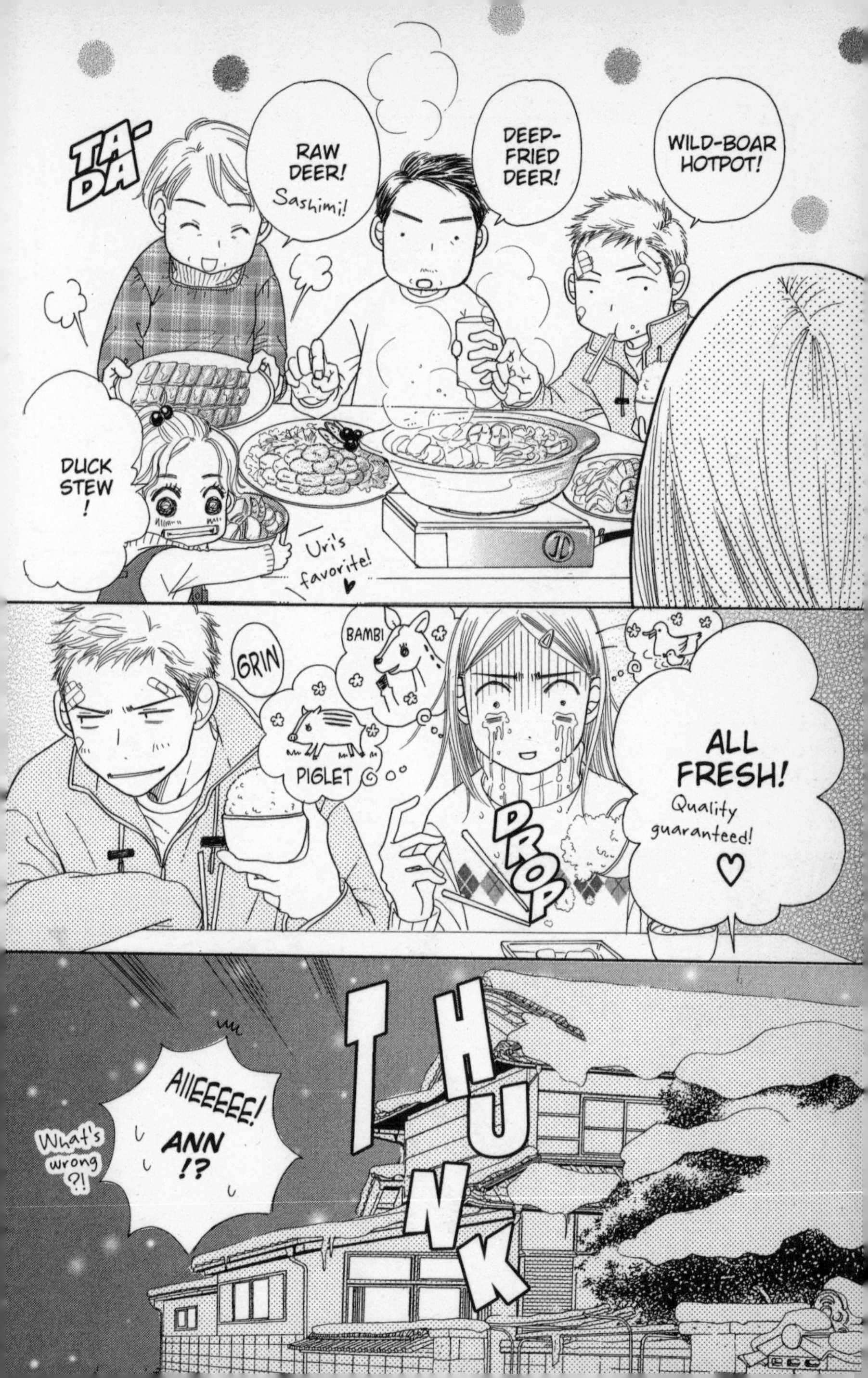
WILD-BOAR HOTPOT!
DEEP-FRIED DEER!
RAW DEER!
Sashimi!
TA-DA
DUCK STEW!
Uri's favorite! ♥
ALL FRESH!
Quality guaranteed! ♡
BAMBI
GRIN
PIGLET
DROP
THUNK
AIIEEEEE!
ANN!?
What's wrong?!

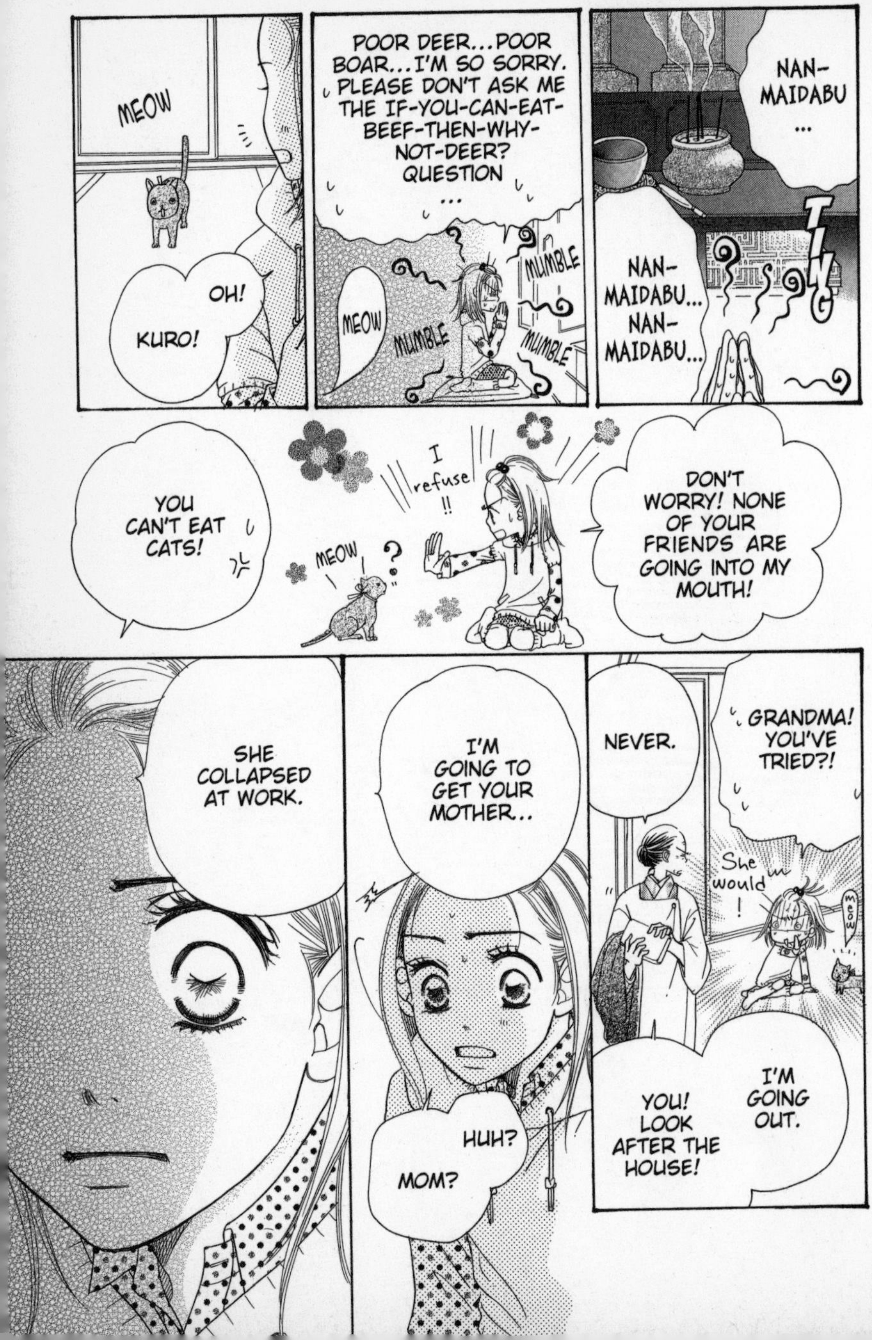
NAN-MAIDABU...
TING
NAN-MAIDABU... NAN-MAIDABU...
POOR DEER...POOR BOAR...I'M SO SORRY. PLEASE DON'T ASK ME THE IF-YOU-CAN-EAT-BEEF-THEN-WHY-NOT-DEER? QUESTION...
MUMBLE
MUMBLE
MEOW
MUMBLE
MEOW
OH!
KURO!
DON'T WORRY! NONE OF YOUR FRIENDS ARE GOING INTO MY MOUTH!
I refuse!!
MEOW
YOU CAN'T EAT CATS!
GRANDMA! YOU'VE TRIED?!
NEVER.
She would!
meow
I'M GOING OUT.
YOU! LOOK AFTER THE HOUSE!
I'M GOING TO GET YOUR MOTHER...
HUH?
MOM?
SHE COLLAPSED AT WORK.

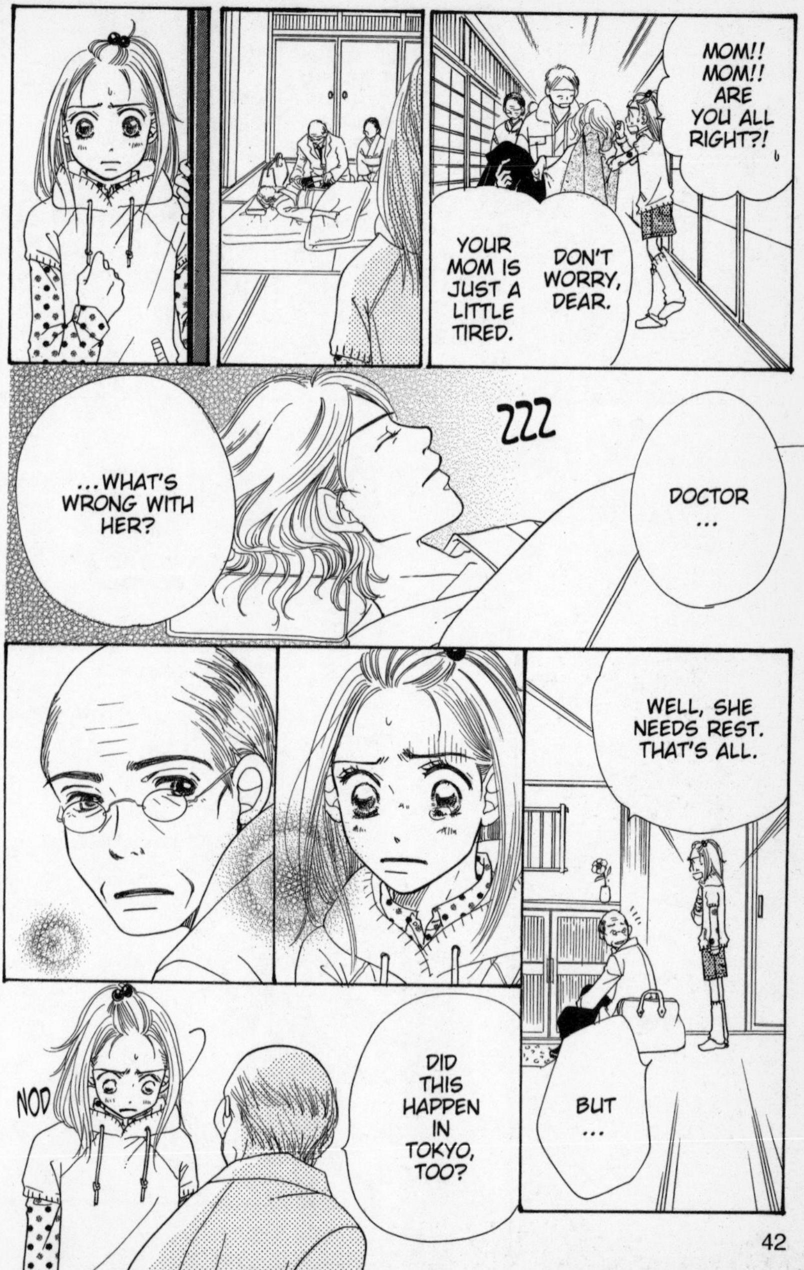
MOM!! MOM!! ARE YOU ALL RIGHT?!
DON'T WORRY, DEAR.
YOUR MOM IS JUST A LITTLE TIRED.
DOCTOR ...
ZZZ
...WHAT'S WRONG WITH HER?
WELL, SHE NEEDS REST. THAT'S ALL.
BUT ...
DID THIS HAPPEN IN TOKYO, TOO?
NOD

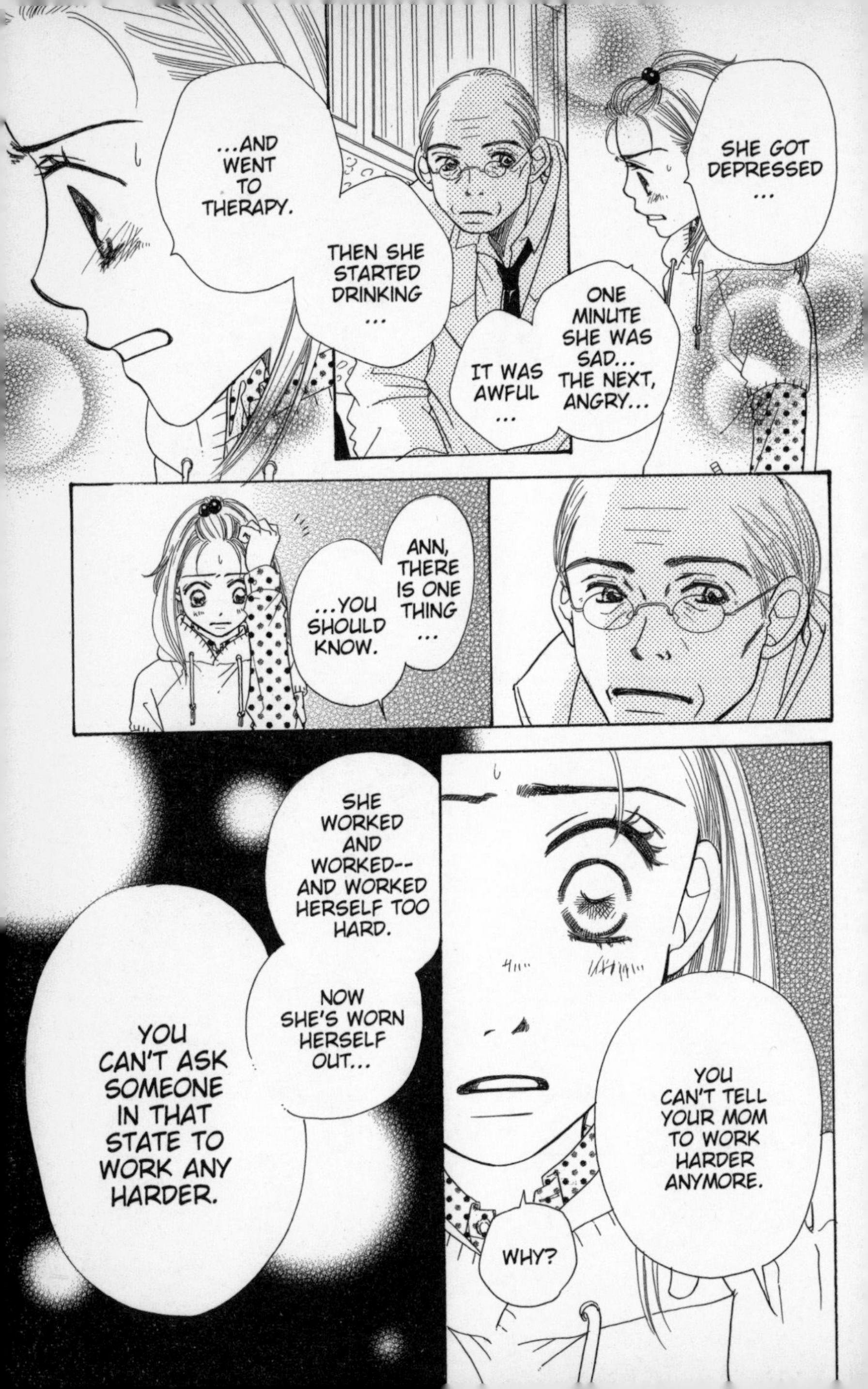
SHE GOT DEPRESSED...
ONE MINUTE SHE WAS SAD... THE NEXT, ANGRY...
IT WAS AWFUL...
THEN SHE STARTED DRINKING...
...AND WENT TO THERAPY.
ANN, THERE IS ONE THING...
...YOU SHOULD KNOW.
YOU CAN'T TELL YOUR MOM TO WORK HARDER ANYMORE.
WHY?
SHE WORKED AND WORKED--AND WORKED HERSELF TOO HARD.
NOW SHE'S WORN HERSELF OUT...
YOU CAN'T ASK SOMEONE IN THAT STATE TO WORK ANY HARDER.

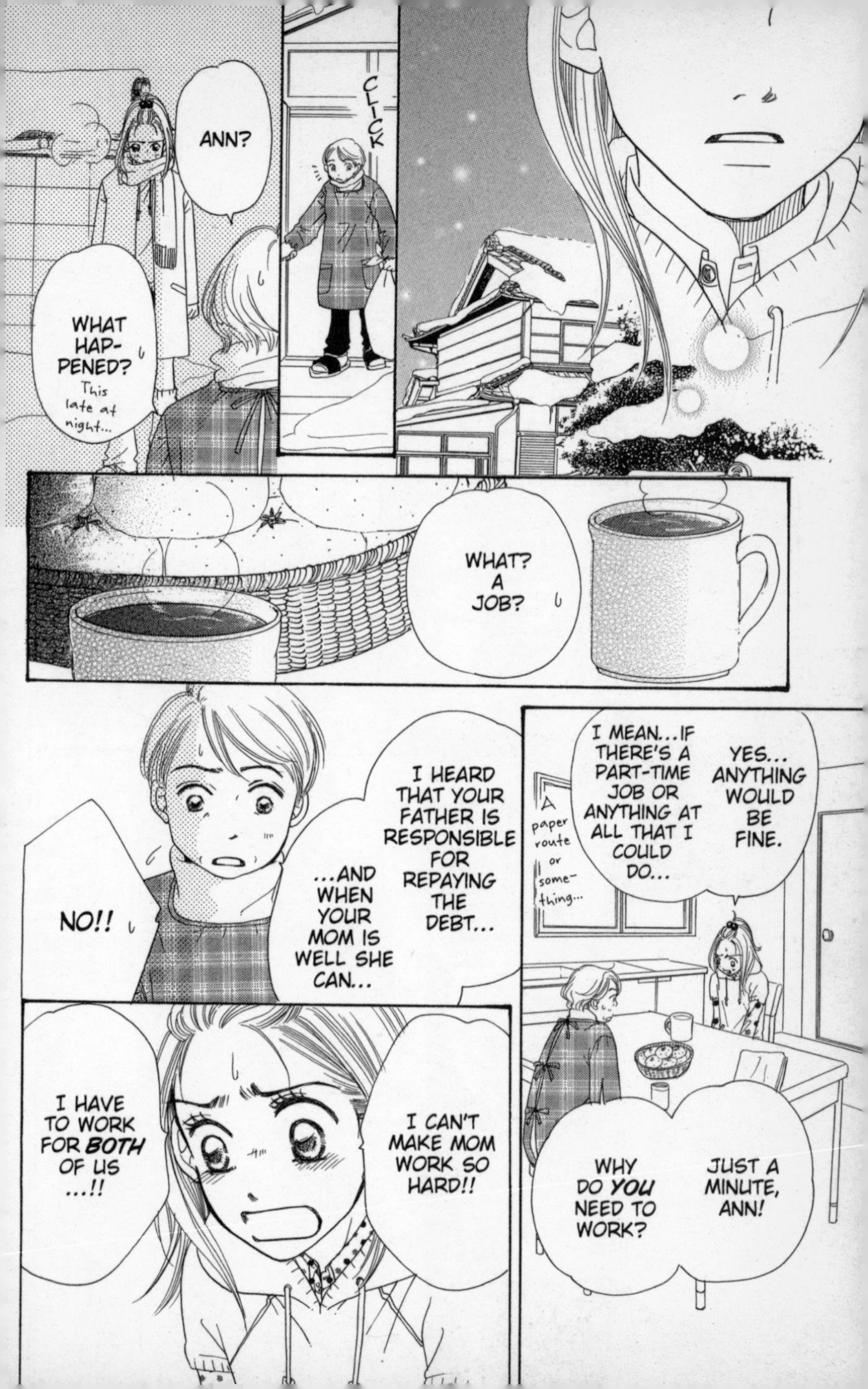
CLICK
ANN?
WHAT HAP-PENED?
This late at night...
WHAT? A JOB?
YES... ANYTHING WOULD BE FINE.
I MEAN... IF THERE'S A PART-TIME JOB OR ANYTHING AT ALL THAT I COULD DO...
A paper route or some-thing...
JUST A MINUTE, ANN!
WHY DO *YOU* NEED TO WORK?
I HEARD THAT YOUR FATHER IS RESPONSIBLE FOR REPAYING THE DEBT...
...AND WHEN YOUR MOM IS WELL SHE CAN...
NO!!
I CAN'T MAKE MOM WORK SO HARD!!
I HAVE TO WORK FOR ***BOTH*** OF US ...!!

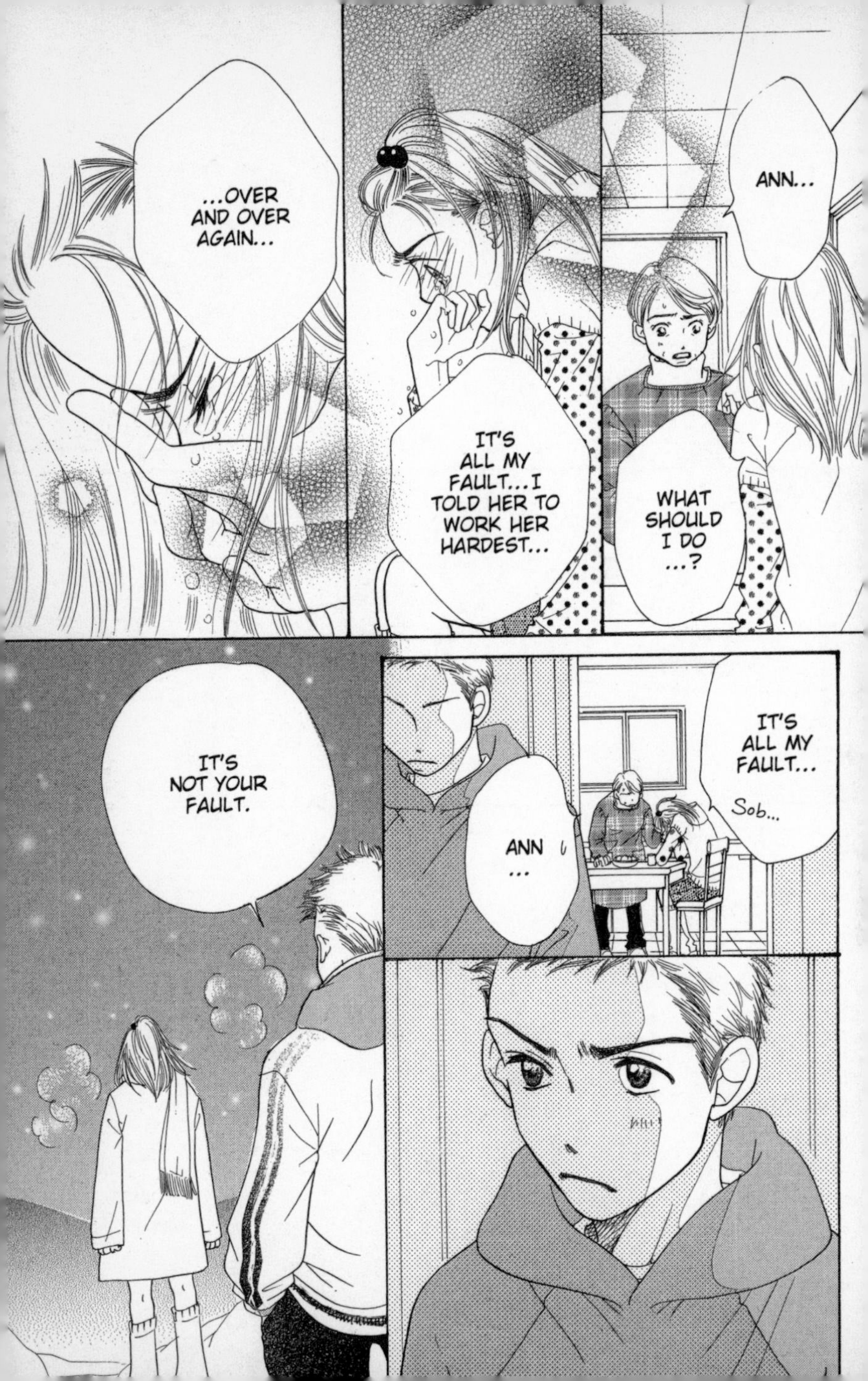
ANN...
WHAT SHOULD I DO ...?
IT'S ALL MY FAULT... I TOLD HER TO WORK HER HARDEST...
...OVER AND OVER AGAIN...
IT'S ALL MY FAULT...
Sob...
ANN ...
IT'S NOT YOUR FAULT.

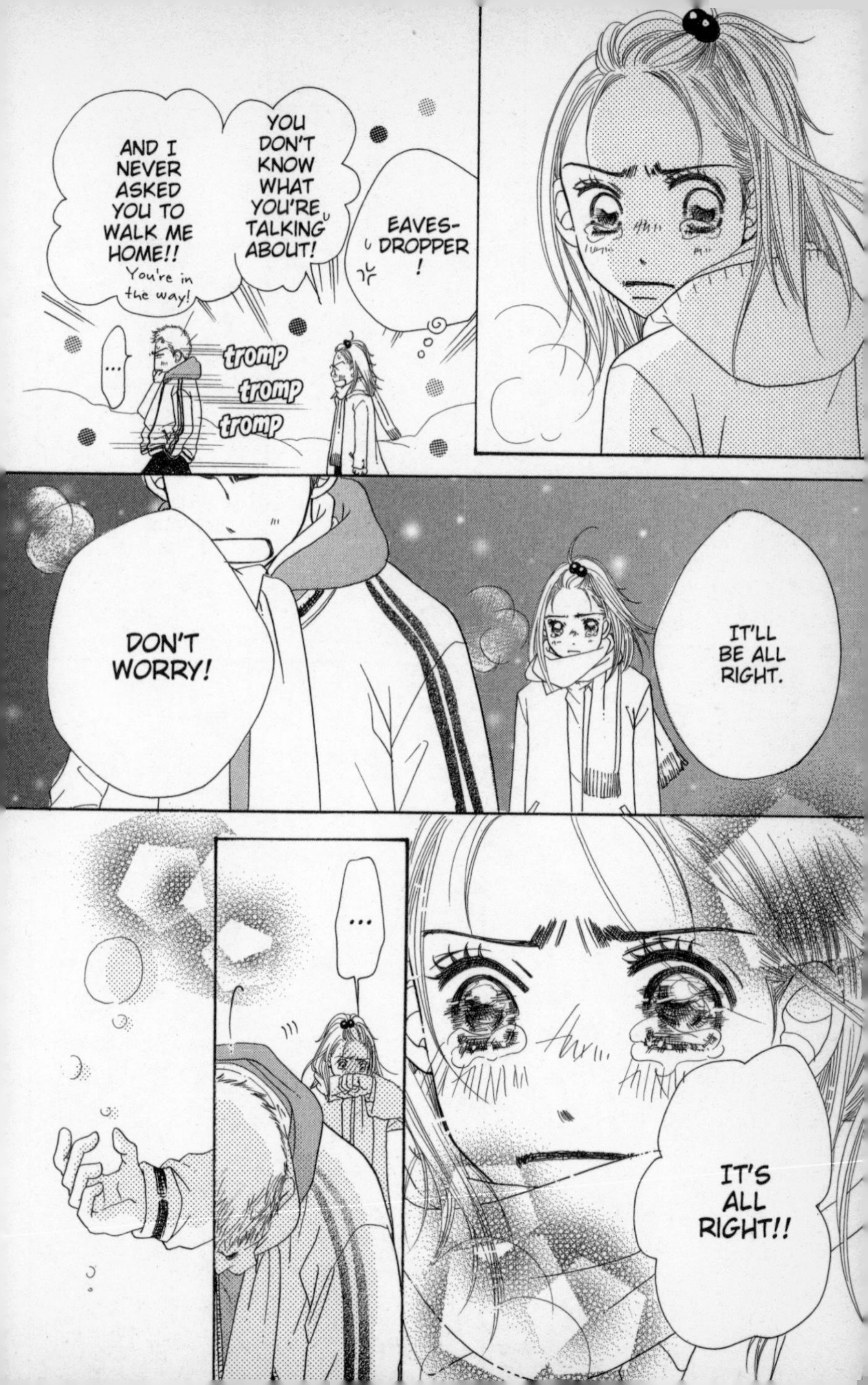
EAVES-DROPPER!
YOU DON'T KNOW WHAT YOU'RE TALKING ABOUT!
AND I NEVER ASKED YOU TO WALK ME HOME!!
You're in the way!
...
tromp
tromp
tromp
IT'LL BE ALL RIGHT.
DON'T WORRY!
IT'S ALL RIGHT!!
...

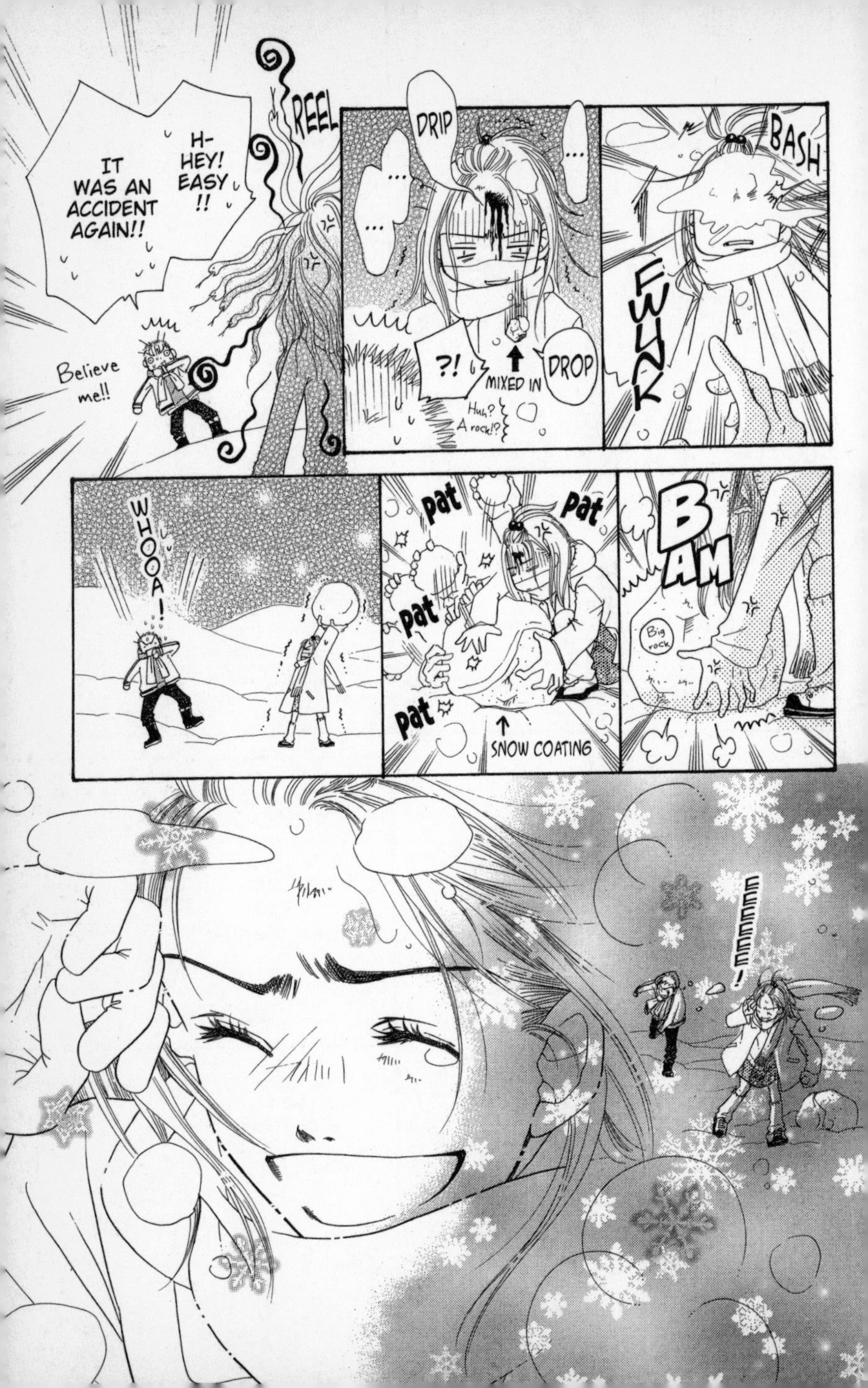
BASH
FWUNK
...
DRIP
...
...
DROP
MIXED IN
?!
Huh? A rock!?
REEL
H- HEY! EASY!!
IT WAS AN ACCIDENT AGAIN!!
Believe me!!
BAM
Big rock
pat
pat
pat
pat
SNOW COATING
WHOOA!
EEEEEE!

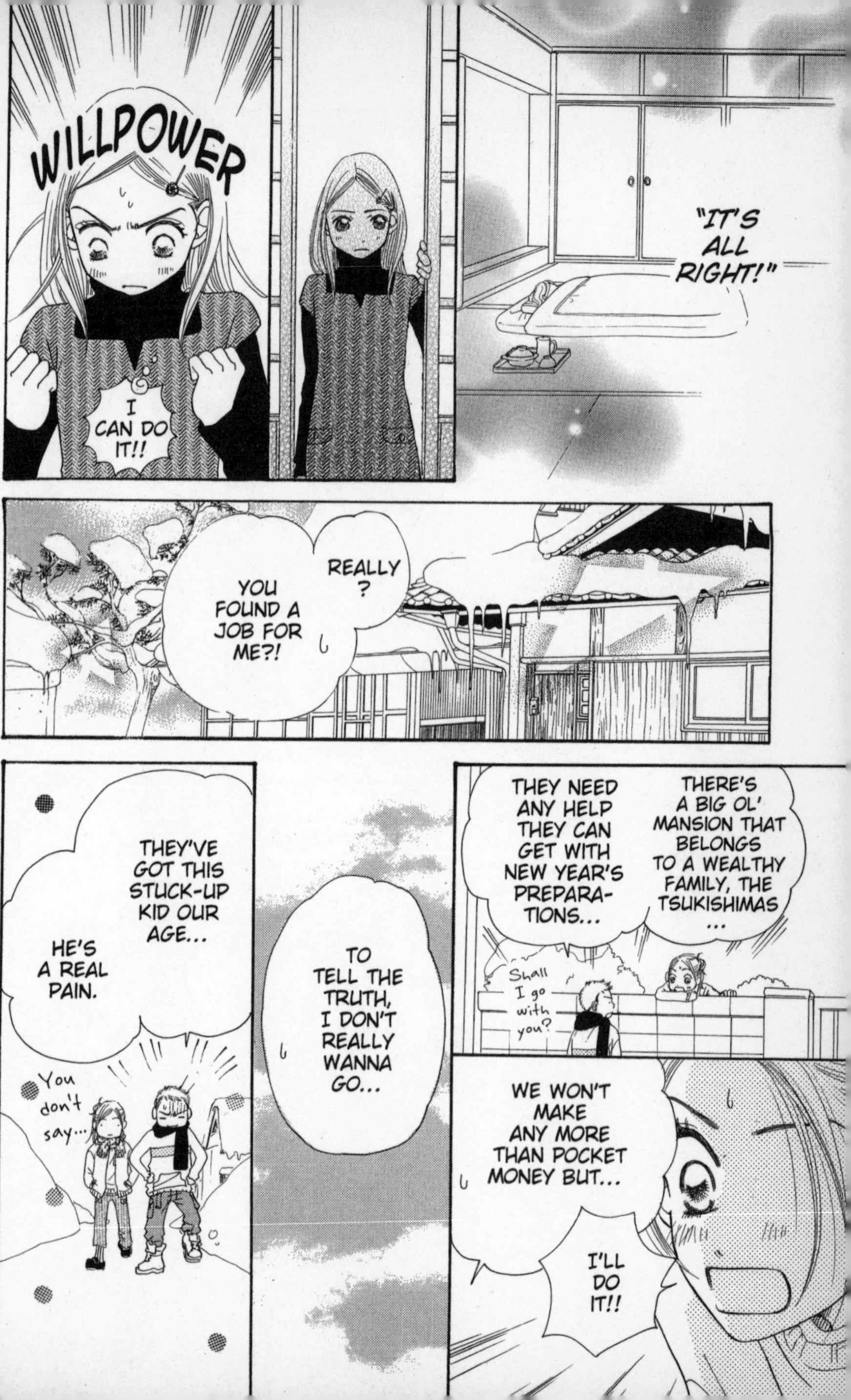
"IT'S ALL RIGHT!"
WILLPOWER
I CAN DO IT!!
REALLY?
YOU FOUND A JOB FOR ME?!
THERE'S A BIG OL' MANSION THAT BELONGS TO A WEALTHY FAMILY, THE TSUKISHIMAS...
THEY NEED ANY HELP THEY CAN GET WITH NEW YEAR'S PREPARATIONS...
Shall I go with you?
WE WON'T MAKE ANY MORE THAN POCKET MONEY BUT...
I'LL DO IT!!
TO TELL THE TRUTH, I DON'T REALLY WANNA GO...
THEY'VE GOT THIS STUCK-UP KID OUR AGE...
HE'S A REAL PAIN.
You don't say...

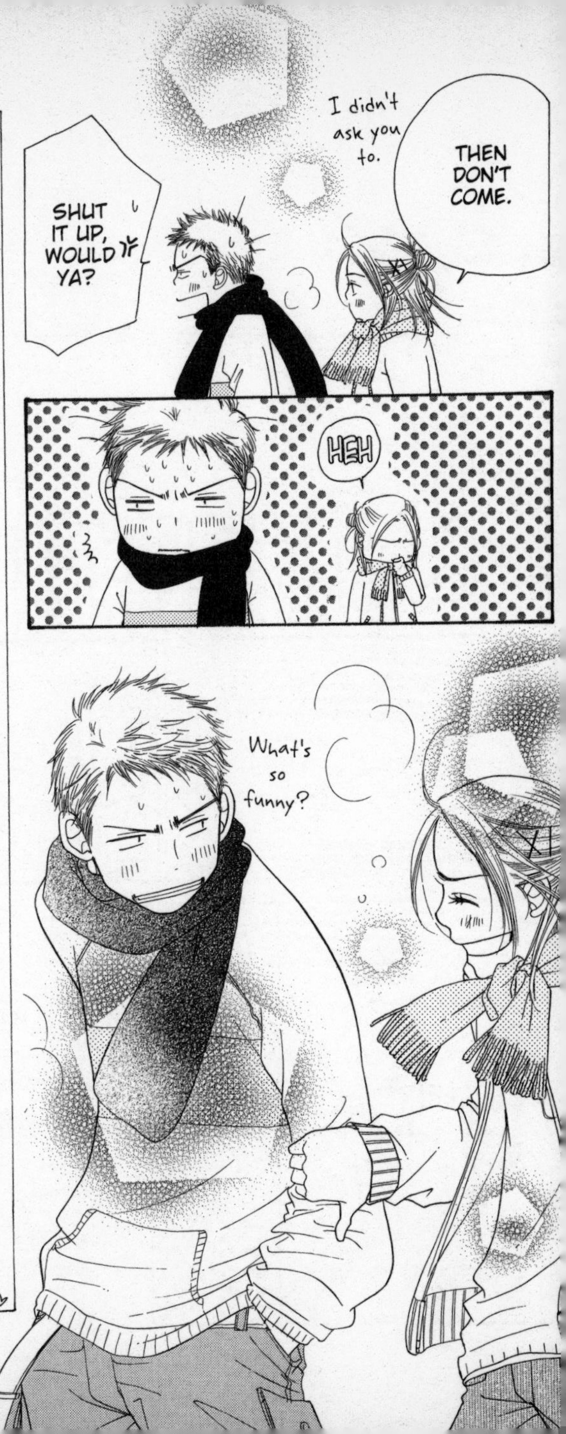
THEN DON'T COME.
I didn't ask you to.
SHUT IT UP, WOULD YA?
HEH
What's so funny?

About Winter, Age 12: Making a Wish

I like writing about boys and girls this age. They're so pure and honest. But there's something more. In some ways they will change, but in other ways they won't...I hope I can draw them all the way through those changes...

I asked a friend to help me with the Shimane dialect, got pictures from my father of his hunting gun, dragged my sister around with me on research trips, borrowed a number of materials on villages from my uncle, and had my assistants draw lots of complicated background images... to eventually finish the book.

Thank you, guys!!

By the way, the main characters are speaking in the Izumo dialect. It's been toned down a little, though. Anyway, I have to say that I like the way this dialect sounds!

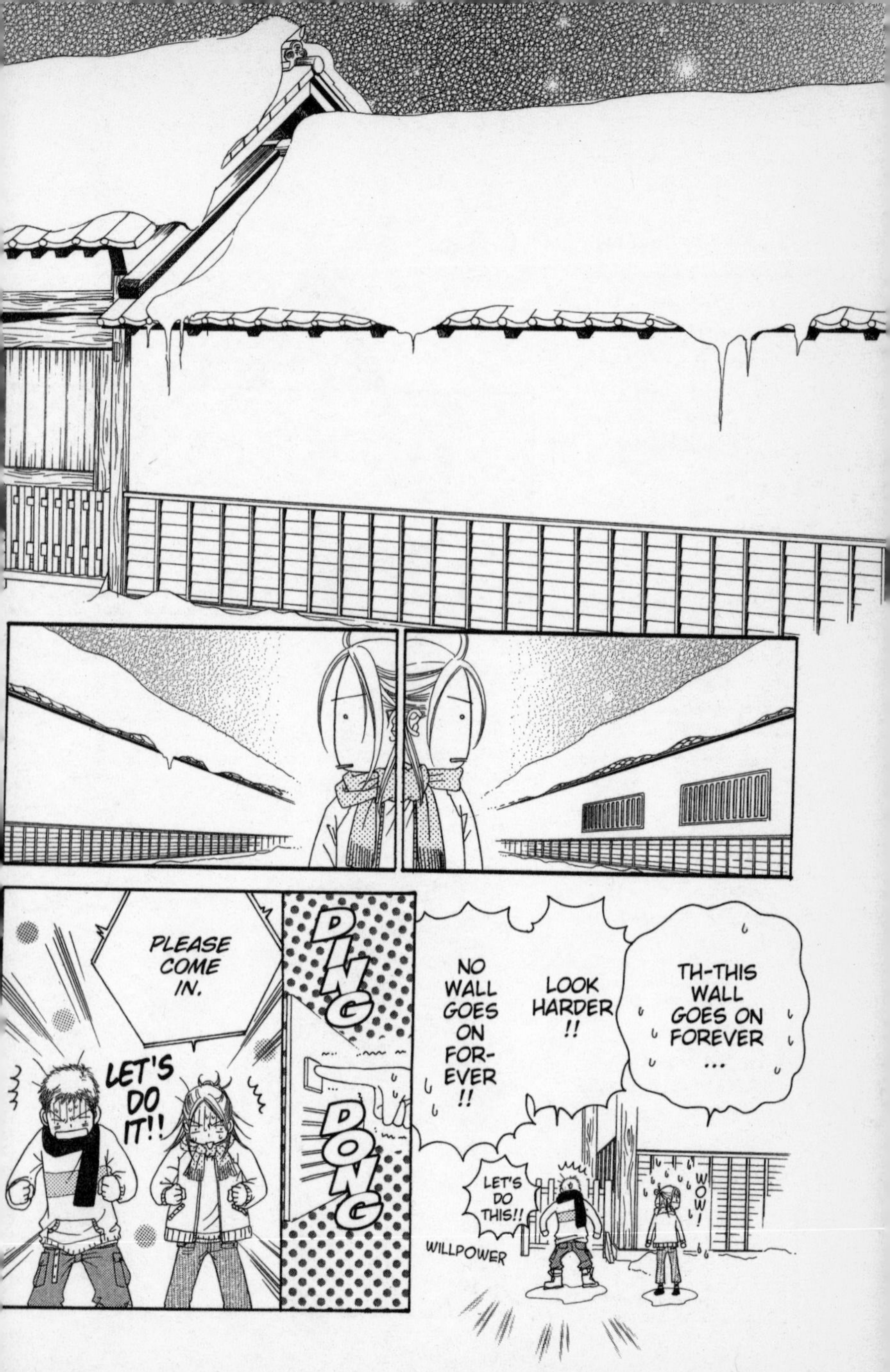
TH-THIS WALL GOES ON FOREVER...
LOOK HARDER!!
NO WALL GOES ON FOR-EVER!!
WOW!
LET'S DO THIS!!
WILLPOWER
DING
DONG
PLEASE COME IN.
LET'S DO IT!!

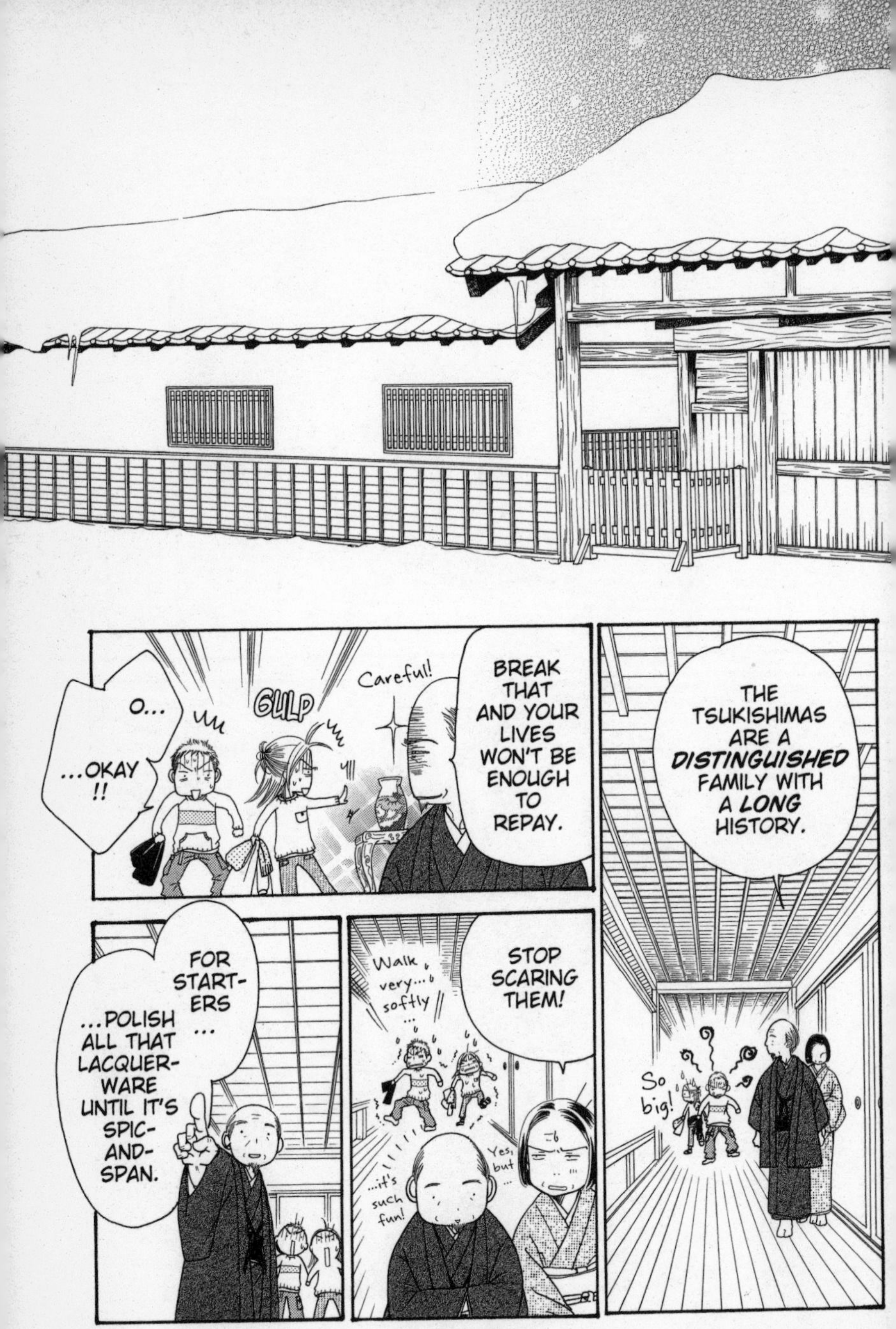
THE TSUKISHIMAS ARE A DISTINGUISHED FAMILY WITH A LONG HISTORY.
So big!
BREAK THAT AND YOUR LIVES WON'T BE ENOUGH TO REPAY.
Careful!
GULP
O...
...OKAY!!
STOP SCARING THEM!
Walk very... softly...
Yes, but...
...it's such fun!
FOR STARTERS...
...POLISH ALL THAT LACQUERWARE UNTIL IT'S SPIC-AND-SPAN.

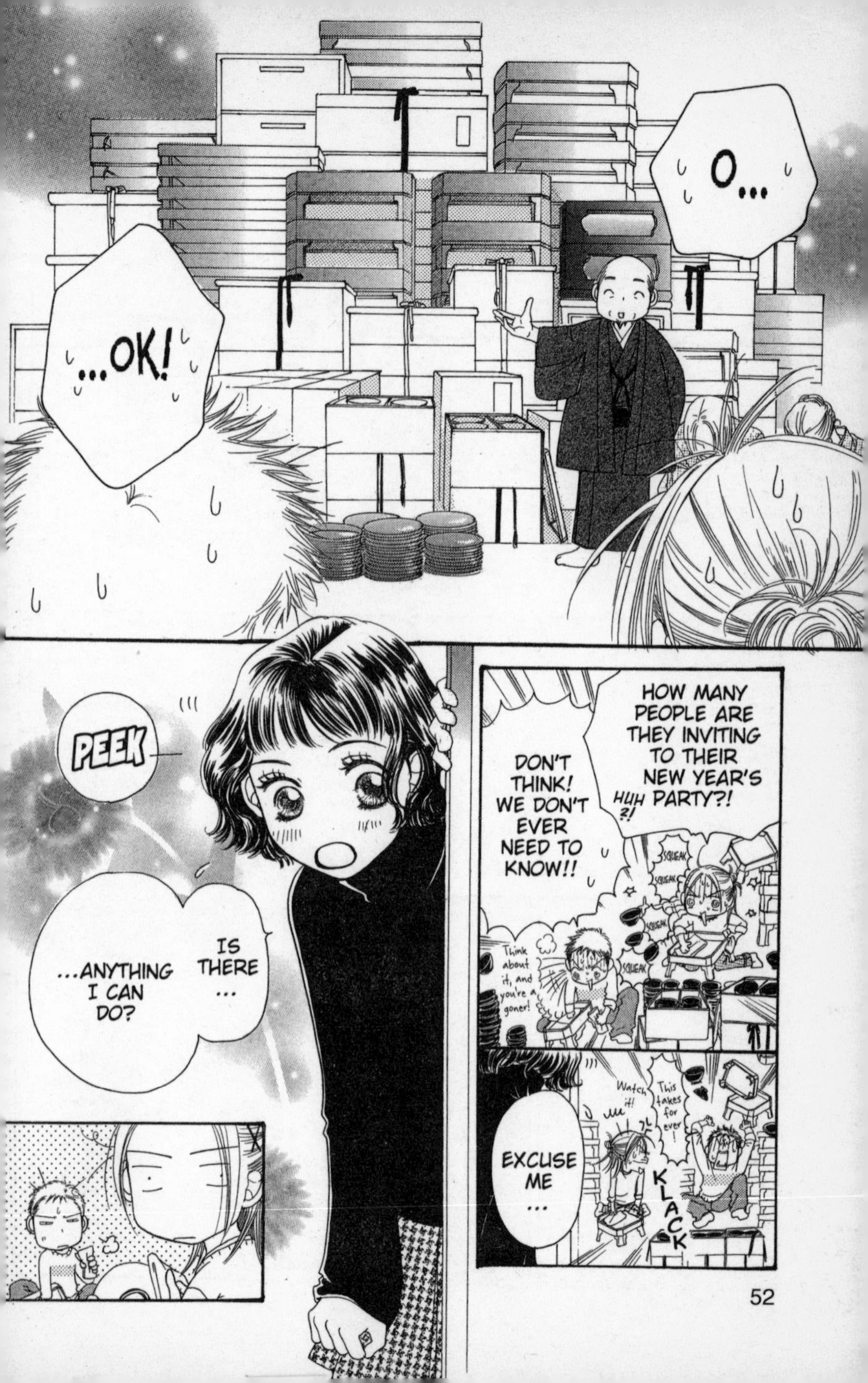

O...
...OK!
HOW MANY PEOPLE ARE THEY INVITING TO THEIR NEW YEAR'S PARTY?!
HUH ?!
DON'T THINK! WE DON'T EVER NEED TO KNOW!!
SQUEAK
SQUEAK
SQUEAK
SQUEAK
Think about it, and you're a goner!
This takes for ever!
Watch it!
KLACK
EXCUSE ME ...
PEEK
IS THERE ...
...ANYTHING I CAN DO?

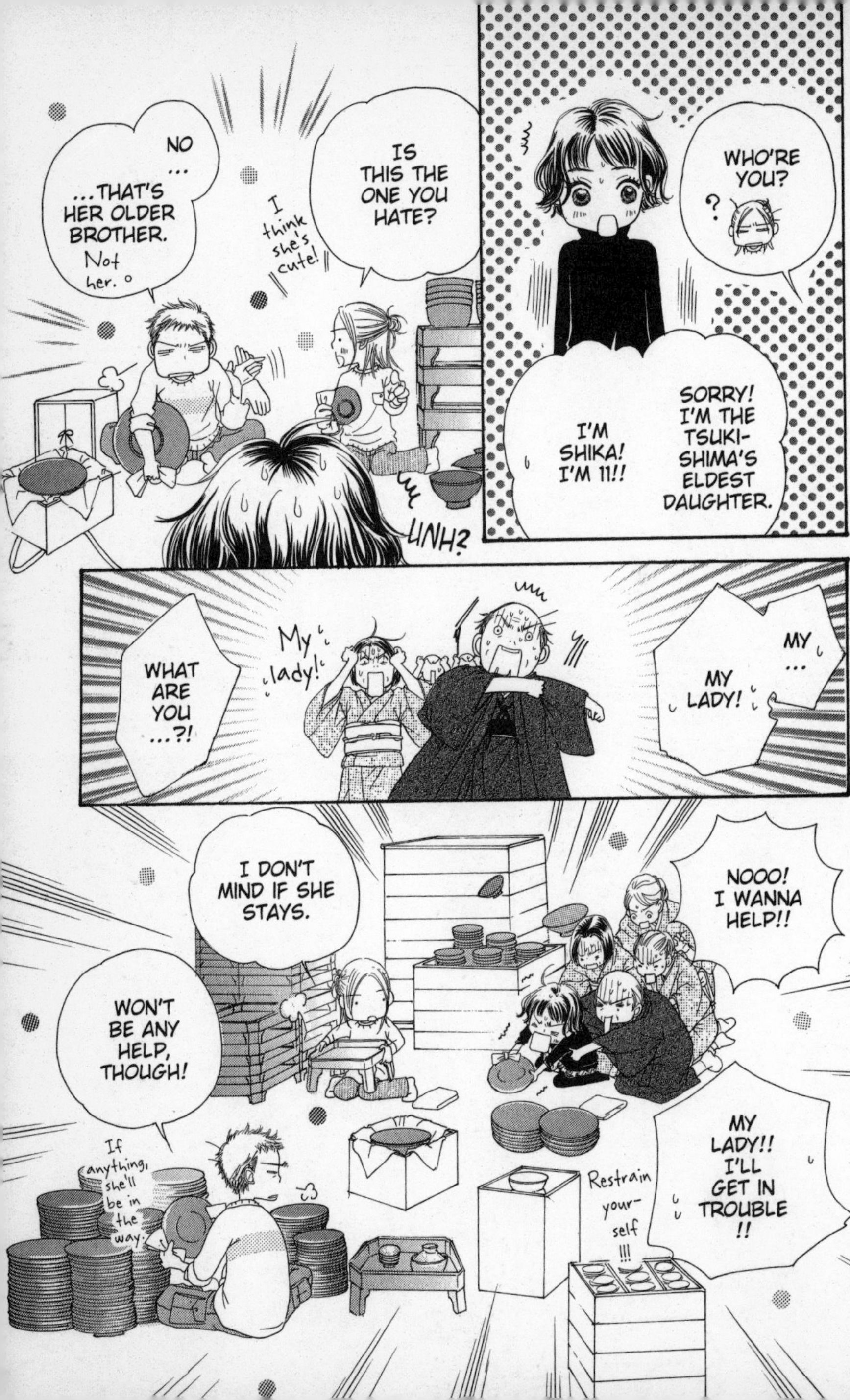
WHO'RE YOU?
SORRY! I'M THE TSUKI-SHIMA'S ELDEST DAUGHTER.
I'M SHIKA! I'M 11!!
UNH?
IS THIS THE ONE YOU HATE?
I think she's cute!
NO ... ...THAT'S HER OLDER BROTHER.
Not her.
MY ... MY LADY!
My lady!
WHAT ARE YOU ...?!
NOOO! I WANNA HELP!!
MY LADY!! I'LL GET IN TROUBLE!!
Restrain your-self!!!
I DON'T MIND IF SHE STAYS.
WON'T BE ANY HELP, THOUGH!
If anything, she'll be in the way.

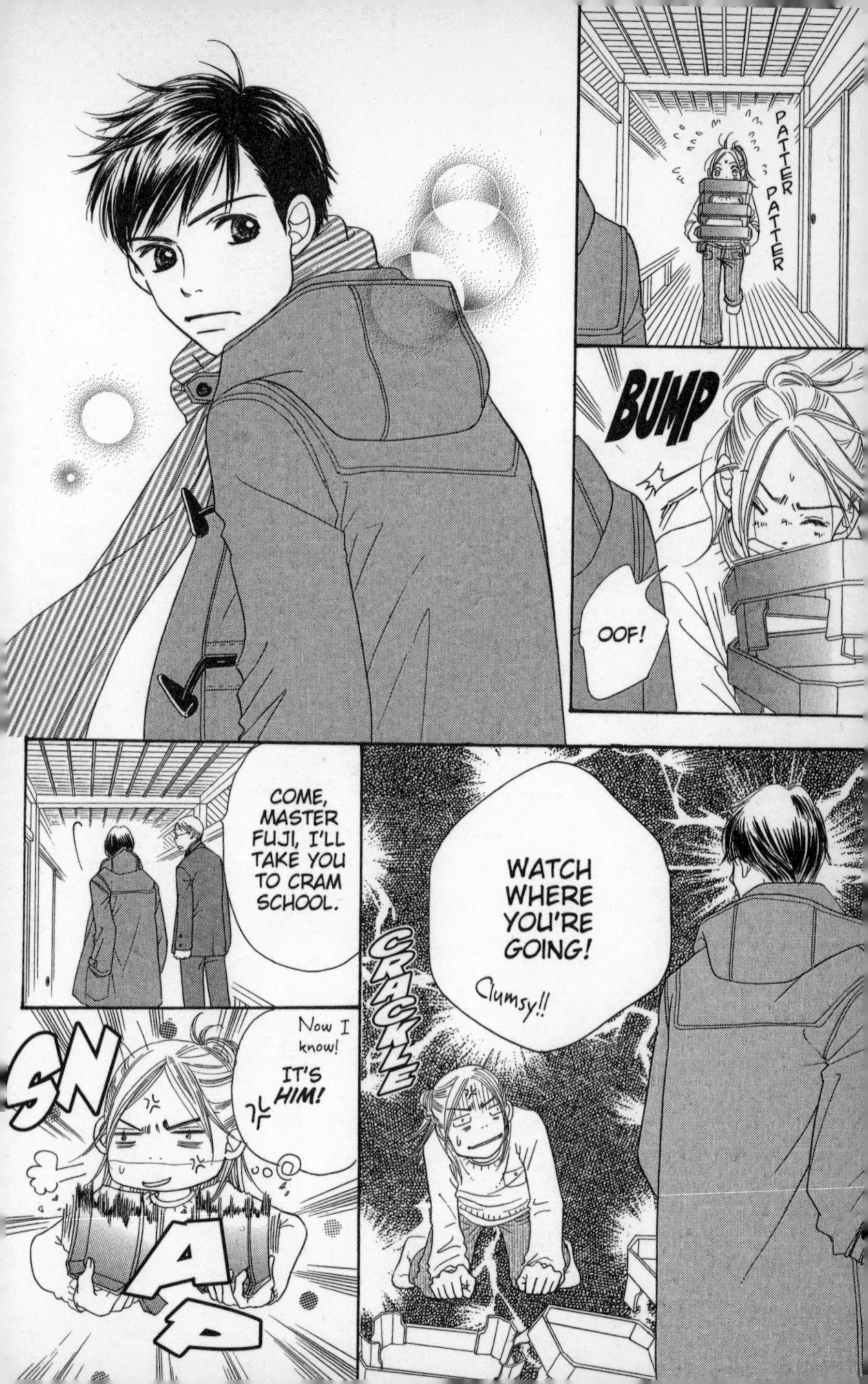
PATTER PATTER
BUMP
OOF!
WATCH WHERE YOU'RE GOING!
Clumsy!!
CRACKLE
COME, MASTER FUJI, I'LL TAKE YOU TO CRAM SCHOOL.
Now I know!
IT'S HIM!
SNAP

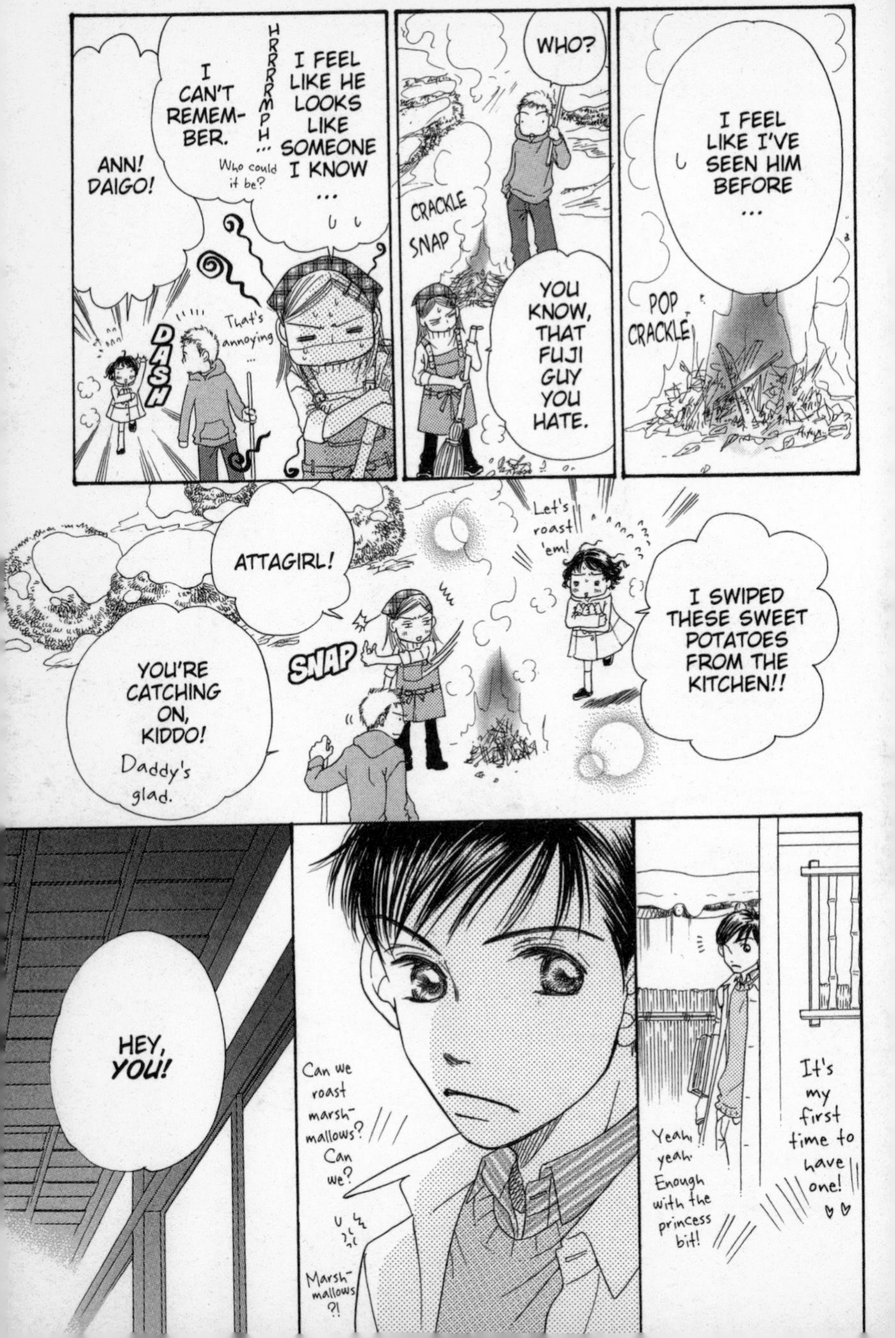
I FEEL LIKE I'VE SEEN HIM BEFORE ...
POP CRACKLE
WHO?
CRACKLE SNAP
YOU KNOW, THAT FUJI GUY YOU HATE.
I FEEL LIKE HE LOOKS LIKE SOMEONE I KNOW ...
HRRRRMPH...
Who could it be?
I CAN'T REMEMBER.
ANN! DAIGO!
That's annoying ...
DASH
Let's roast 'em!
I SWIPED THESE SWEET POTATOES FROM THE KITCHEN!!
ATTAGIRL!
SNAP
YOU'RE CATCHING ON, KIDDO!
Daddy's glad.
It's my first time to have one!
Yeah yeah. Enough with the princess bit!
Can we roast marsh-mallows? Can we?
Marsh-mallows?!
HEY, YOU!

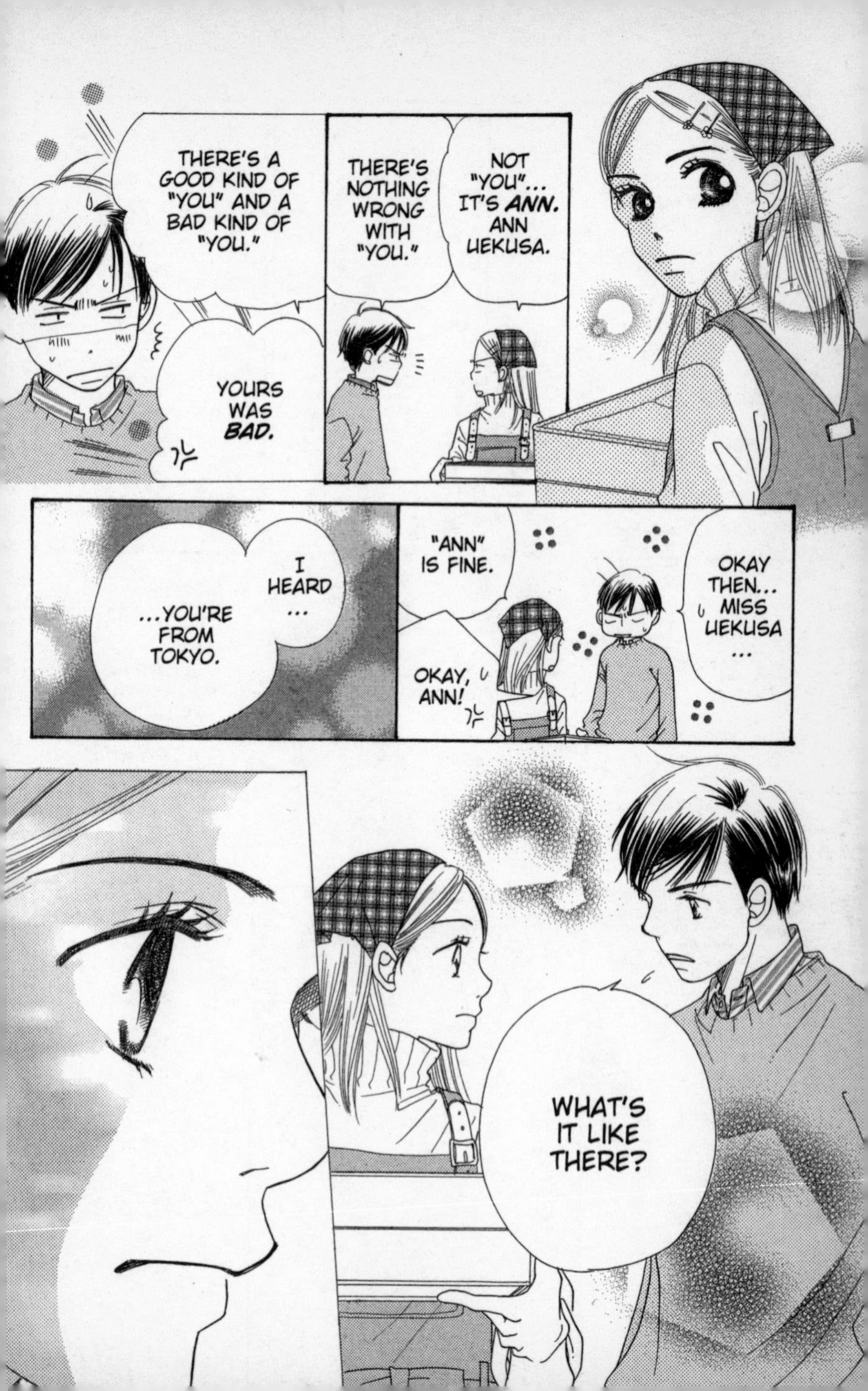
NOT "YOU"... IT'S ANN. ANN UEKUSA.
THERE'S NOTHING WRONG WITH "YOU."
THERE'S A GOOD KIND OF "YOU" AND A BAD KIND OF "YOU."
YOURS WAS BAD.
OKAY THEN... MISS UEKUSA ...
"ANN" IS FINE.
OKAY, ANN!
I HEARD ...
...YOU'RE FROM TOKYO.
WHAT'S IT LIKE THERE?

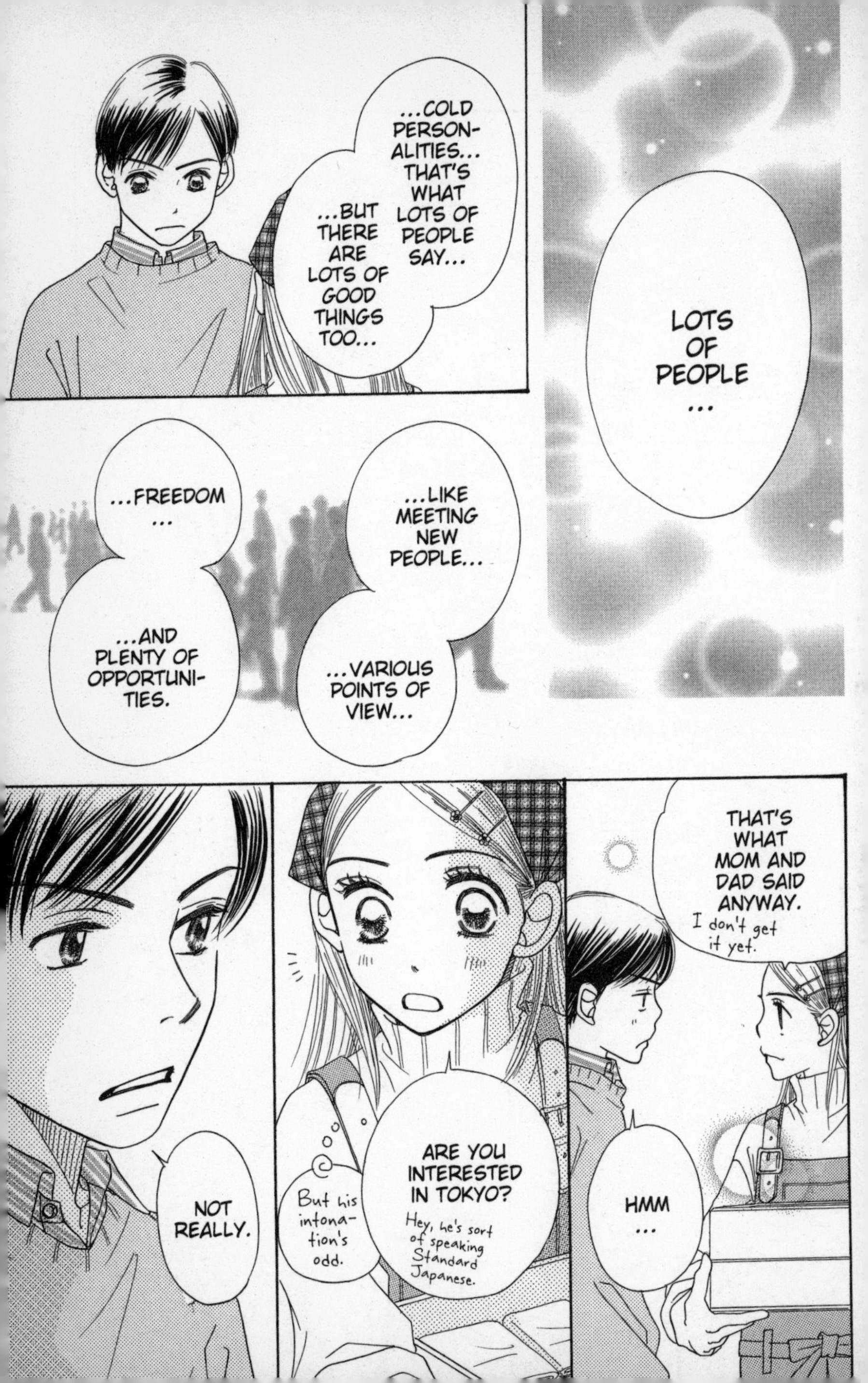
LOTS OF PEOPLE ...
...COLD PERSONALITIES... THAT'S WHAT LOTS OF PEOPLE SAY...
...BUT THERE ARE LOTS OF GOOD THINGS TOO...
...LIKE MEETING NEW PEOPLE...
...VARIOUS POINTS OF VIEW...
...FREEDOM ...
...AND PLENTY OF OPPORTUNITIES.
THAT'S WHAT MOM AND DAD SAID ANYWAY.
I don't get it yet.
HMM ...
ARE YOU INTERESTED IN TOKYO?
Hey, he's sort of speaking Standard Japanese.
But his intonation's odd.
NOT REALLY.

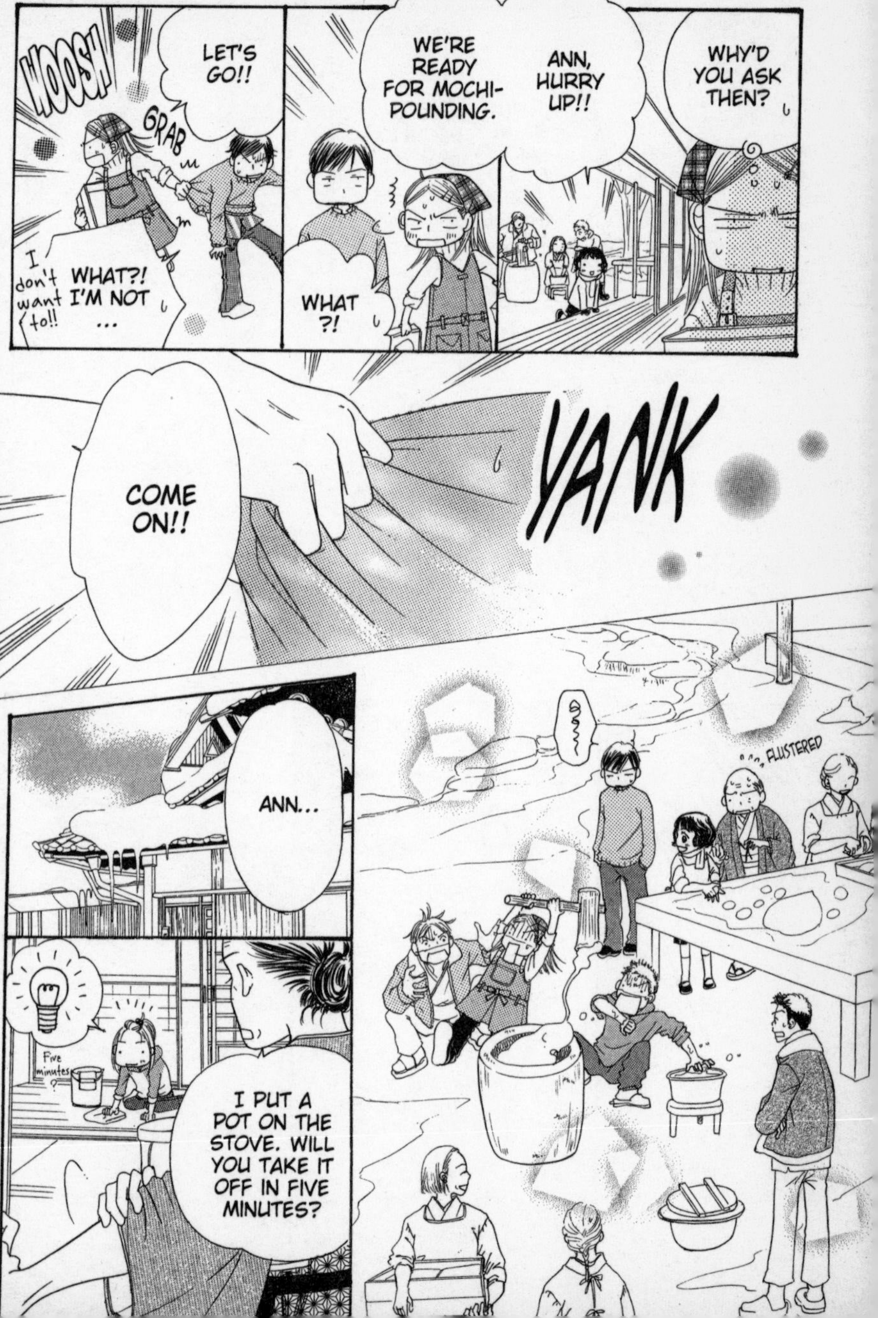
WHY'D YOU ASK THEN?
ANN, HURRY UP!!
WE'RE READY FOR MOCHI-POUNDING.
WHAT ?!
LET'S GO!!
WHOOSH
GRAB
WHAT?! I'M NOT ...
I don't want to!!
YANK
COME ON!!
FLUSTERED
ANN...
I PUT A POT ON THE STOVE. WILL YOU TAKE IT OFF IN FIVE MINUTES?
Five minutes?

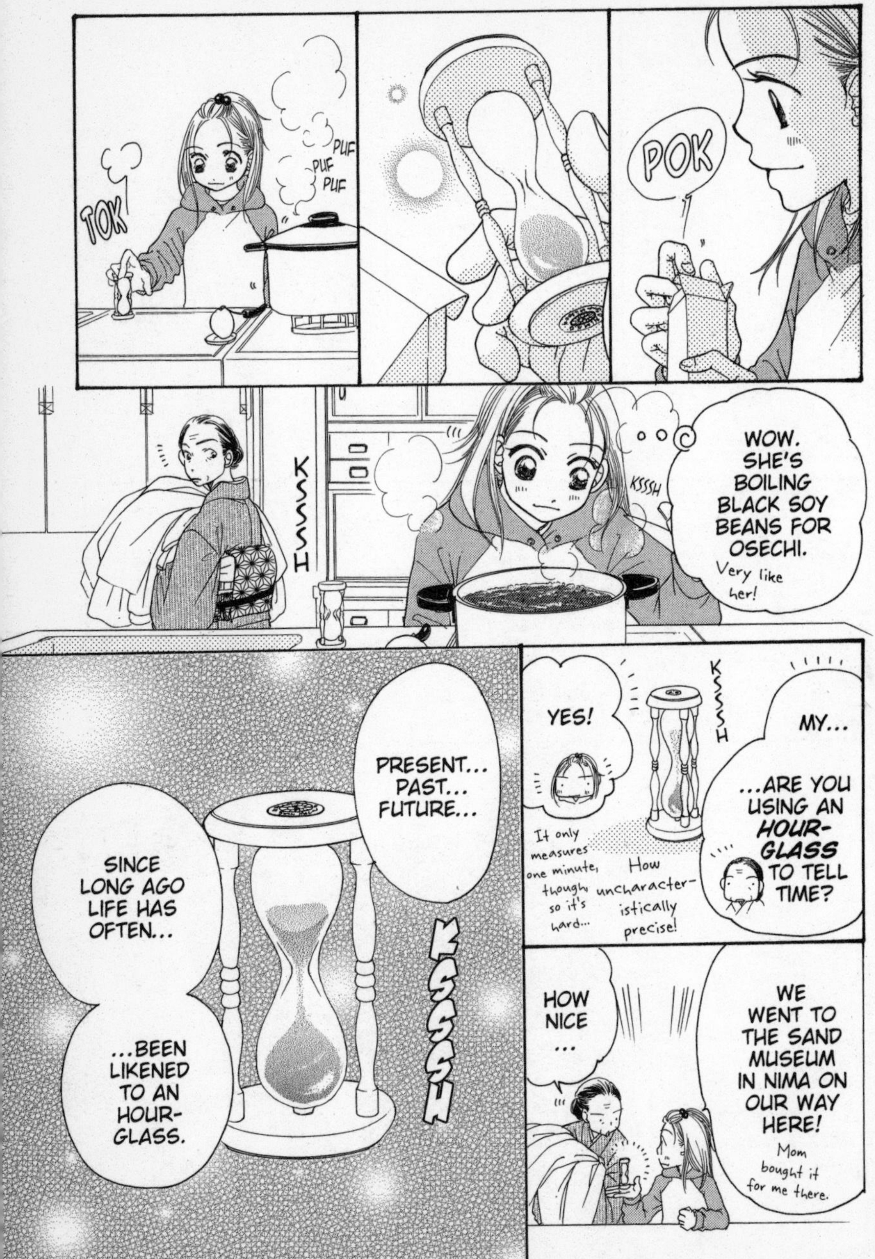
POK
PUF PUF PUF
TOK
WOW. SHE'S BOILING BLACK SOY BEANS FOR OSECHI.
Very like her!
KSSSH
KSSSH
MY...
...ARE YOU USING AN ***HOUR-GLASS*** TO TELL TIME?
KSSSH
YES!
It only measures one minute, though so it's hard...
How uncharacter-istically precise!
WE WENT TO THE SAND MUSEUM IN NIMA ON OUR WAY HERE!
Mom bought it for me there.
HOW NICE ...
PRESENT... PAST... FUTURE...
KSSSH
SINCE LONG AGO LIFE HAS OFTEN...
...BEEN LIKENED TO AN HOUR-GLASS.

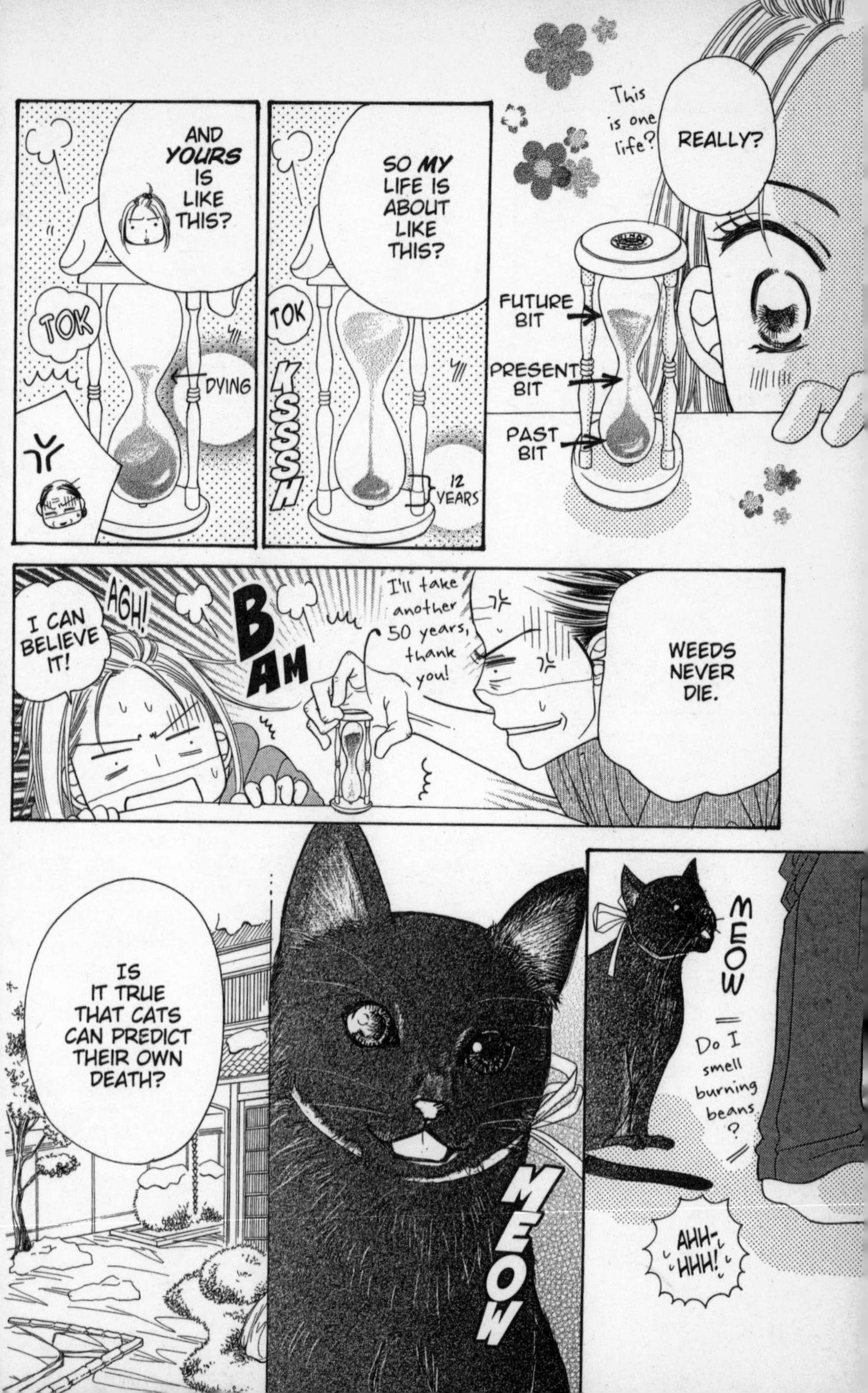
This is one life?
REALLY?
FUTURE BIT
PRESENT BIT
PAST BIT
SO MY LIFE IS ABOUT LIKE THIS?
TOK
KSSSH
12 YEARS
AND YOURS IS LIKE THIS?
TOK
DYING
WEEDS NEVER DIE.
I'll take another 50 years, thank you!
BAM
AGH!
I CAN BELIEVE IT!
MEOW
=
Do I smell burning beans?
=
AHH-HHH!
MEOW
IS IT TRUE THAT CATS CAN PREDICT THEIR OWN DEATH?

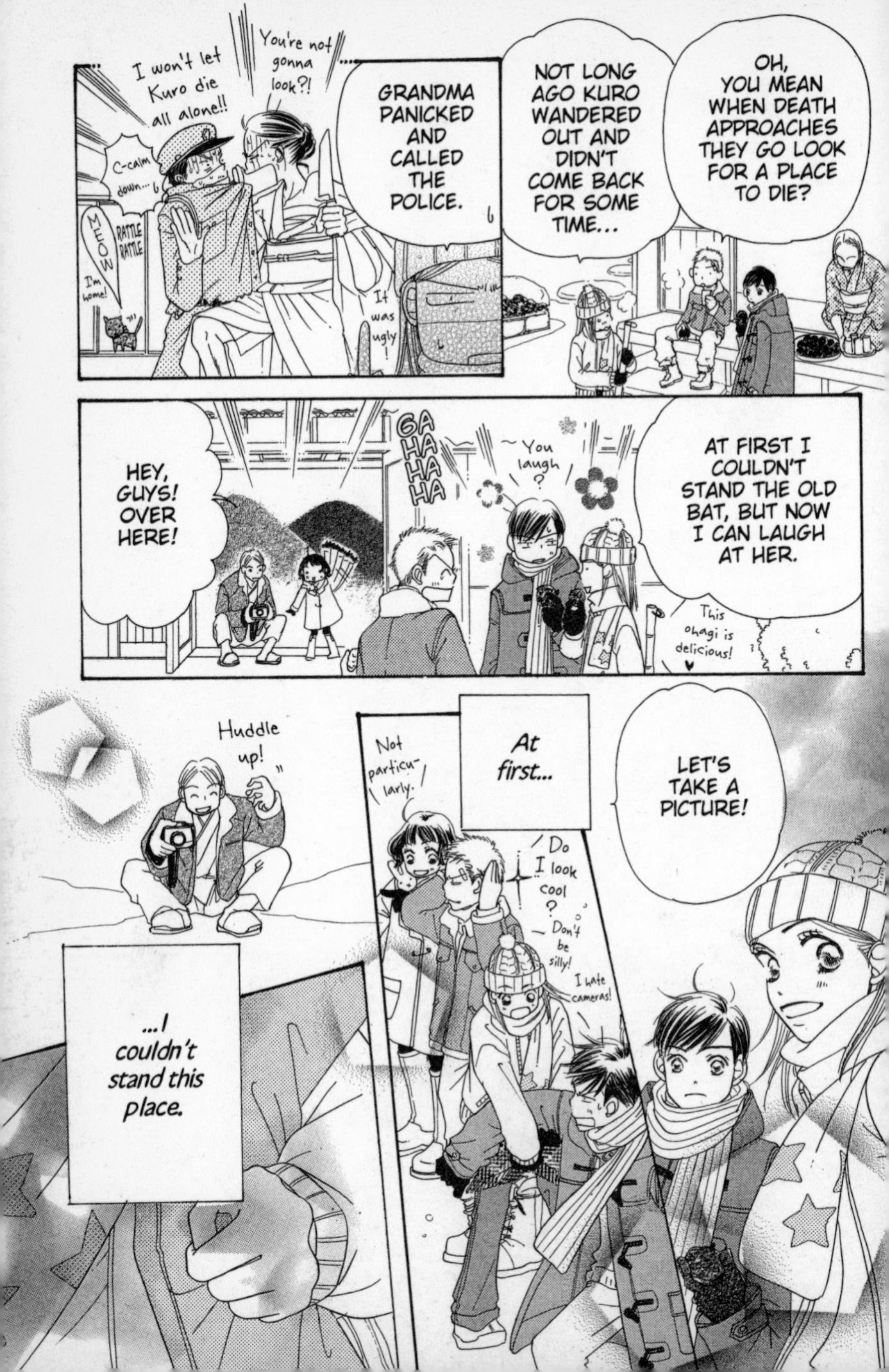
OH, YOU MEAN WHEN DEATH APPROACHES THEY GO LOOK FOR A PLACE TO DIE?
NOT LONG AGO KURO WANDERED OUT AND DIDN'T COME BACK FOR SOME TIME...
GRANDMA PANICKED AND CALLED THE POLICE.
It was ugly!
You're not gonna look?!
I won't let Kuro die all alone!!
C-calm down...
RATTLE RATTLE
MEOW
I'm home!
AT FIRST I COULDN'T STAND THE OLD BAT, BUT NOW I CAN LAUGH AT HER.
This ohagi is delicious!
~You laugh?
GAHAHAHA
HEY, GUYS! OVER HERE!
LET'S TAKE A PICTURE!
At first...
Do I look cool?
Don't be silly!
I hate cameras!
Not particu-larly.
Huddle up!
...I couldn't stand this place.

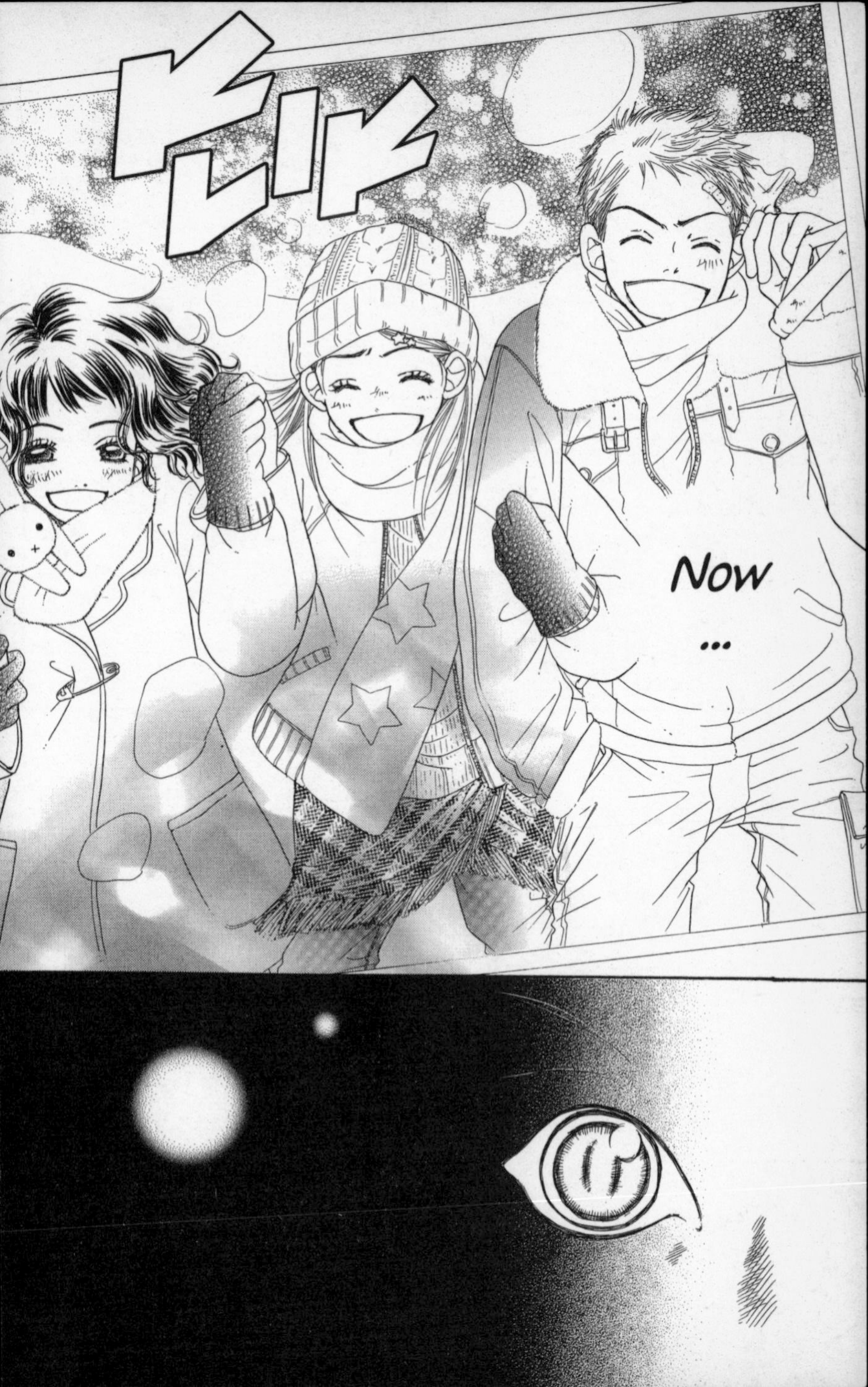
Now
...

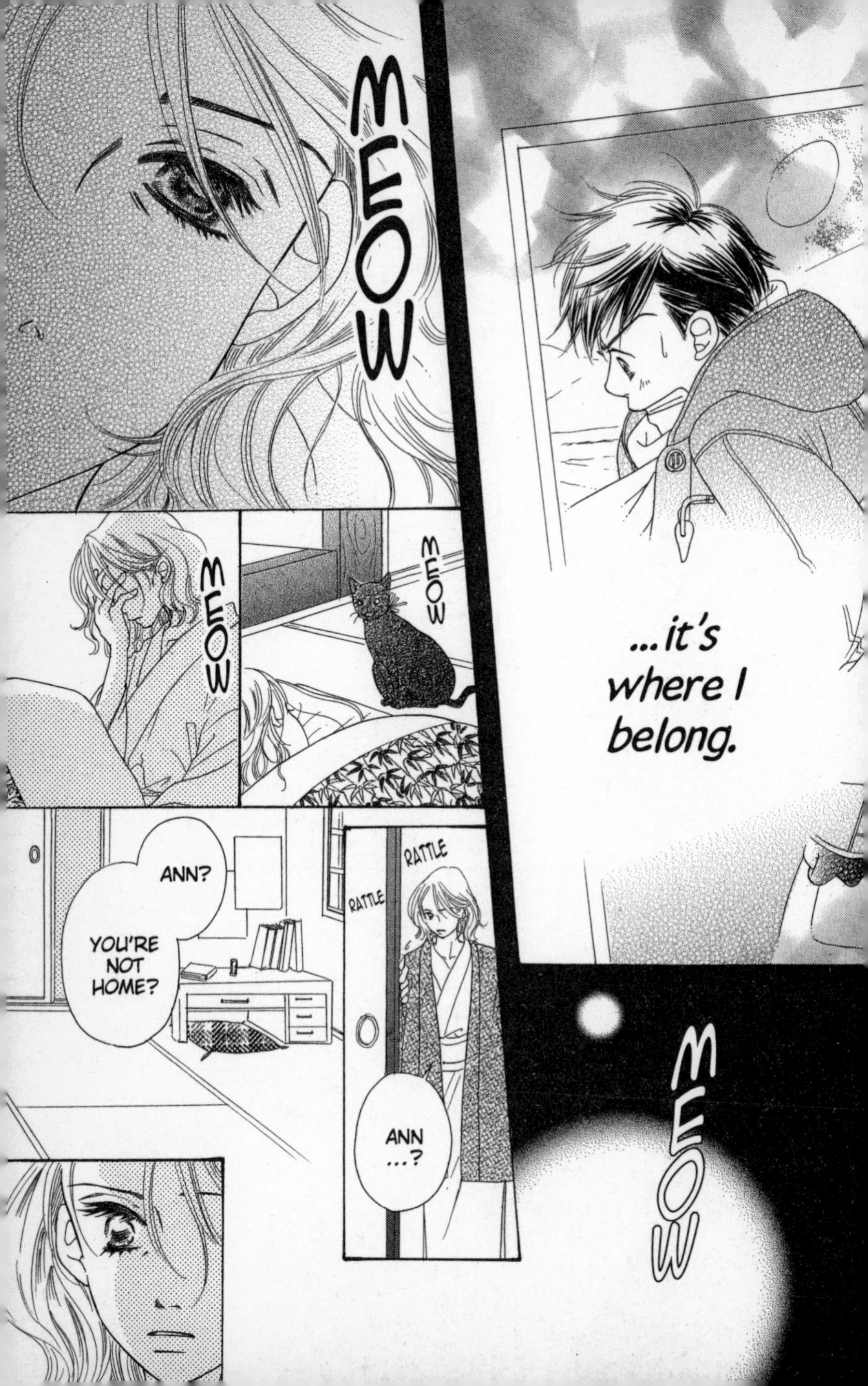
...it's where I belong.
MEOW
MEOW
MEOW
MEOW
RATTLE
RATTLE
ANN ...?
ANN?
YOU'RE NOT HOME?

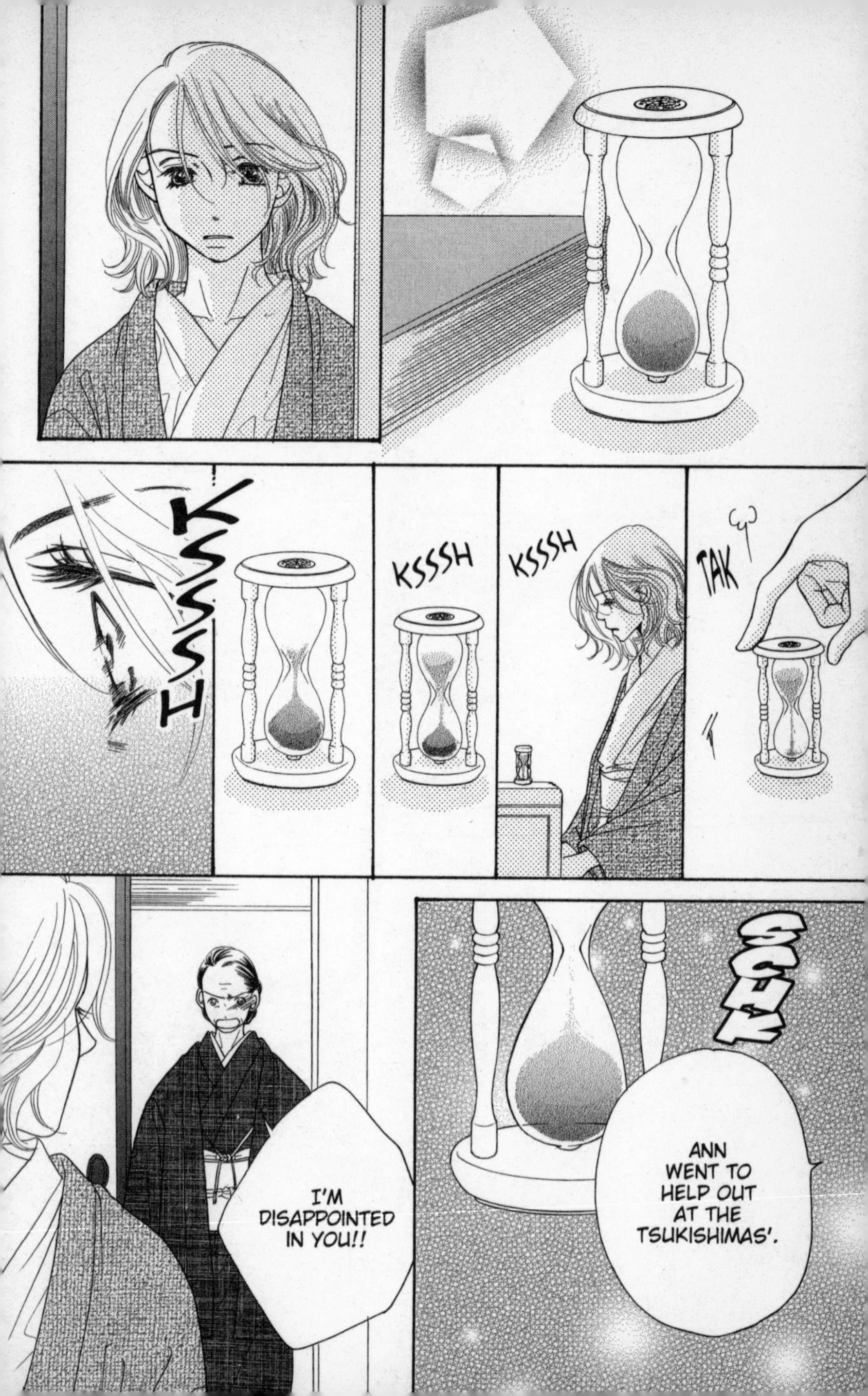
TAK
KSSSH
KSSSH
KSSSH
SCHY
ANN WENT TO HELP OUT AT THE TSUKISHIMAS'.
I'M DISAPPOINTED IN YOU!!

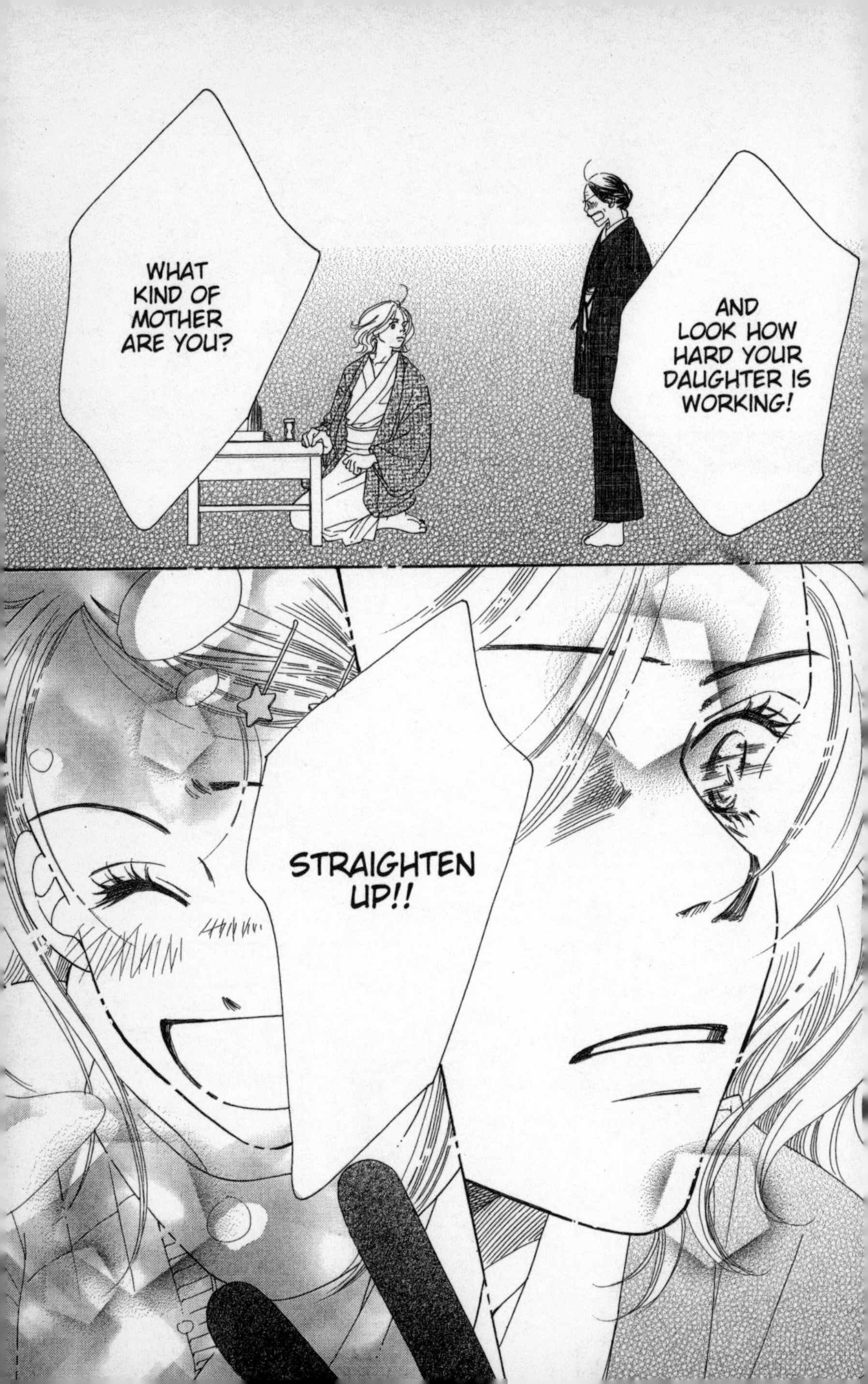
AND LOOK HOW HARD YOUR DAUGHTER IS WORKING!
WHAT KIND OF MOTHER ARE YOU?
STRAIGHTEN UP!!

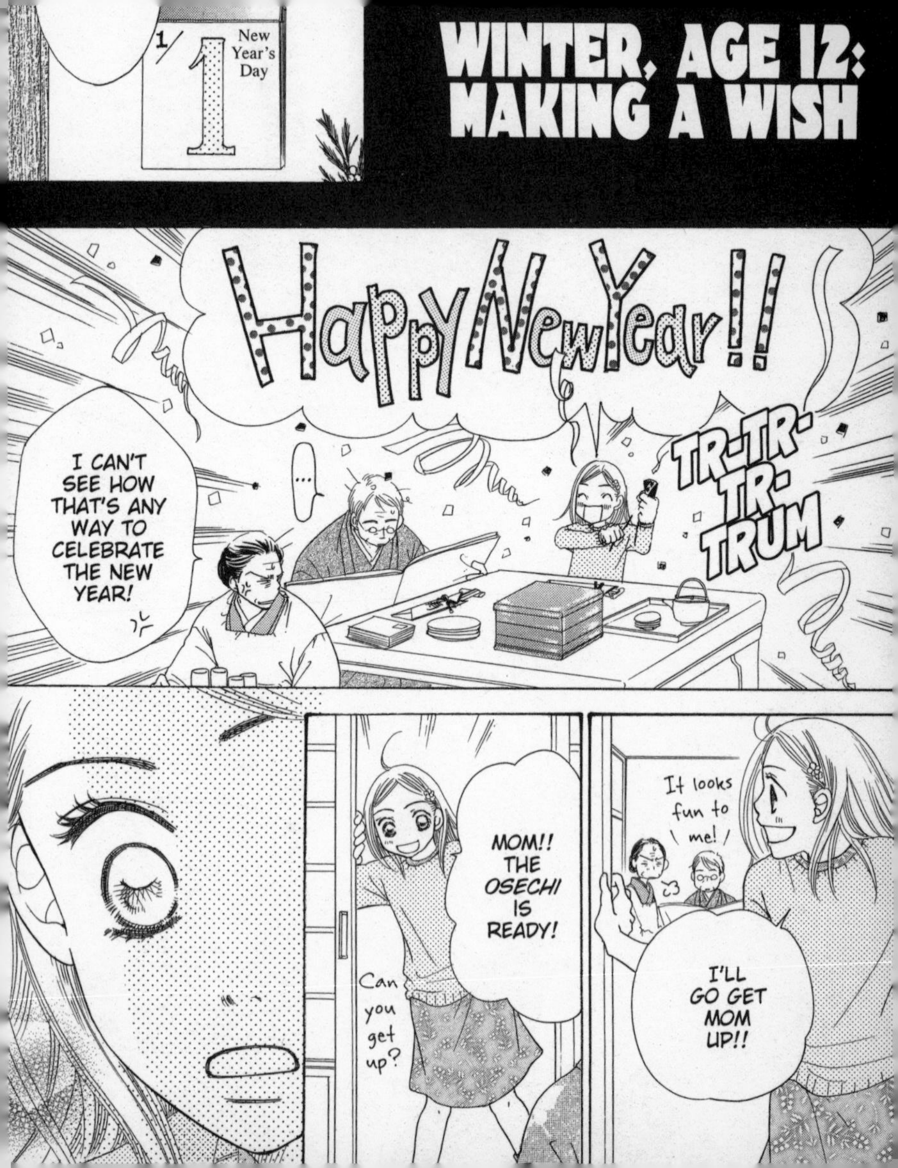
WINTER, AGE 12: MAKING A WISH
1/1 New Year's Day
Happy New Year!!
TR-TR-TR-TRUM
...
I CAN'T SEE HOW THAT'S ANY WAY TO CELEBRATE THE NEW YEAR!
It looks fun to me!
I'LL GO GET MOM UP!!
MOM!! THE OSECHI IS READY!
Can you get up?

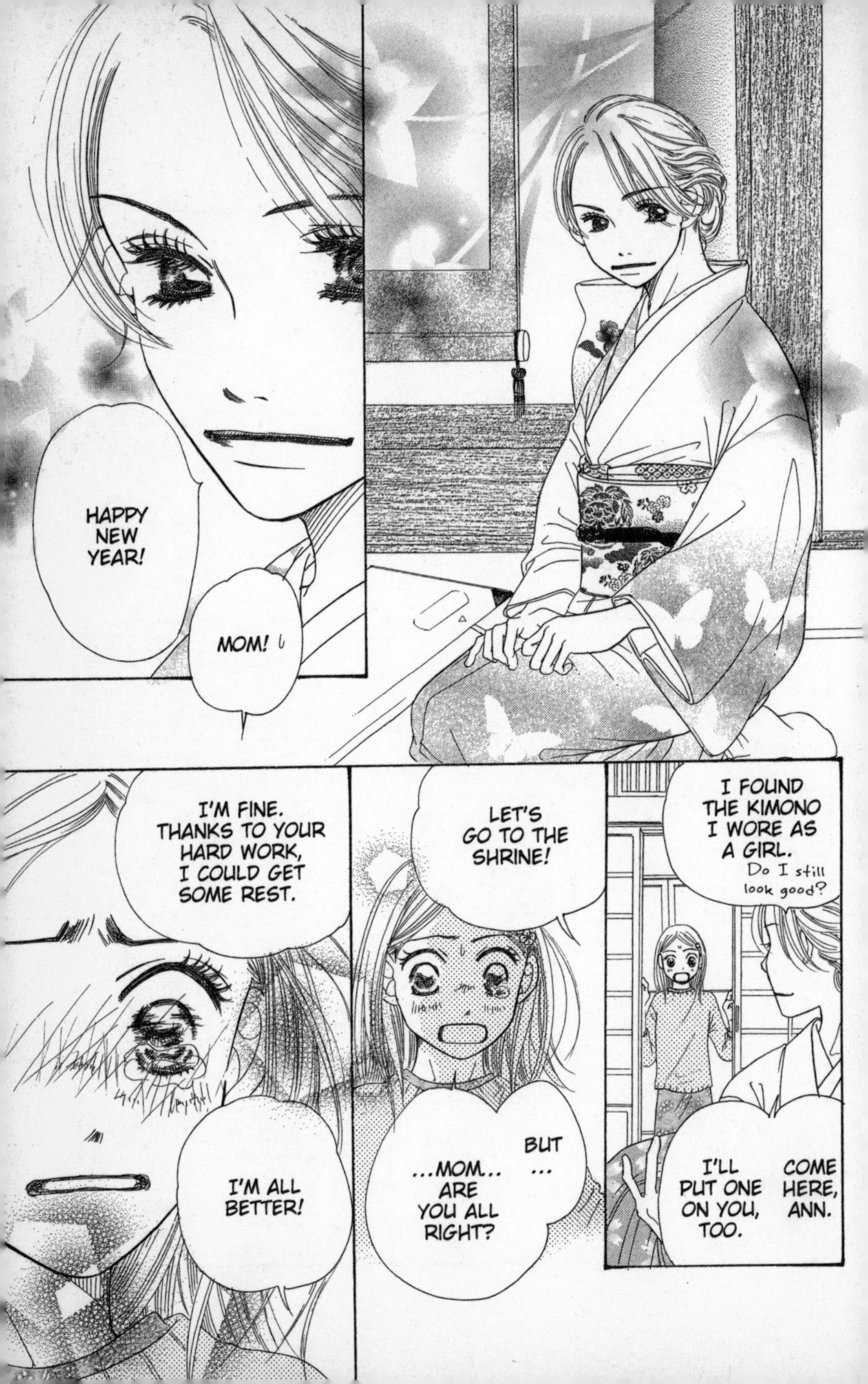
HAPPY NEW YEAR!
MOM!
I FOUND THE KIMONO I WORE AS A GIRL.
Do I still look good?
COME HERE, ANN.
I'LL PUT ONE ON YOU, TOO.
LET'S GO TO THE SHRINE!
BUT ...
...MOM... ARE YOU ALL RIGHT?
I'M FINE. THANKS TO YOUR HARD WORK, I COULD GET SOME REST.
I'M ALL BETTER!

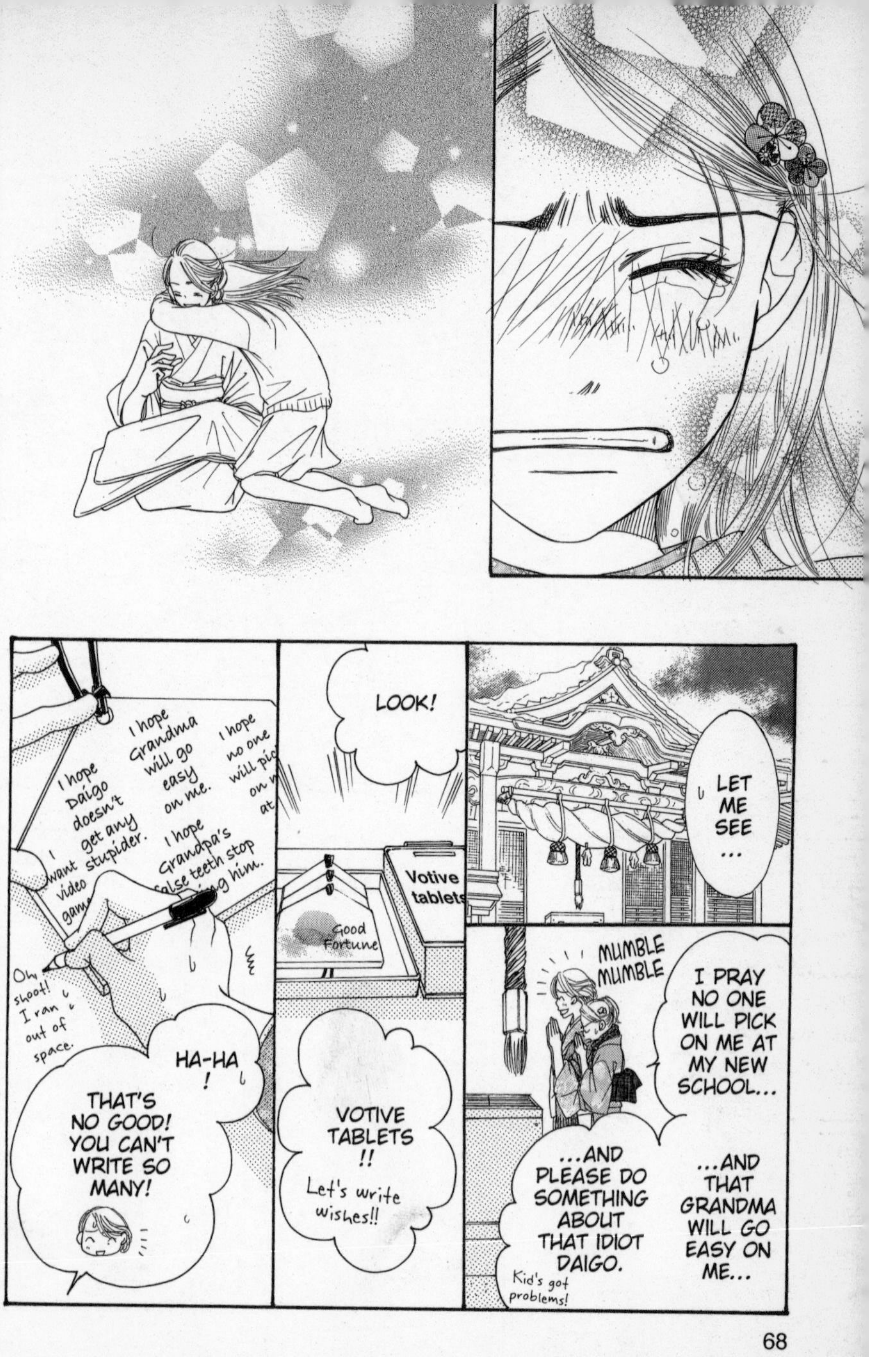
LET ME SEE...
MUMBLE MUMBLE
I PRAY NO ONE WILL PICK ON ME AT MY NEW SCHOOL...
...AND THAT GRANDMA WILL GO EASY ON ME...
...AND PLEASE DO SOMETHING ABOUT THAT IDIOT DAIGO.
Kid's got problems!
LOOK!
Votive tablets
Good Fortune
VOTIVE TABLETS!!
Let's write wishes!!
I hope Daigo doesn't get any stupider.
I hope Grandma will go easy on me.
I hope Grandpa's false teeth stop
Oh shoot! I ran out of space.
HA-HA!
THAT'S NO GOOD! YOU CAN'T WRITE SO MANY!

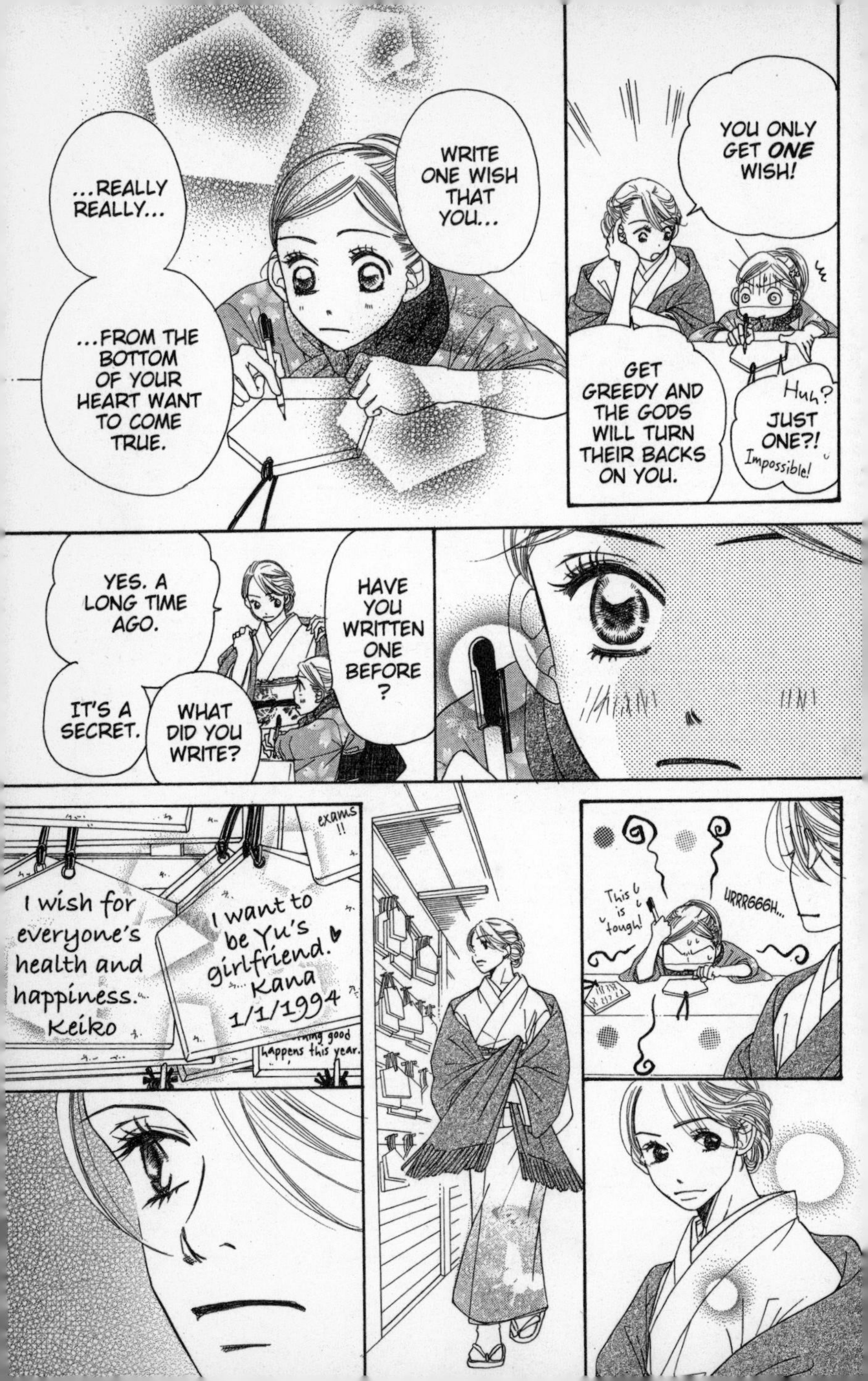
YOU ONLY GET ONE WISH!
GET GREEDY AND THE GODS WILL TURN THEIR BACKS ON YOU.
Huh? JUST ONE?! Impossible!
WRITE ONE WISH THAT YOU...
...REALLY REALLY...
...FROM THE BOTTOM OF YOUR HEART WANT TO COME TRUE.
HAVE YOU WRITTEN ONE BEFORE?
YES. A LONG TIME AGO.
WHAT DID YOU WRITE?
IT'S A SECRET.
This is tough!
URRRGGGH...
exams!!
I wish for everyone's health and happiness. Keiko
I want to be Yu's girlfriend! Kana 1/1/1994
thing good happens this year.

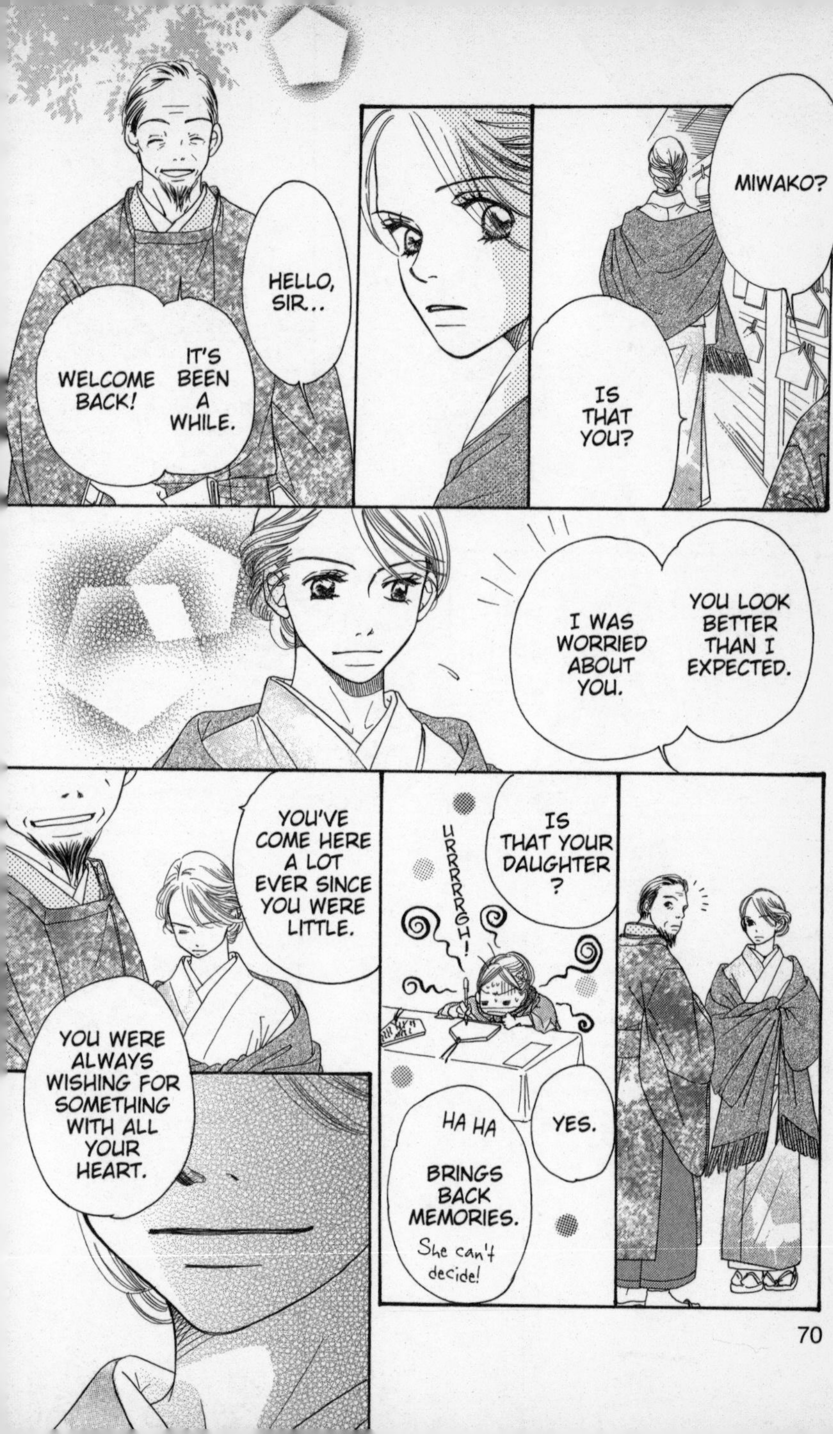
MIWAKO?
IS THAT YOU?
HELLO, SIR...
IT'S BEEN A WHILE.
WELCOME BACK!
YOU LOOK BETTER THAN I EXPECTED.
I WAS WORRIED ABOUT YOU.
IS THAT YOUR DAUGHTER?
URRRRRGH!
YES.
HA HA
BRINGS BACK MEMORIES.
She can't decide!
YOU'VE COME HERE A LOT EVER SINCE YOU WERE LITTLE.
YOU WERE ALWAYS WISHING FOR SOMETHING WITH ALL YOUR HEART.

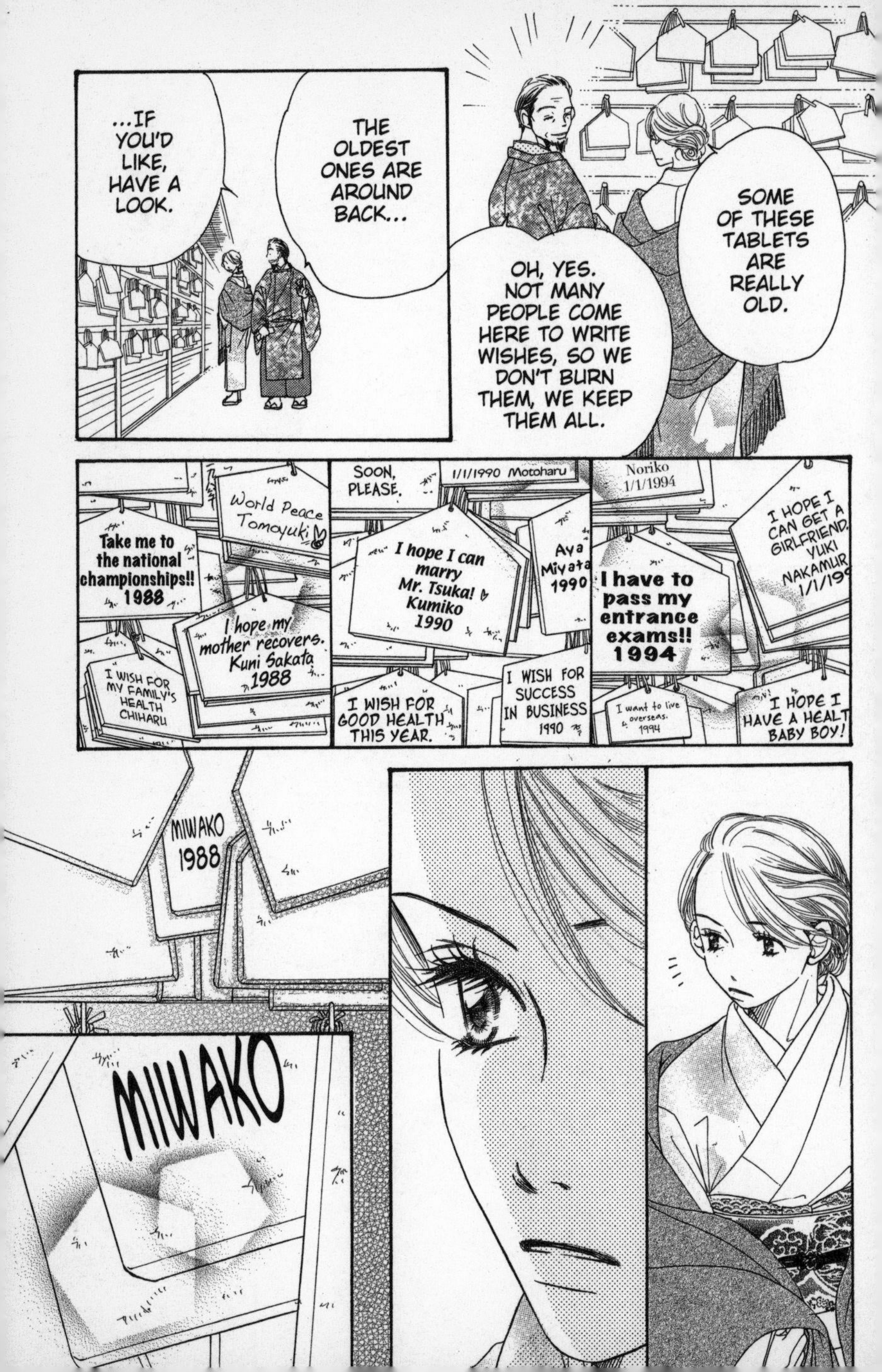
SOME OF THESE TABLETS ARE REALLY OLD.
OH, YES. NOT MANY PEOPLE COME HERE TO WRITE WISHES, SO WE DON'T BURN THEM, WE KEEP THEM ALL.
THE OLDEST ONES ARE AROUND BACK...
...IF YOU'D LIKE, HAVE A LOOK.
Noriko 1/1/1994
I HOPE I CAN GET A GIRLFRIEND. YUKI NAKAMUR 1/1/19
I have to pass my entrance exams!! 1994
I want to live overseas. 1994
I HOPE I HAVE A HEALT BABY BOY!
SOON, PLEASE.
1/1/1990 Motoharu
I hope I can marry Mr. Tsuka! Kumiko 1990
Aya Miyata 1990
I WISH FOR SUCCESS IN BUSINESS 1990
I WISH FOR GOOD HEALTH THIS YEAR.
World Peace Tomoyuki
Take me to the national championships!! 1988
I hope my mother recovers. Kuni Sakata 1988
I WISH FOR MY FAMILY'S HEALTH CHIHARU
MIWAKO 1988
MIWAKO

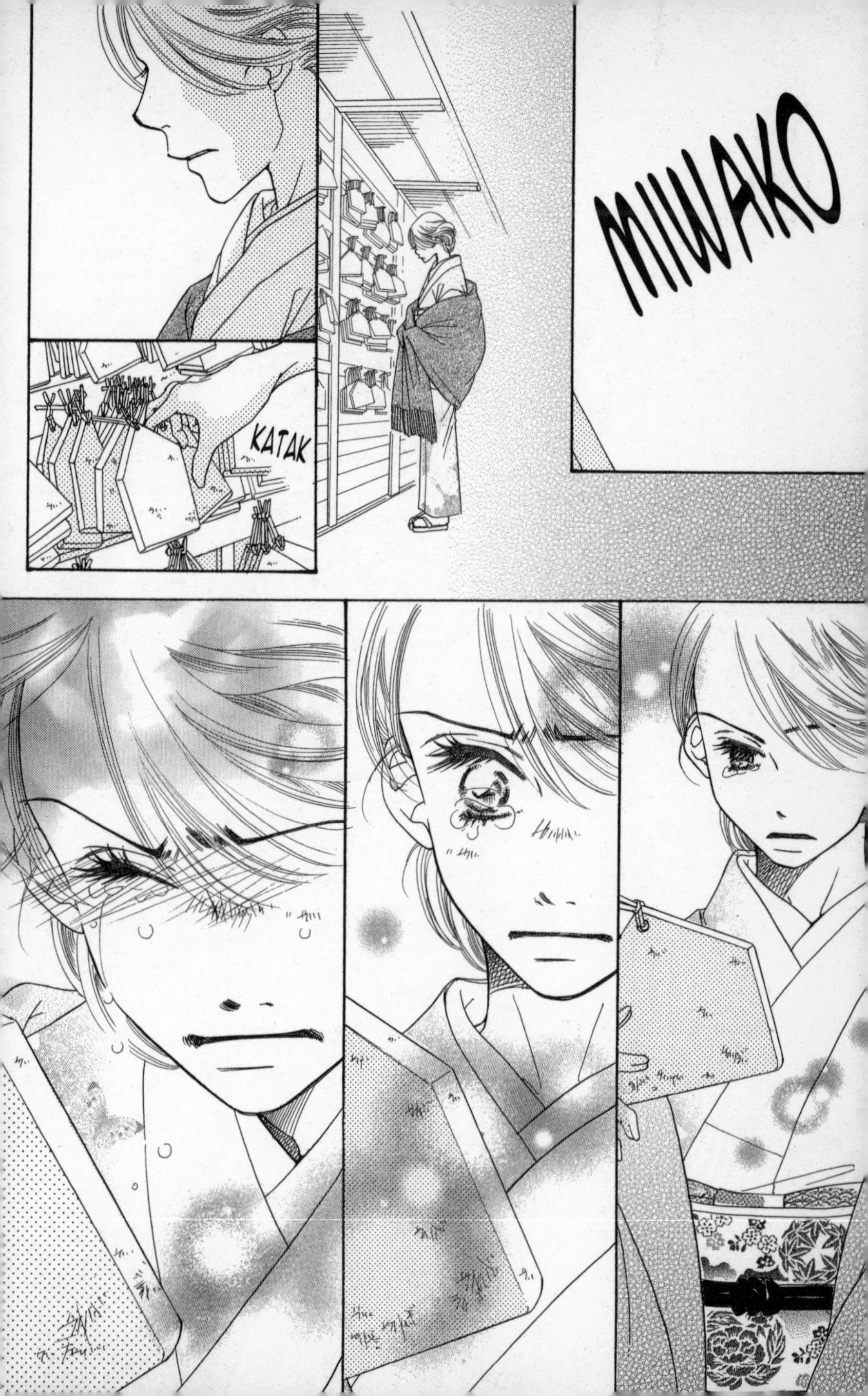
MIWAKO
KATAK

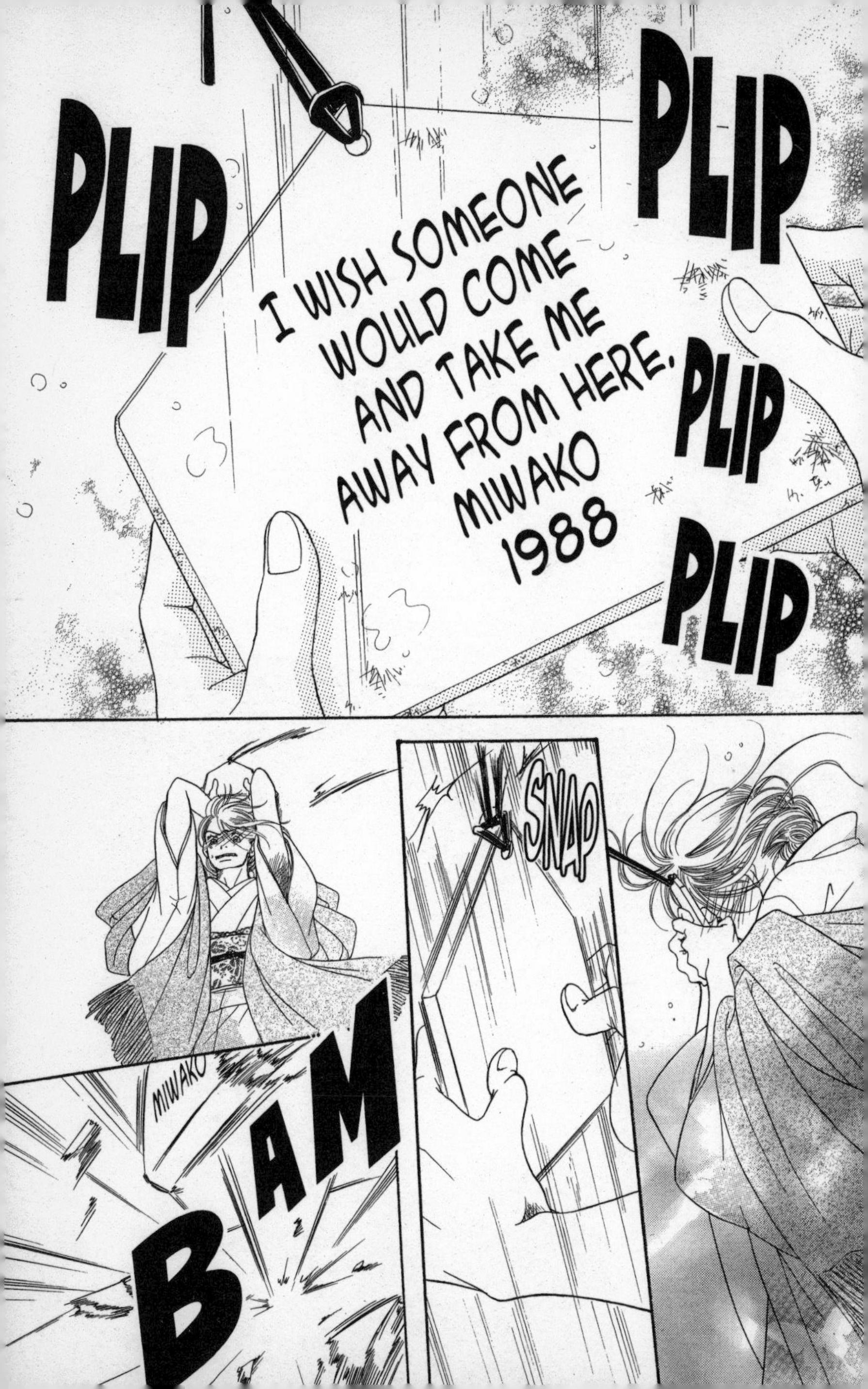
PLIP
PLIP
I WISH SOMEONE WOULD COME AND TAKE ME AWAY FROM HERE.
MIWAKO
1988
PLIP
PLIP
SNAP
MIWAKO
BAM

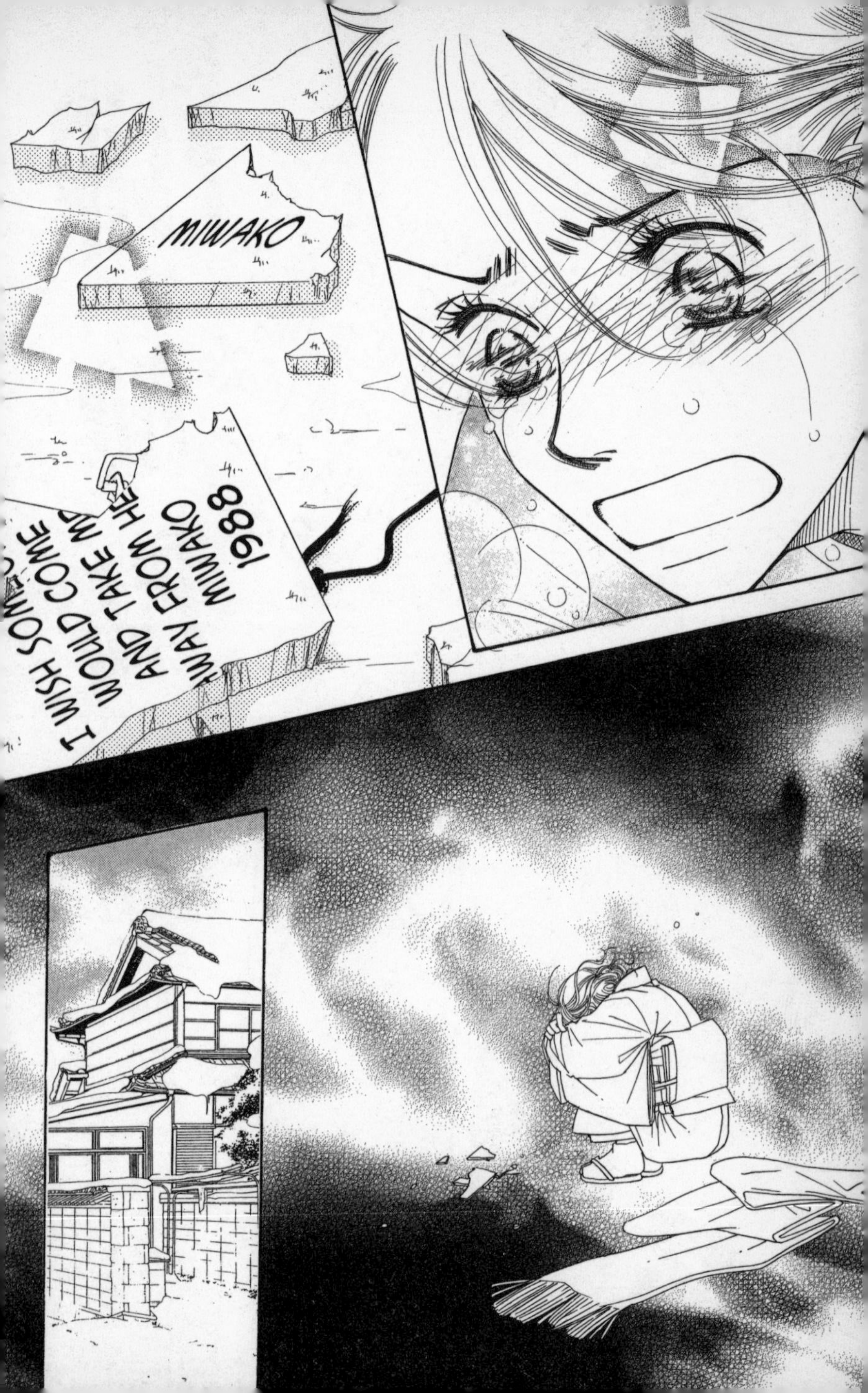
MIWAKO
I WISH SOME
WOULD COME
AND TAKE M
AWAY FROM HE
MIWAKO
1988

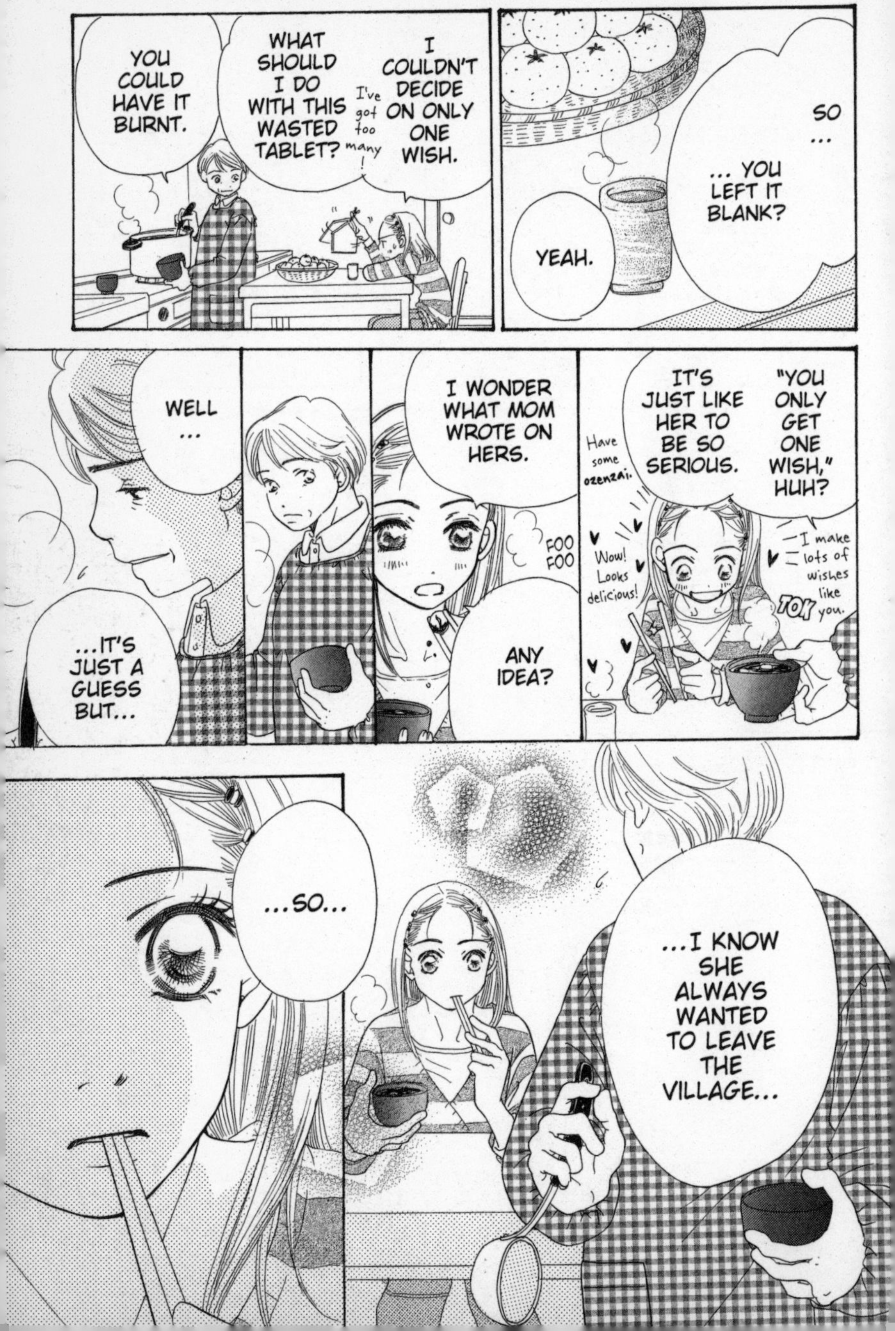
SO ...
... YOU LEFT IT BLANK?
YEAH.
I COULDN'T DECIDE ON ONLY ONE WISH.
I've got too many!
WHAT SHOULD I DO WITH THIS WASTED TABLET?
YOU COULD HAVE IT BURNT.
"YOU ONLY GET ONE WISH," HUH?
IT'S JUST LIKE HER TO BE SO SERIOUS.
I make lots of wishes like you.
TOK
Have some ozenzai.
Wow! Looks delicious!
I WONDER WHAT MOM WROTE ON HERS.
FOO FOO
ANY IDEA?
WELL ...
...IT'S JUST A GUESS BUT...
...I KNOW SHE ALWAYS WANTED TO LEAVE THE VILLAGE...
...SO...

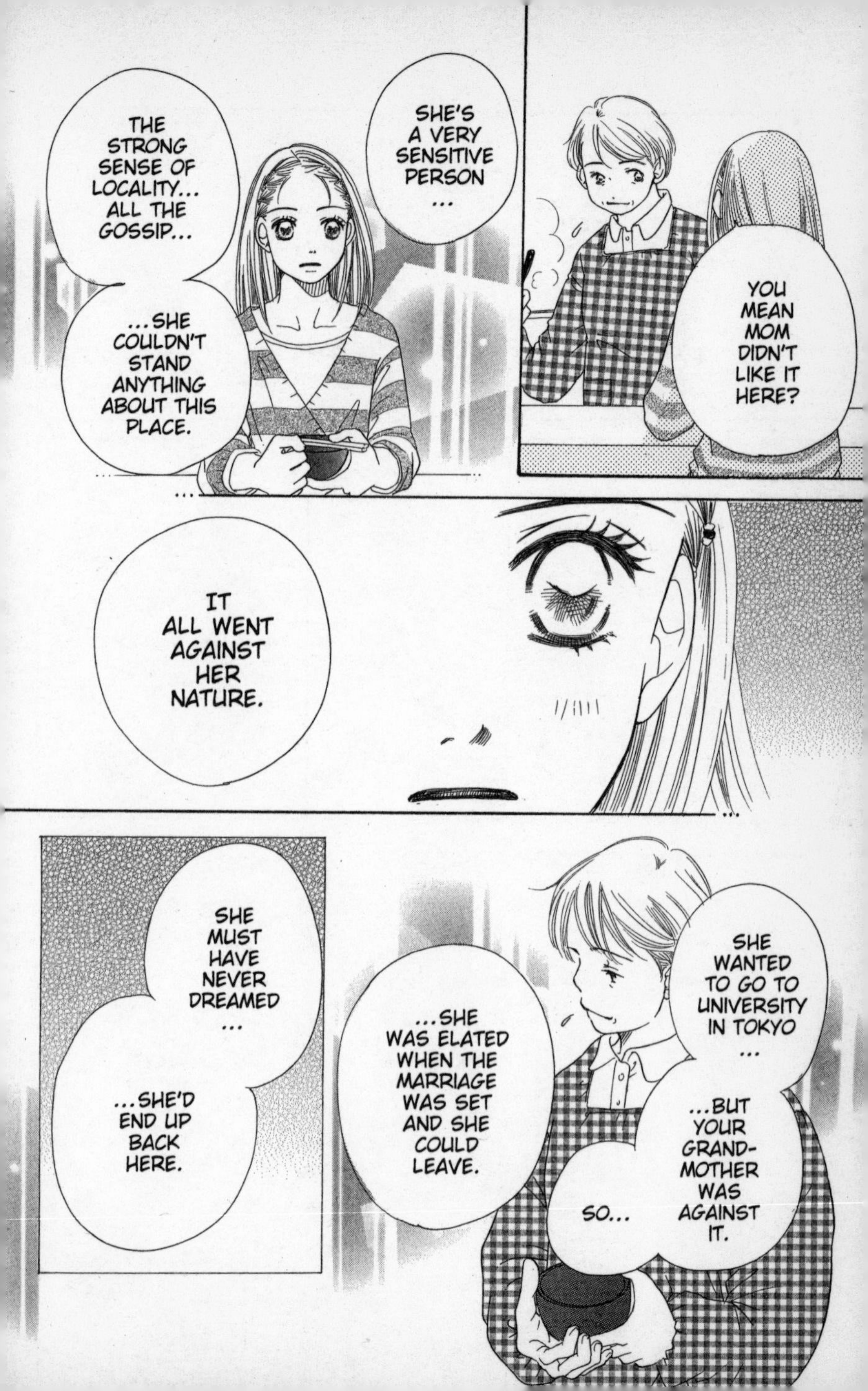
YOU MEAN MOM DIDN'T LIKE IT HERE?
SHE'S A VERY SENSITIVE PERSON...
THE STRONG SENSE OF LOCALITY... ALL THE GOSSIP...
...SHE COULDN'T STAND ANYTHING ABOUT THIS PLACE.
IT ALL WENT AGAINST HER NATURE.
SHE WANTED TO GO TO UNIVERSITY IN TOKYO...
...BUT YOUR GRAND-MOTHER WAS AGAINST IT.
SO...
...SHE WAS ELATED WHEN THE MARRIAGE WAS SET AND SHE COULD LEAVE.
SHE MUST HAVE NEVER DREAMED...
...SHE'D END UP BACK HERE.

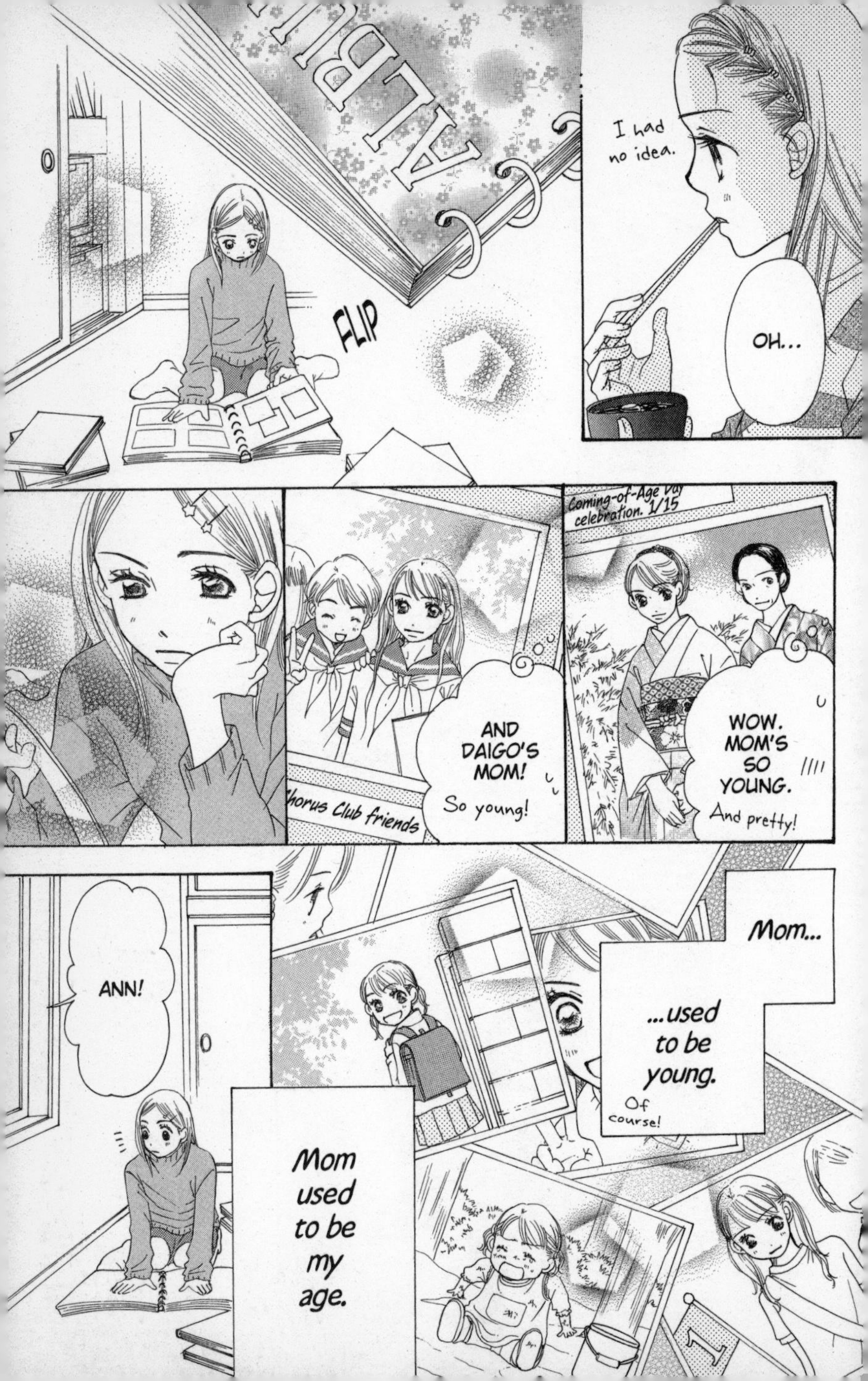
I had no idea.
OH...
FLIP
Coming-of-Age Day celebration. 1/15
WOW. MOM'S SO YOUNG.
And pretty!
AND DAIGO'S MOM!
So young!
Chorus Club friends
Mom...
...used to be young.
Of course!
ANN!
Mom used to be my age.

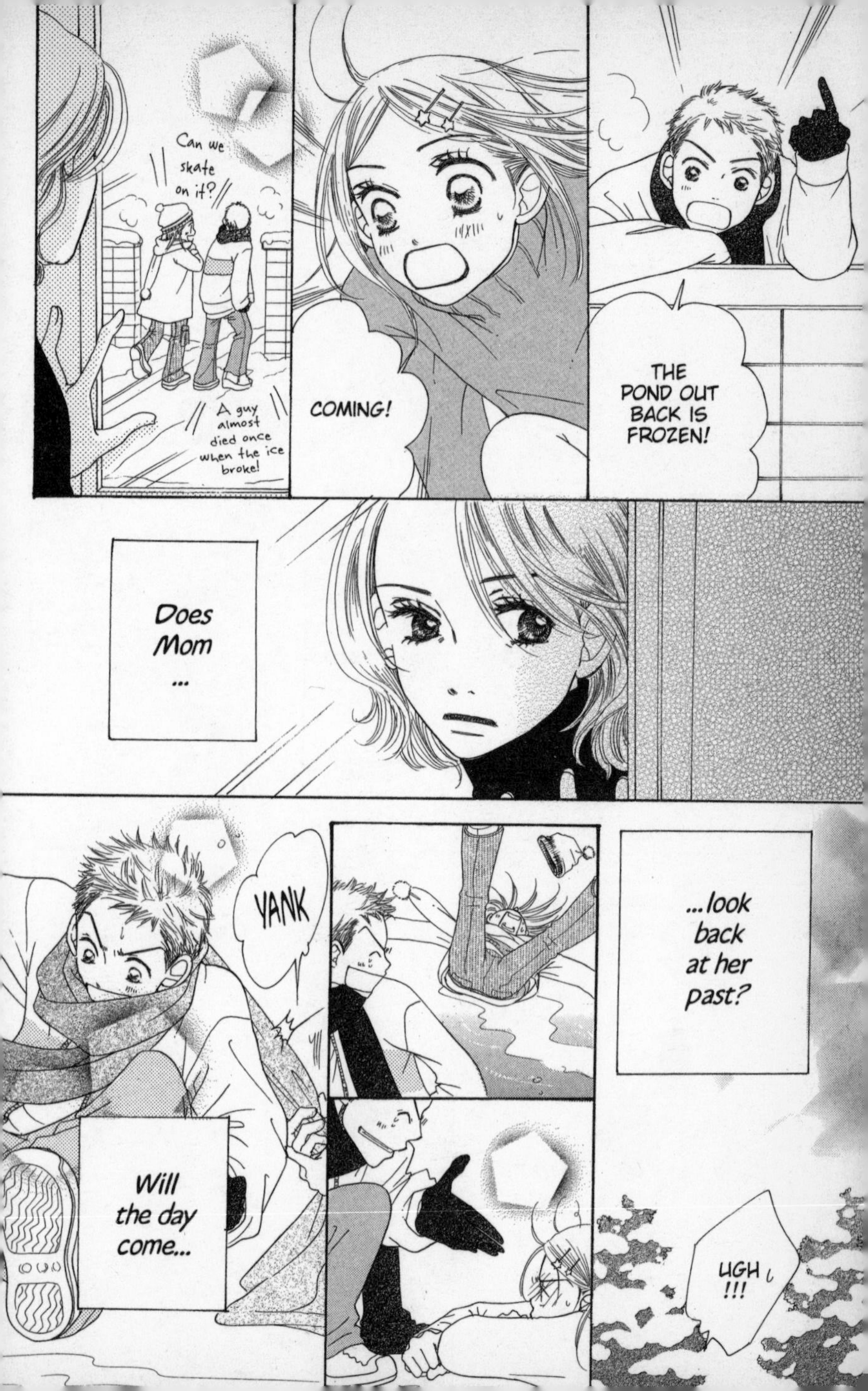
THE POND OUT BACK IS FROZEN!
COMING!
Can we skate on it?
A guy almost died once when the ice broke!
Does Mom ...
...look back at her past?
UGH !!!
YANK
Will the day come...

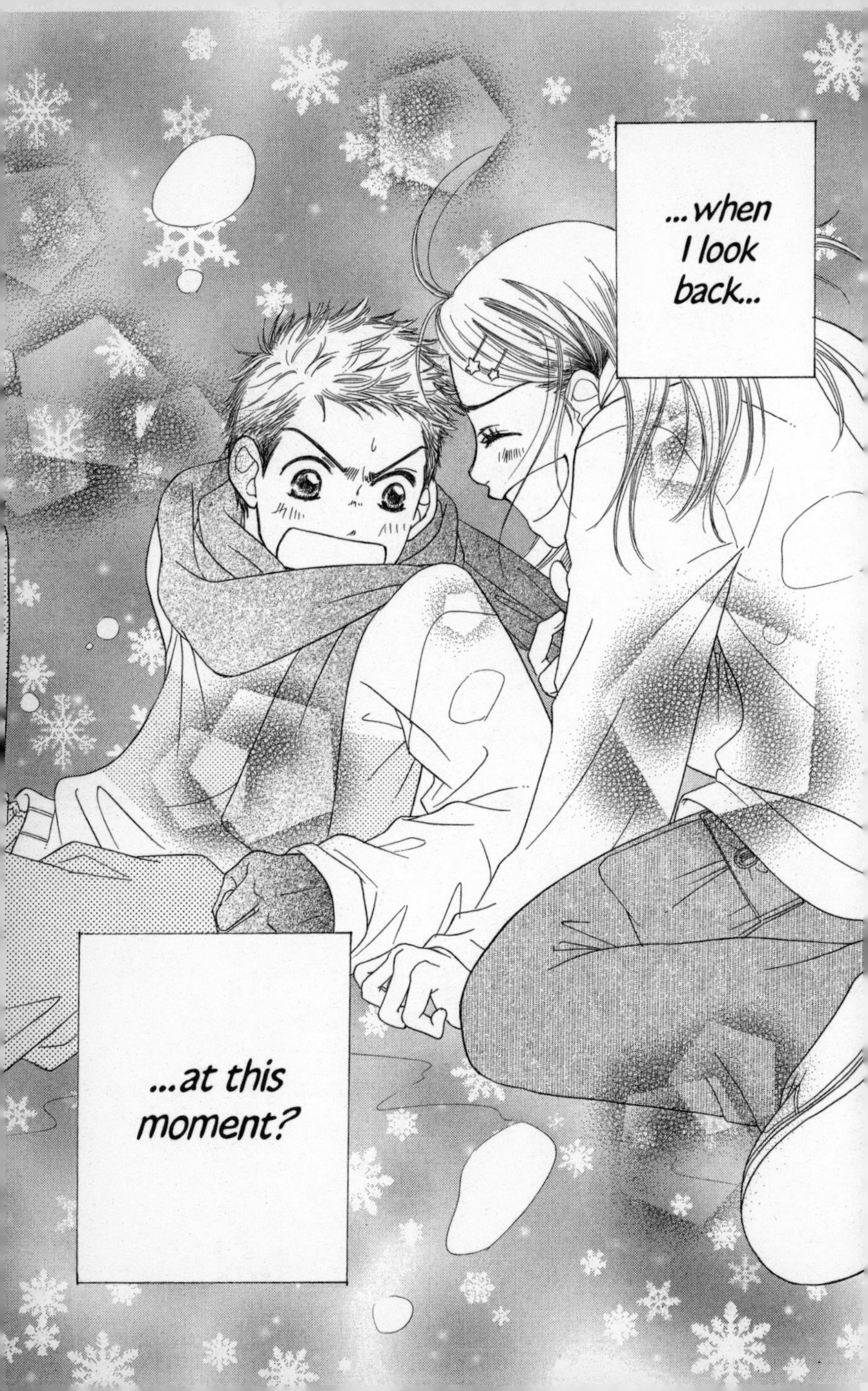
...when I look back...
...at this moment?

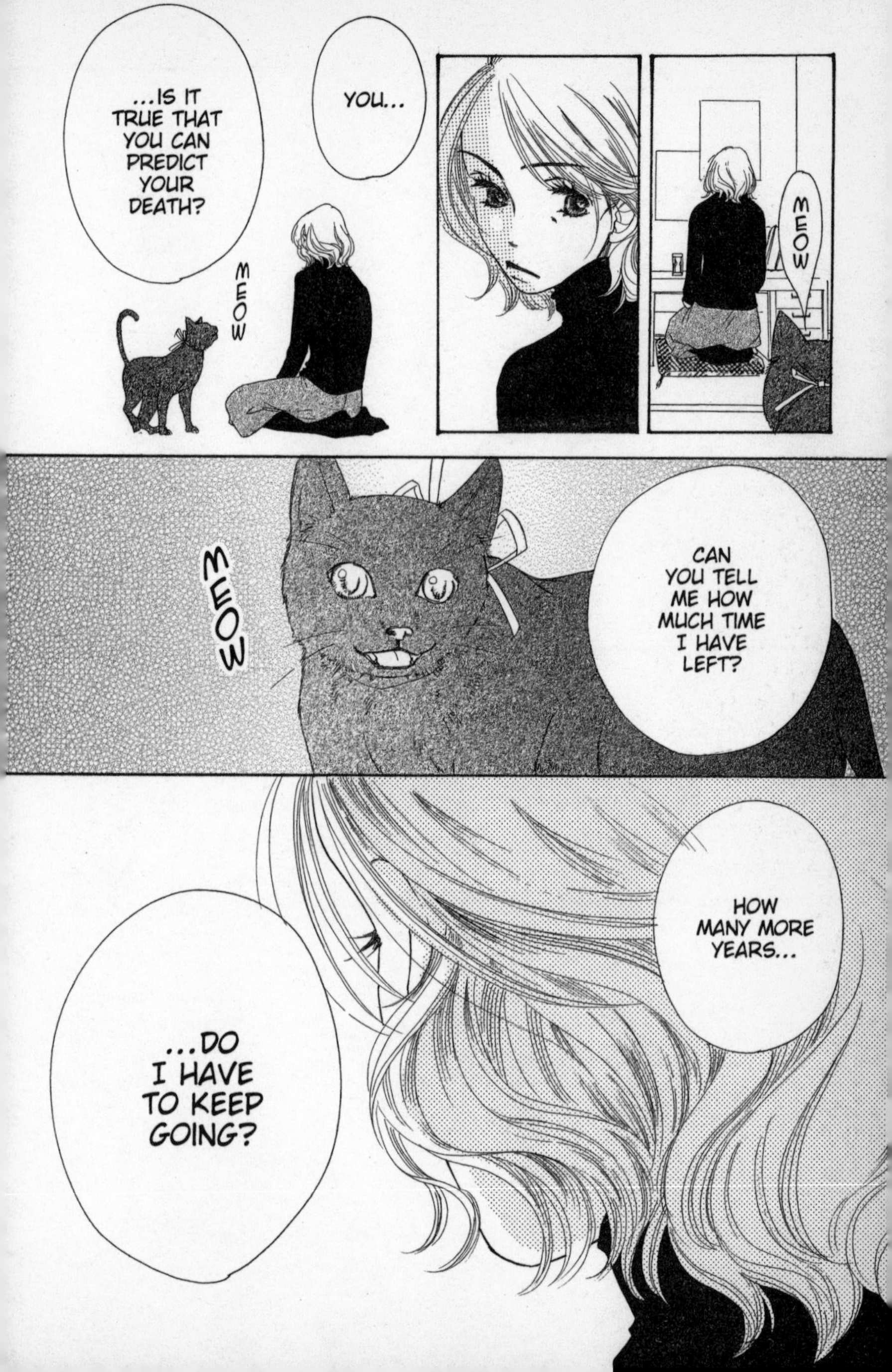
MEOW
YOU...
...IS IT TRUE THAT YOU CAN PREDICT YOUR DEATH?
MEOW
CAN YOU TELL ME HOW MUCH TIME I HAVE LEFT?
MEOW
HOW MANY MORE YEARS...
...DO I HAVE TO KEEP GOING?

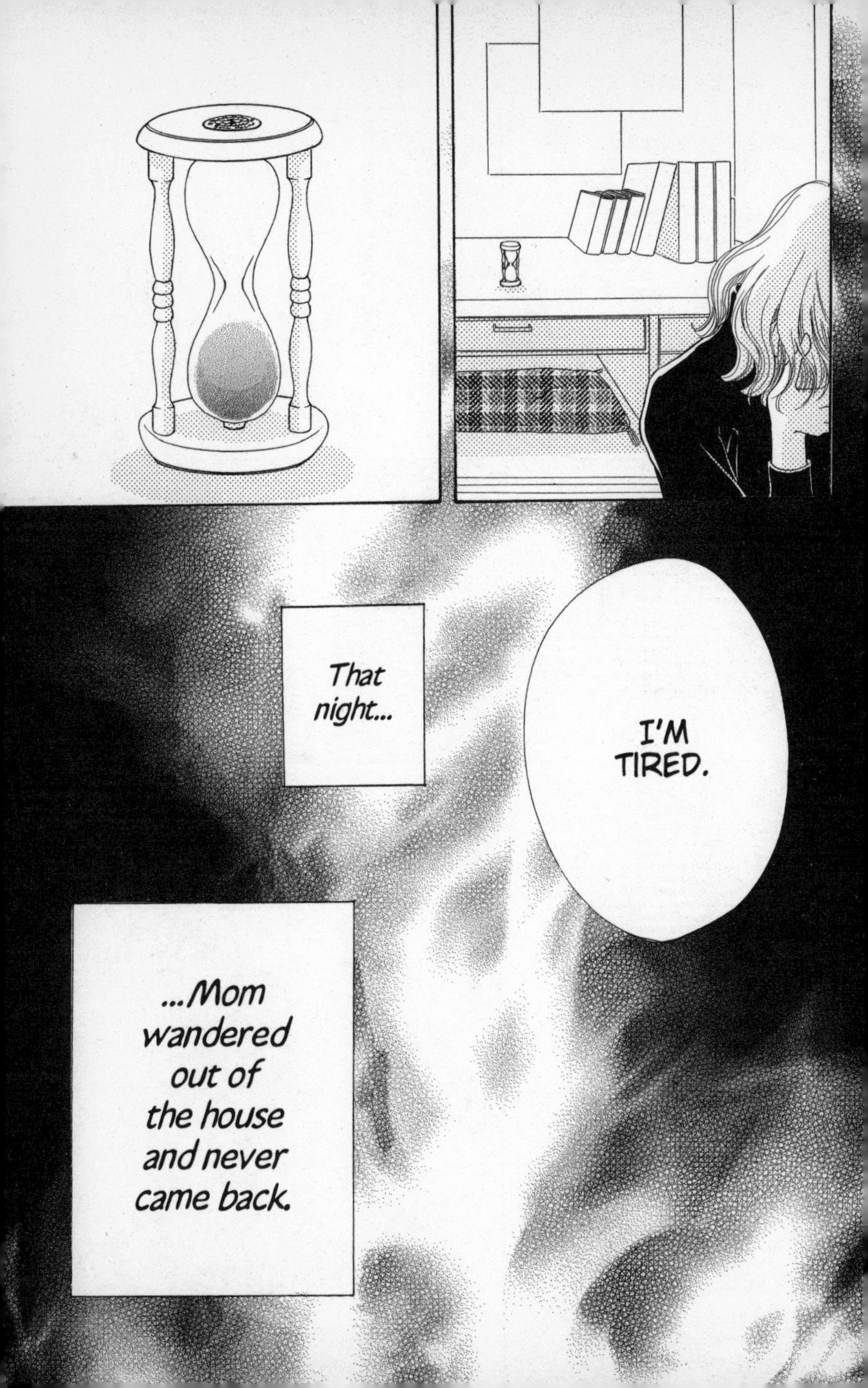
I'M TIRED.
That night...
...Mom wandered out of the house and never came back.

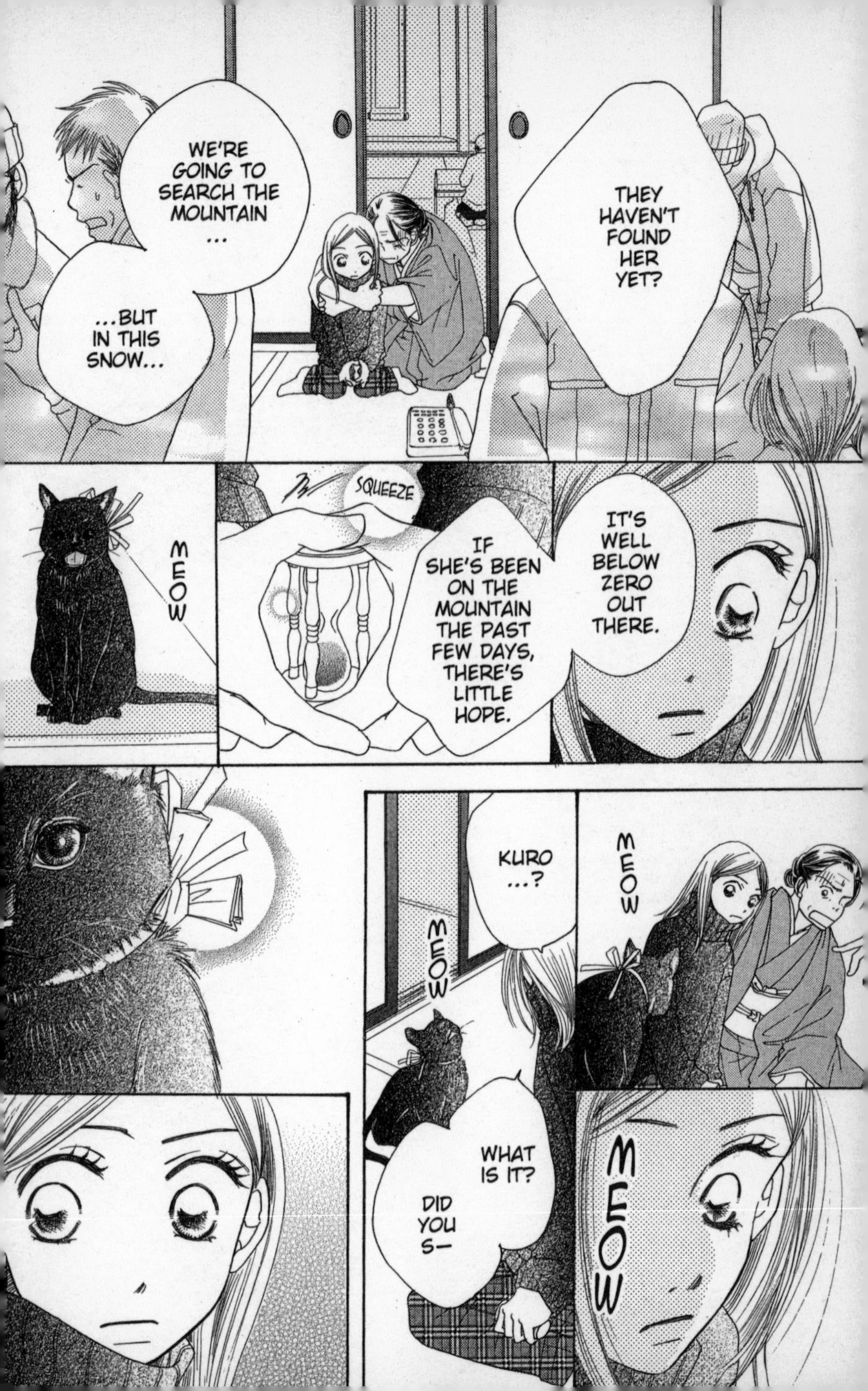
THEY HAVEN'T FOUND HER YET?
WE'RE GOING TO SEARCH THE MOUNTAIN ...
...BUT IN THIS SNOW...
IT'S WELL BELOW ZERO OUT THERE.
SQUEEZE
IF SHE'S BEEN ON THE MOUNTAIN THE PAST FEW DAYS, THERE'S LITTLE HOPE.
MEOW
MEOW
MEOW
KURO ...?
MEOW
WHAT IS IT?
DID YOU S—

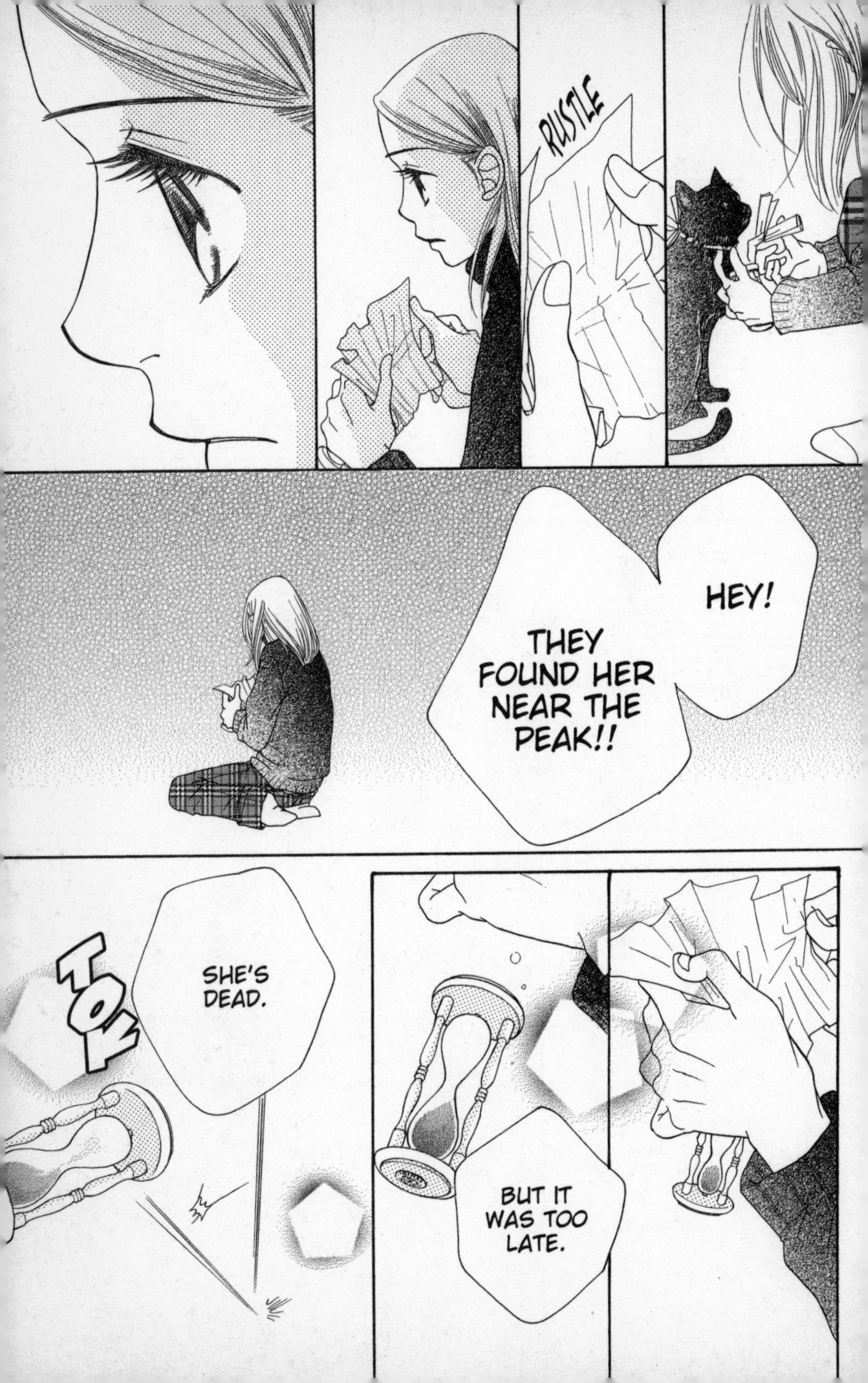
RUSTLE
HEY!
THEY FOUND HER NEAR THE PEAK!!
BUT IT WAS TOO LATE.
SHE'S DEAD.
TOK

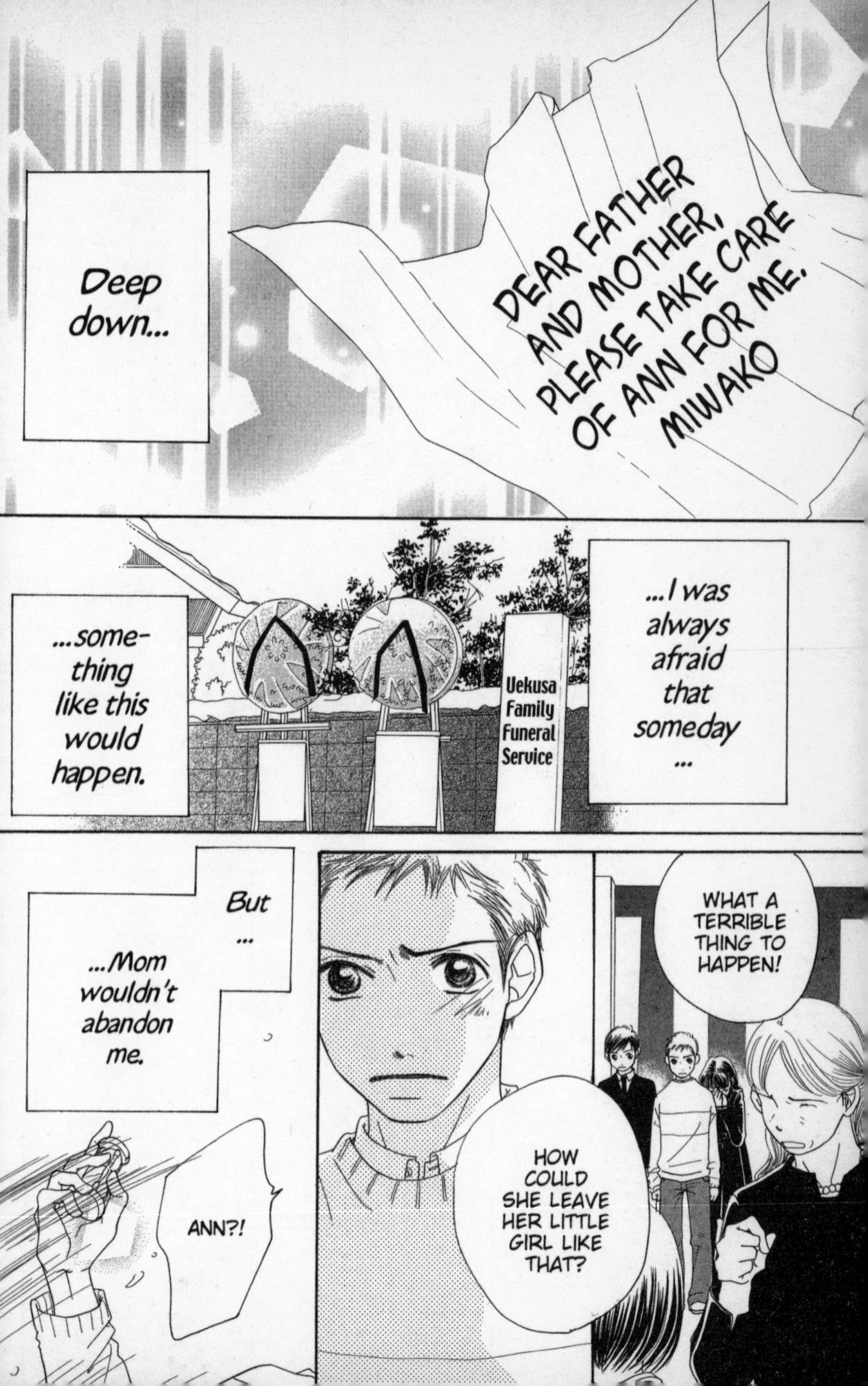
DEAR FATHER AND MOTHER, PLEASE TAKE CARE OF ANN FOR ME. MIWAKO
Deep down...
...I was always afraid that someday ...
Uekusa Family Funeral Service
...some-thing like this would happen.
WHAT A TERRIBLE THING TO HAPPEN!
HOW COULD SHE LEAVE HER LITTLE GIRL LIKE THAT?
But ...
...Mom wouldn't abandon me.
ANN?!

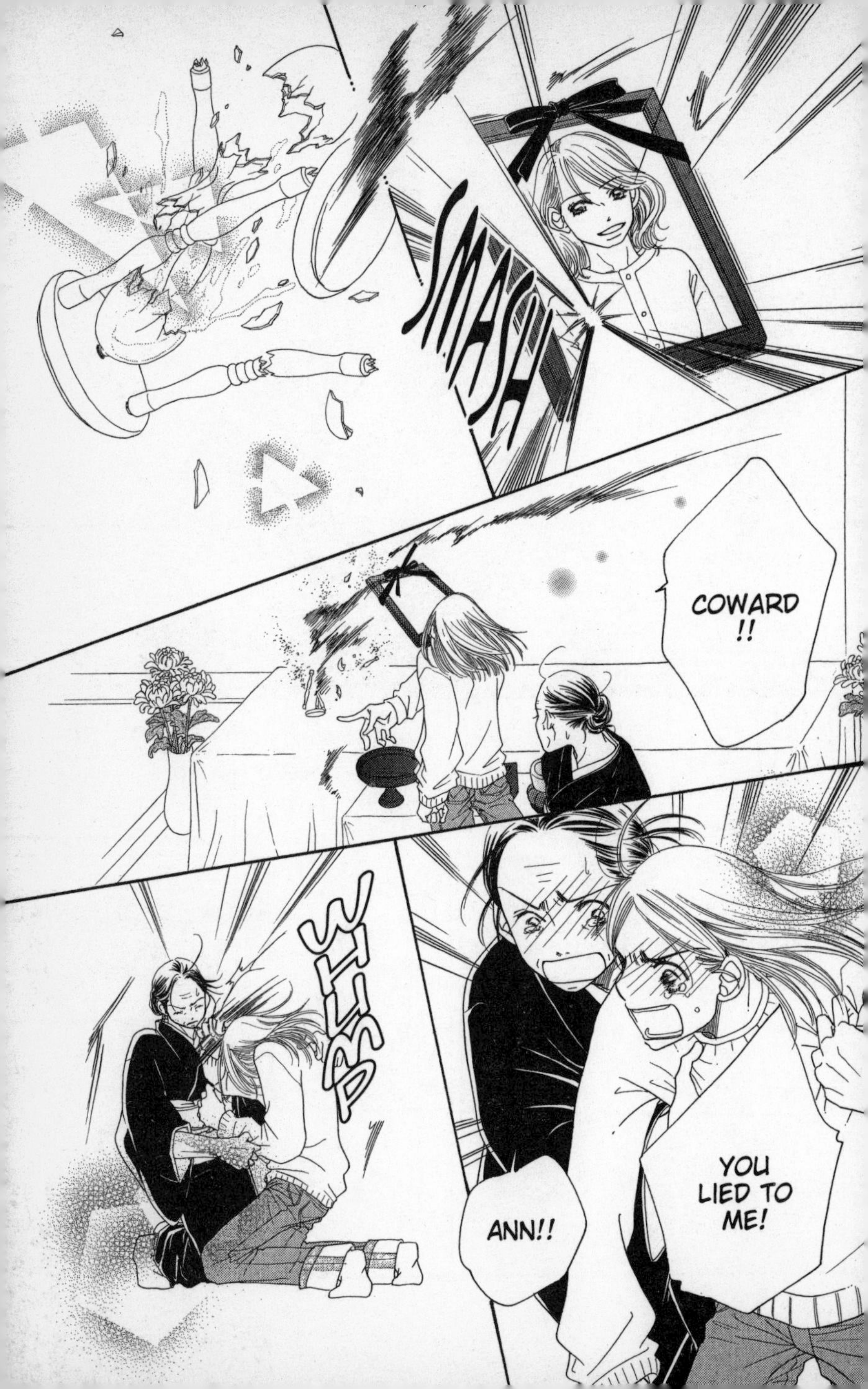
SMASH
COWARD !!
YOU LIED TO ME!
ANN!!
WHAP

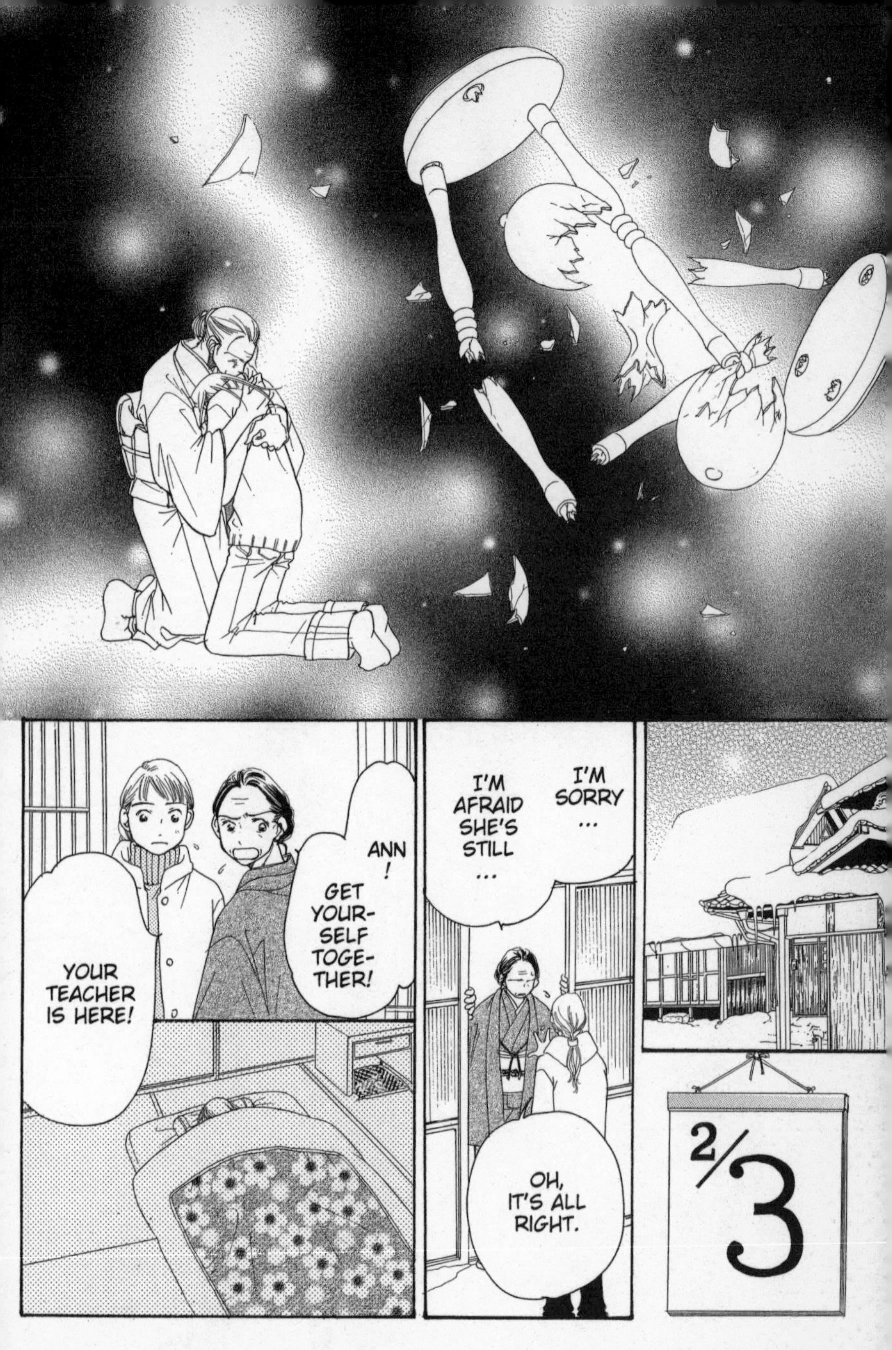
2/3
I'M SORRY ...
I'M AFRAID SHE'S STILL ...
OH, IT'S ALL RIGHT.
ANN! GET YOURSELF TOGETHER!
YOUR TEACHER IS HERE!

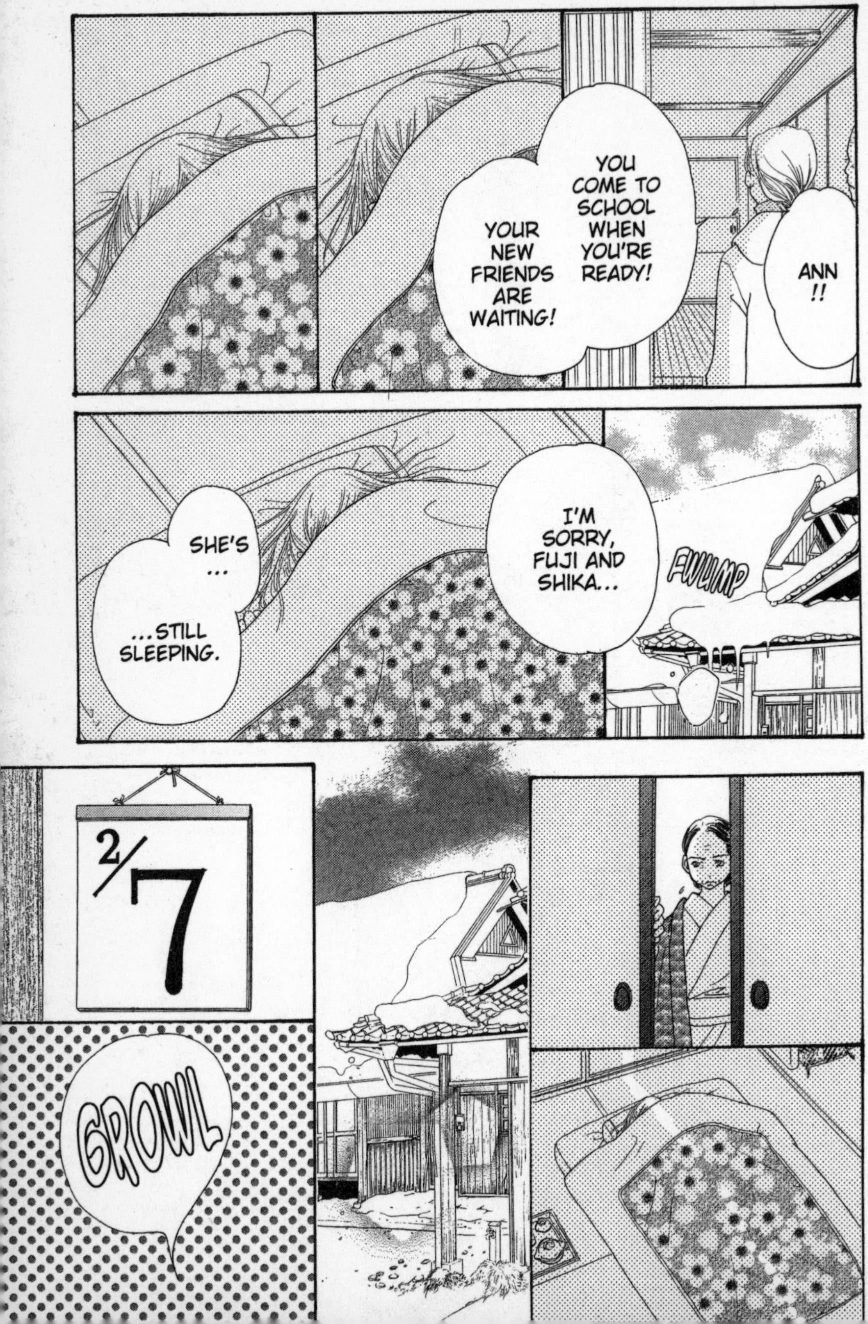
ANN !!
YOU COME TO SCHOOL WHEN YOU'RE READY!
YOUR NEW FRIENDS ARE WAITING!
FWUMP
I'M SORRY, FUJI AND SHIKA...
SHE'S ...
...STILL SLEEPING.
2/7
GROWL

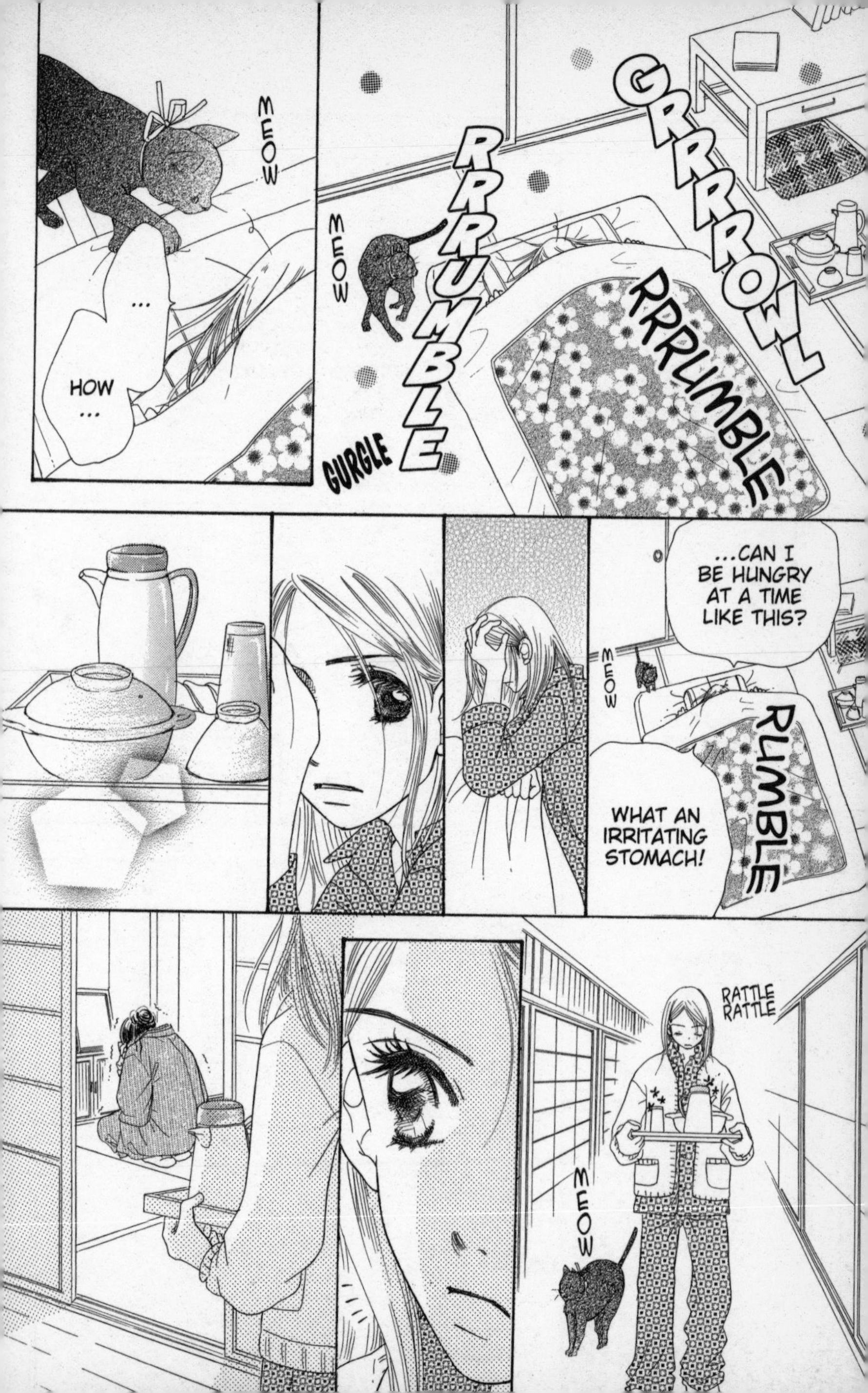
GRRRROWL
RRRUMBLE
RRRUMBLE
MEOW
GURGLE
MEOW
...
HOW ...
...CAN I BE HUNGRY AT A TIME LIKE THIS?
MEOW
RUMBLE
WHAT AN IRRITATING STOMACH!
RATTLE RATTLE
MEOW

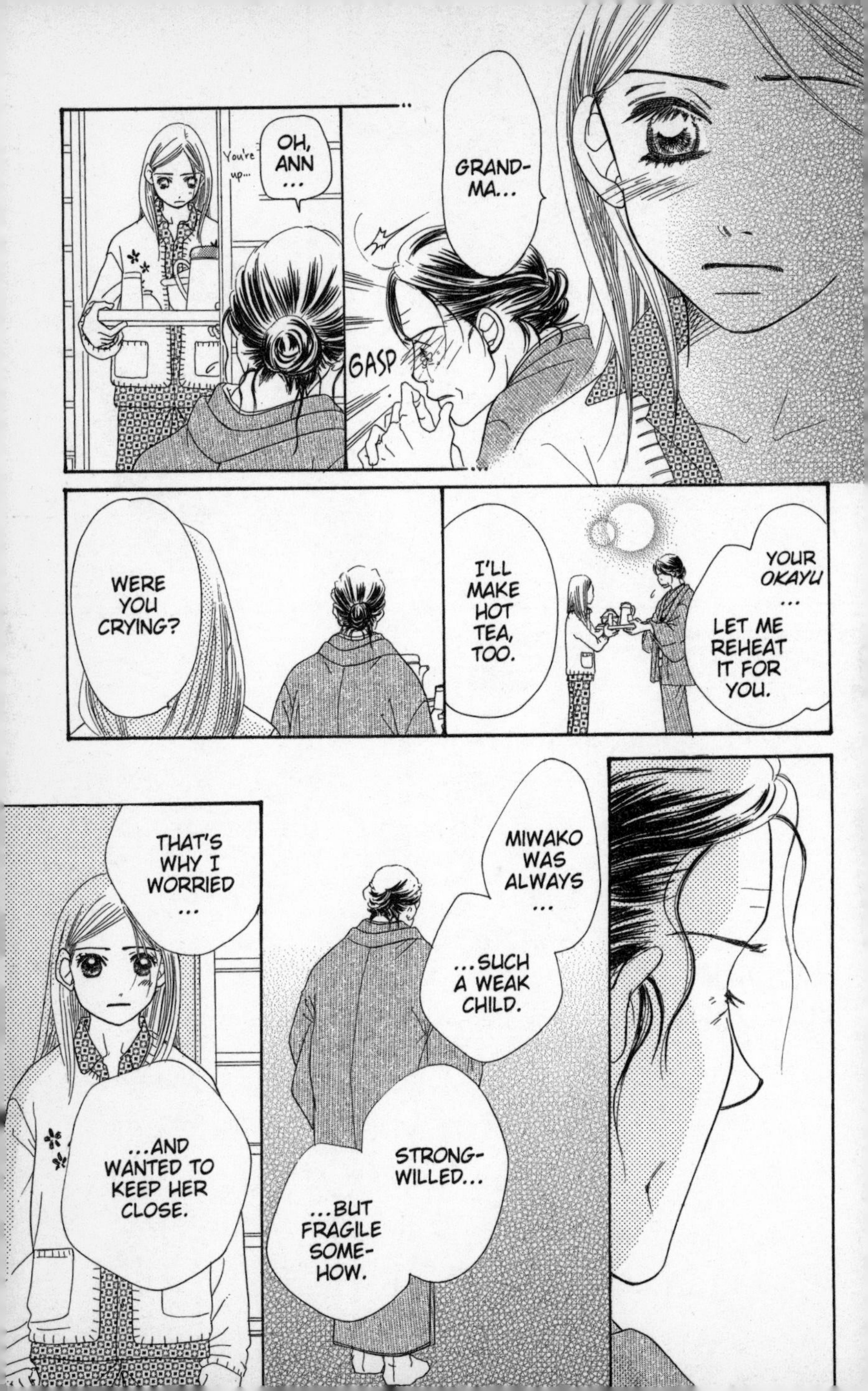
GRAND-MA...
GASP
OH, ANN...
You're up...
YOUR OKAYU...
LET ME REHEAT IT FOR YOU.
I'LL MAKE HOT TEA, TOO.
WERE YOU CRYING?
MIWAKO WAS ALWAYS...
...SUCH A WEAK CHILD.
STRONG-WILLED...
...BUT FRAGILE SOME-HOW.
THAT'S WHY I WORRIED...
...AND WANTED TO KEEP HER CLOSE.

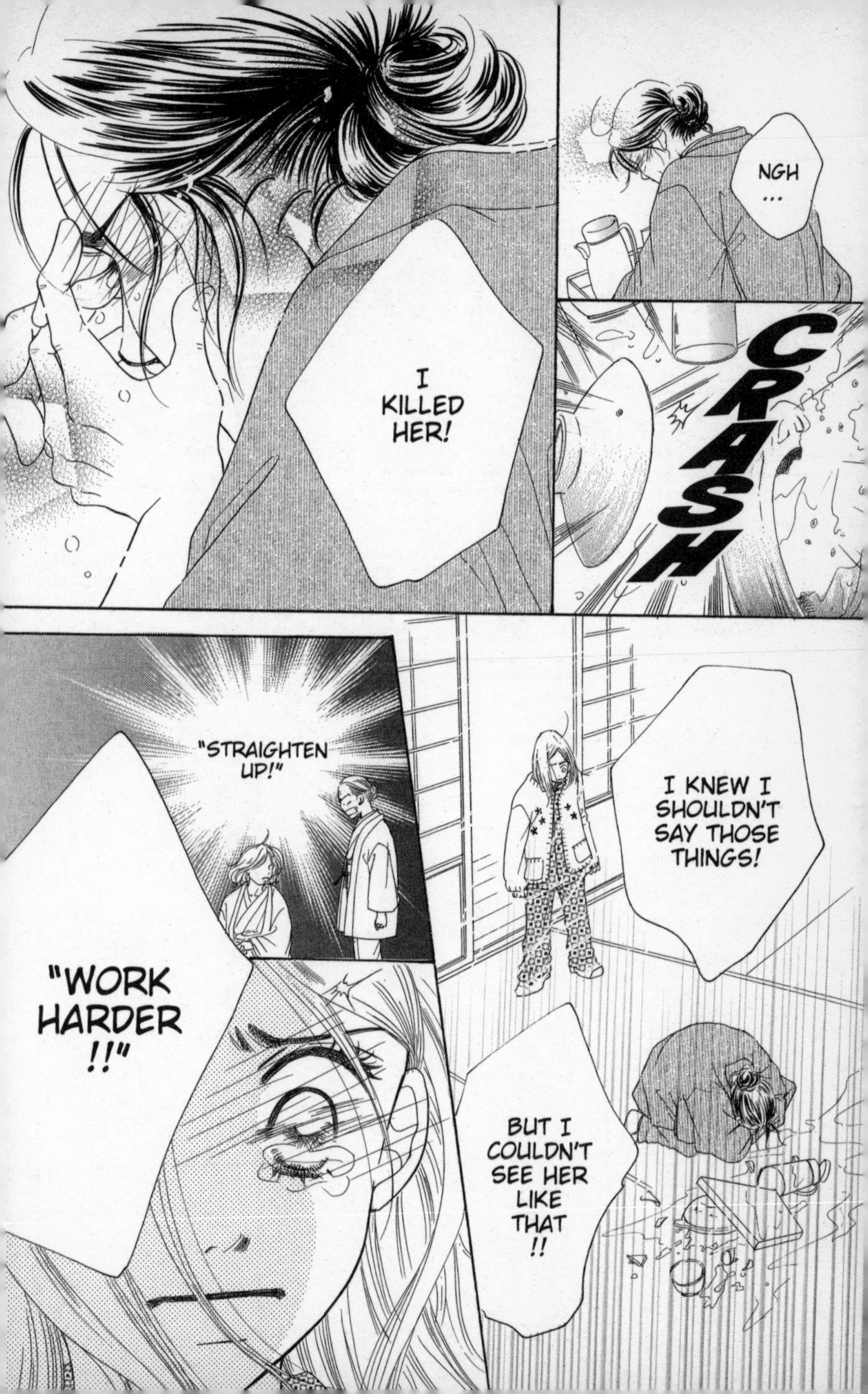
NGH ...
CRASH
I KILLED HER!
I KNEW I SHOULDN'T SAY THOSE THINGS!
BUT I COULDN'T SEE HER LIKE THAT !!
"STRAIGHTEN UP!"
"WORK HARDER !!"

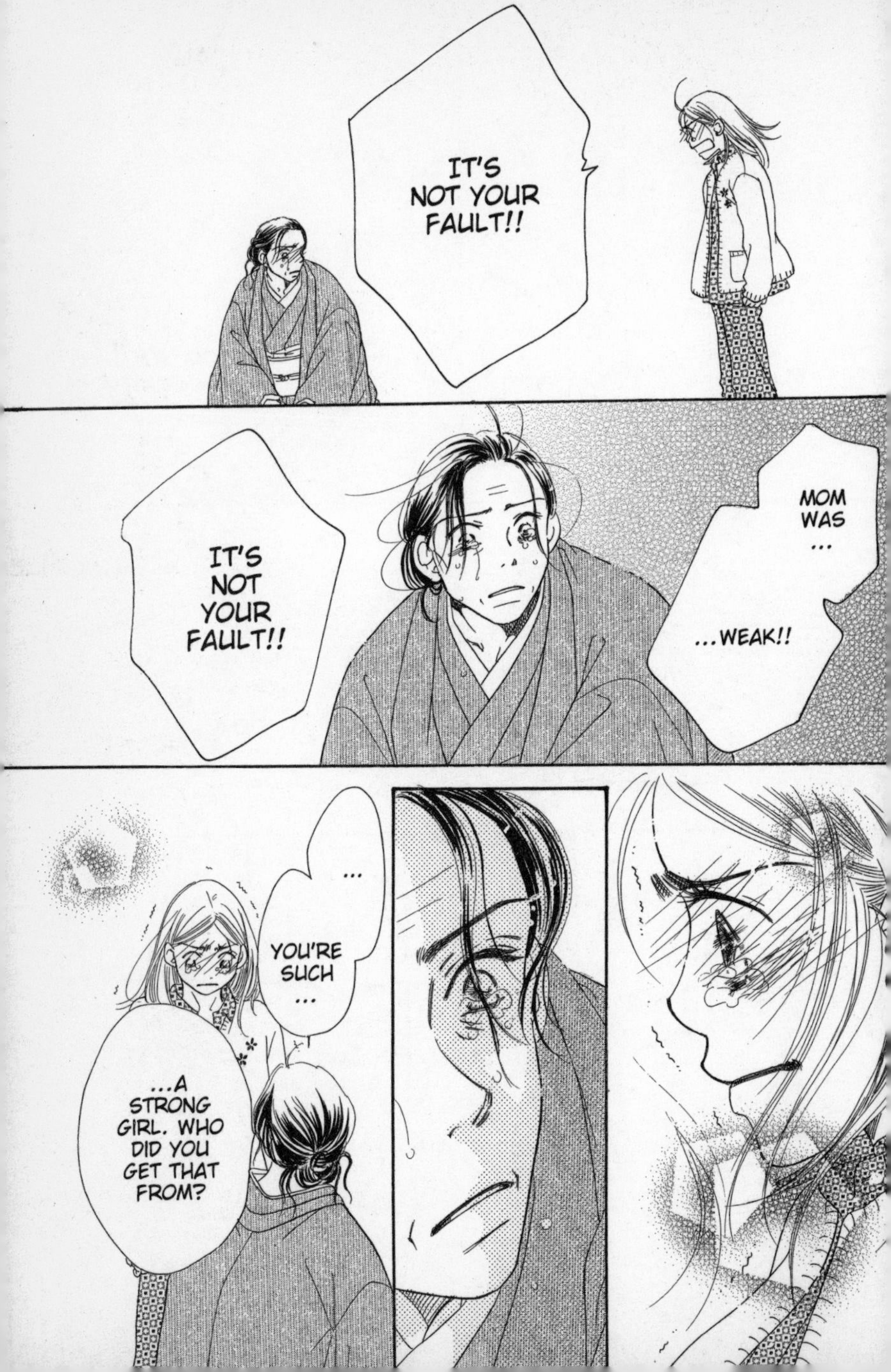
IT'S NOT YOUR FAULT!!
MOM WAS ...
...WEAK!!
IT'S NOT YOUR FAULT!!
... YOU'RE SUCH ...
...A STRONG GIRL. WHO DID YOU GET THAT FROM?

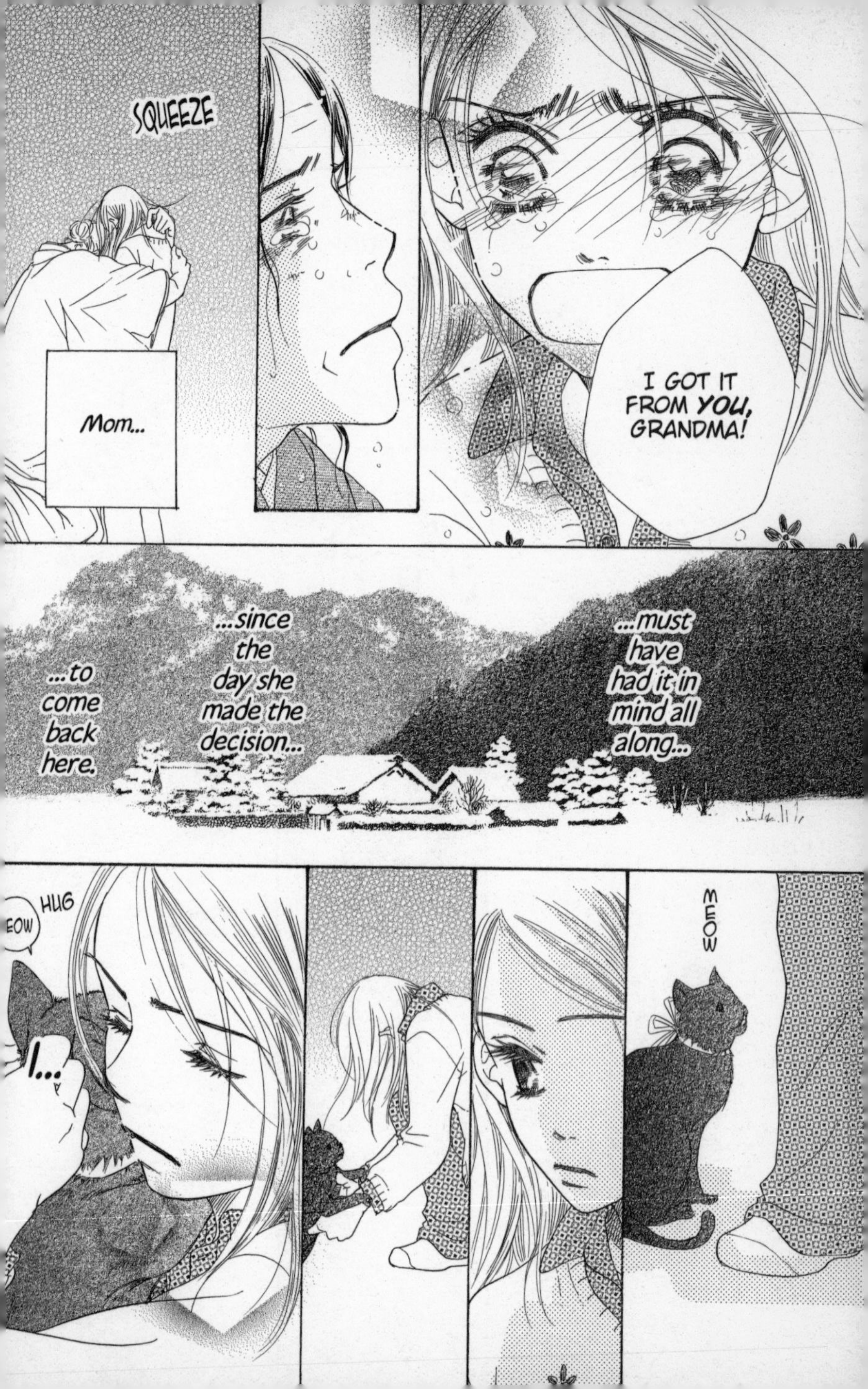
I GOT IT FROM YOU, GRANDMA!
SQUEEZE
Mom...
...must have had it in mind all along...
...since the day she made the decision...
...to come back here.
MEOW
HUG
EOW
I...

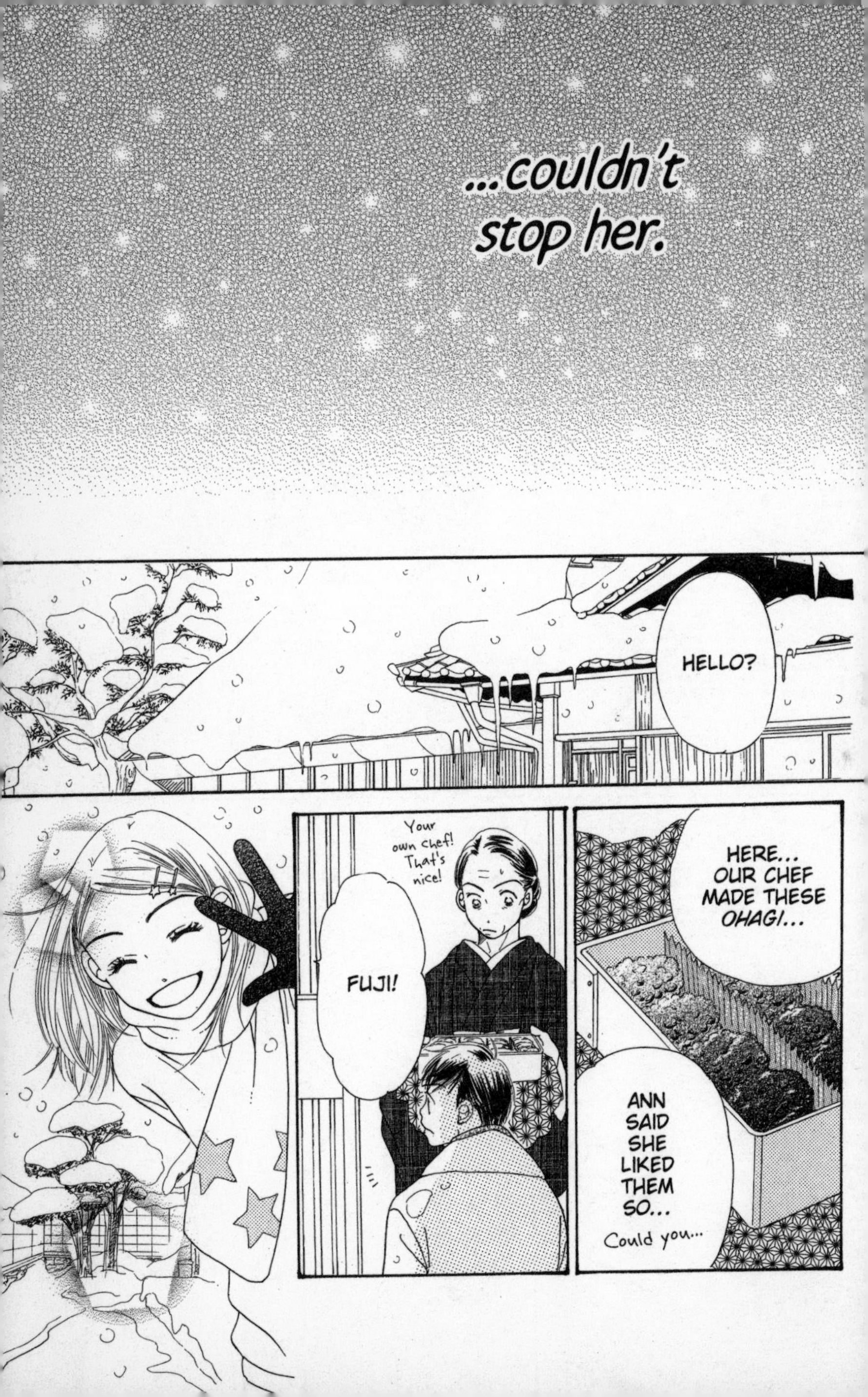
...couldn't stop her.
HELLO?
HERE... OUR CHEF MADE THESE OHAGI...
ANN SAID SHE LIKED THEM SO...
Could you...
Your own chef! That's nice!
FUJI!

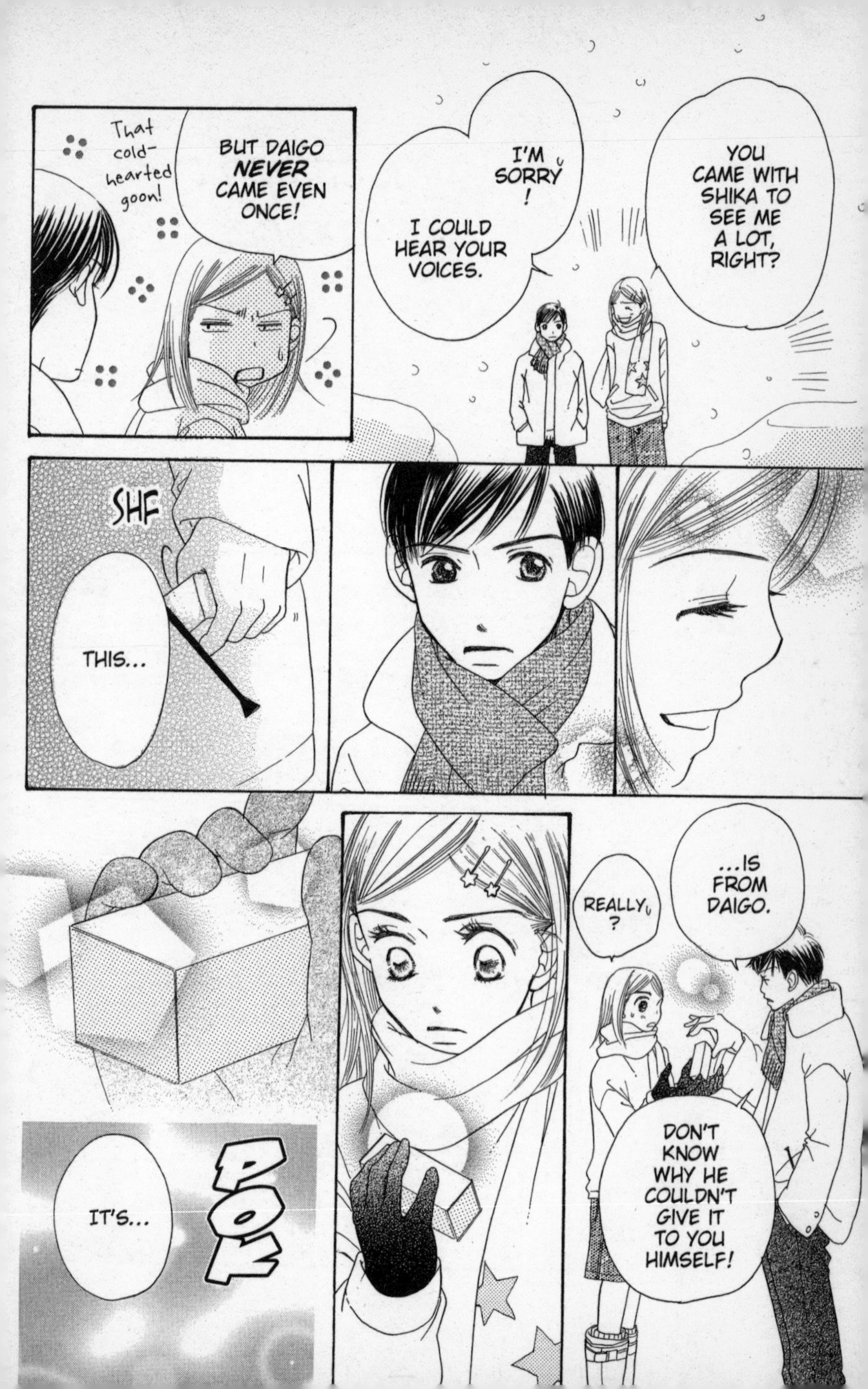
YOU CAME WITH SHIKA TO SEE ME A LOT, RIGHT?
I'M SORRY!
I COULD HEAR YOUR VOICES.
BUT DAIGO **NEVER** CAME EVEN ONCE!
That cold-hearted goon!
SHF
THIS...
...IS FROM DAIGO.
REALLY?
DON'T KNOW WHY HE COULDN'T GIVE IT TO YOU HIMSELF!
POP
IT'S...

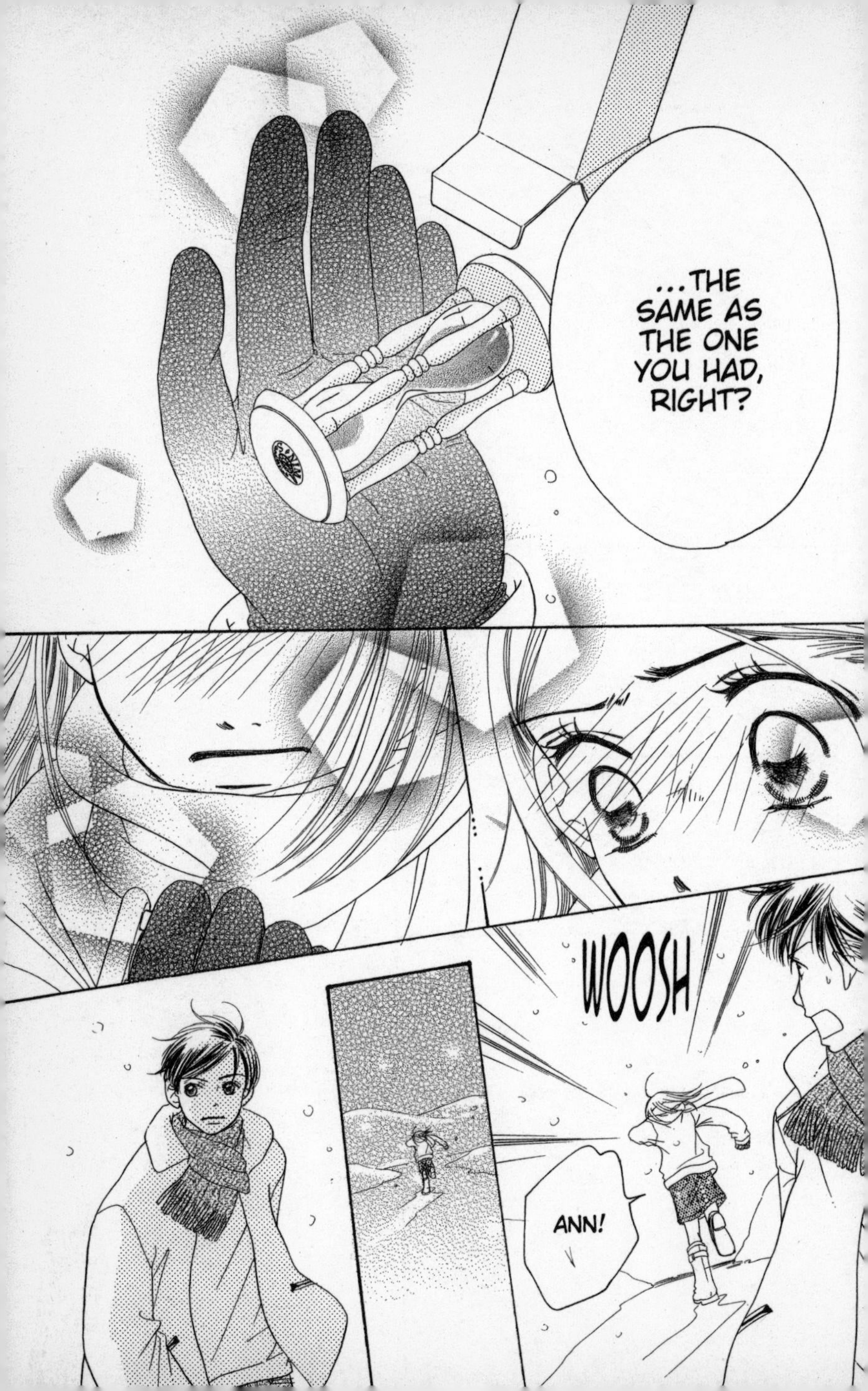
...THE SAME AS THE ONE YOU HAD, RIGHT?
WOOSH
ANN!

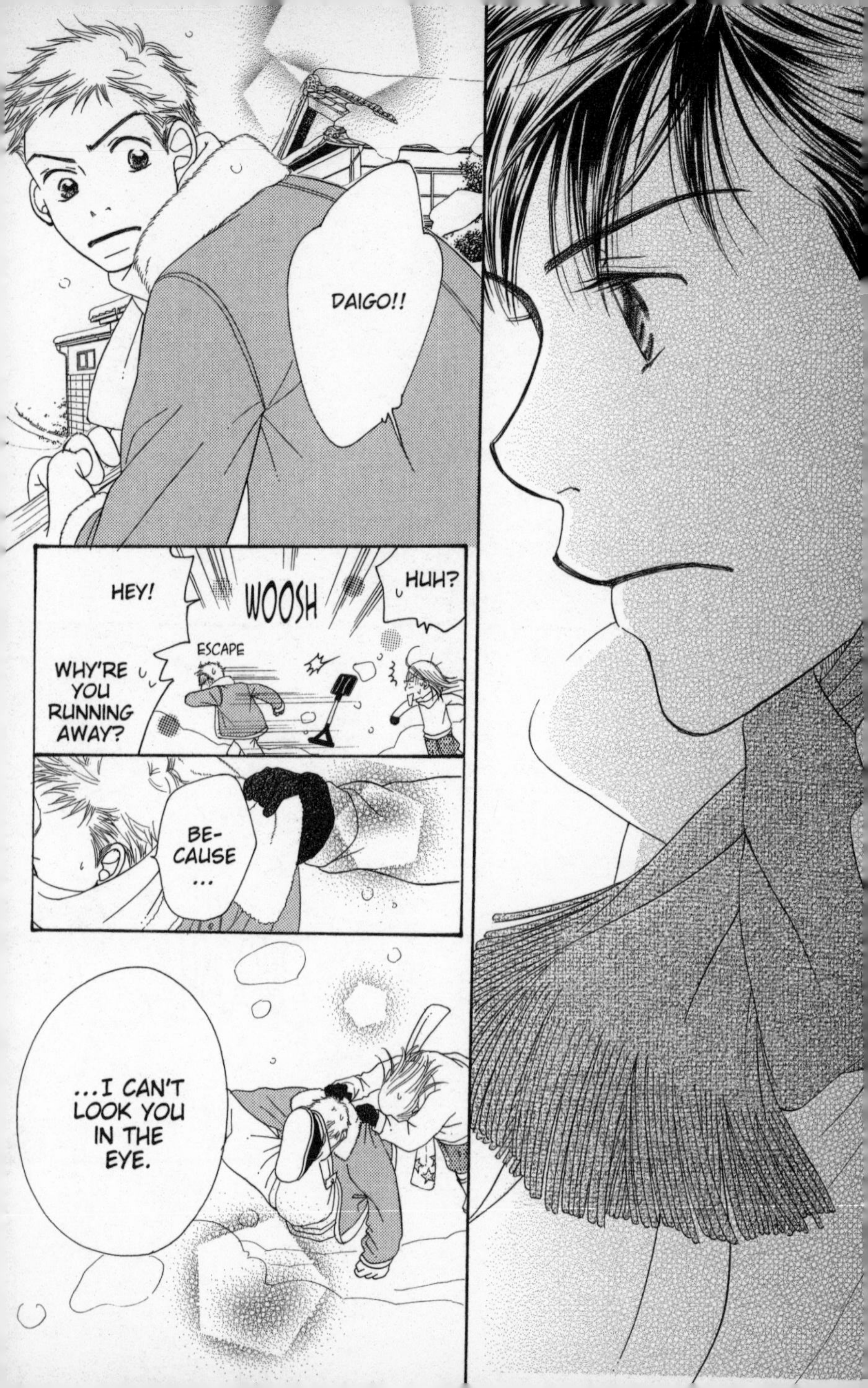
DAIGO!!
HUH?
WOOSH
HEY!
ESCAPE
WHY'RE YOU RUNNING AWAY?
BE-CAUSE ...
...I CAN'T LOOK YOU IN THE EYE.

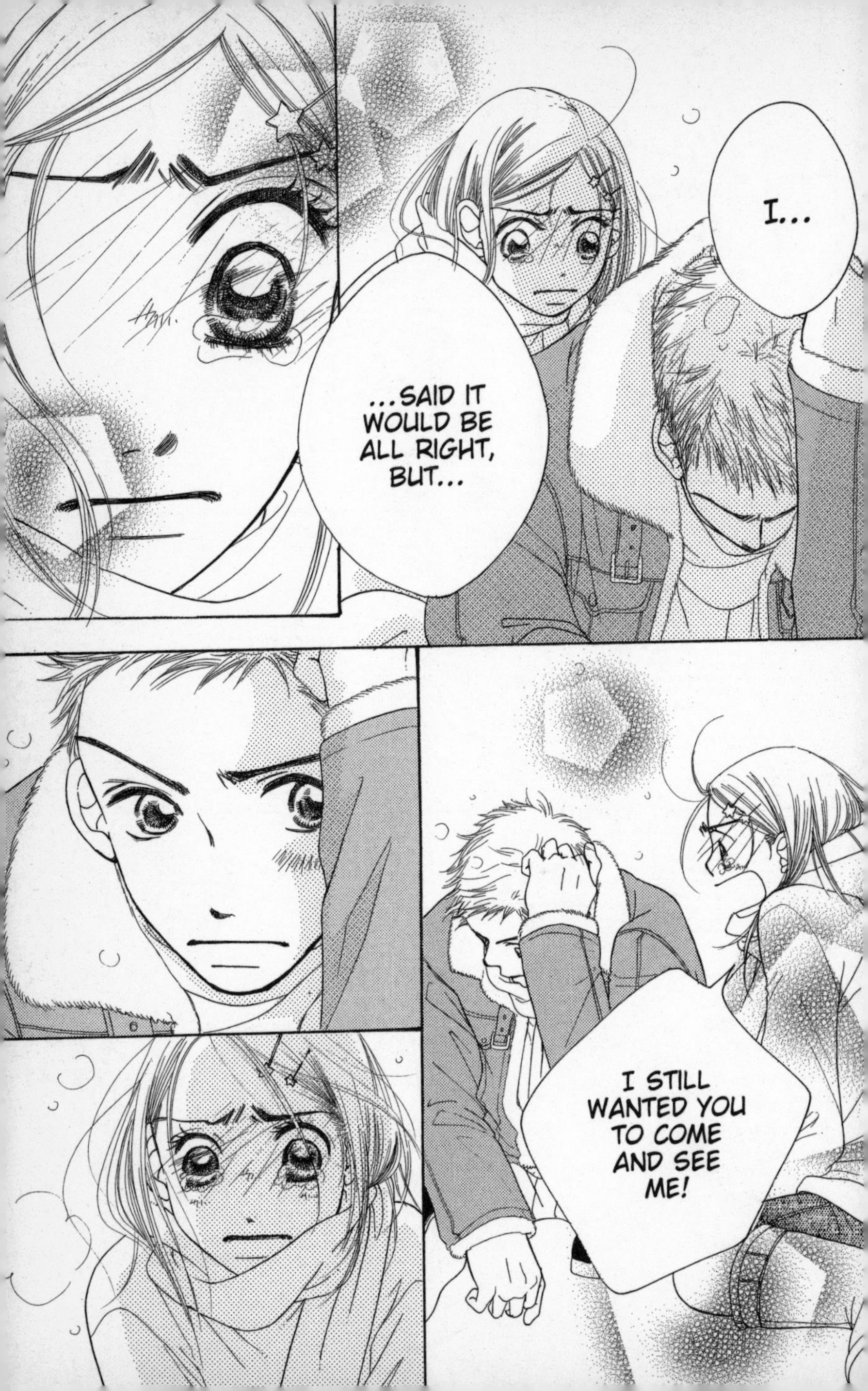
I...
...SAID IT WOULD BE ALL RIGHT, BUT...
I STILL WANTED YOU TO COME AND SEE ME!

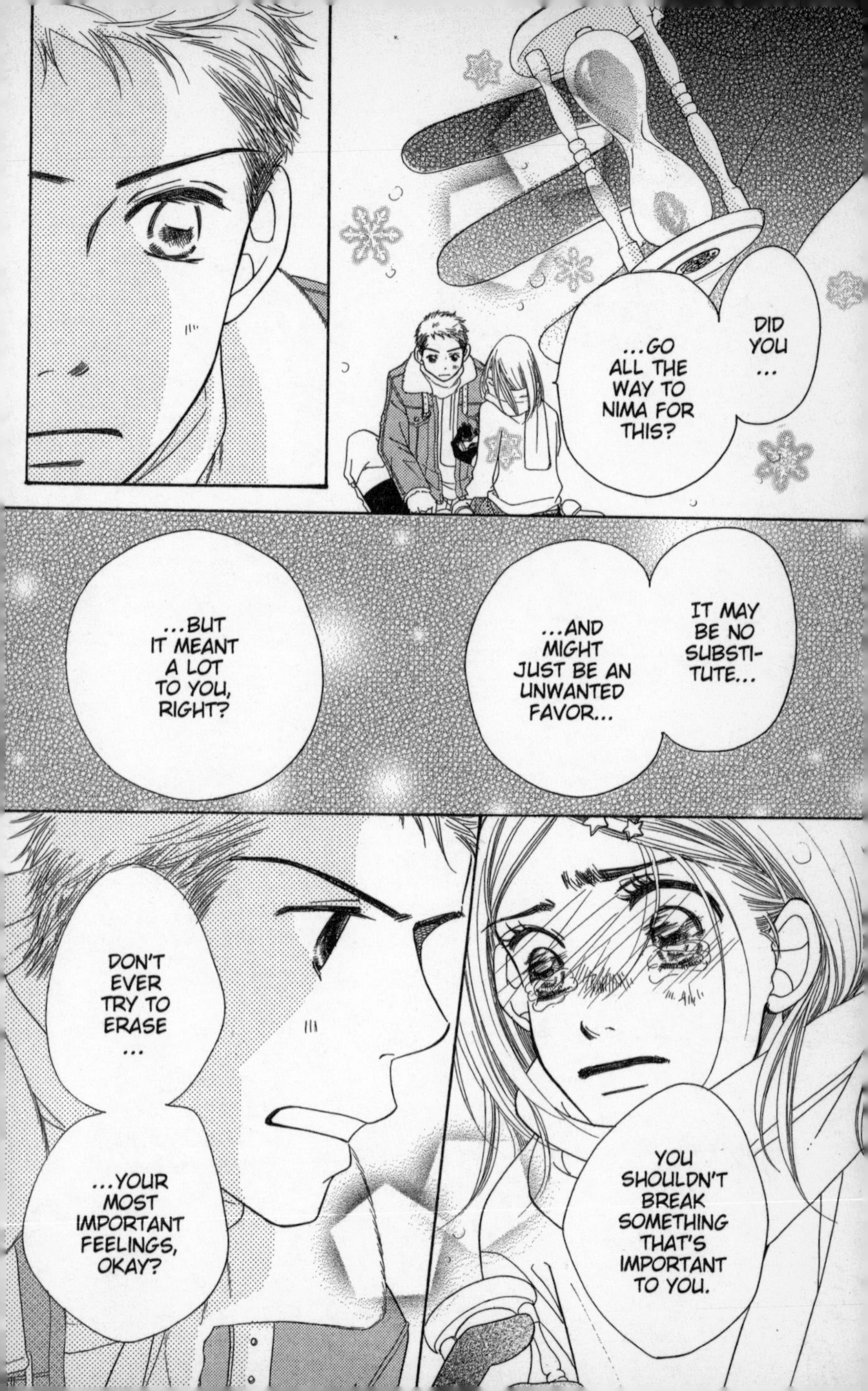
DID YOU ...
...GO ALL THE WAY TO NIMA FOR THIS?
IT MAY BE NO SUBSTI-TUTE...
...AND MIGHT JUST BE AN UNWANTED FAVOR...
...BUT IT MEANT A LOT TO YOU, RIGHT?
YOU SHOULDN'T BREAK SOMETHING THAT'S IMPORTANT TO YOU.
DON'T EVER TRY TO ERASE ...
...YOUR MOST IMPORTANT FEELINGS, OKAY?

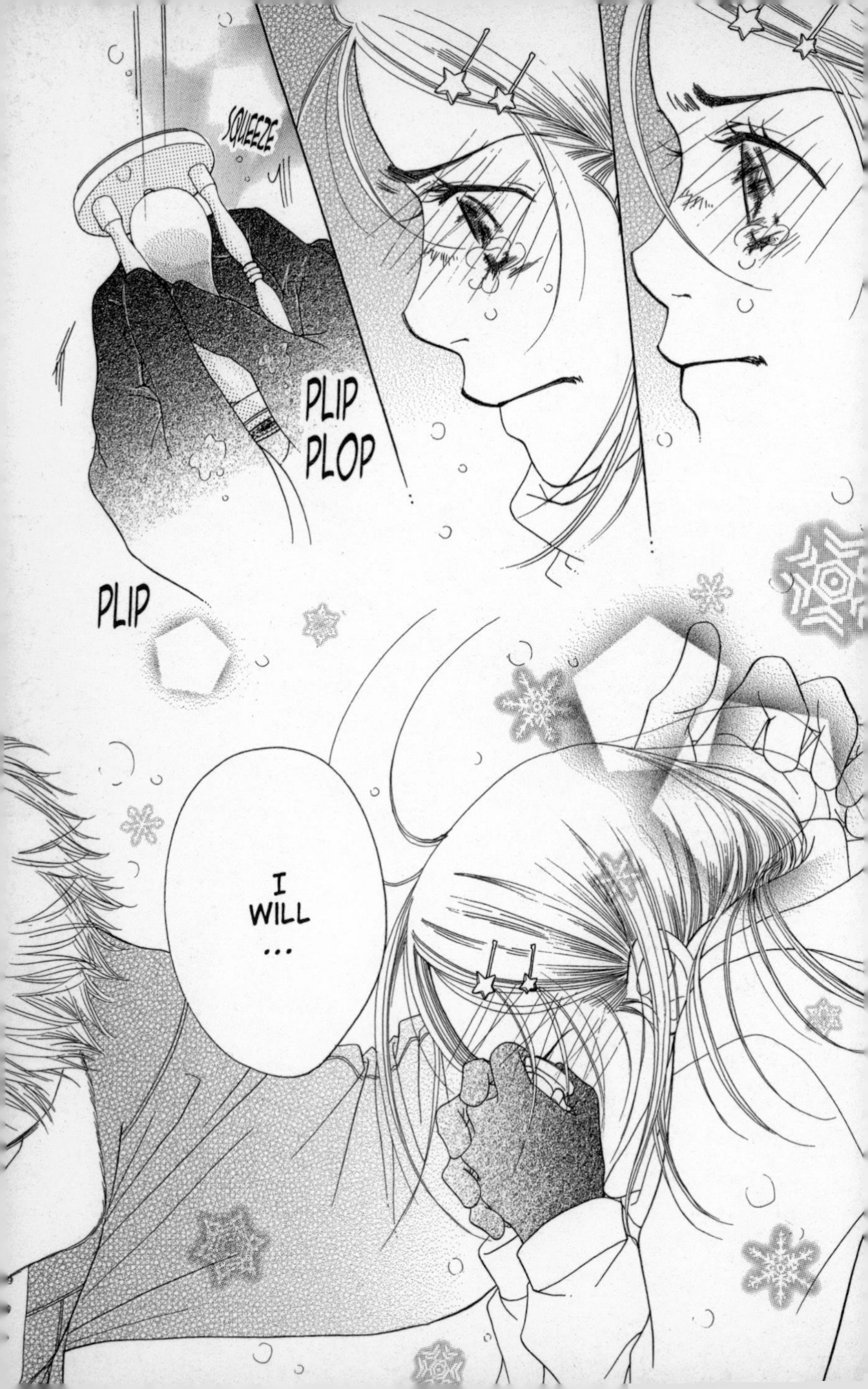
SQUEEZE
PLIP PLOP
PLIP
I WILL ...

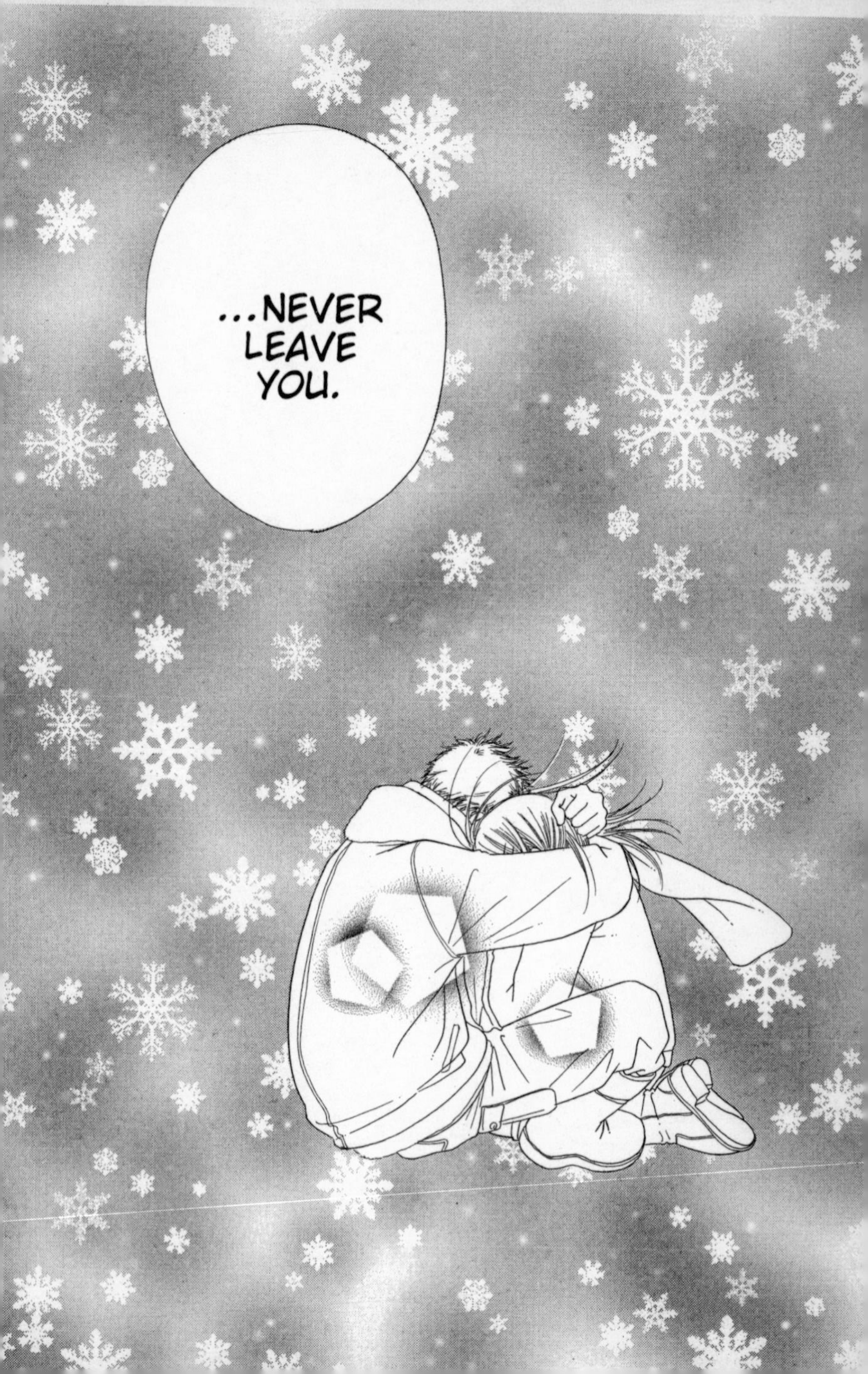
...NEVER LEAVE YOU.

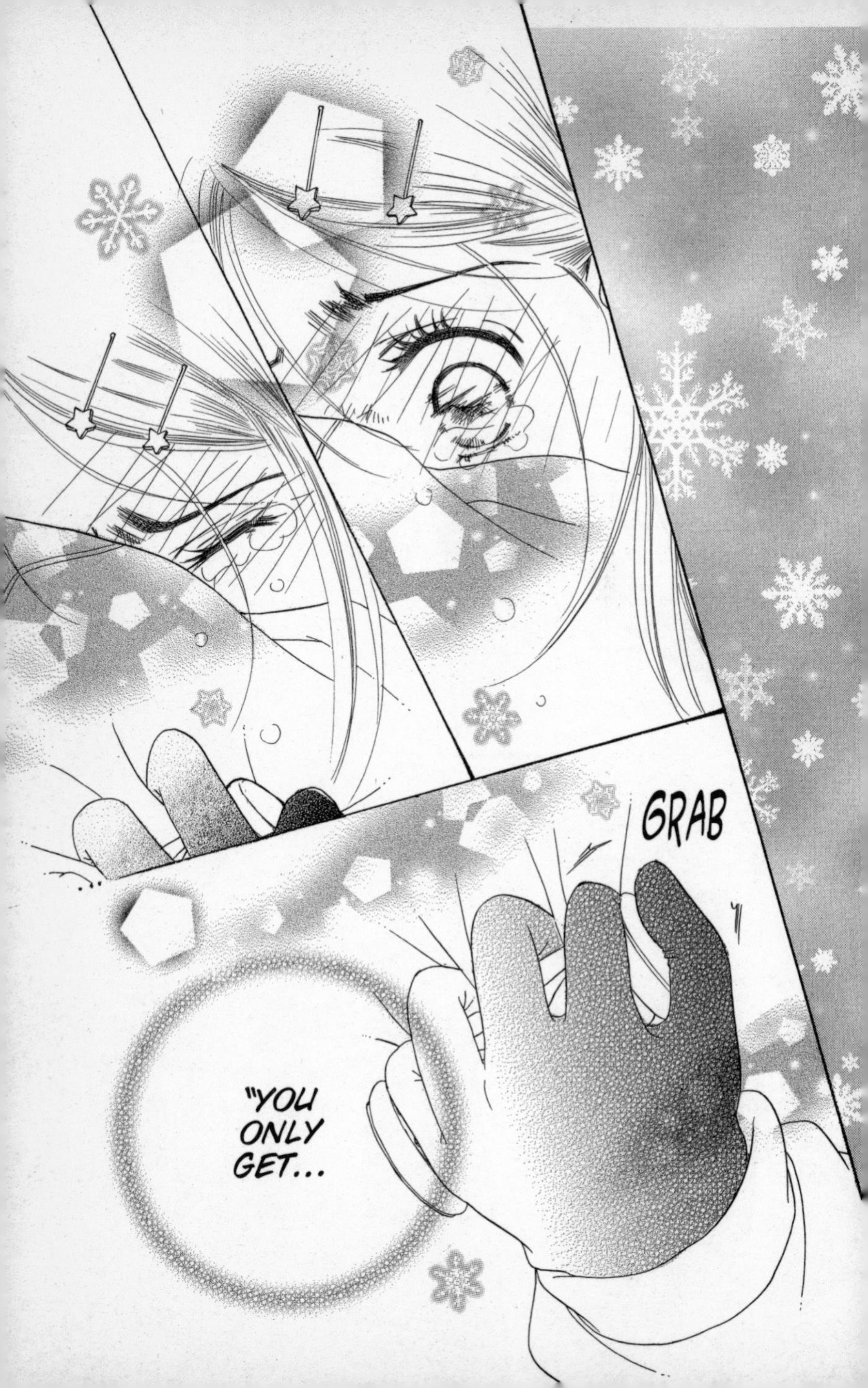
GRAB
"YOU ONLY GET...

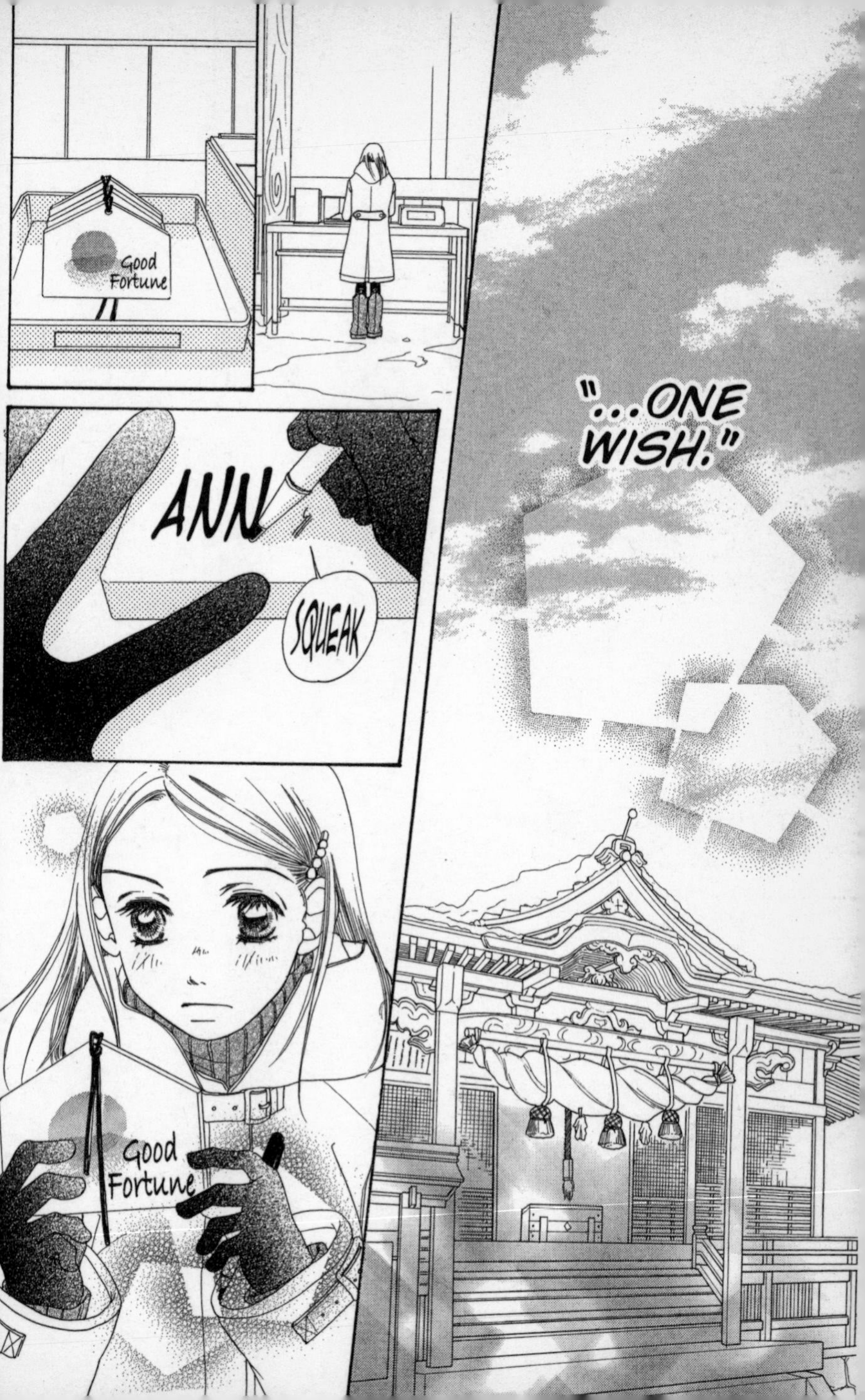
"...ONE WISH."
Good Fortune
ANN
SQUEAK
Good Fortune

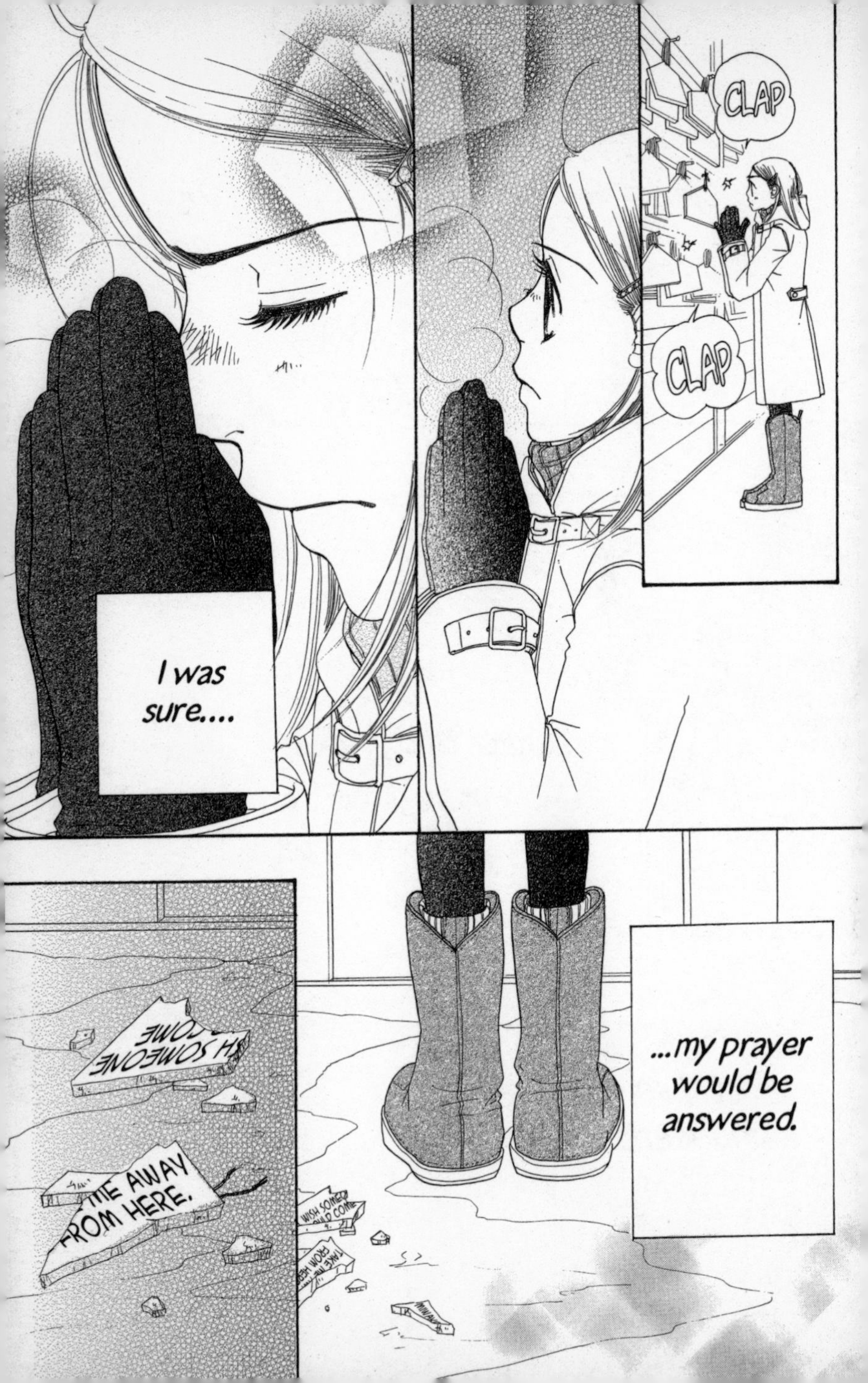
CLAP
CLAP
I was sure....
...my prayer would be answered.
ME AWAY FROM HERE.

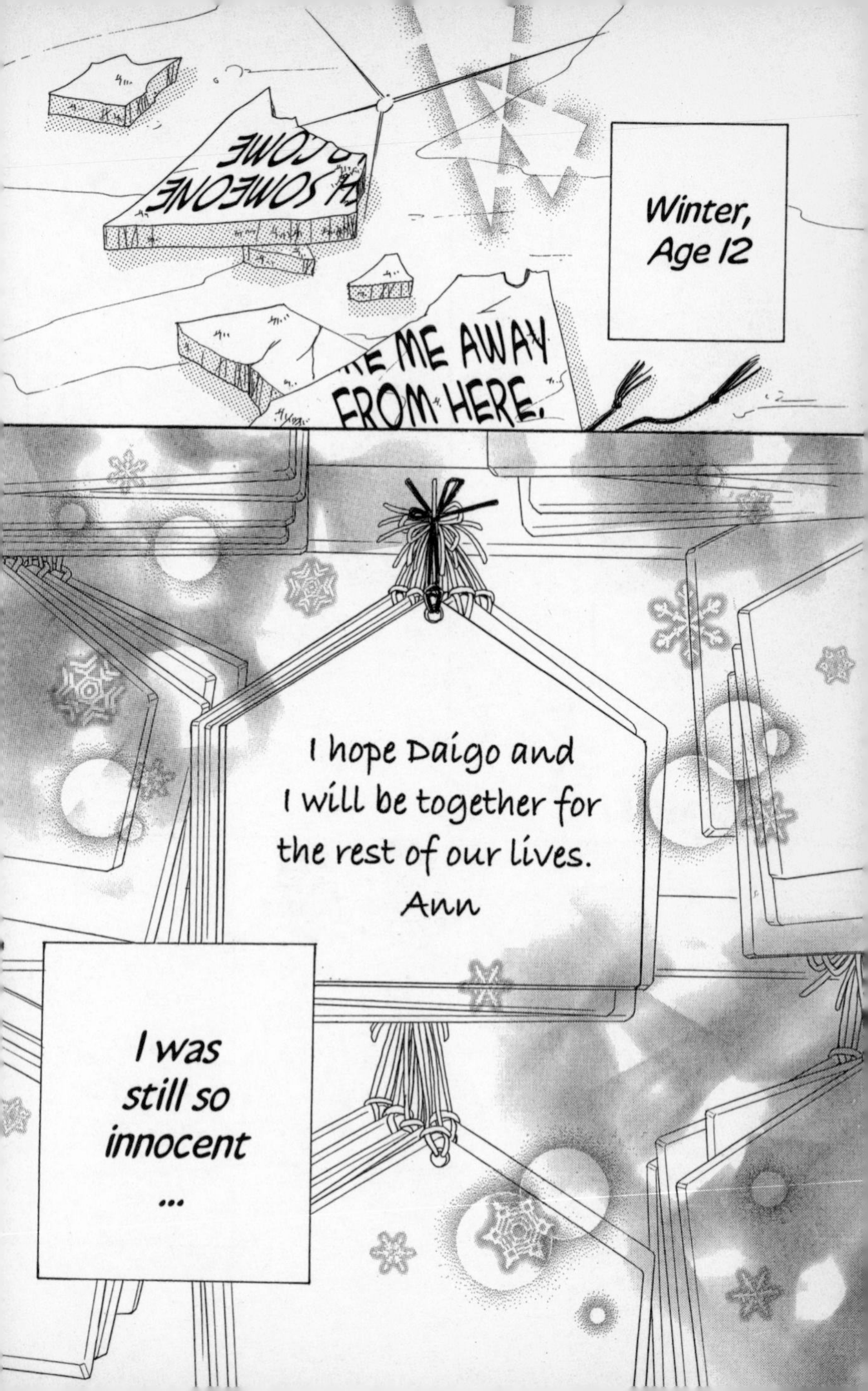

Winter, Age 12
SOMEONE
ME AWAY
FROM HERE.
I hope Daigo and I will be together for the rest of our lives. Ann
I was still so innocent ...

Sand Chronicles

Ann Uekusa, Age 12

An honest girl with a strong will. At least that's what she is right now...

About the World's Biggest One-year Hourglass

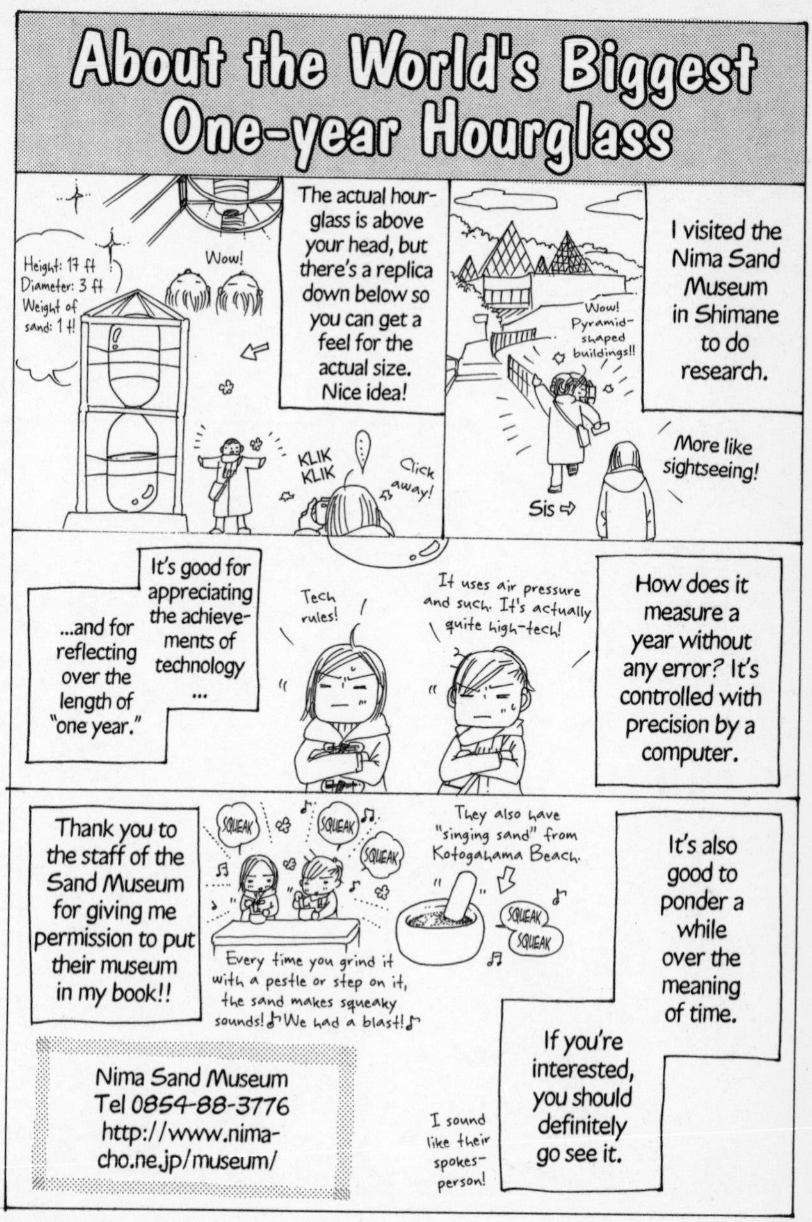

I visited the Nima Sand Museum in Shimane to do research.
Wow! Pyramid-shaped buildings!!
More like sightseeing!
Sis
The actual hourglass is above your head, but there's a replica down below so you can get a feel for the actual size. Nice idea!
KLIK KLIK
Click away!
Wow!
Height: 17 ft
Diameter: 3 ft
Weight of sand: 1 t!
How does it measure a year without any error? It's controlled with precision by a computer.
It uses air pressure and such. It's actually quite high-tech!
Tech rules!
It's good for appreciating the achievements of technology ...
...and for reflecting over the length of "one year."
It's also good to ponder a while over the meaning of time.
If you're interested, you should definitely go see it.
I sound like their spokesperson!
They also have "singing sand" from Kotogahama Beach.
SQUEAK
SQUEAK
SQUEAK
SQUEAK
SQUEAK
Every time you grind it with a pestle or step on it, the sand makes squeaky sounds! ♪ We had a blast! ♪
Thank you to the staff of the Sand Museum for giving me permission to put their museum in my book!!
Nima Sand Museum
Tel 0854-88-3776
http://www.nima-cho.ne.jp/museum/

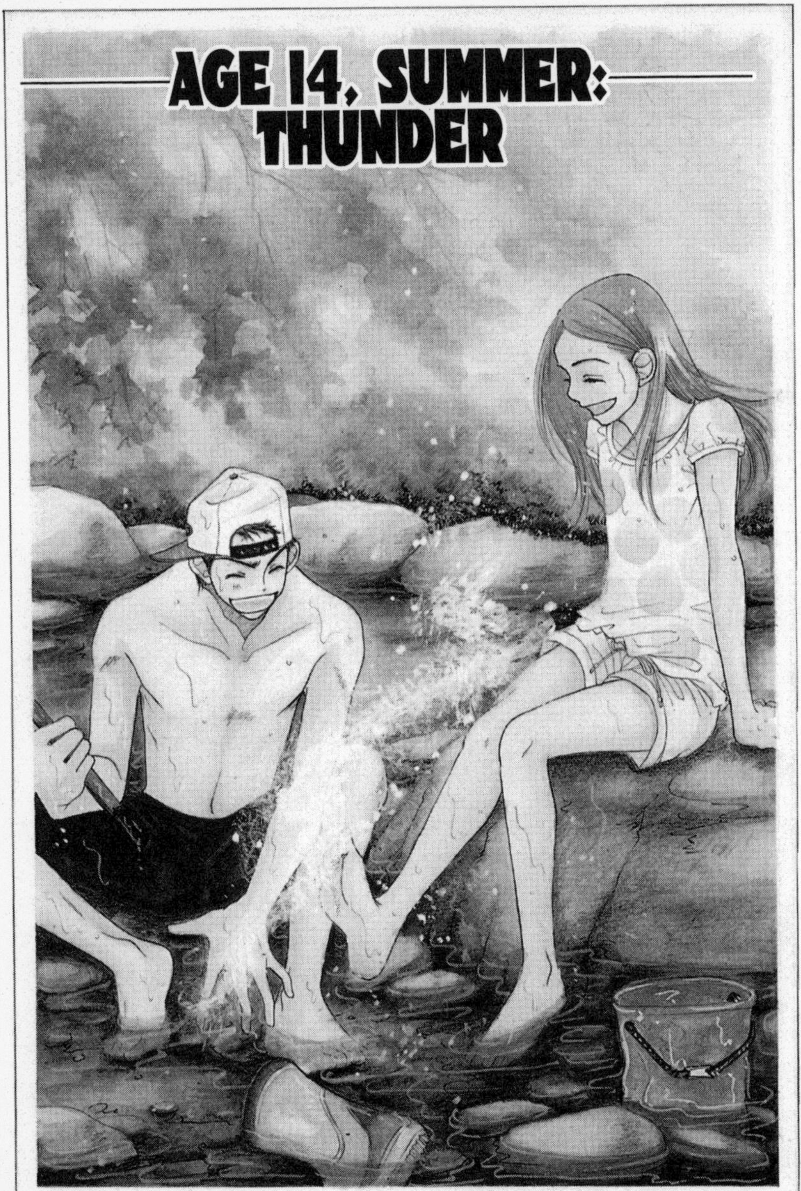
AGE 14, SUMMER:
THUNDER

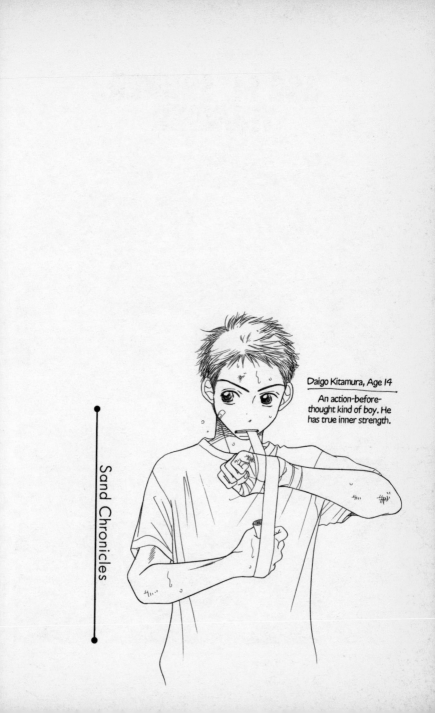

Daigo Kitamura, Age 14

An action-before-thought kind of boy. He has true inner strength.

Sand Chronicles

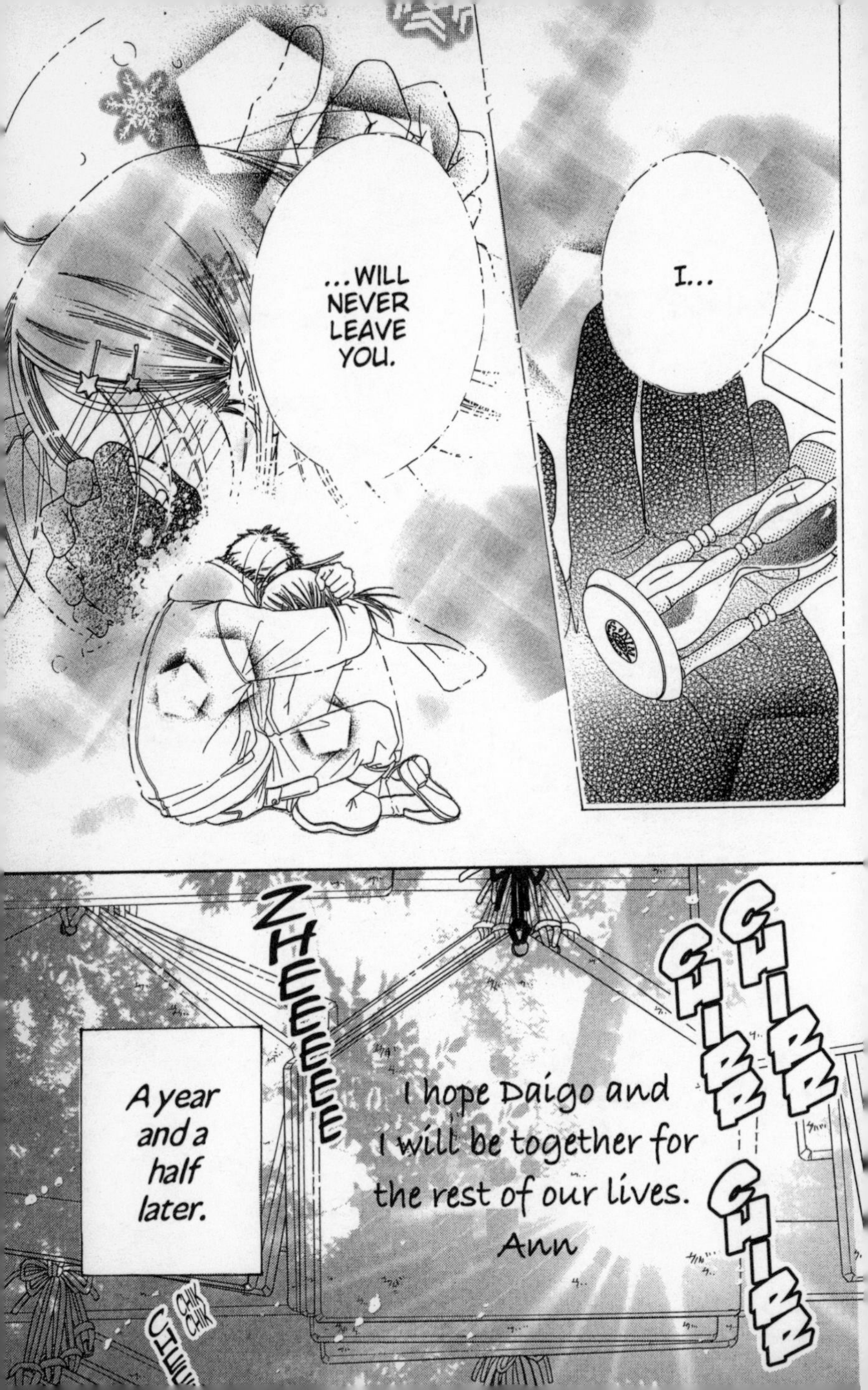
I...
...WILL NEVER LEAVE YOU.
CHIRR
CHIRR
CHIRR
I hope Daigo and I will be together for the rest of our lives.
Ann
ZHEEEEEEE
A year and a half later.
CHIK CHIK

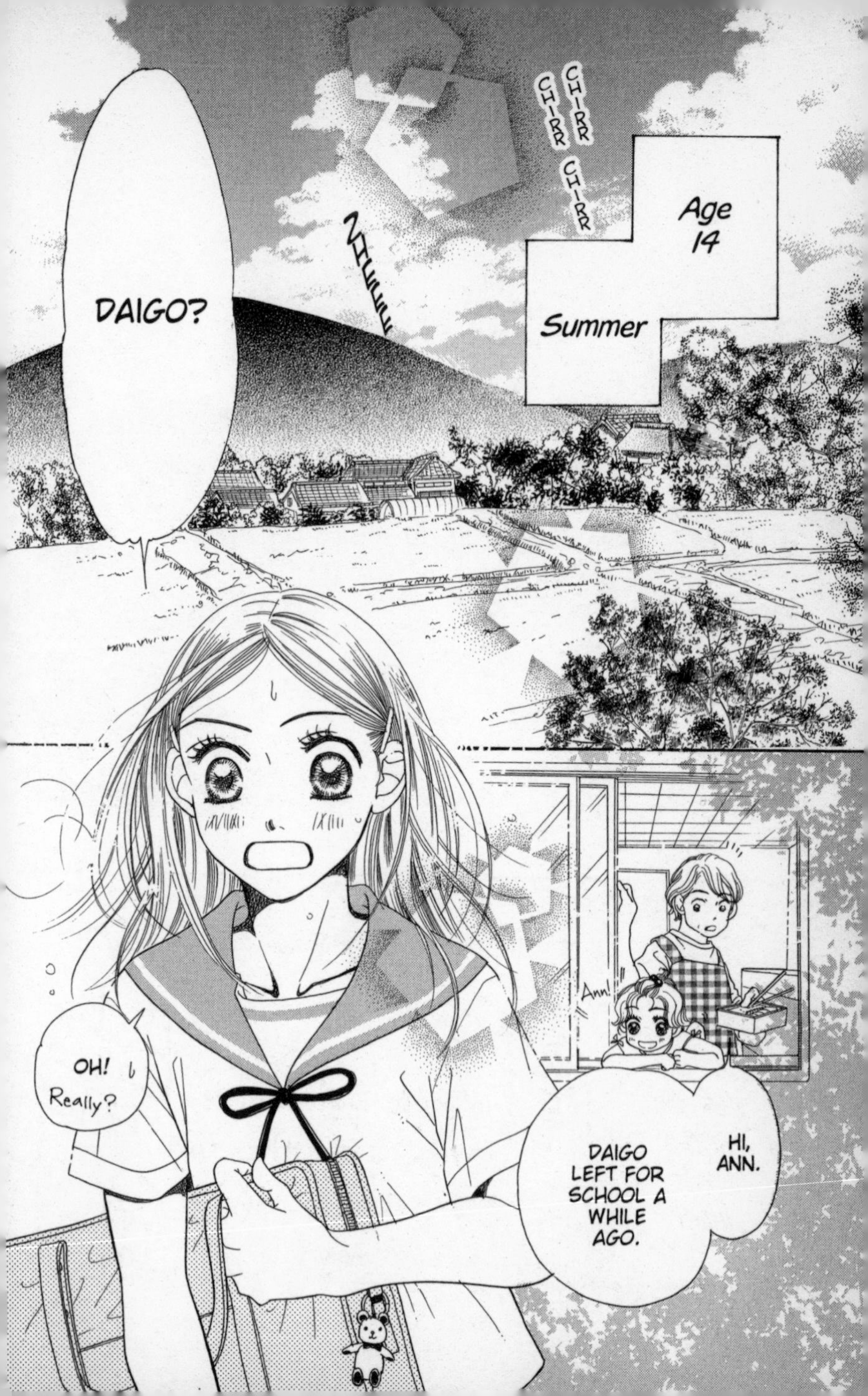
CHIRR CHIRR
CHIRR CHIRR
Age 14
Summer
ZHUUUU
DAIGO?
HI, ANN.
DAIGO LEFT FOR SCHOOL A WHILE AGO.
Ann!
OH! Really?

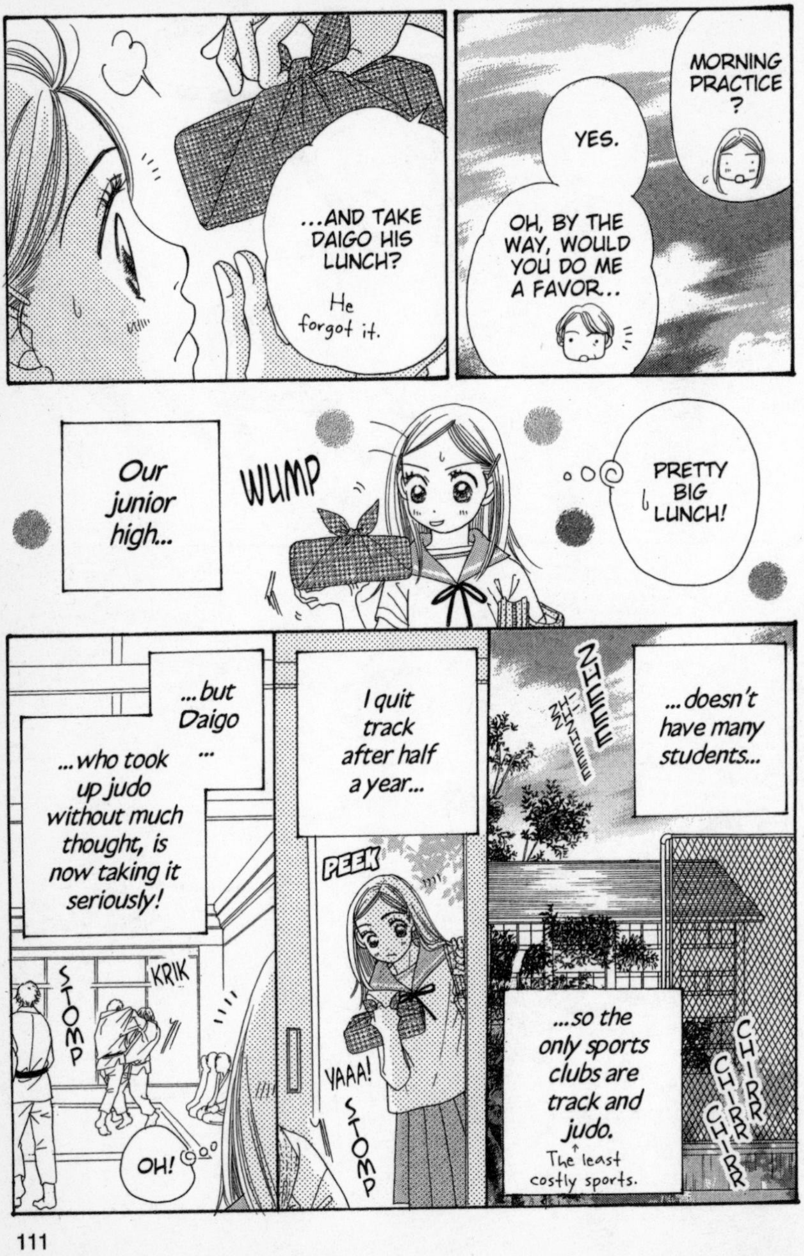
MORNING PRACTICE ?
YES.
OH, BY THE WAY, WOULD YOU DO ME A FAVOR..
...AND TAKE DAIGO HIS LUNCH?
He forgot it.
PRETTY BIG LUNCH!
WUMP
Our junior high...
ZHEEE
ZHEEEEE
...doesn't have many students...
...so the only sports clubs are track and judo.
The least costly sports.
CHIRR
CHIRR
CHIRR
I quit track after half a year...
PEEK
YAAA!
STOMP
...but Daigo ...
...who took up judo without much thought, is now taking it seriously!
KRIK
STOMP
OH!

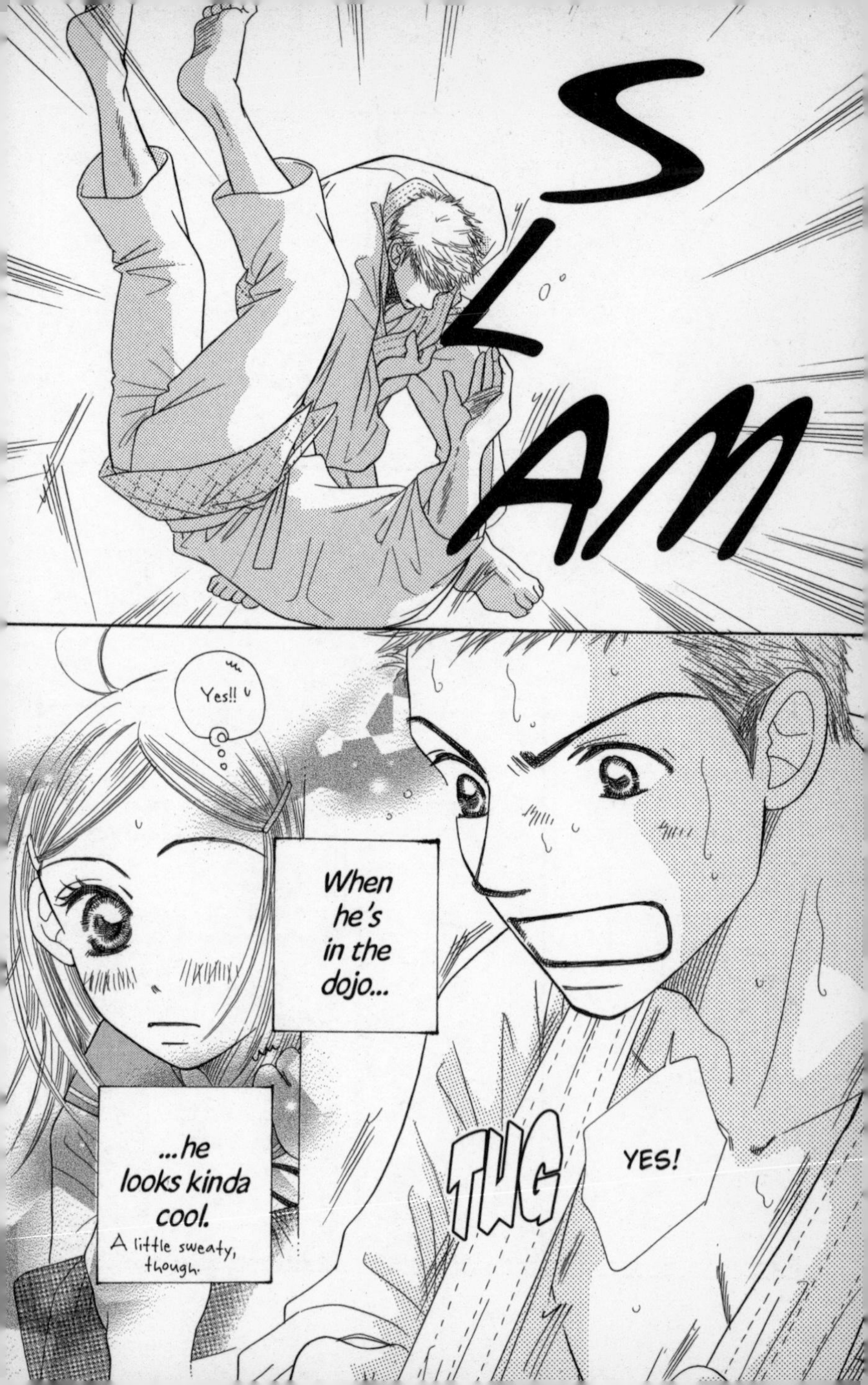
SLAM
YES!
TUG
When he's in the dojo...
Yes!!
...he looks kinda cool.
A little sweaty, though.

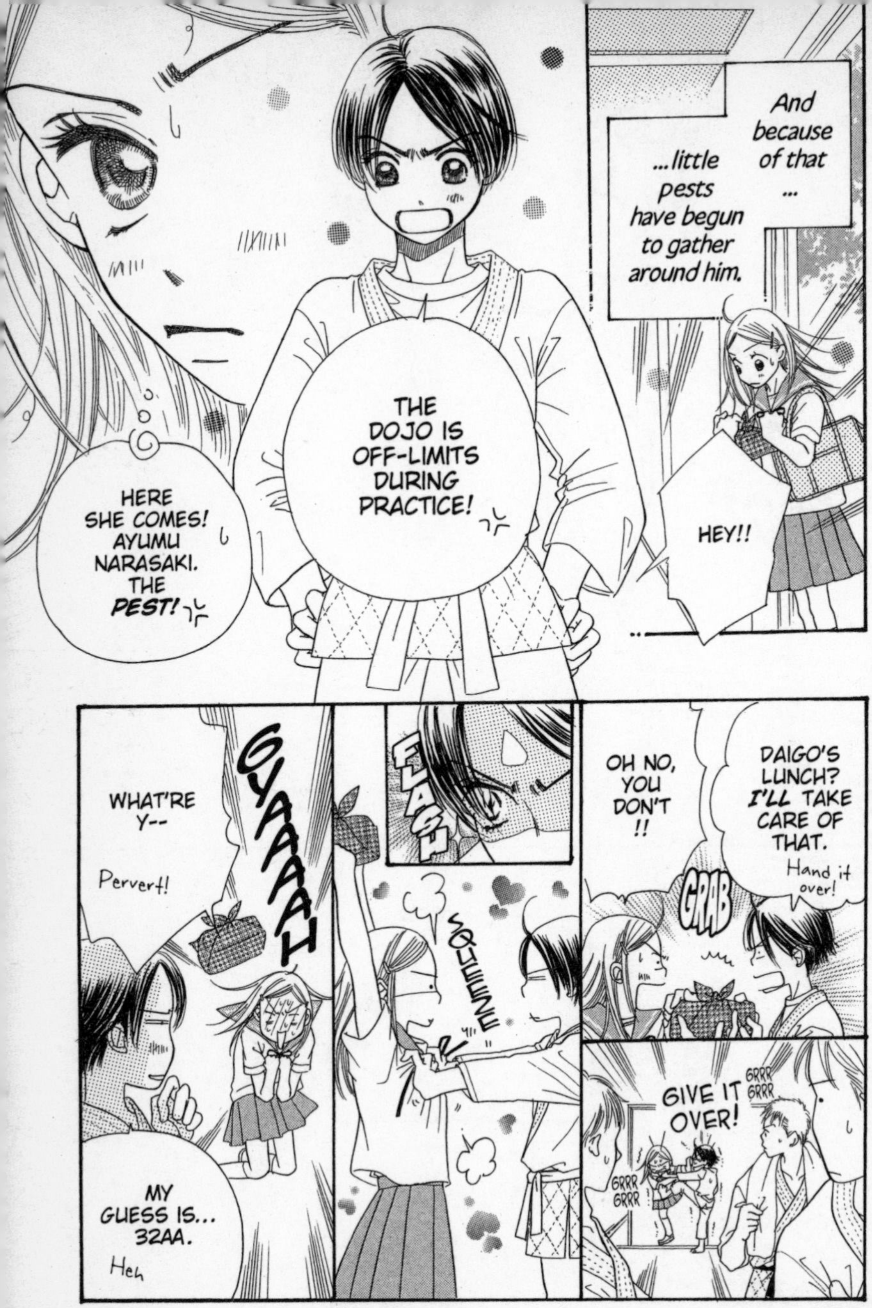
And because of that ...
...little pests have begun to gather around him.
HEY!!
THE DOJO IS OFF-LIMITS DURING PRACTICE!
HERE SHE COMES! AYUMU NARASAKI. THE ***PEST!***
DAIGO'S LUNCH? ***I'LL*** TAKE CARE OF THAT.
Hand it over!
OH NO, YOU DON'T !!
GRAB
GIVE IT OVER!
GRRR GRRR
GRRR GRRR
FLASH
SQUEEZE
WHAT'RE Y--
GYAAAAAH
Pervert!
MY GUESS IS... 32AA.
Heh

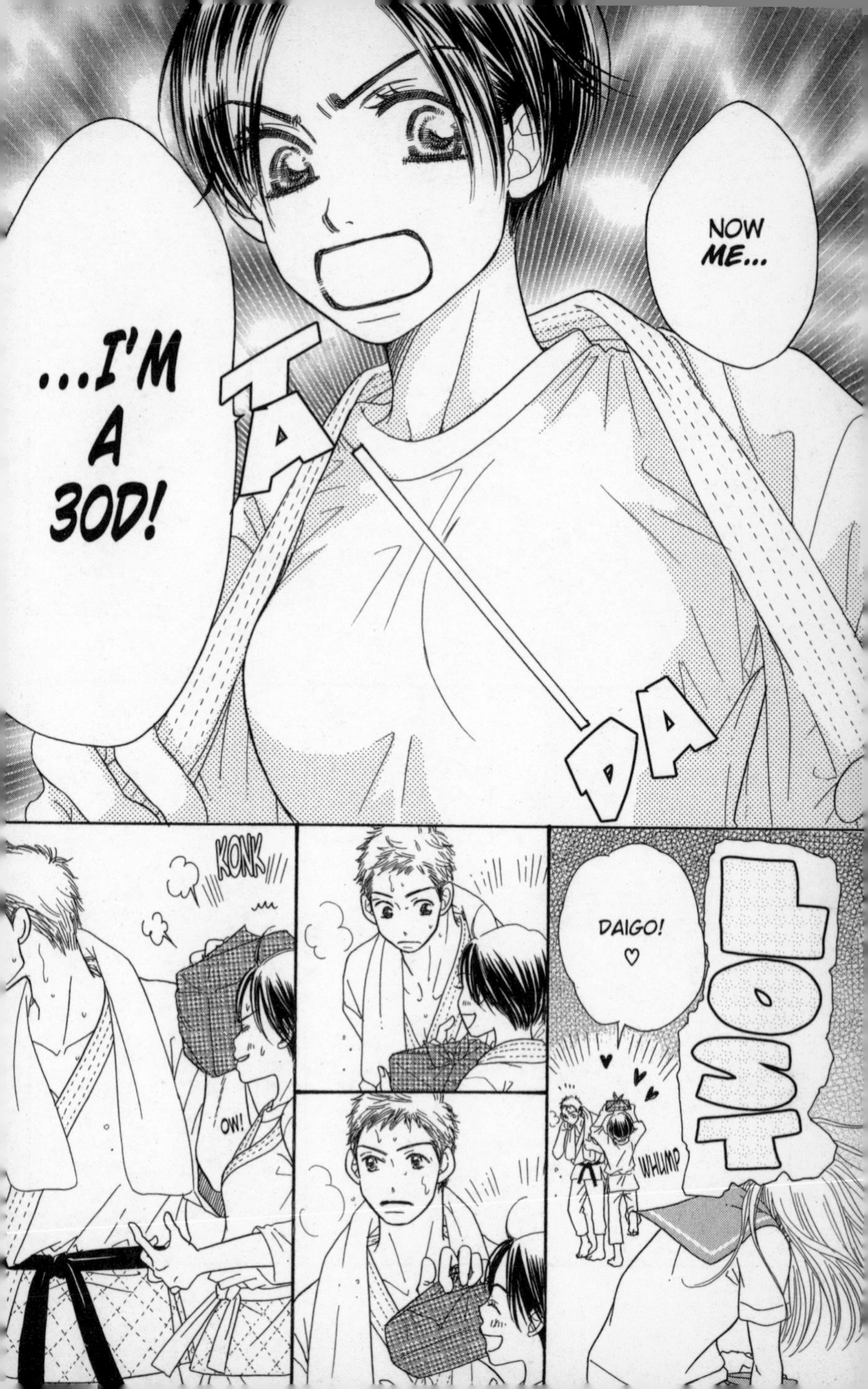
NOW ME...
...I'M A 30D!
TA
DA
THWOMP
DAIGO! ♡
WHUMP
KONK
OW!

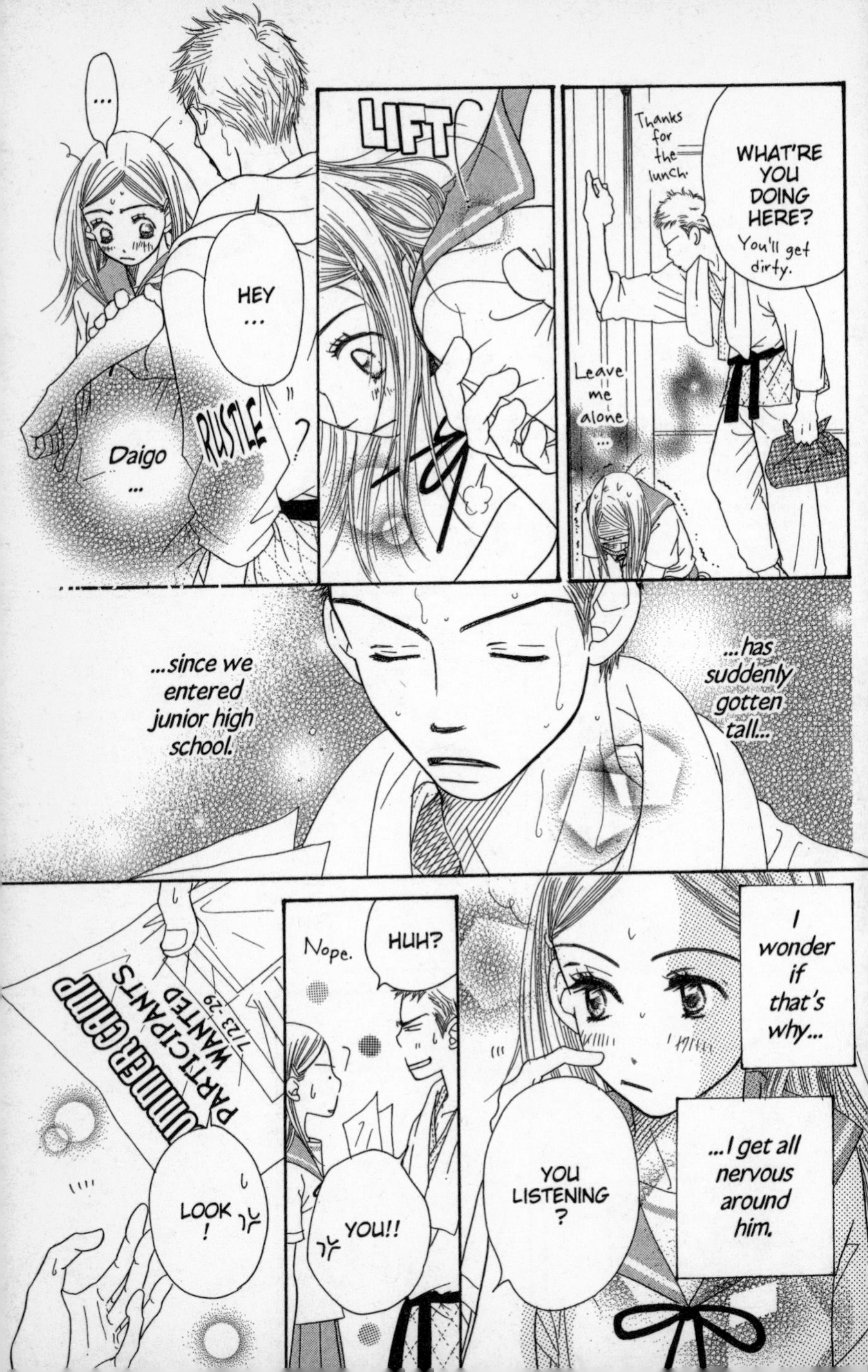
WHAT'RE YOU DOING HERE?
You'll get dirty.
Thanks for the lunch.
Leave me alone...
LIFT
HEY...
RUSTLE
...
Daigo...
...has suddenly gotten tall...
...since we entered junior high school.
I wonder if that's why...
...I get all nervous around him.
YOU LISTENING?
HUH?
Nope.
YOU!!
SUMMER CAMP
PARTICIPANTS WANTED
7/23-29
LOOK!

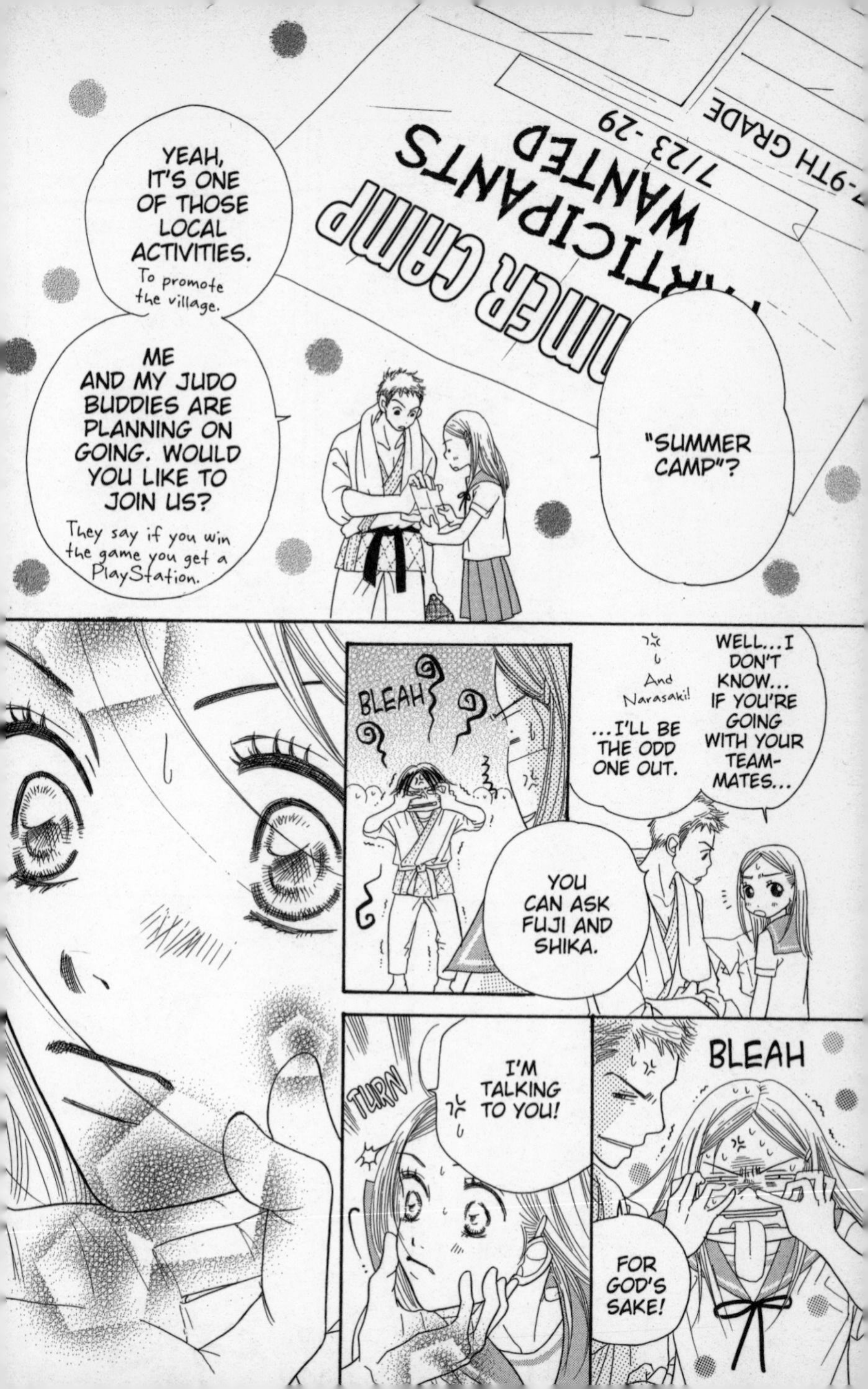

WANTED
7/23 -29
-9TH GRADE
"SUMMER CAMP"?
YEAH, IT'S ONE OF THOSE LOCAL ACTIVITIES.
To promote the village.
ME AND MY JUDO BUDDIES ARE PLANNING ON GOING. WOULD YOU LIKE TO JOIN US?
They say if you win the game you get a PlayStation.
WELL...I DON'T KNOW... IF YOU'RE GOING WITH YOUR TEAM-MATES...
...I'LL BE THE ODD ONE OUT.
And Narasaki!
YOU CAN ASK FUJI AND SHIKA.
BLEAH
BLEAH
FOR GOD'S SAKE!
TURN
I'M TALKING TO YOU!

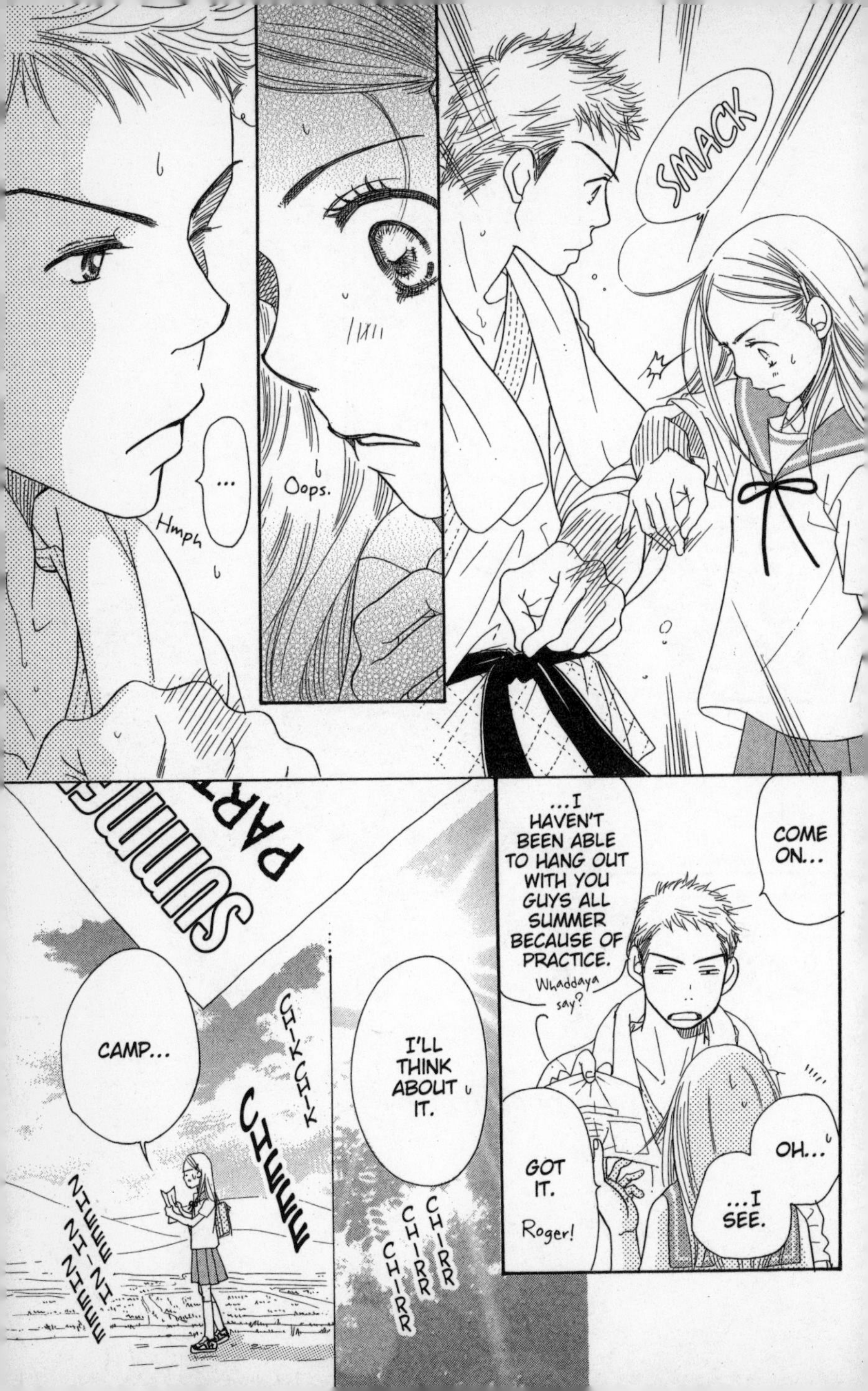
SMACK
Oops.
...
Hmph
COME ON...
...I HAVEN'T BEEN ABLE TO HANG OUT WITH YOU GUYS ALL SUMMER BECAUSE OF PRACTICE.
Whaddaya say?
OH...
...I SEE.
GOT IT.
Roger!
I'LL THINK ABOUT IT.
CHIRR CHIRR CHIRR CHIRR
CAMP...
CHIK CHIK
CHUUUU
NIEEE NI-NI NIEEE

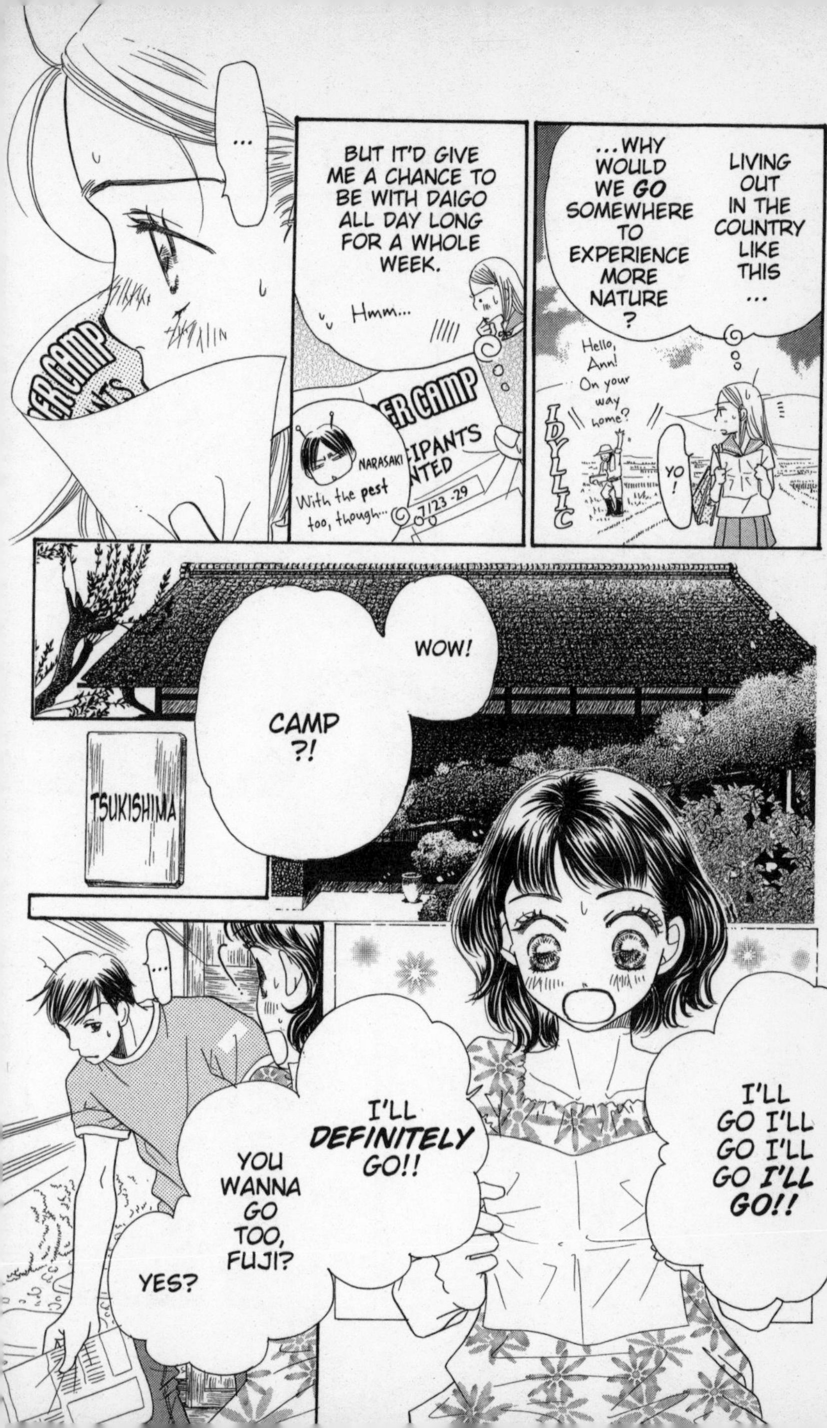
LIVING OUT IN THE COUNTRY LIKE THIS ...
...WHY WOULD WE GO SOMEWHERE TO EXPERIENCE MORE NATURE?
IDYLLIC
Hello, Ann! On your way home?
YO!
BUT IT'D GIVE ME A CHANCE TO BE WITH DAIGO ALL DAY LONG FOR A WHOLE WEEK.
Hmm...
ER CAMP
CIPANTS
NTED
7/23-29
NARASAKI
With the pest too, though...
...
ER CAMP
WOW!
CAMP?!
TSUKISHIMA
I'LL GO I'LL GO I'LL GO I'LL GO!!
I'LL DEFINITELY GO!!
YOU WANNA GO TOO, FUJI?
YES?
...

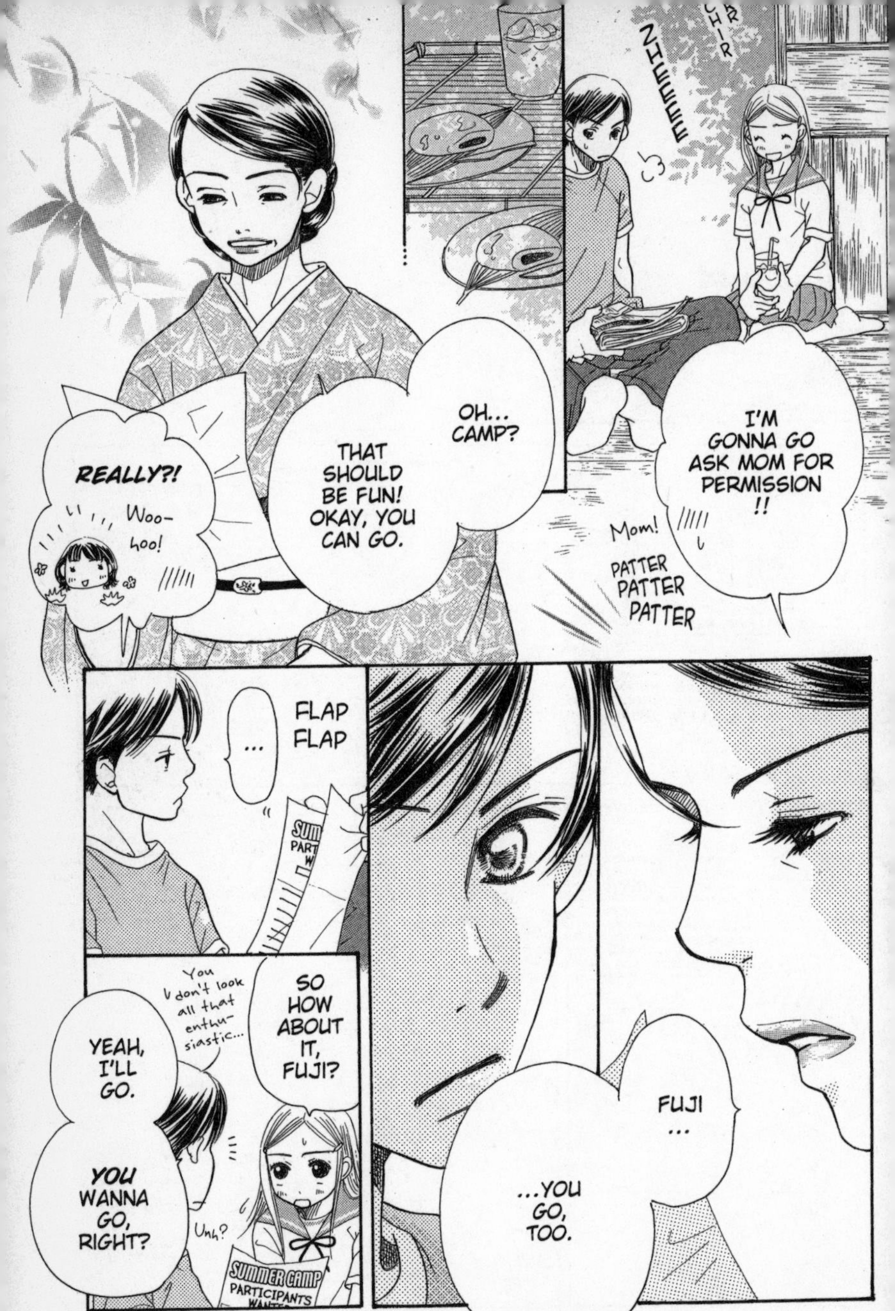
CHIR
ZHEEEE
I'M GONNA GO ASK MOM FOR PERMISSION!!
Mom!
PATTER PATTER PATTER
OH... CAMP?
THAT SHOULD BE FUN! OKAY, YOU CAN GO.
REALLY?!
Woo-hoo!
FUJI ...
...YOU GO, TOO.
...
FLAP FLAP
SO HOW ABOUT IT, FUJI?
You don't look all that enthu-siastic...
YEAH, I'LL GO.
YOU WANNA GO, RIGHT?
Unh?
SUMMER CAMP
PARTICIPANTS

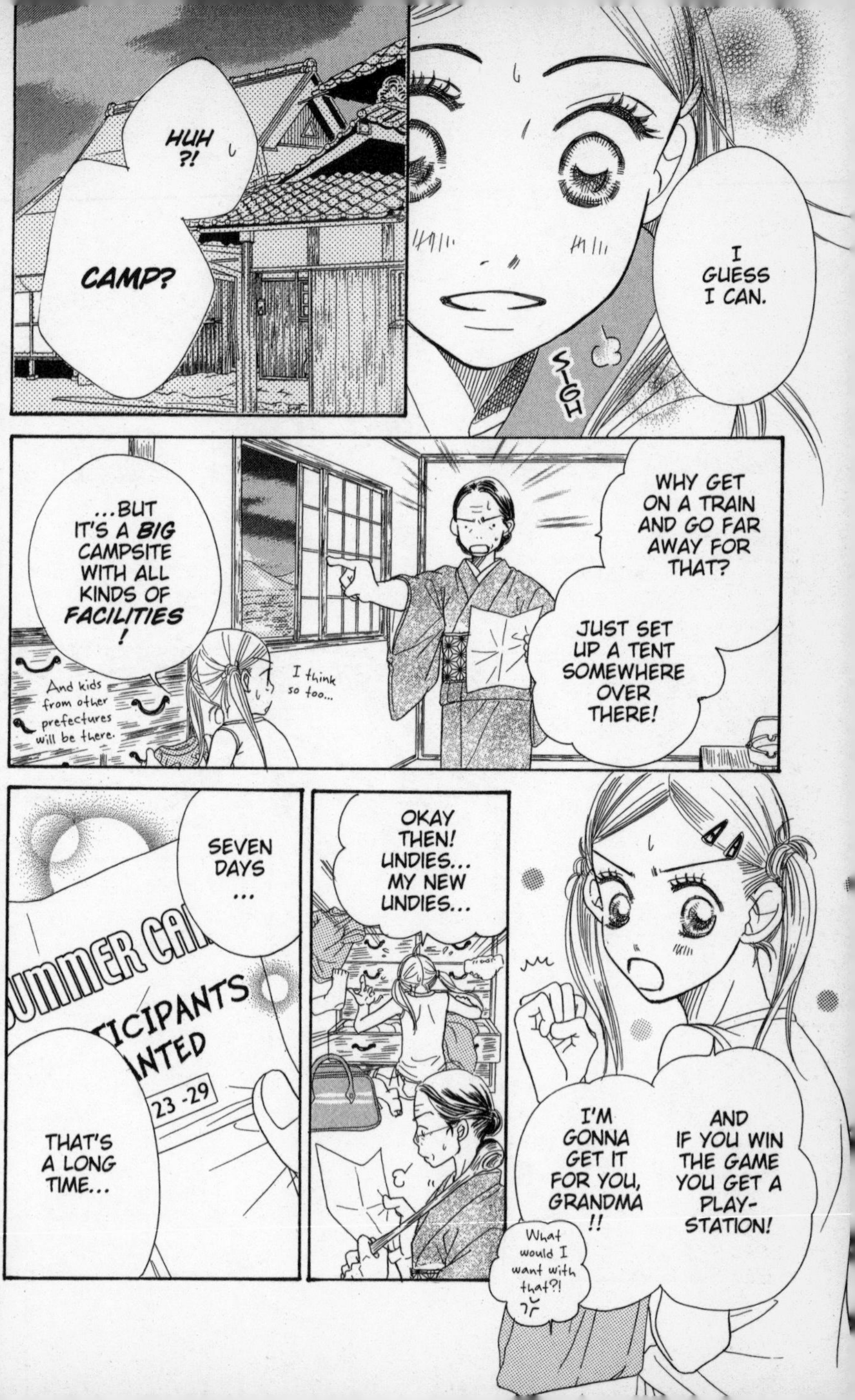
I GUESS I CAN.
SIGH
HUH ?!
CAMP?
WHY GET ON A TRAIN AND GO FAR AWAY FOR THAT?
JUST SET UP A TENT SOMEWHERE OVER THERE!
I think so too...
...BUT IT'S A BIG CAMPSITE WITH ALL KINDS OF FACILITIES!
And kids from other prefectures will be there.
AND IF YOU WIN THE GAME YOU GET A PLAY-STATION!
I'M GONNA GET IT FOR YOU, GRANDMA!!
What would I want with that?!
OKAY THEN! UNDIES... MY NEW UNDIES...
SEVEN DAYS...
23 -29
THAT'S A LONG TIME...

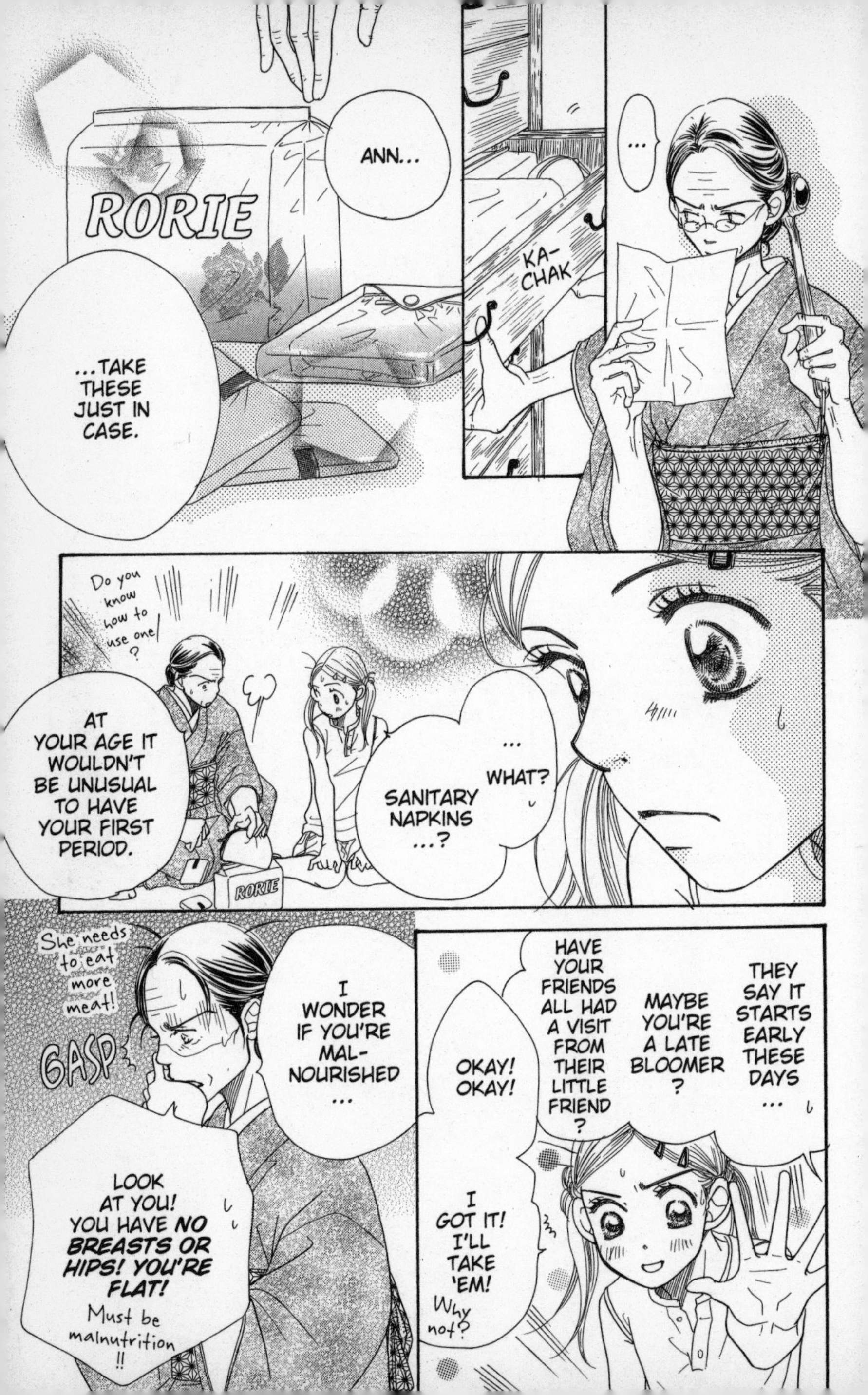
...
KA-CHAK
ANN...
RORIE
...TAKE THESE JUST IN CASE.
... WHAT?
SANITARY NAPKINS ...?
Do you know how to use one/?
AT YOUR AGE IT WOULDN'T BE UNUSUAL TO HAVE YOUR FIRST PERIOD.
RORIE
THEY SAY IT STARTS EARLY THESE DAYS...
MAYBE YOU'RE A LATE BLOOMER?
HAVE YOUR FRIENDS ALL HAD A VISIT FROM THEIR LITTLE FRIEND?
OKAY! OKAY!
I GOT IT! I'LL TAKE 'EM!
Why not?
I WONDER IF YOU'RE MAL-NOURISHED...
She needs to eat more meat!
GASP
LOOK AT YOU! YOU HAVE NO BREASTS OR HIPS! YOU'RE FLAT!
Must be malnutrition!!

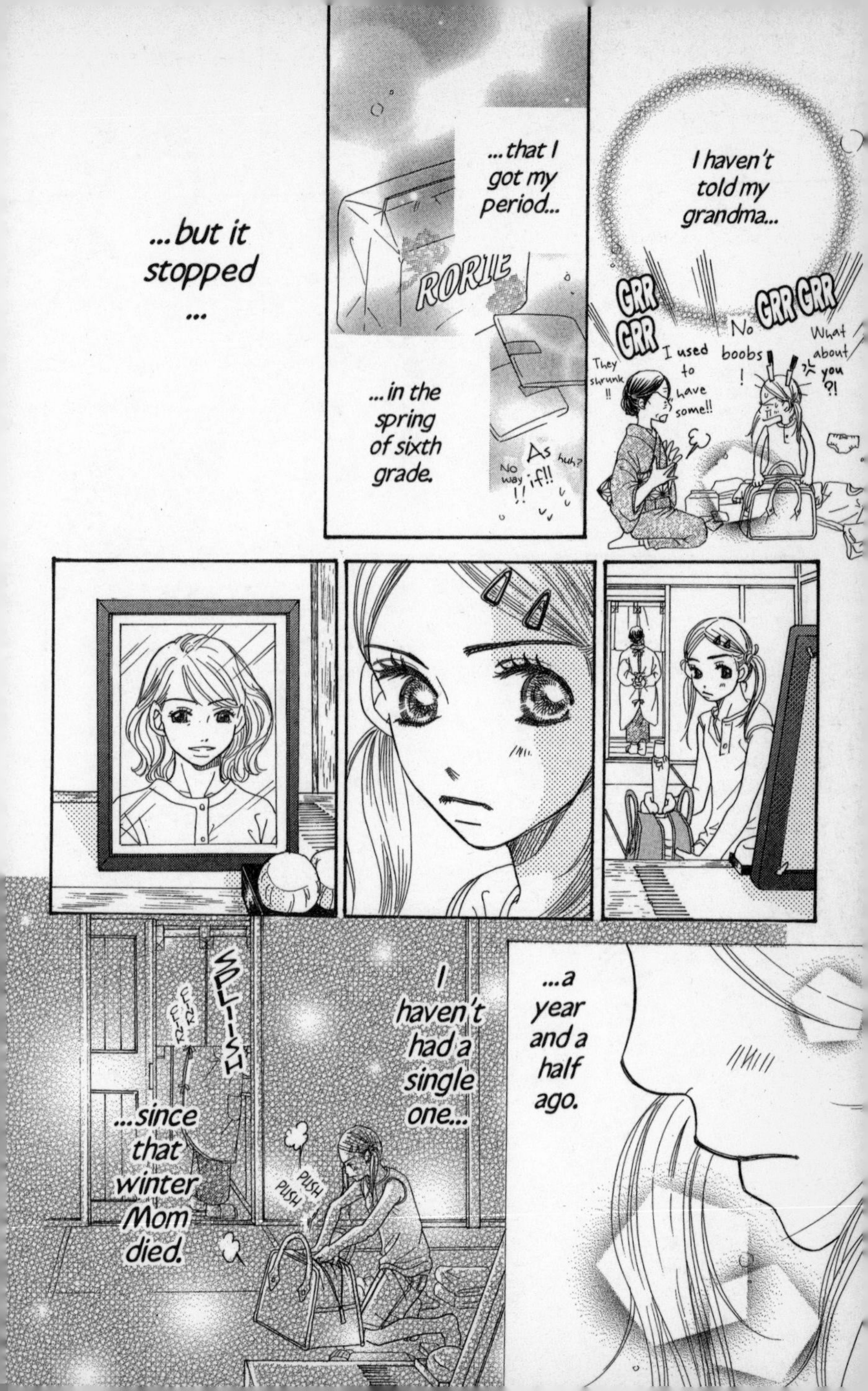
I haven't told my grandma...
GRR GRR
No boobs!
What about you ?!
GRR GRR
I used to have some!!
They shrunk!!
...that I got my period...
RORIE
...in the spring of sixth grade.
As if!!
huh?
No way!!
...but it stopped ...
...a year and a half ago.
I haven't had a single one...
SPLISH
PUSH PUSH
...since that winter Mom died.

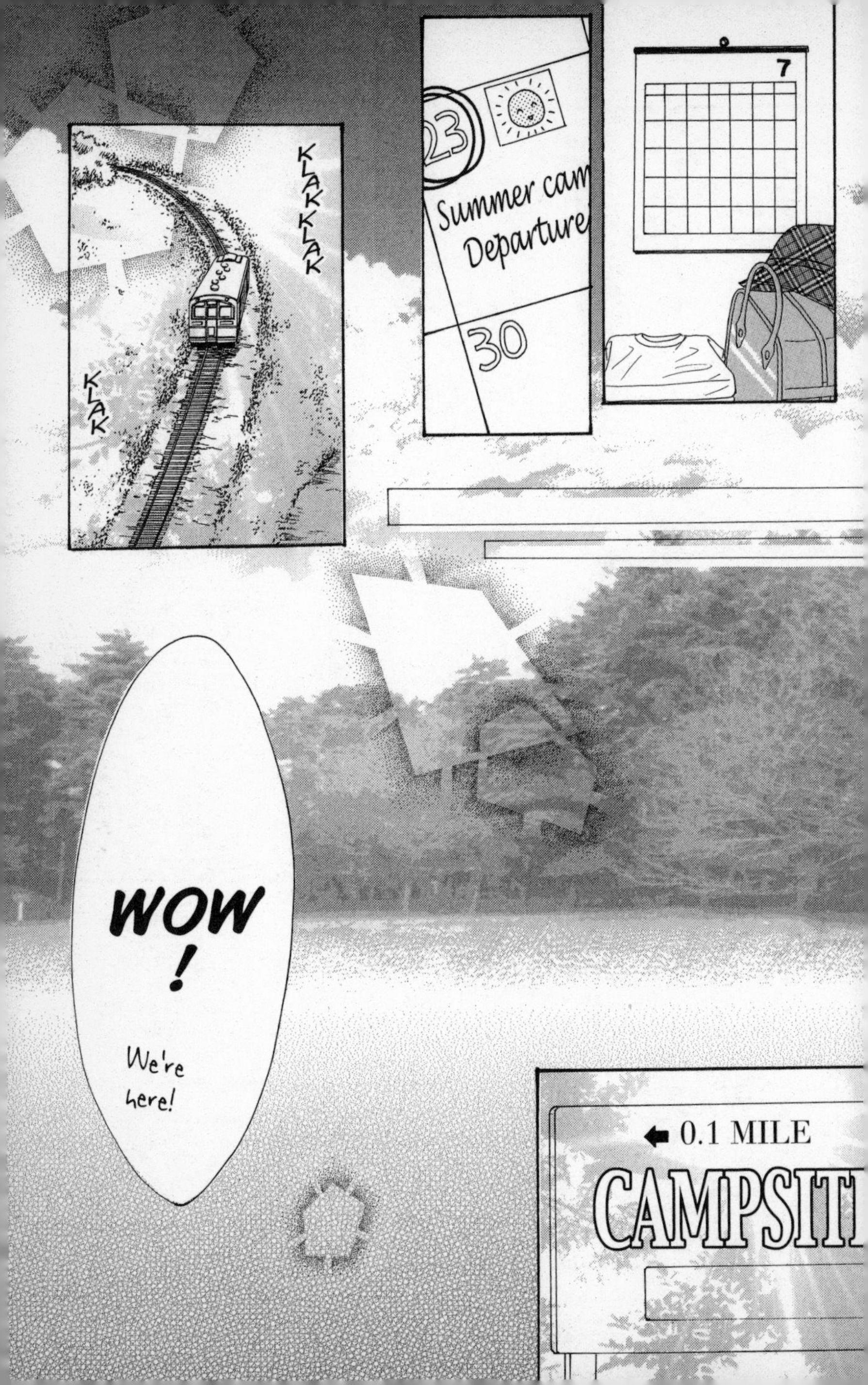

7
23
Summer cam
Departure
30
KLAK KLAK
KLAK
WOW!
We're here!
0.1 MILE
CAMPSIT

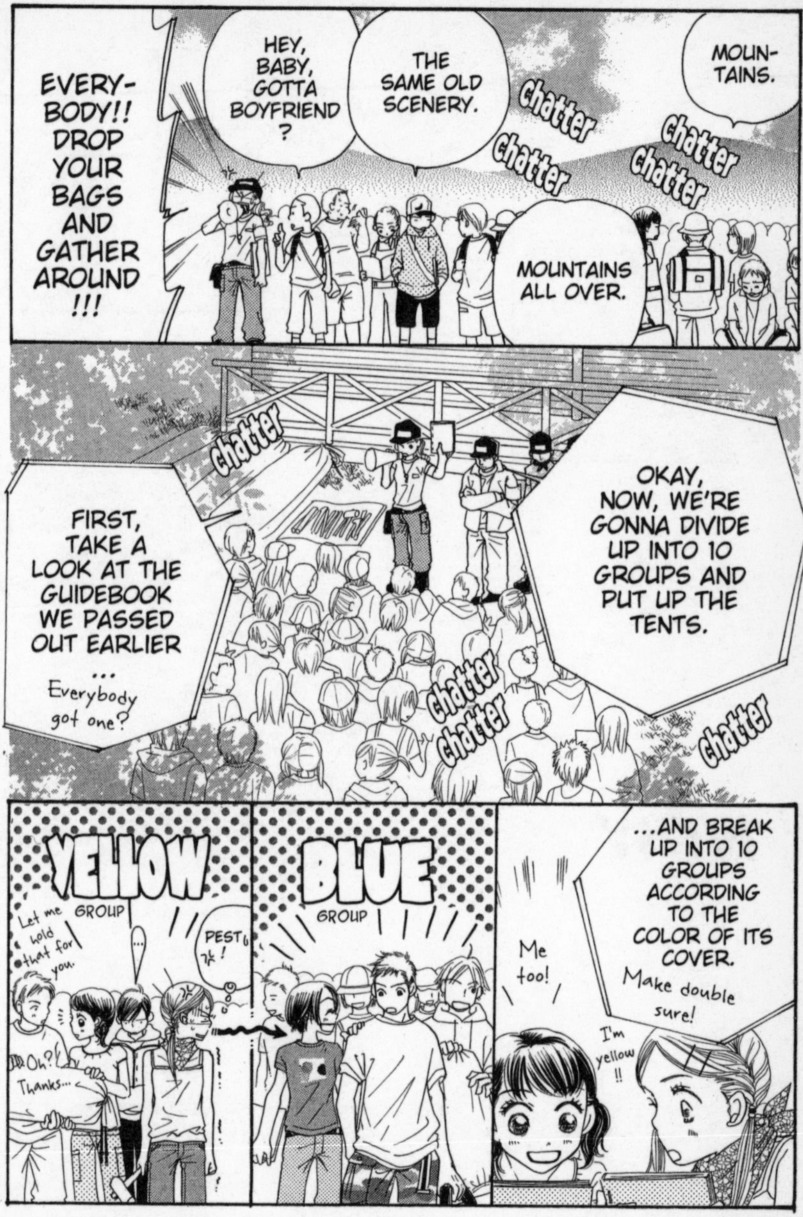
MOUN-TAINS.
Chatter
Chatter
MOUNTAINS ALL OVER.
Chatter
Chatter
THE SAME OLD SCENERY.
HEY, BABY, GOTTA BOYFRIEND?
EVERY-BODY!! DROP YOUR BAGS AND GATHER AROUND!!!
OKAY, NOW, WE'RE GONNA DIVIDE UP INTO 10 GROUPS AND PUT UP THE TENTS.
chatter
chatter
chatter
chatter
FIRST, TAKE A LOOK AT THE GUIDEBOOK WE PASSED OUT EARLIER...
Everybody got one?
...AND BREAK UP INTO 10 GROUPS ACCORDING TO THE COLOR OF ITS COVER.
Make double sure!
I'm yellow!!
Me too!
BLUE
GROUP
YELLOW
GROUP
PEST
...
Let me hold that for you.
Oh? Thanks...

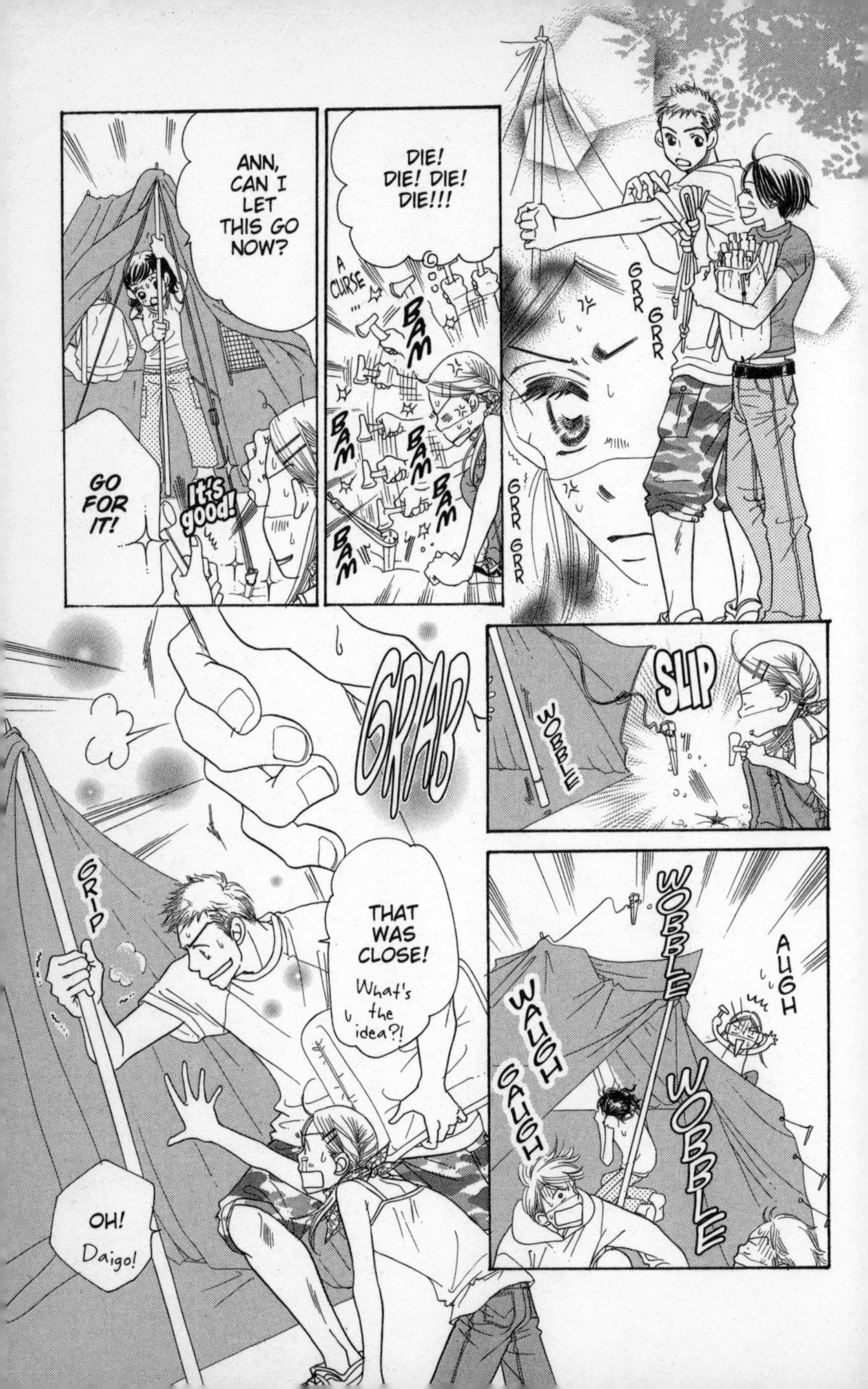
GRR GRR
GRR GRR
DIE! DIE! DIE! DIE!!!
A CURSE ...
BAM
BAM
BAM
BAM
BAM
ANN, CAN I LET THIS GO NOW?
It's good!
GO FOR IT!
SLIP
WOBBLE
WOBBLE
AUGH
WAUGH
GAUGH
WOBBLE
GRAB
GRIP
THAT WAS CLOSE!
What's the idea?!
OH!
Daigo!

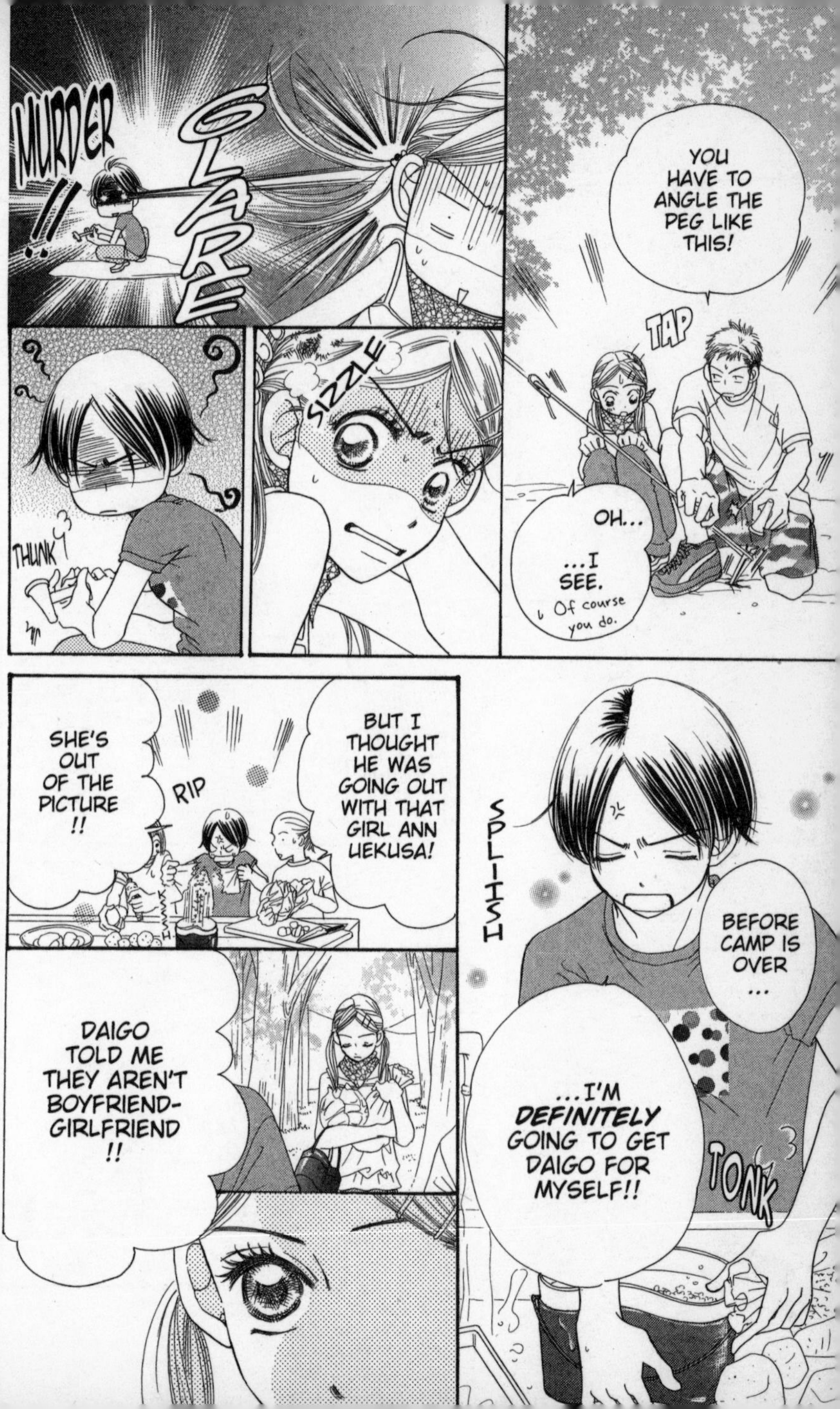
YOU HAVE TO ANGLE THE PEG LIKE THIS!
TAP
OH...
...I SEE.
Of course you do.
MURDER!!
GLARE
SIZZLE
THUNK
SPLISH
BEFORE CAMP IS OVER...
...I'M DEFINITELY GOING TO GET DAIGO FOR MYSELF!!
TONK
BUT I THOUGHT HE WAS GOING OUT WITH THAT GIRL ANN UEKUSA!
RIP
SHE'S OUT OF THE PICTURE!!
KSSH
DAIGO TOLD ME THEY AREN'T BOYFRIEND-GIRLFRIEND!!

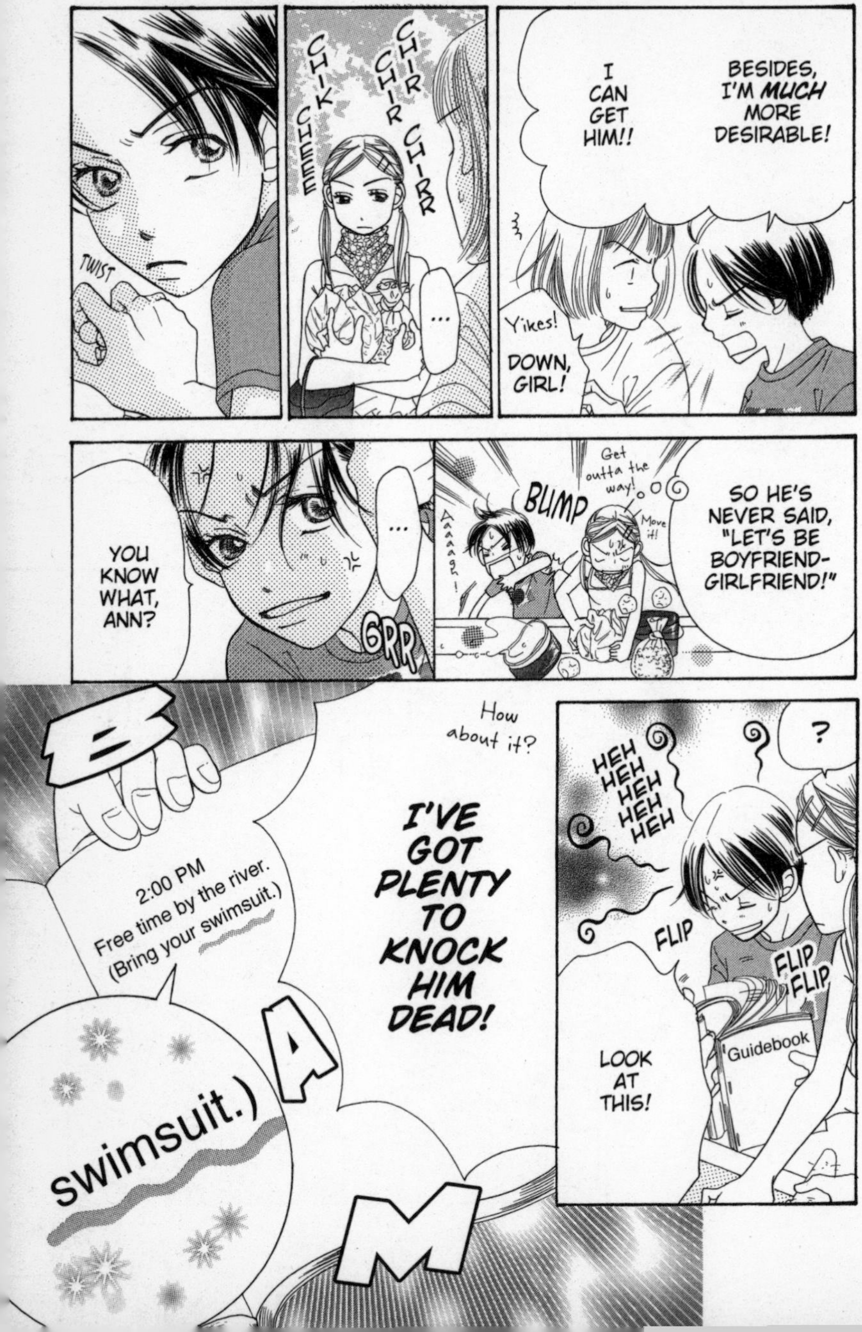

BESIDES, I'M *MUCH* MORE DESIRABLE!
I CAN GET HIM!!
Yikes!
DOWN, GIRL!
CHIR CHIR CHIRR
CHIK CHEEE
...
TWIST
SO HE'S NEVER SAID, "LET'S BE BOYFRIEND-GIRLFRIEND!"
Get outta the way!
Move it!
BUMP
Aaaaagh!
...
YOU KNOW WHAT, ANN?
GRR
?
HEH HEH HEH HEH HEH
FLIP
FLIP FLIP
Guidebook
LOOK AT THIS!
How about it?
I'VE GOT PLENTY TO KNOCK HIM DEAD!
2:00 PM
Free time by the river.
(Bring your swimsuit.)
swimsuit.)
B
A
M

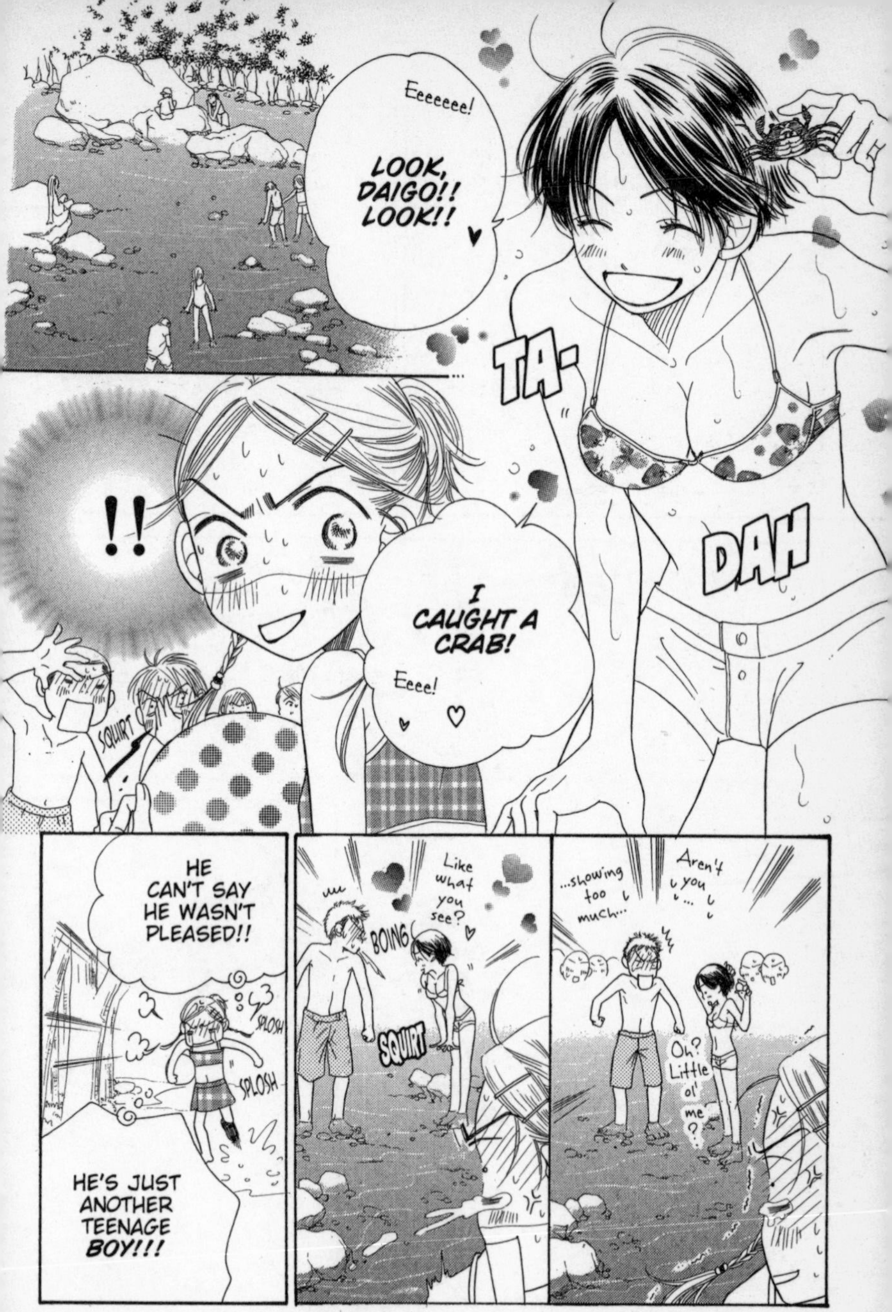
Eeeeeee!
LOOK, DAIGO!! LOOK!!
TA-
DAH
!!
I CAUGHT A CRAB!
Eeee!
SQUIRT
Aren't you...
...showing too much...
Oh? Little ol' me?
Like what you see?
BOING
SQUIRT
HE CAN'T SAY HE WASN'T PLEASED!!
SPLOSH
SPLOSH
HE'S JUST ANOTHER TEENAGE BOY!!!

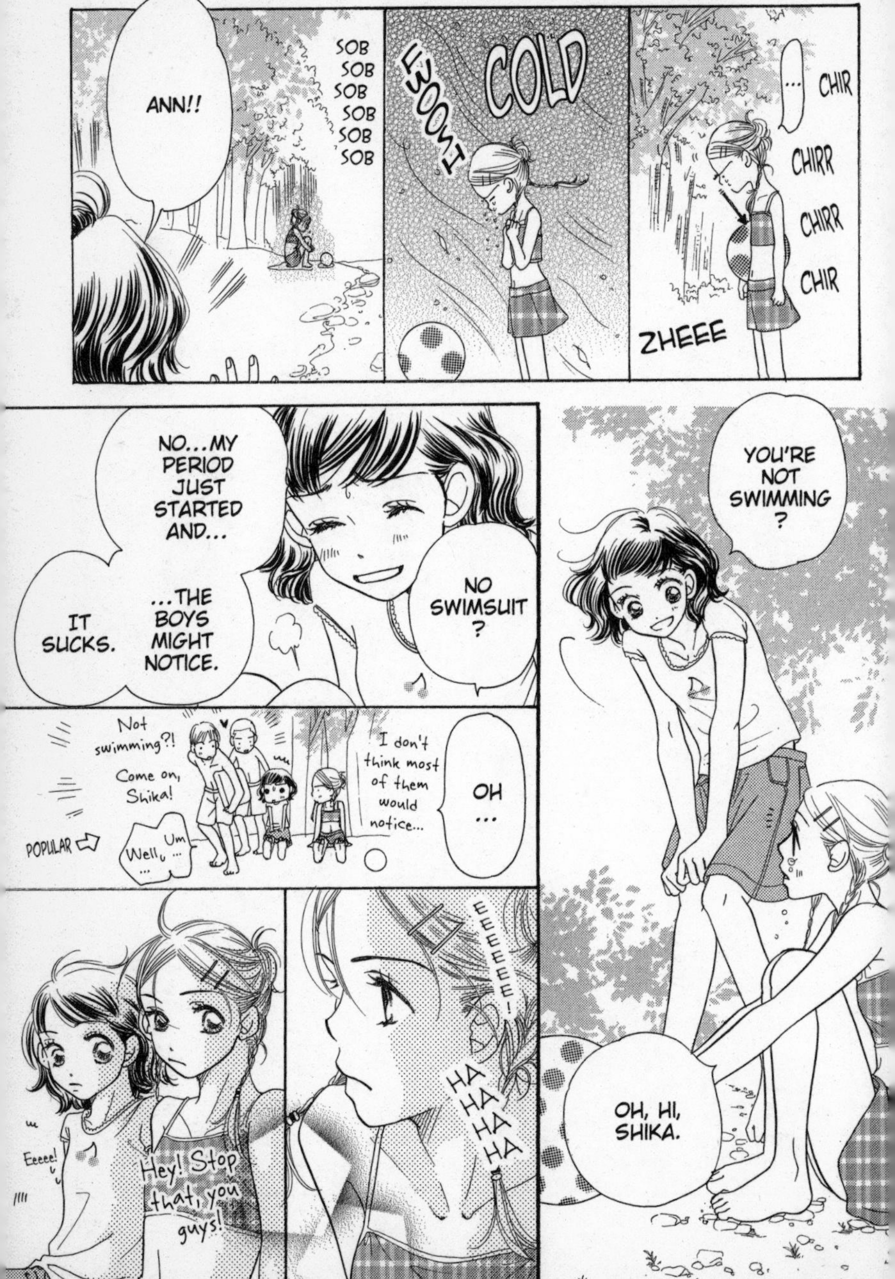
...
CHIR
CHIRR
CHIRR
CHIR
ZHEEE
COLD
ANN!!
SOB
SOB
SOB
SOB
SOB
SOB
YOU'RE NOT SWIMMING?
OH, HI, SHIKA.
NO SWIMSUIT?
NO... MY PERIOD JUST STARTED AND...
...THE BOYS MIGHT NOTICE.
IT SUCKS.
OH...
I don't think most of them would notice...
Not swimming?!
Come on, Shika!
Um...
Well, ...
POPULAR
EEEEEEE!
HA HA HA HA
Hey! Stop that, you guys!
Eeeee!

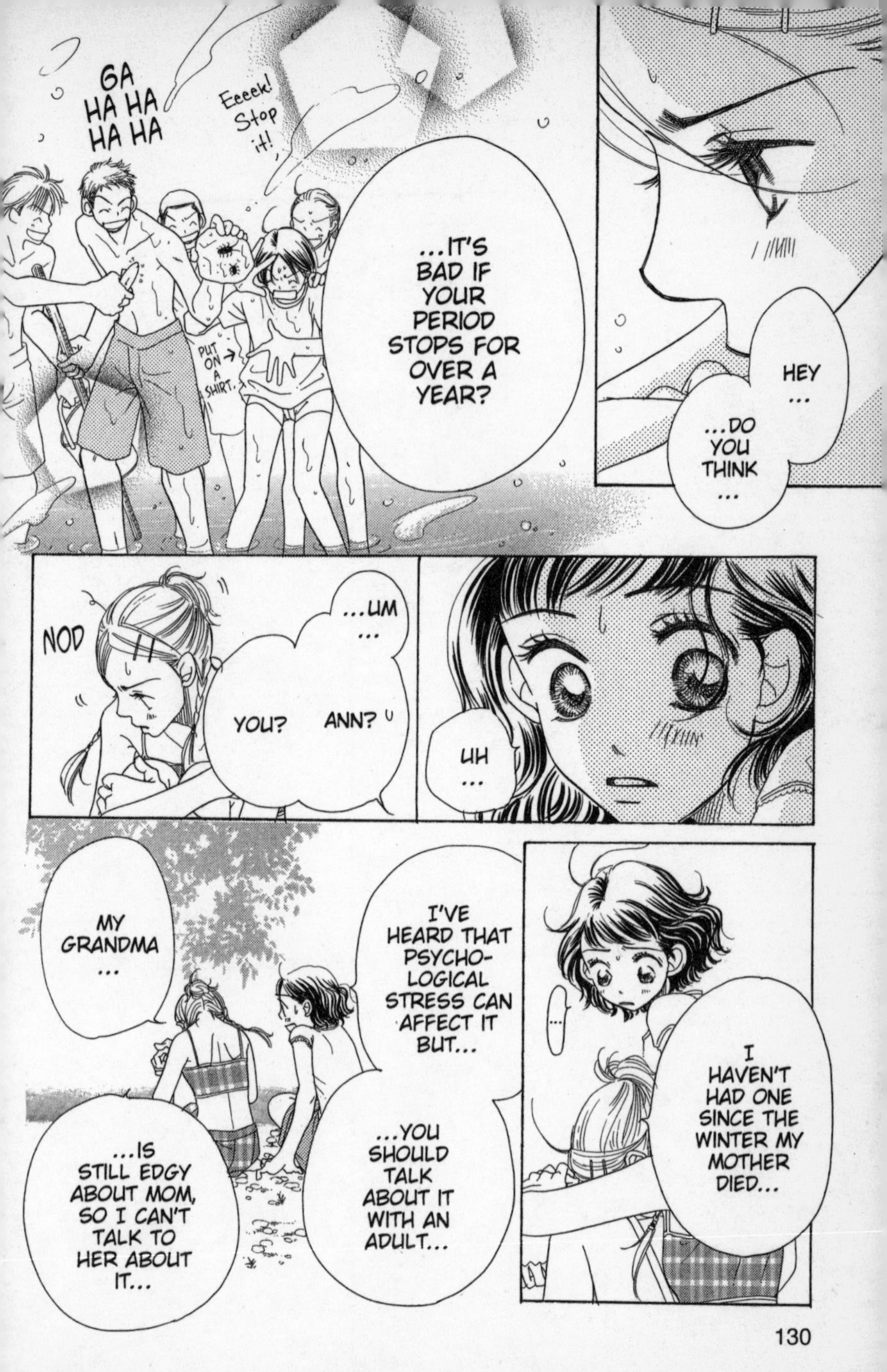
HEY ...
...DO YOU THINK ...
...IT'S BAD IF YOUR PERIOD STOPS FOR OVER A YEAR?
Eeeek! Stop it!
GA HA HA HA HA
PUT ON A SHIRT.
UH ...
...UM ...
ANN?
YOU?
NOD
...
I HAVEN'T HAD ONE SINCE THE WINTER MY MOTHER DIED...
I'VE HEARD THAT PSYCHO-LOGICAL STRESS CAN AFFECT IT BUT...
...YOU SHOULD TALK ABOUT IT WITH AN ADULT...
MY GRANDMA ...
...IS STILL EDGY ABOUT MOM, SO I CAN'T TALK TO HER ABOUT IT...

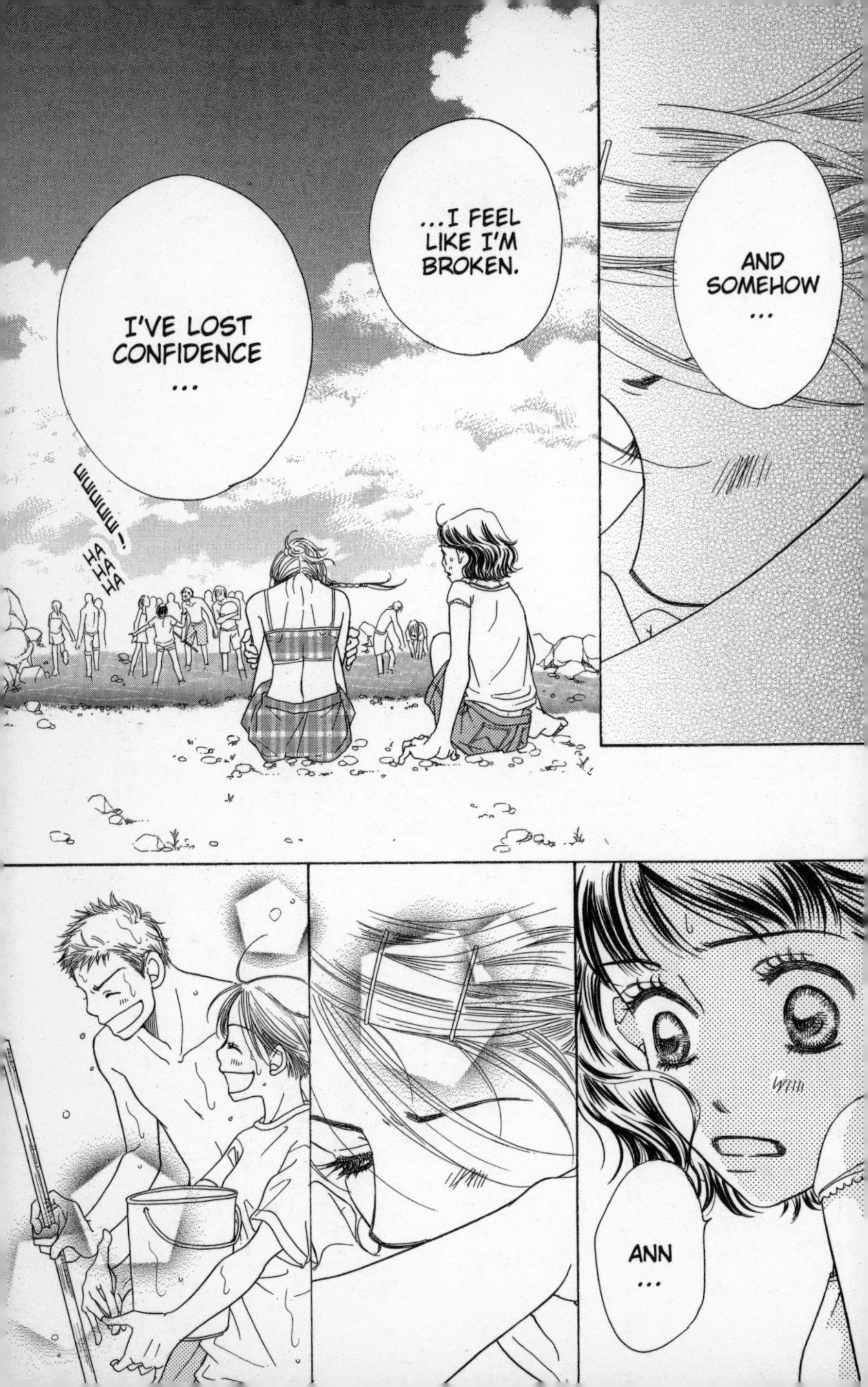
AND SOMEHOW ...
...I FEEL LIKE I'M BROKEN.
I'VE LOST CONFIDENCE ...
EEEEE!
HA HA HA
ANN ...

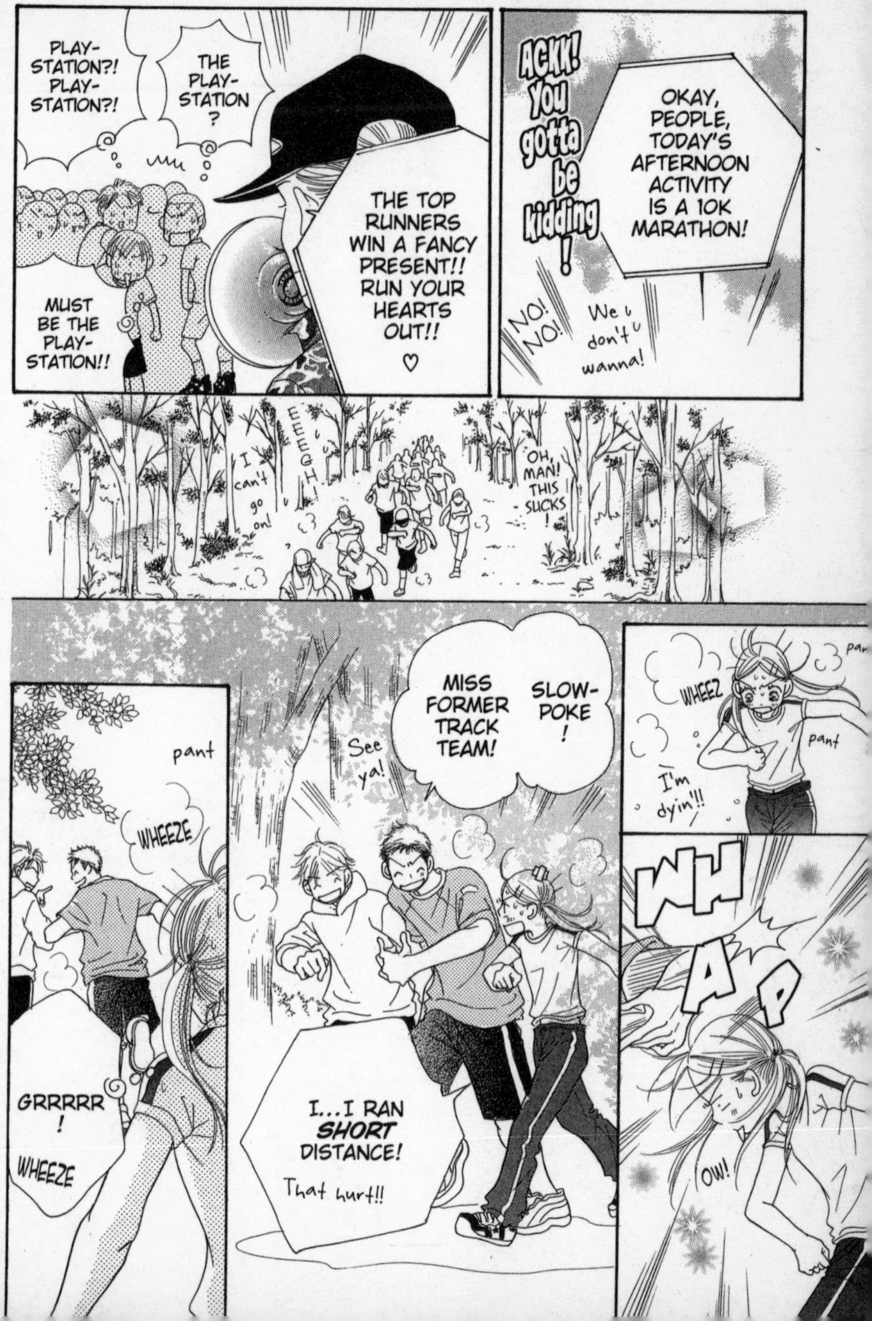
OKAY, PEOPLE, TODAY'S AFTERNOON ACTIVITY IS A 10K MARATHON!
ACKK! You gotta be kidding!
NO! NO!
We don't wanna!
THE TOP RUNNERS WIN A FANCY PRESENT!! RUN YOUR HEARTS OUT!! ♡
THE PLAY-STATION?
PLAY-STATION?! PLAY-STATION?!
MUST BE THE PLAY-STATION!!
OH, MAN! THIS SUCKS!
EEEGH!
I can't go on!
WHEEZ
pant
I'm dyin'!!
WHAP
OW!
SLOW-POKE!
MISS FORMER TRACK TEAM!
See ya!
I...I RAN SHORT DISTANCE!
That hurt!!
pant
WHEEZE
GRRRRR!
WHEEZE

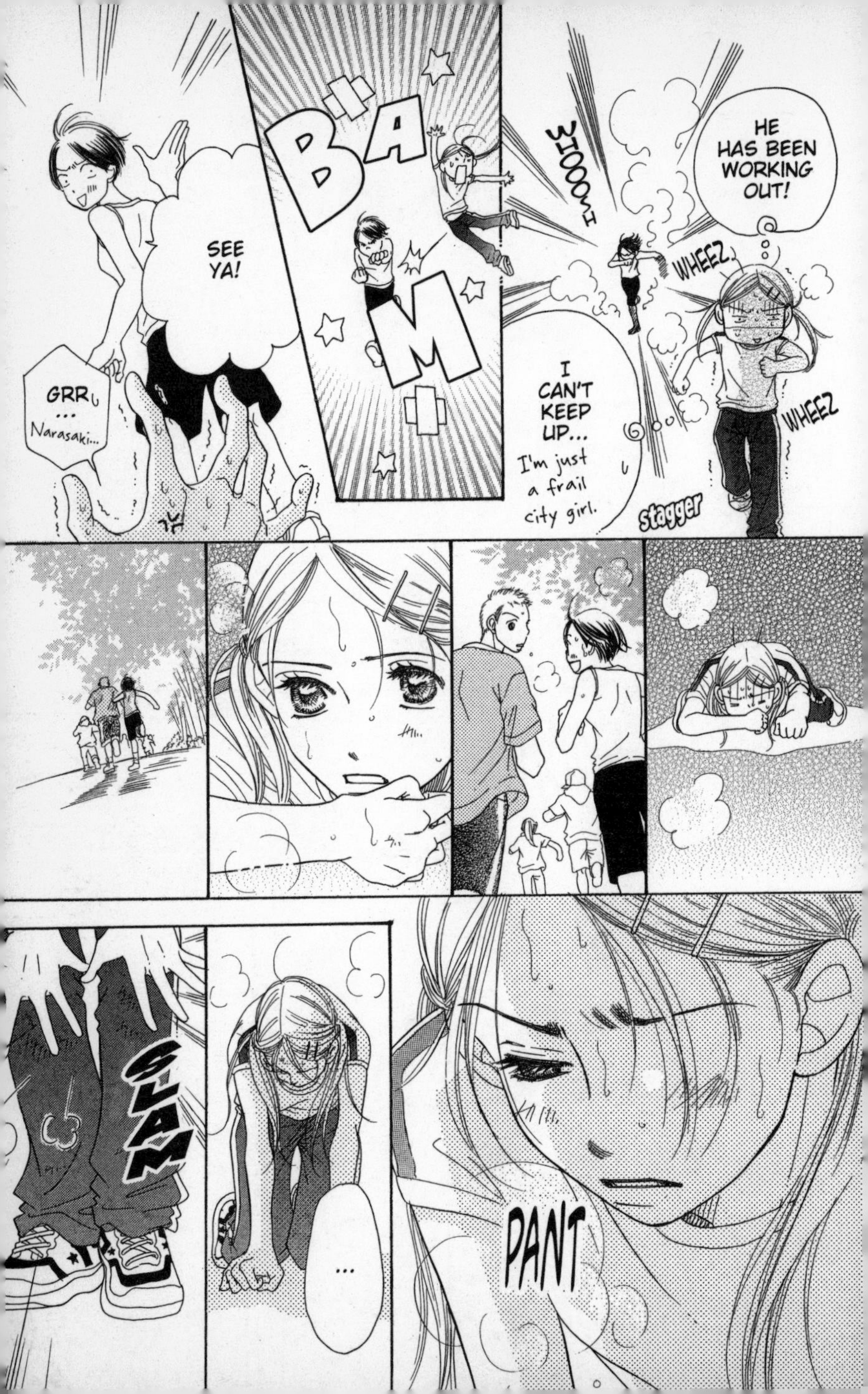
HE HAS BEEN WORKING OUT!
WHOOOSH
WHEEZ
WHEEZ
I CAN'T KEEP UP... I'm just a frail city girl.
stagger
BAM
SEE YA!
GRR... Narasaki...
PANT
...
SLAM

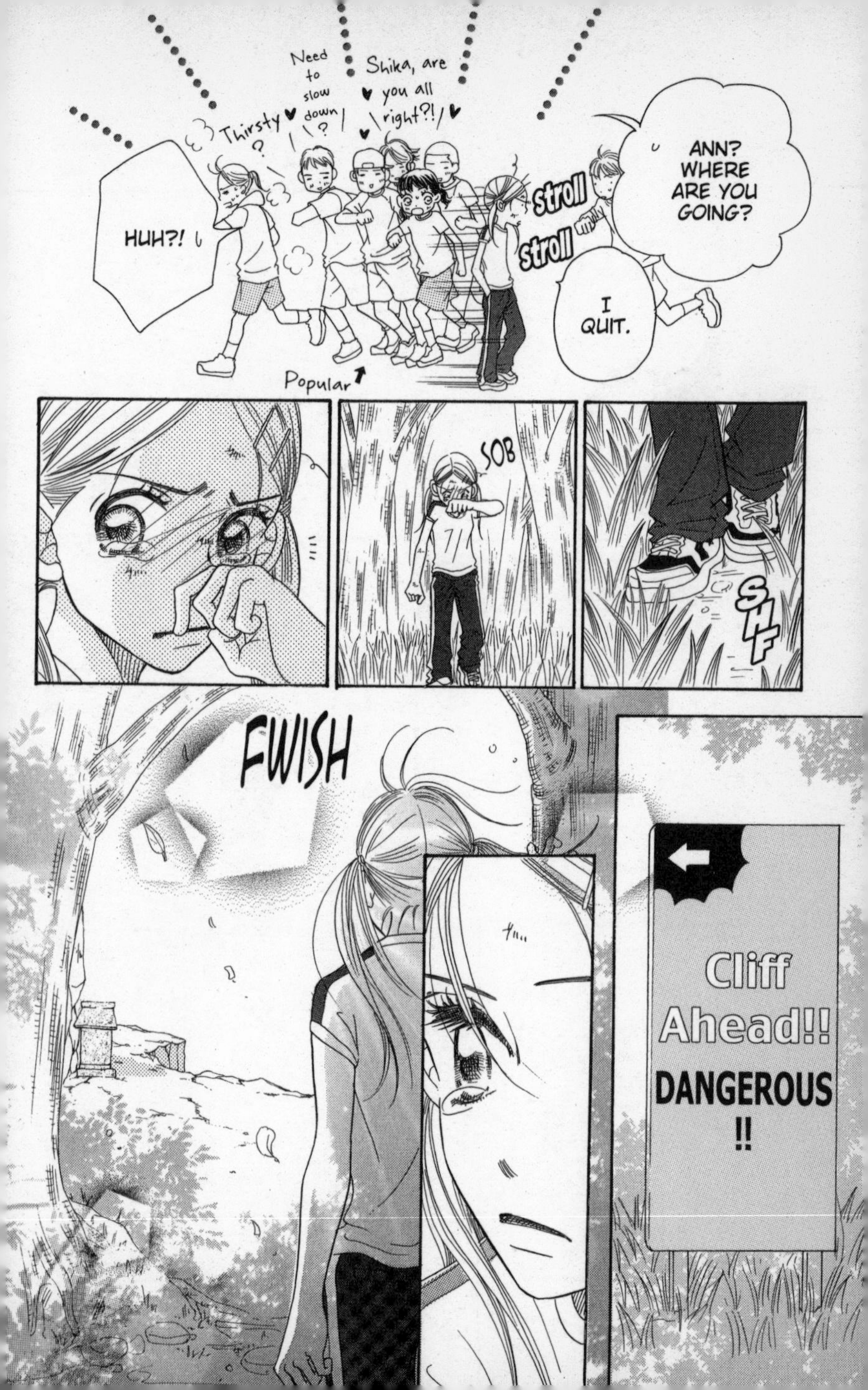
ANN? WHERE ARE YOU GOING?
I QUIT.
stroll
stroll
Shika, are you all right?!
Need to slow down?
Thirsty?
HUH?!
Popular
SHF
SOB
Cliff Ahead!! DANGEROUS !!
FWISH

Age 14, Summer: Thunder.

A tale of summer camp. I was in Girl Scouts as a kid, so camping was a fairly frequent occurrence for me. I had my own cooking pot and sleeping bag. I have lots of pleasant memories... like beautiful starry skies and being attacked by a bunch of red dragonflies!

Being in eighth grade can be a bit hard. It's the time you feel most insecure about yourself physically and mentally... Don't you think so?

I want to thank all the people who have written to me. I have gratefully read your letters, sometimes with teary eyes....Several people e-mailed me saying that they were not sure where to send their letter...so here's the address!!

Sand Chronicles
c/o Shojo Beat
VIZ Media
P.O. Box 77010
San Francisco,
CA 94107

See you in the next Shojo Beat!!
Hinako Ashihara, 5/25/03

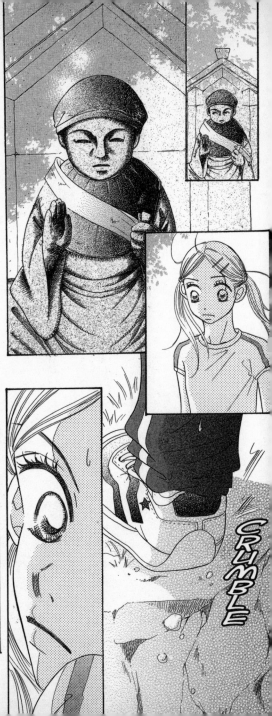

CRUMBLE

135

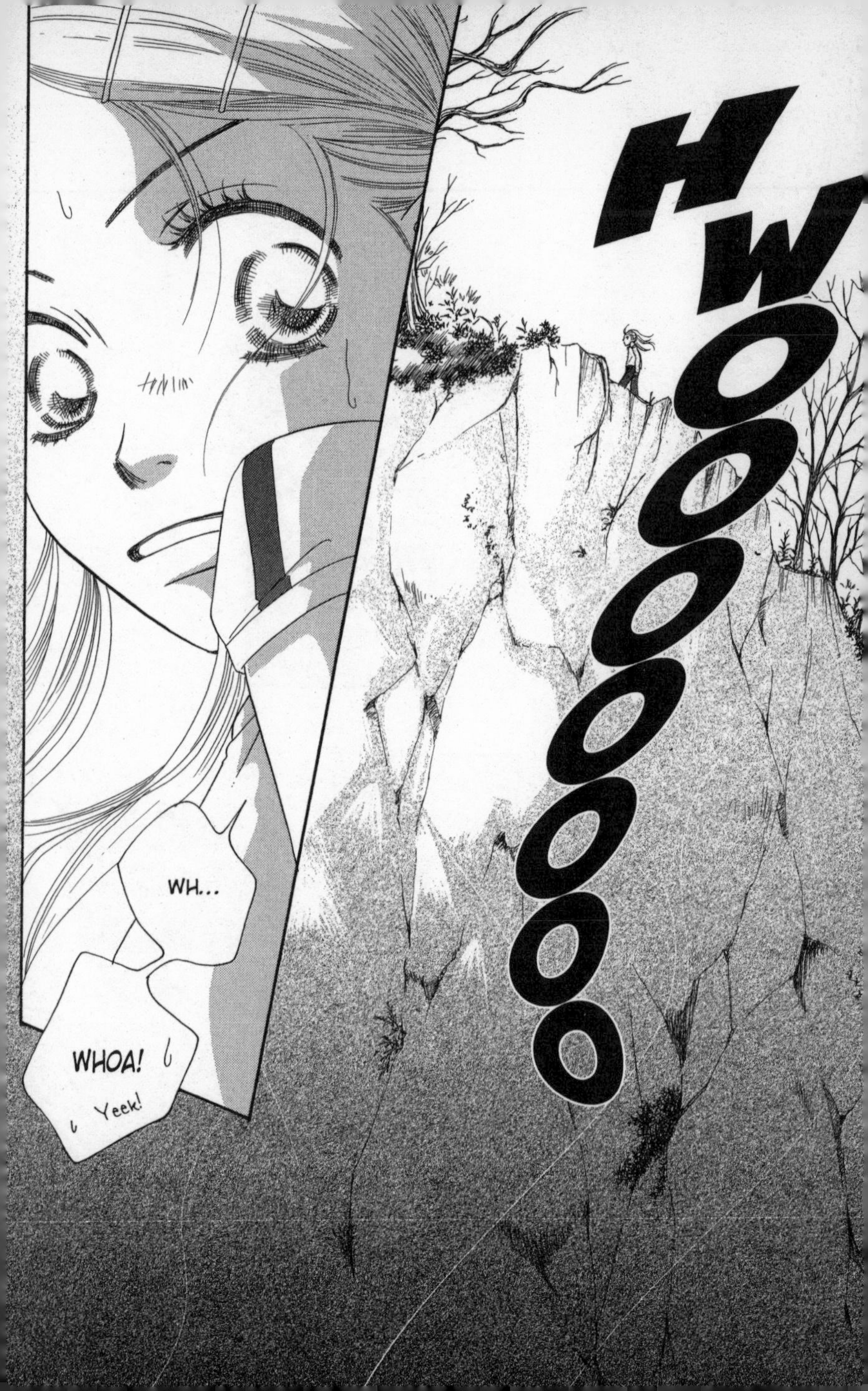
HWOOOOOOO
WH...
WHOA!
Yeek!

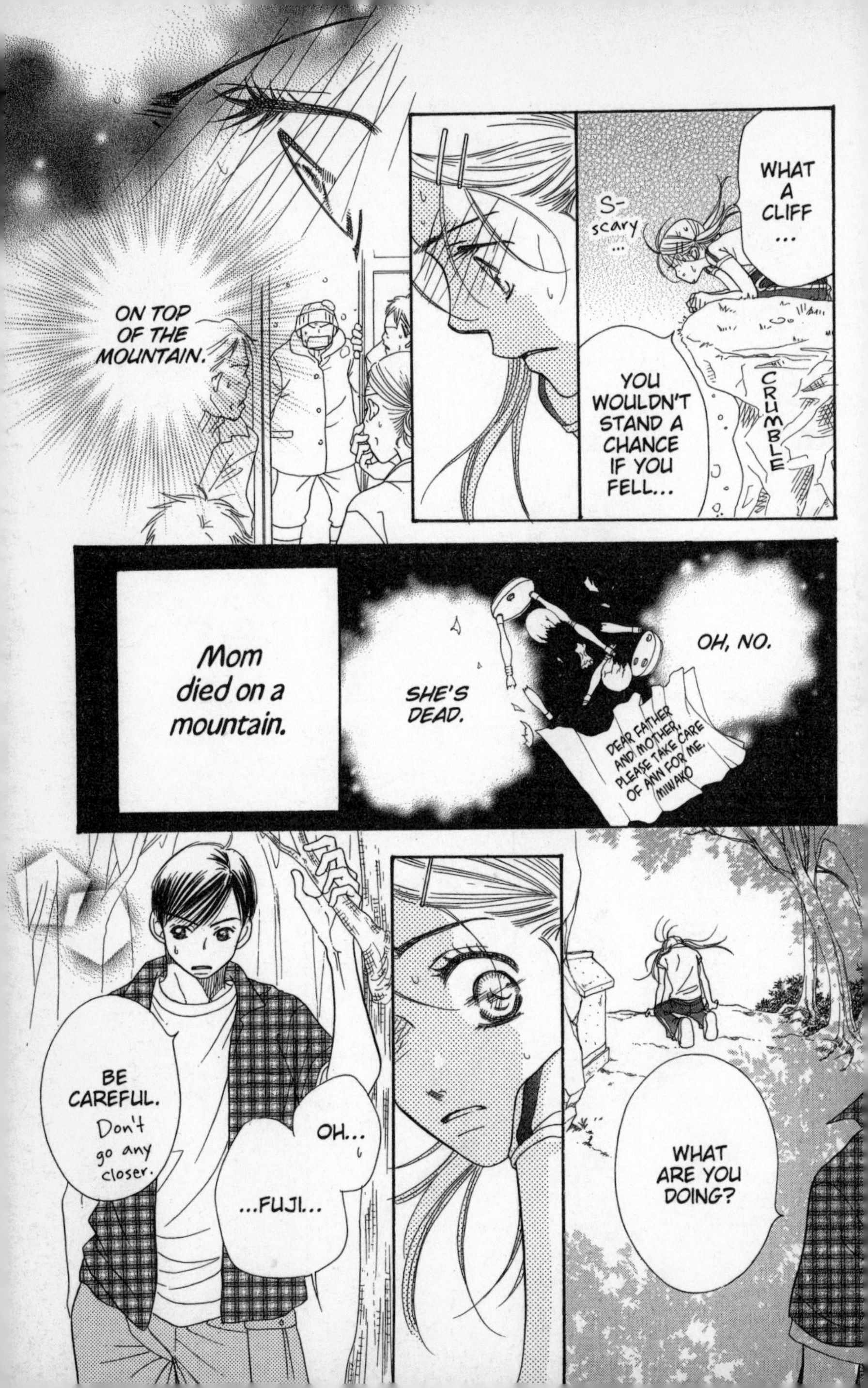
WHAT A CLIFF...
S-scary...
YOU WOULDN'T STAND A CHANCE IF YOU FELL...
CRUMBLE
ON TOP OF THE MOUNTAIN.
OH, NO.
DEAR FATHER AND MOTHER, PLEASE TAKE CARE OF ANN FOR ME. MIWAKO
SHE'S DEAD.
Mom died on a mountain.
WHAT ARE YOU DOING?
OH...
...FUJI...
BE CAREFUL. Don't go any closer.

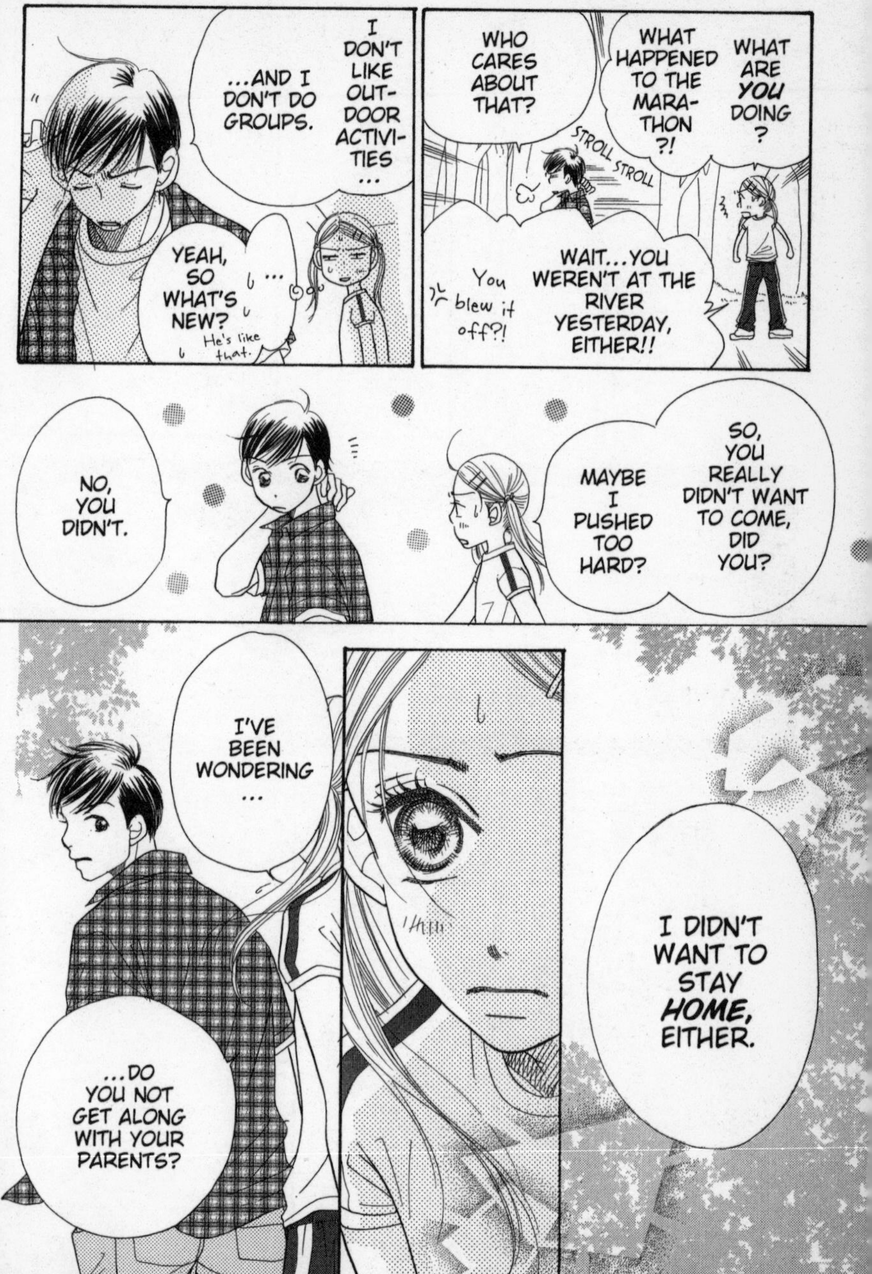
WHAT ARE *YOU* DOING?
WHAT HAPPENED TO THE MARATHON?!
WHO CARES ABOUT THAT?
STROLL STROLL
WAIT...YOU WEREN'T AT THE RIVER YESTERDAY, EITHER!!
You blew it off?!
I DON'T LIKE OUTDOOR ACTIVITIES...
...AND I DON'T DO GROUPS.
YEAH, SO WHAT'S NEW?
He's like that.
SO, YOU REALLY DIDN'T WANT TO COME, DID YOU?
MAYBE I PUSHED TOO HARD?
NO, YOU DIDN'T.
I DIDN'T WANT TO STAY *HOME*, EITHER.
I'VE BEEN WONDERING...
...DO YOU NOT GET ALONG WITH YOUR PARENTS?

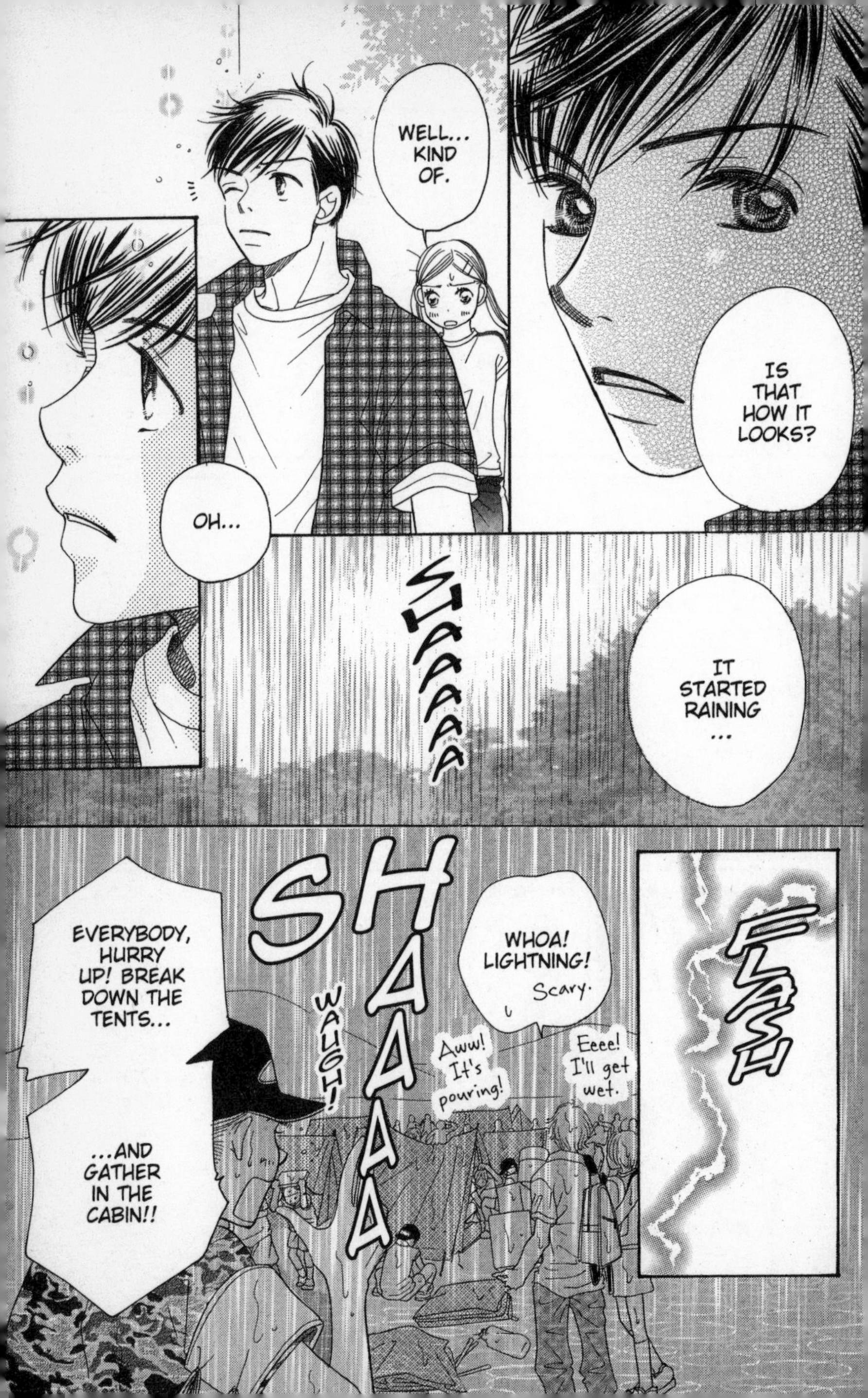
IS THAT HOW IT LOOKS?
WELL... KIND OF.
OH...
IT STARTED RAINING...
SHAAAAAA
FLASH
WHOA! LIGHTNING!
Scary.
Eeee! I'll get wet.
Aww! It's pouring!
SHAAAAA
WAUGH!
EVERYBODY, HURRY UP! BREAK DOWN THE TENTS...
...AND GATHER IN THE CABIN!!

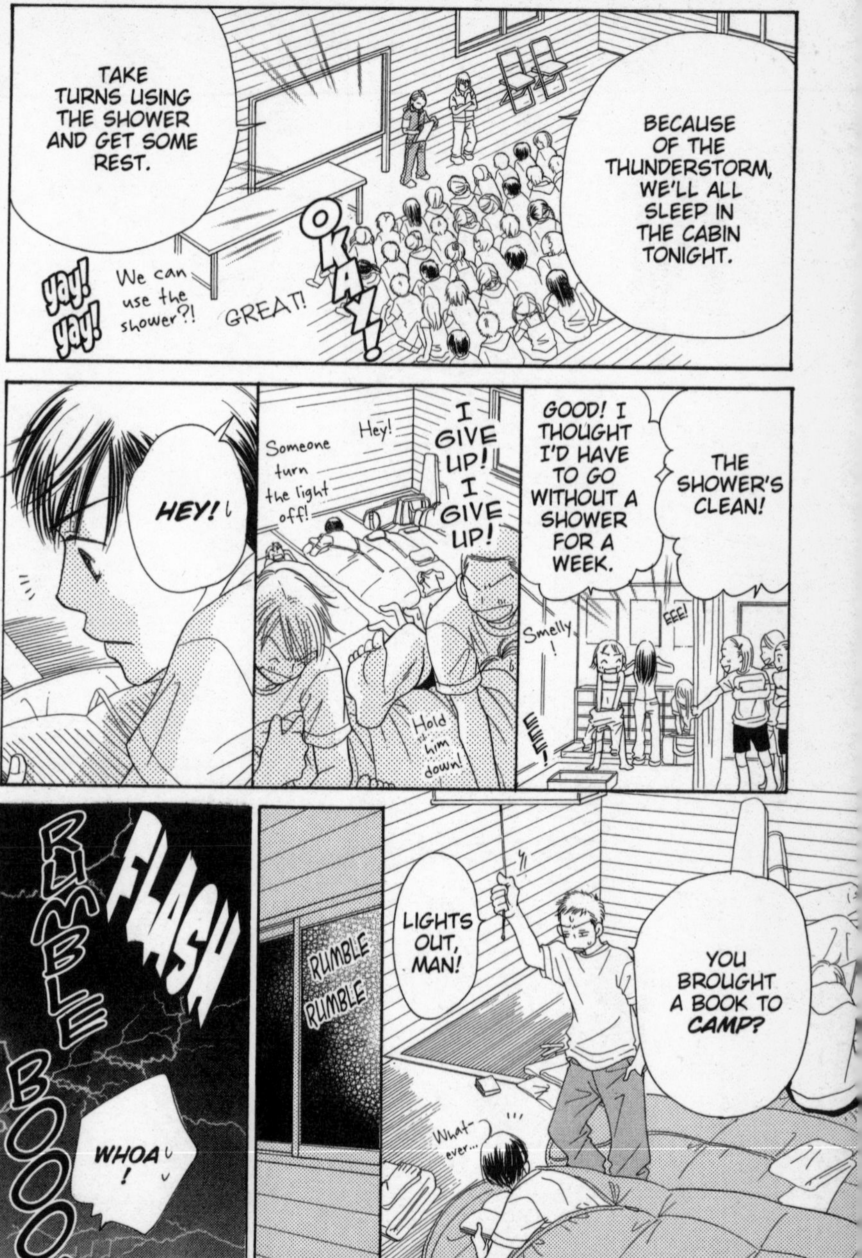
BECAUSE OF THE THUNDERSTORM, WE'LL ALL SLEEP IN THE CABIN TONIGHT.
TAKE TURNS USING THE SHOWER AND GET SOME REST.
OKAY!
GREAT!
We can use the shower?!
yay! yay!
THE SHOWER'S CLEAN!
GOOD! I THOUGHT I'D HAVE TO GO WITHOUT A SHOWER FOR A WEEK.
EEE!
Smelly!
EEEE!
I GIVE UP! I GIVE UP!
Hey!
Someone turn the light off!
Hold him down!
HEY!
YOU BROUGHT A BOOK TO CAMP?
LIGHTS OUT, MAN!
RUMBLE RUMBLE
What-ever...
FLASH
RUMBLE
BOOOOM
WHOA!

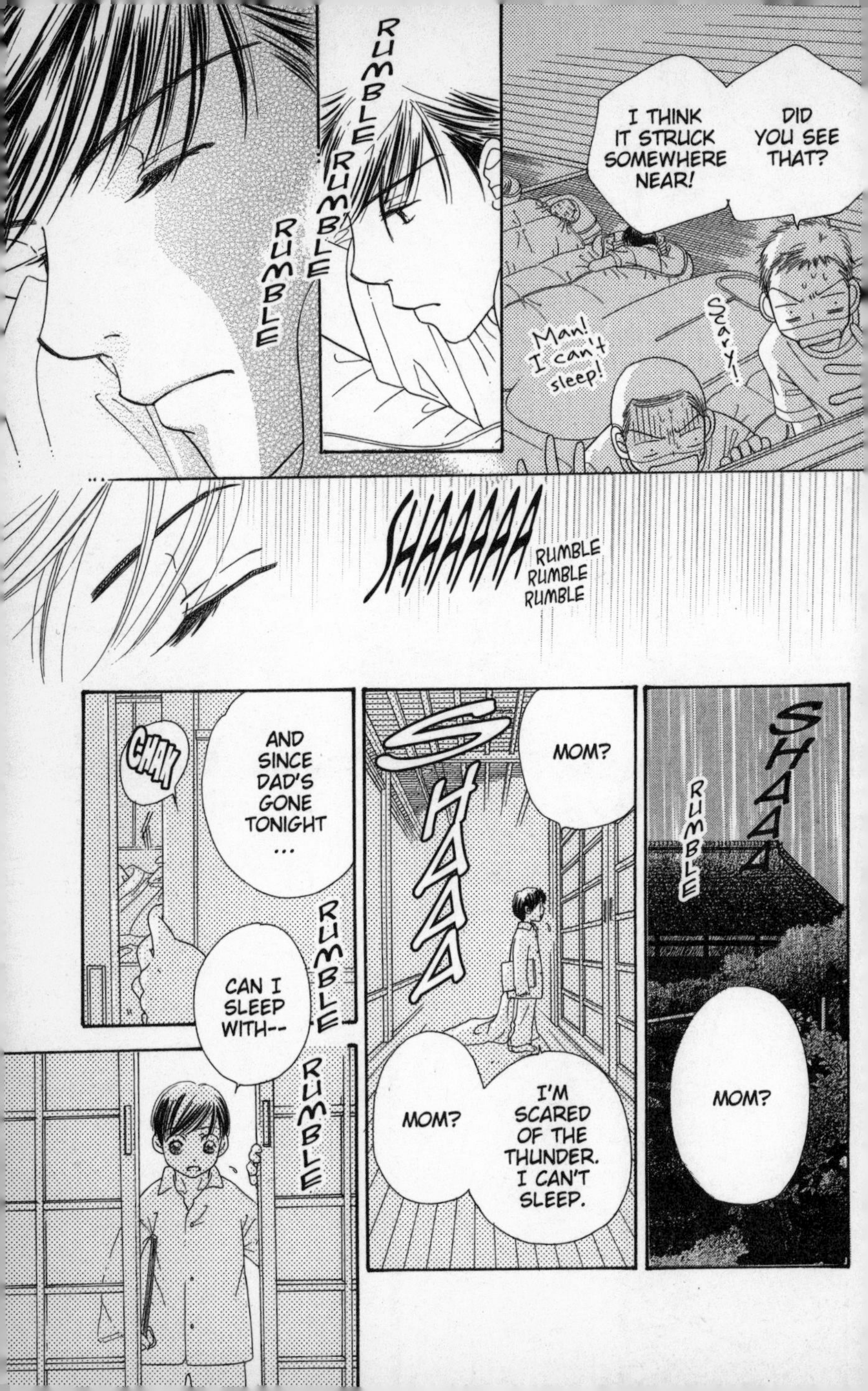
DID YOU SEE THAT?
I THINK IT STRUCK SOMEWHERE NEAR!
Scary!
Man! I can't sleep!
RUMBLE
RUMBLE
RUMBLE
...
SHAAAAA
RUMBLE RUMBLE RUMBLE
SHAAA
RUMBLE
MOM?
MOM?
SHAAAA
MOM?
I'M SCARED OF THE THUNDER. I CAN'T SLEEP.
CHAK
AND SINCE DAD'S GONE TONIGHT ...
RUMBLE
CAN I SLEEP WITH--
RUMBLE

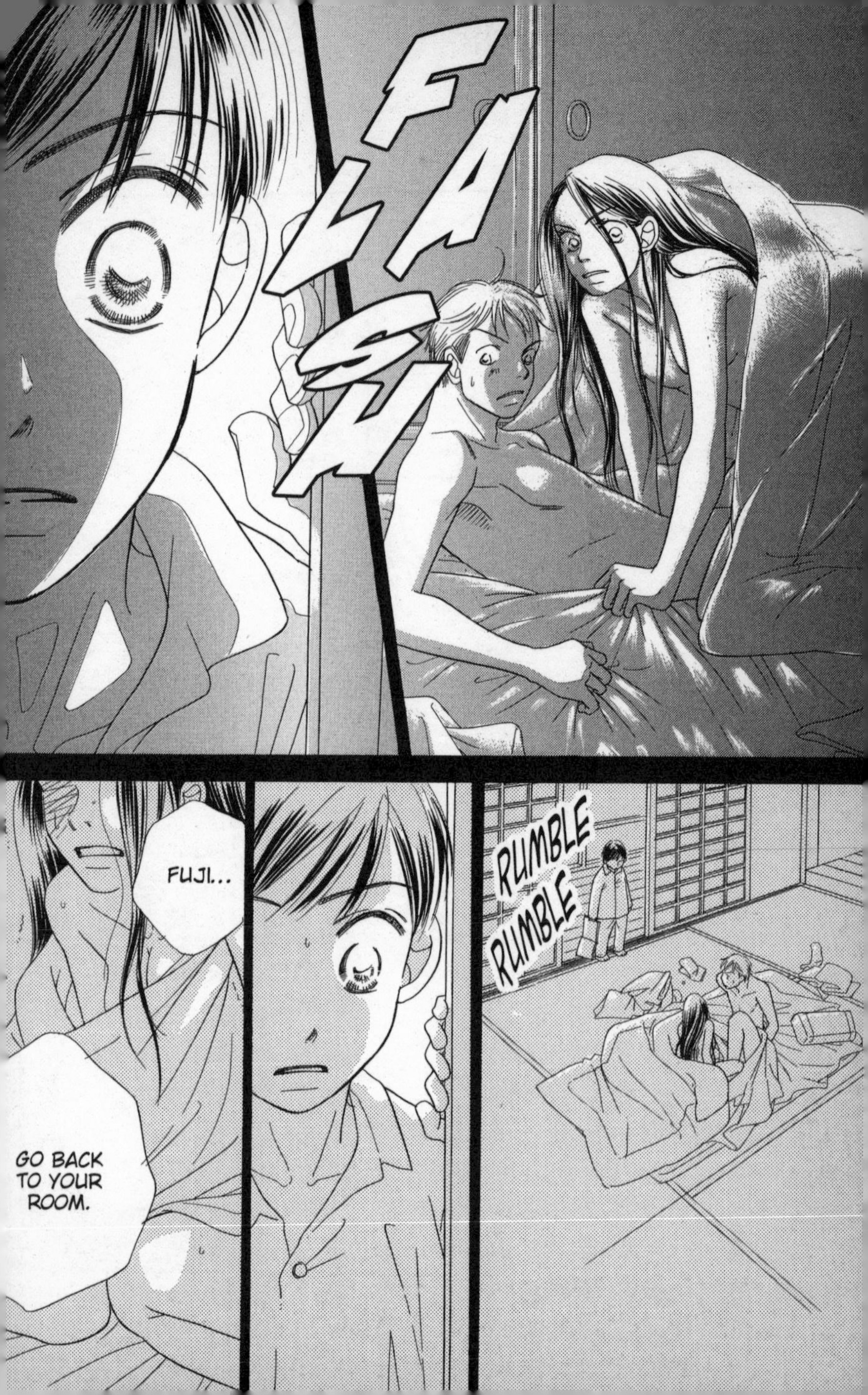
FLASH
RUMBLE RUMBLE
FUJI...
GO BACK TO YOUR ROOM.

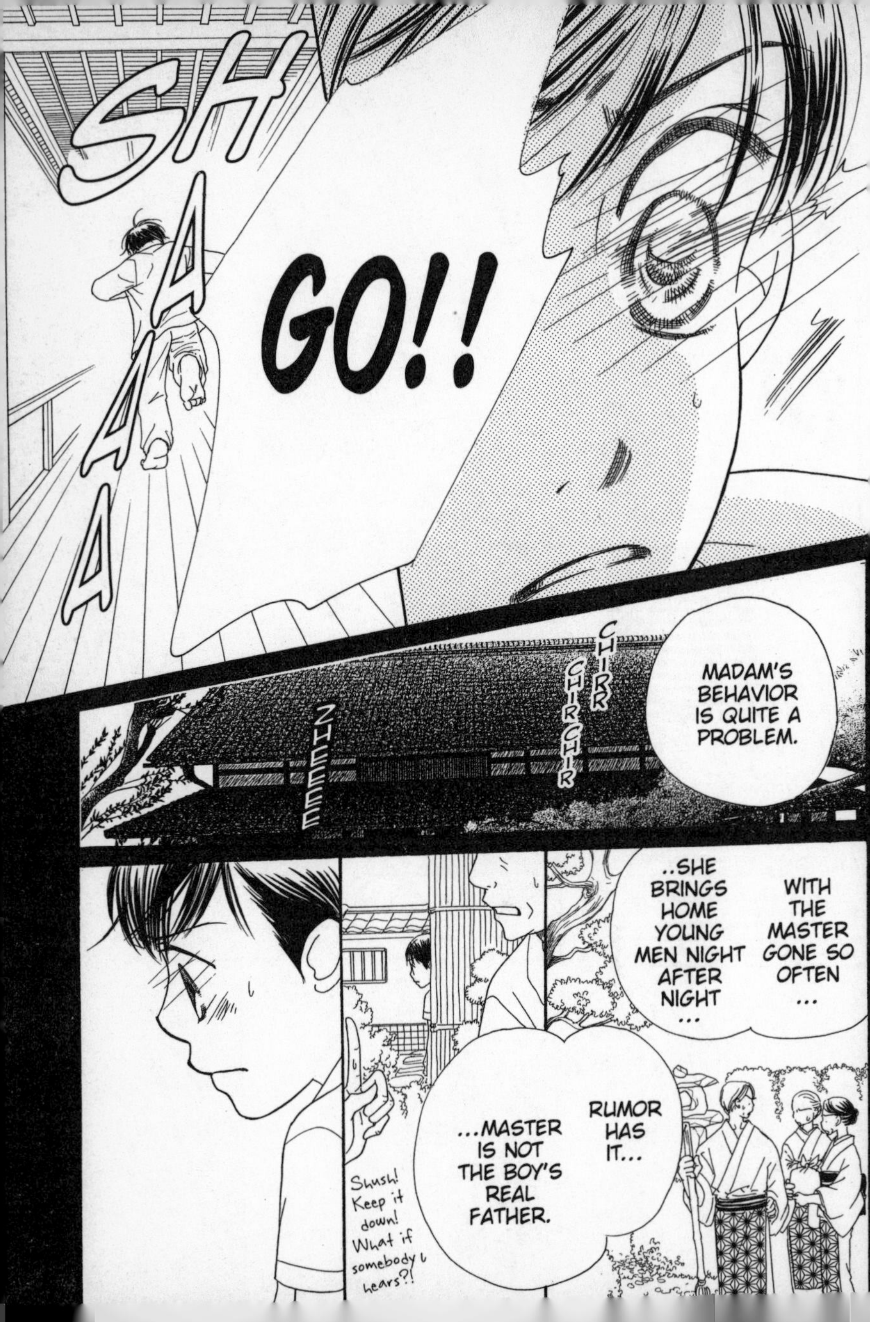
GO!!
SHAAAA
MADAM'S BEHAVIOR IS QUITE A PROBLEM.
CHIRR CHIRCHIR
ZHEEEE
WITH THE MASTER GONE SO OFTEN...
..SHE BRINGS HOME YOUNG MEN NIGHT AFTER NIGHT...
RUMOR HAS IT...
...MASTER IS NOT THE BOY'S REAL FATHER.
Shush! Keep it down! What if somebody hears?!

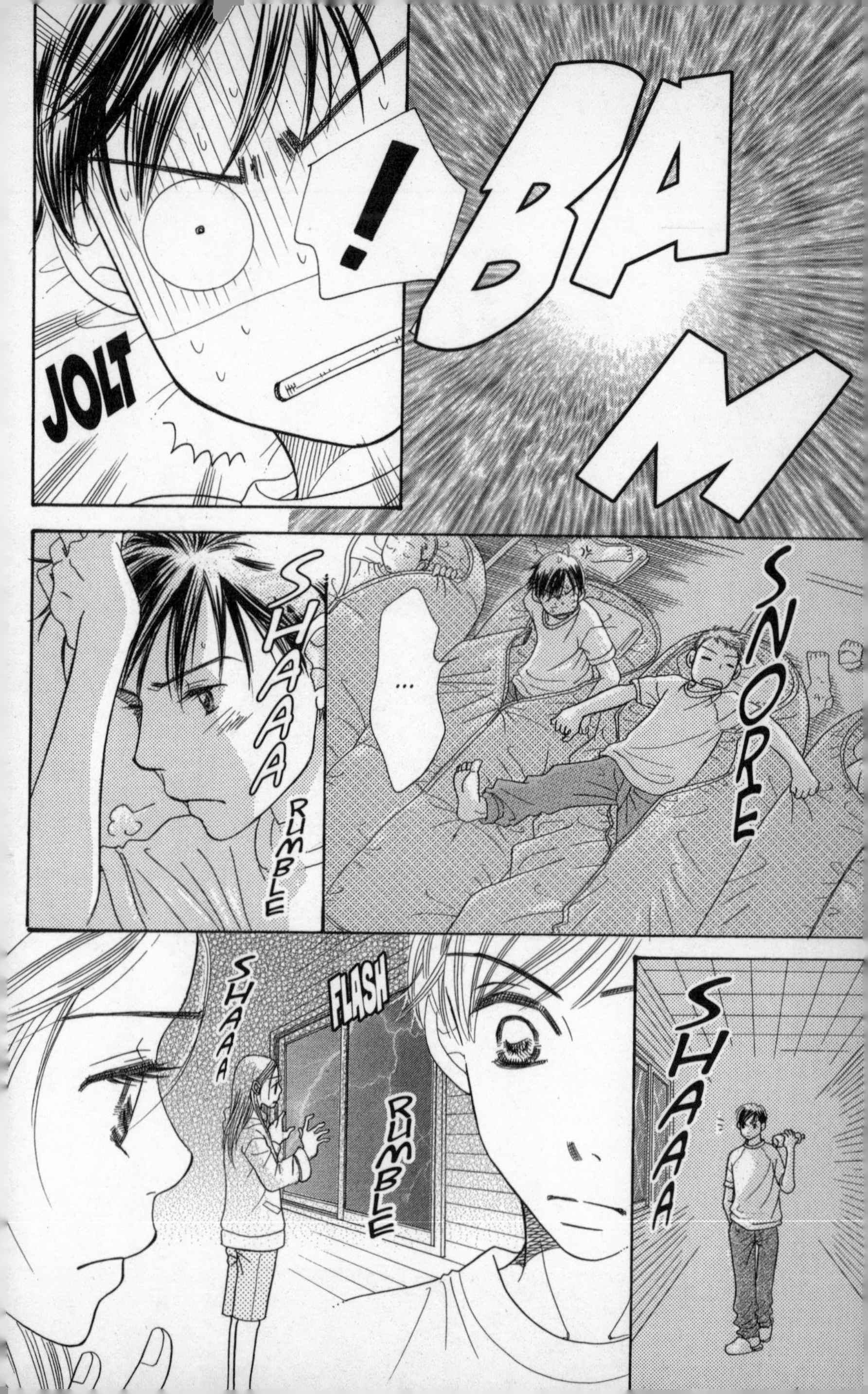
BAM
!
JOLT
SNORE
...
SHAAAA
RUMBLE
SHAAAA
FLASH
RUMBLE
SHAAAA

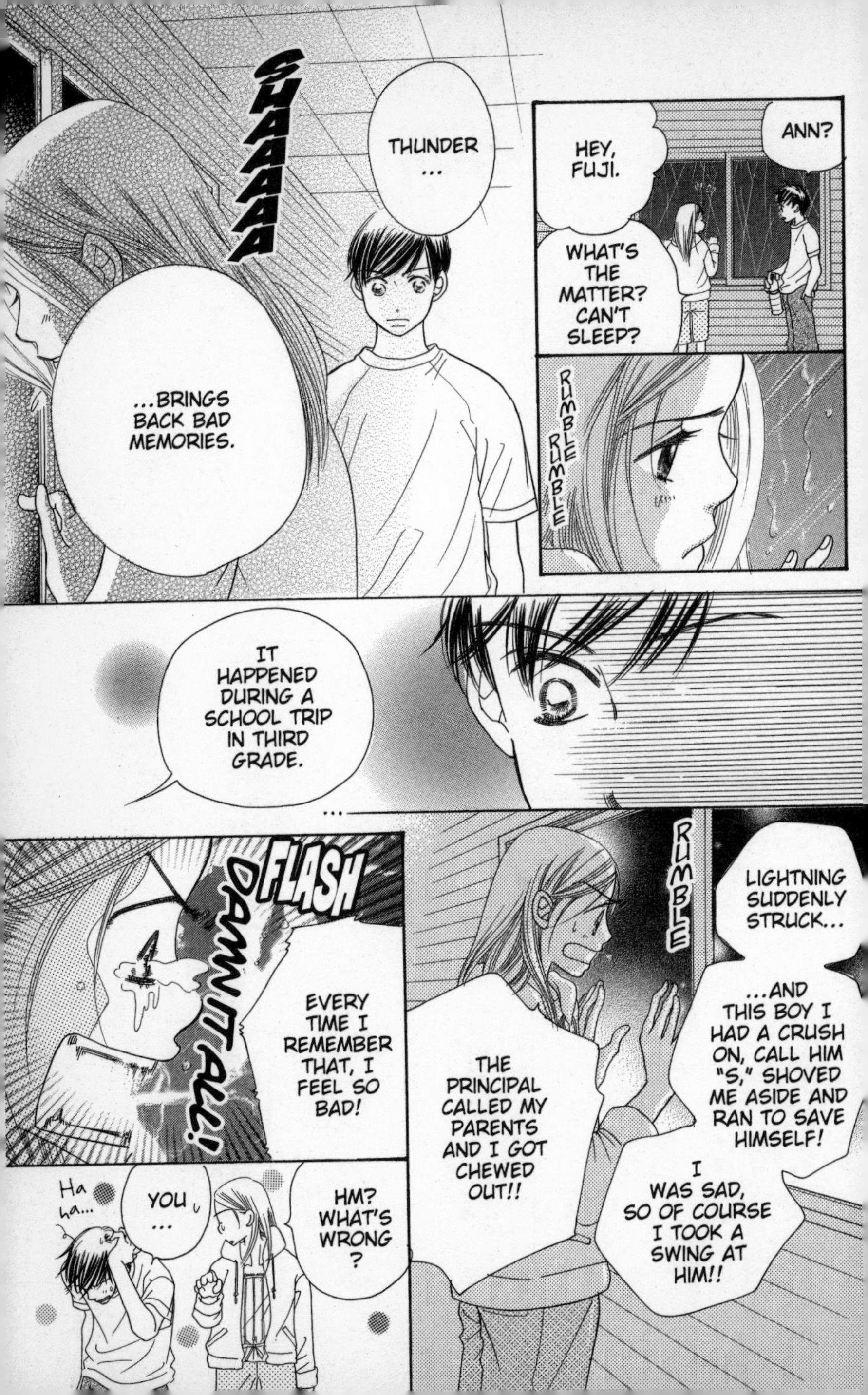
ANN?
HEY, FUJI.
WHAT'S THE MATTER? CAN'T SLEEP?
RUMBLE RUMBLE
THUNDER...
SHAAAAAA
...BRINGS BACK BAD MEMORIES.
IT HAPPENED DURING A SCHOOL TRIP IN THIRD GRADE.
...
LIGHTNING SUDDENLY STRUCK...
RUMBLE
...AND THIS BOY I HAD A CRUSH ON, CALL HIM "S," SHOVED ME ASIDE AND RAN TO SAVE HIMSELF!
I WAS SAD, SO OF COURSE I TOOK A SWING AT HIM!!
THE PRINCIPAL CALLED MY PARENTS AND I GOT CHEWED OUT!!
FLASH
DAMN IT ALL!
EVERY TIME I REMEMBER THAT, I FEEL SO BAD!
HM? WHAT'S WRONG?
YOU...
Ha ha...

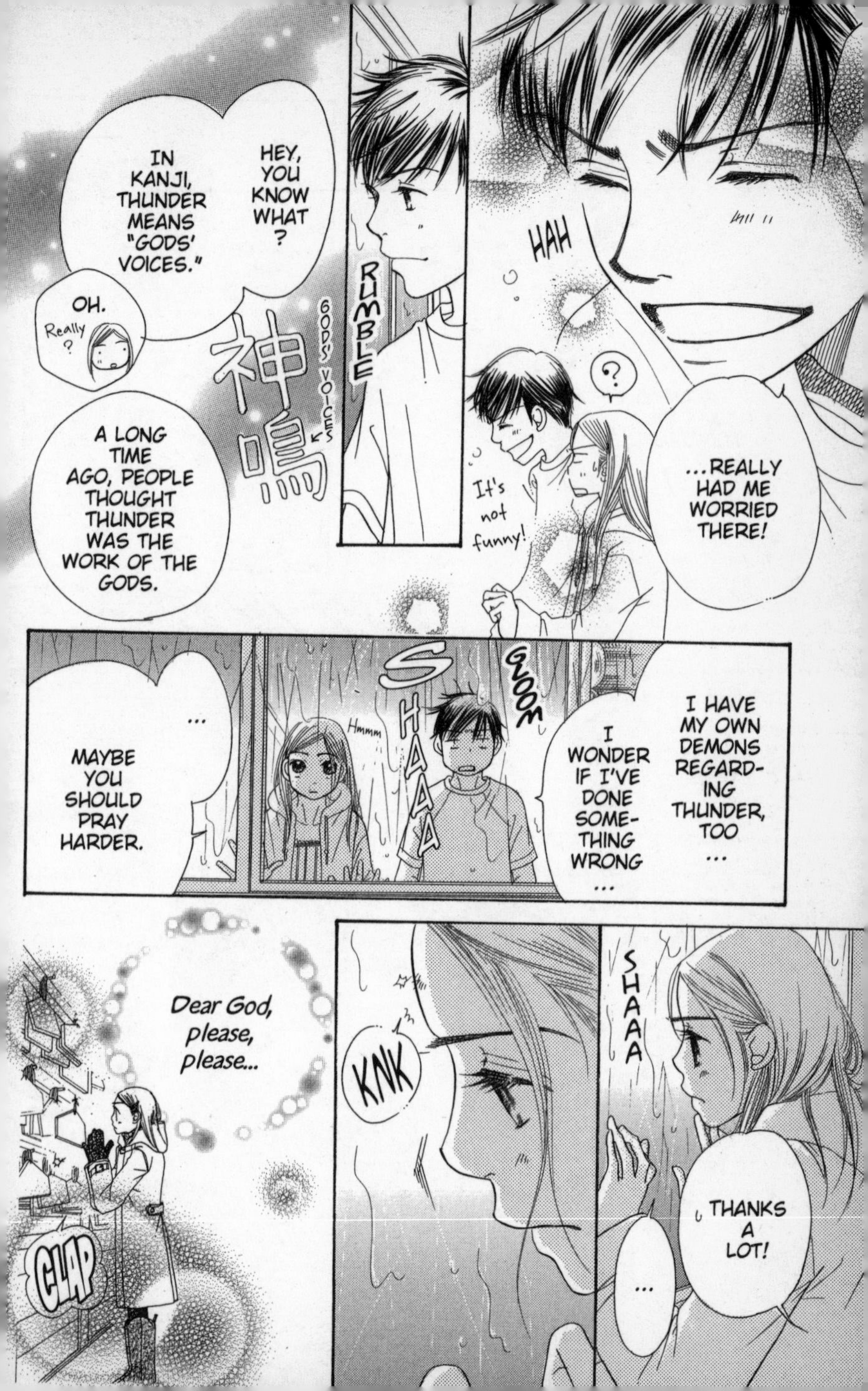
HAH
...REALLY HAD ME WORRIED THERE!
?
It's not funny!
HEY, YOU KNOW WHAT?
RUMBLE
GODS' VOICES
神鳴
IN KANJI, THUNDER MEANS "GODS' VOICES."
OH.
Really?
A LONG TIME AGO, PEOPLE THOUGHT THUNDER WAS THE WORK OF THE GODS.
I HAVE MY OWN DEMONS REGARDING THUNDER, TOO...
I WONDER IF I'VE DONE SOMETHING WRONG...
GLOOM
SHAAAA
Hmmm
...
MAYBE YOU SHOULD PRAY HARDER.
SHAAA
THANKS A LOT!
...
KNK
Dear God, please, please...
CLAP

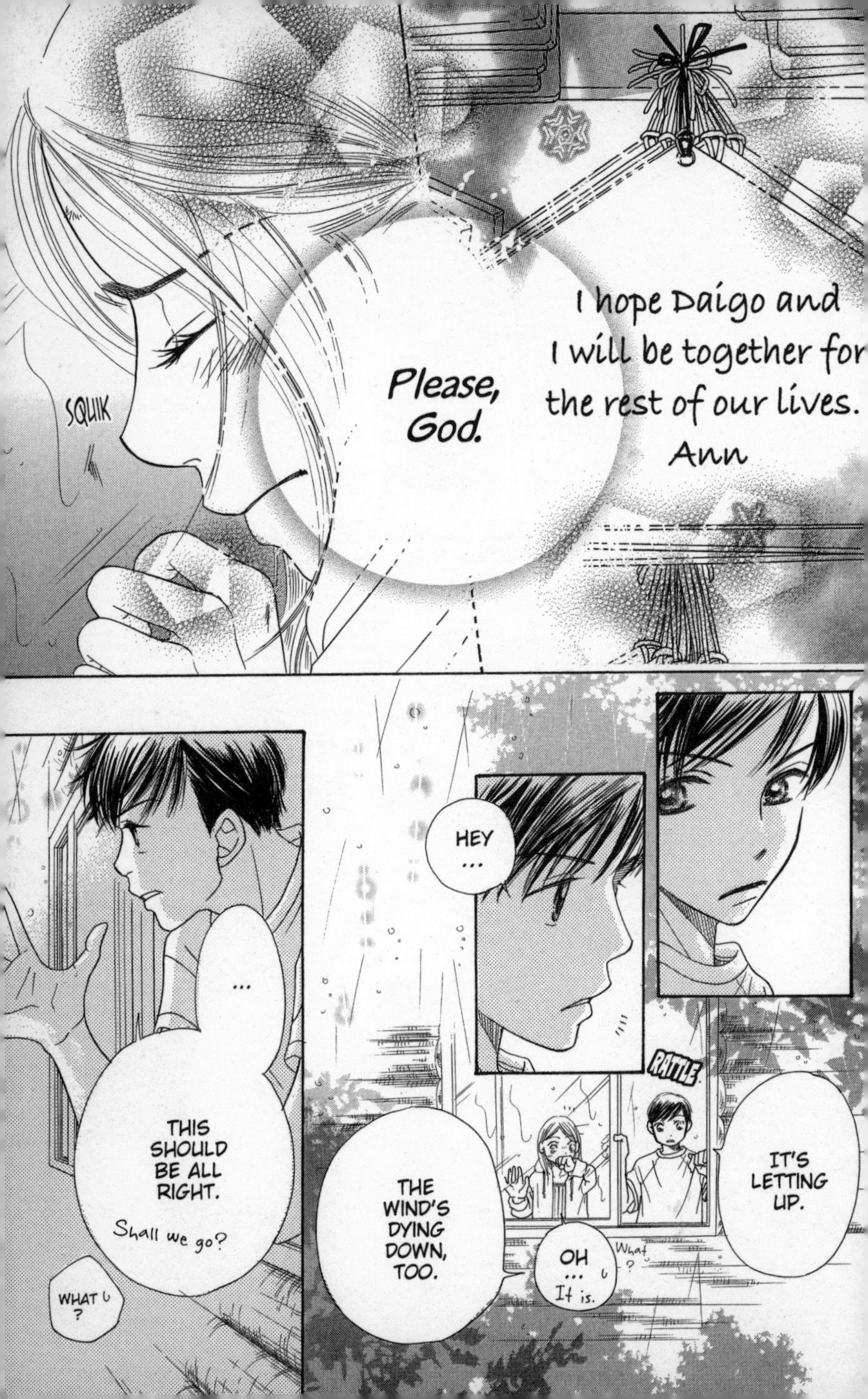

I hope Daigo and I will be together for the rest of our lives. Ann
Please, God.
SQUIK
HEY ...
RATTLE
IT'S LETTING UP.
What ?
OH ... It is.
THE WIND'S DYING DOWN, TOO.
...
THIS SHOULD BE ALL RIGHT.
Shall we go?
WHAT ?

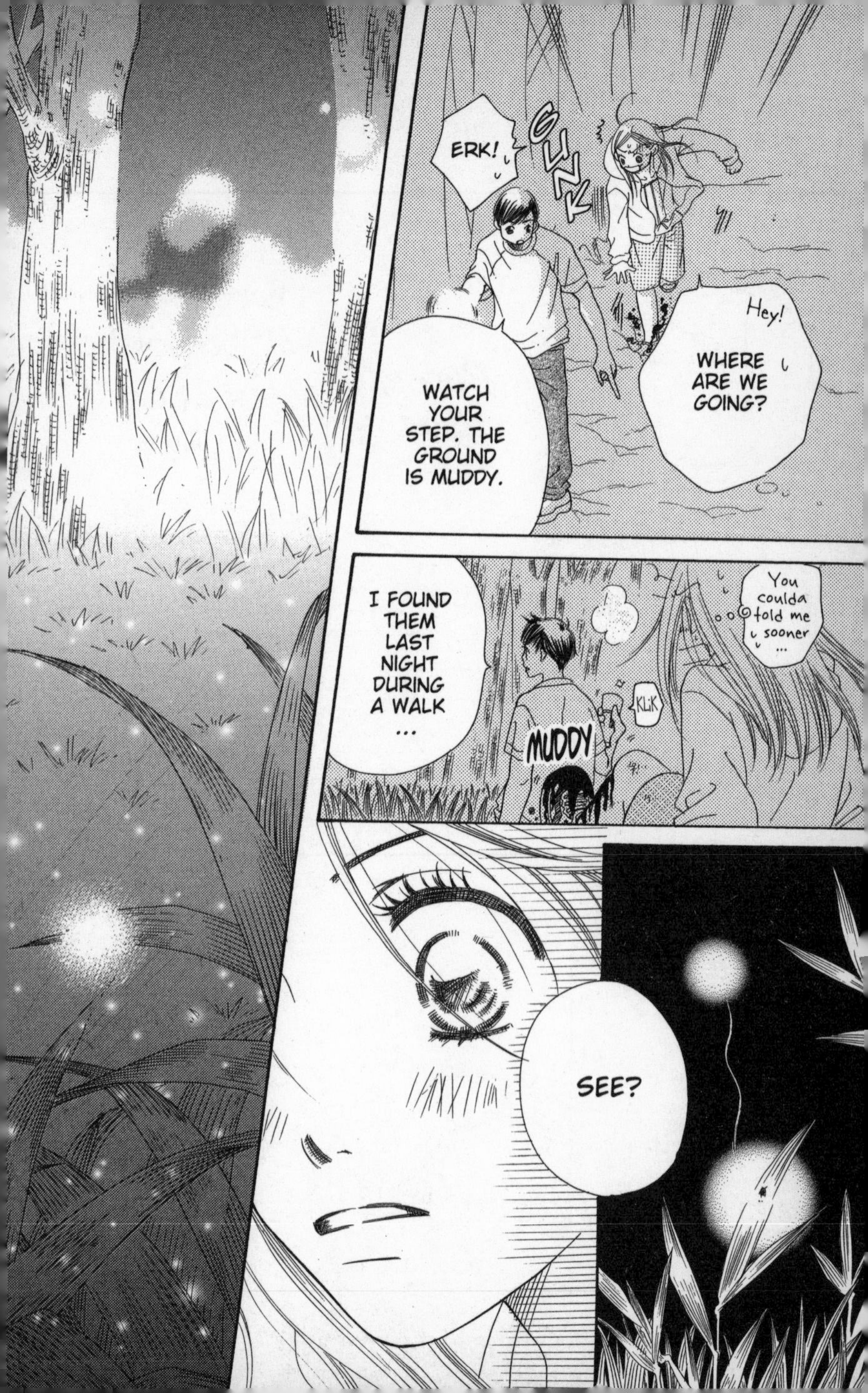
GUNK
ERK!
Hey!
WHERE ARE WE GOING?
WATCH YOUR STEP. THE GROUND IS MUDDY.
You coulda told me sooner ...
KLiK
MUDDY
I FOUND THEM LAST NIGHT DURING A WALK ...
SEE?

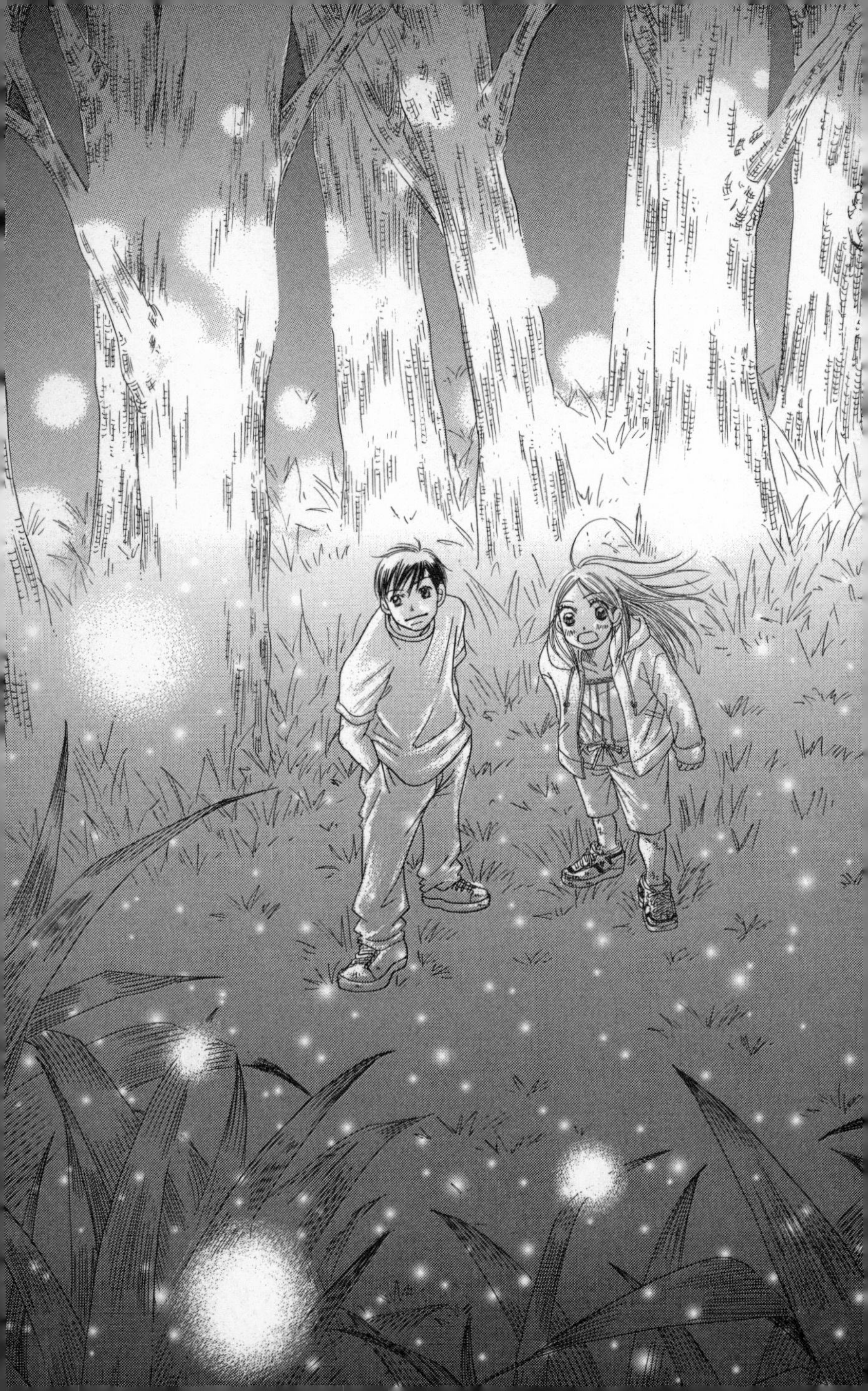

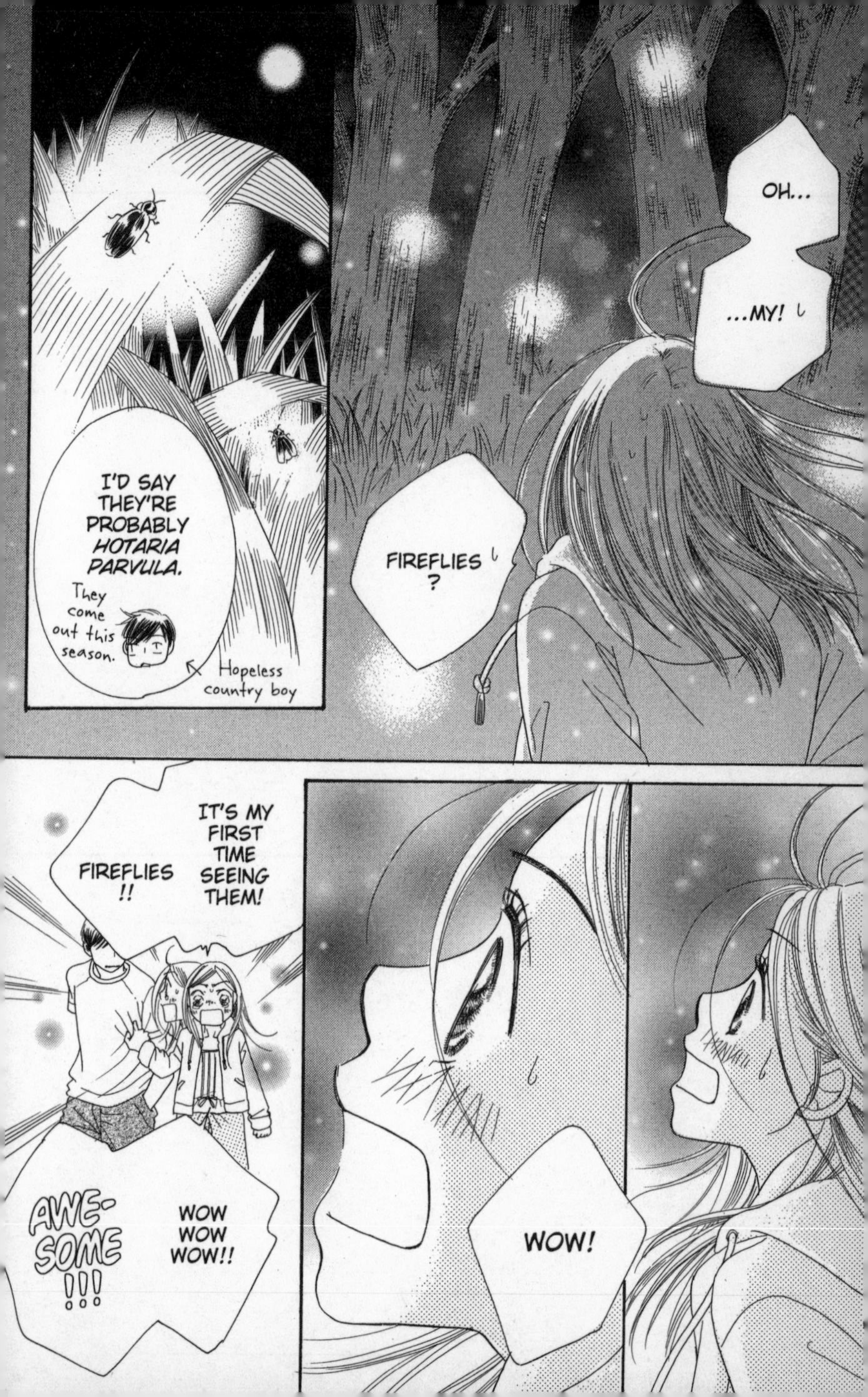
OH...
...MY!
FIREFLIES?
I'D SAY THEY'RE PROBABLY *HOTARIA PARVULA.*
They come out this season.
Hopeless country boy
WOW!
IT'S MY FIRST TIME SEEING THEM!
FIREFLIES!!
WOW WOW WOW!!
AWE-SOME!!!

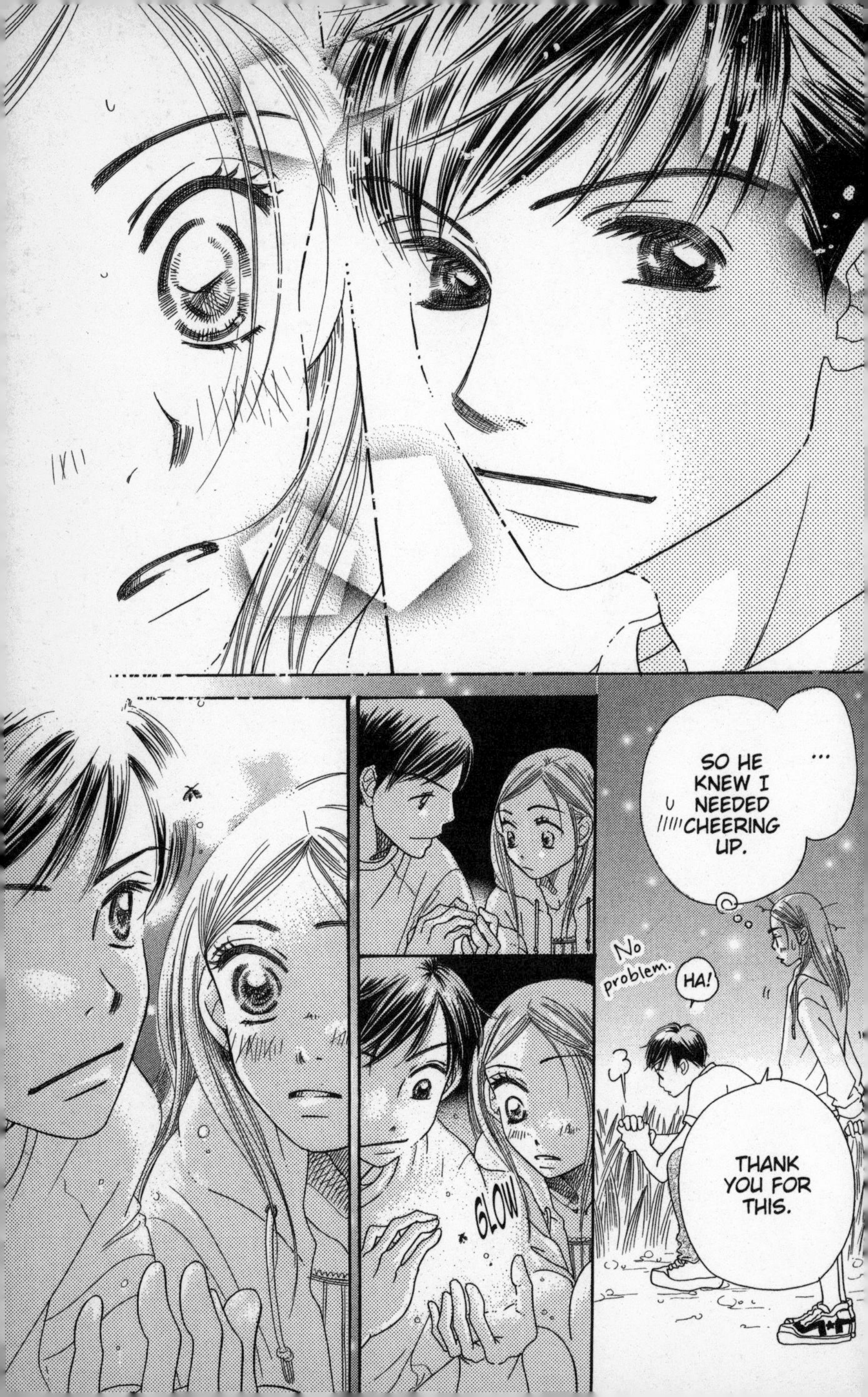
...
SO HE KNEW I NEEDED CHEERING UP.
HA!
No problem.
THANK YOU FOR THIS.
GLOW

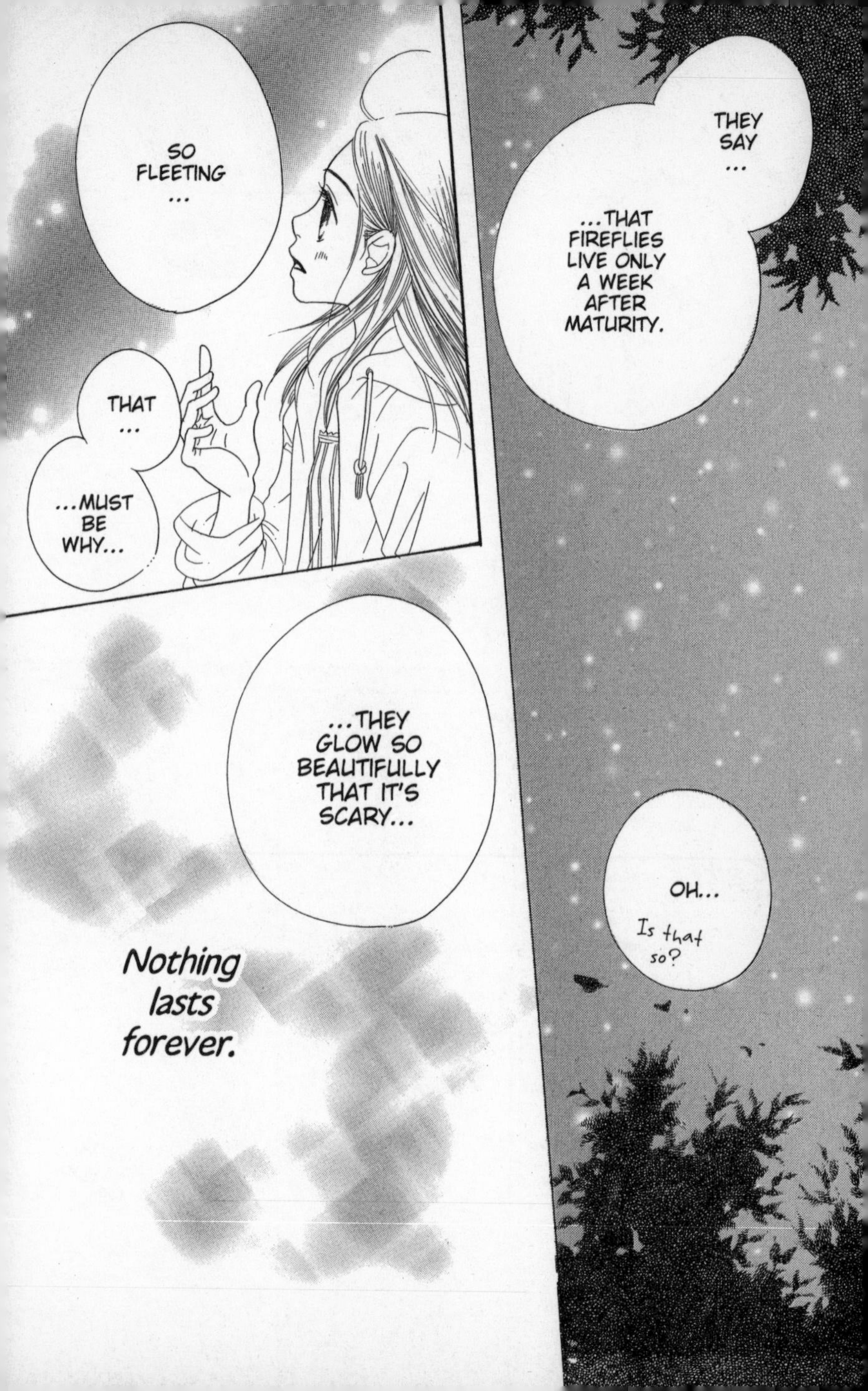
THEY SAY ...
...THAT FIREFLIES LIVE ONLY A WEEK AFTER MATURITY.
OH...
Is that so?
SO FLEETING ...
THAT ...
...MUST BE WHY...
...THEY GLOW SO BEAUTIFULLY THAT IT'S SCARY...
Nothing lasts forever.

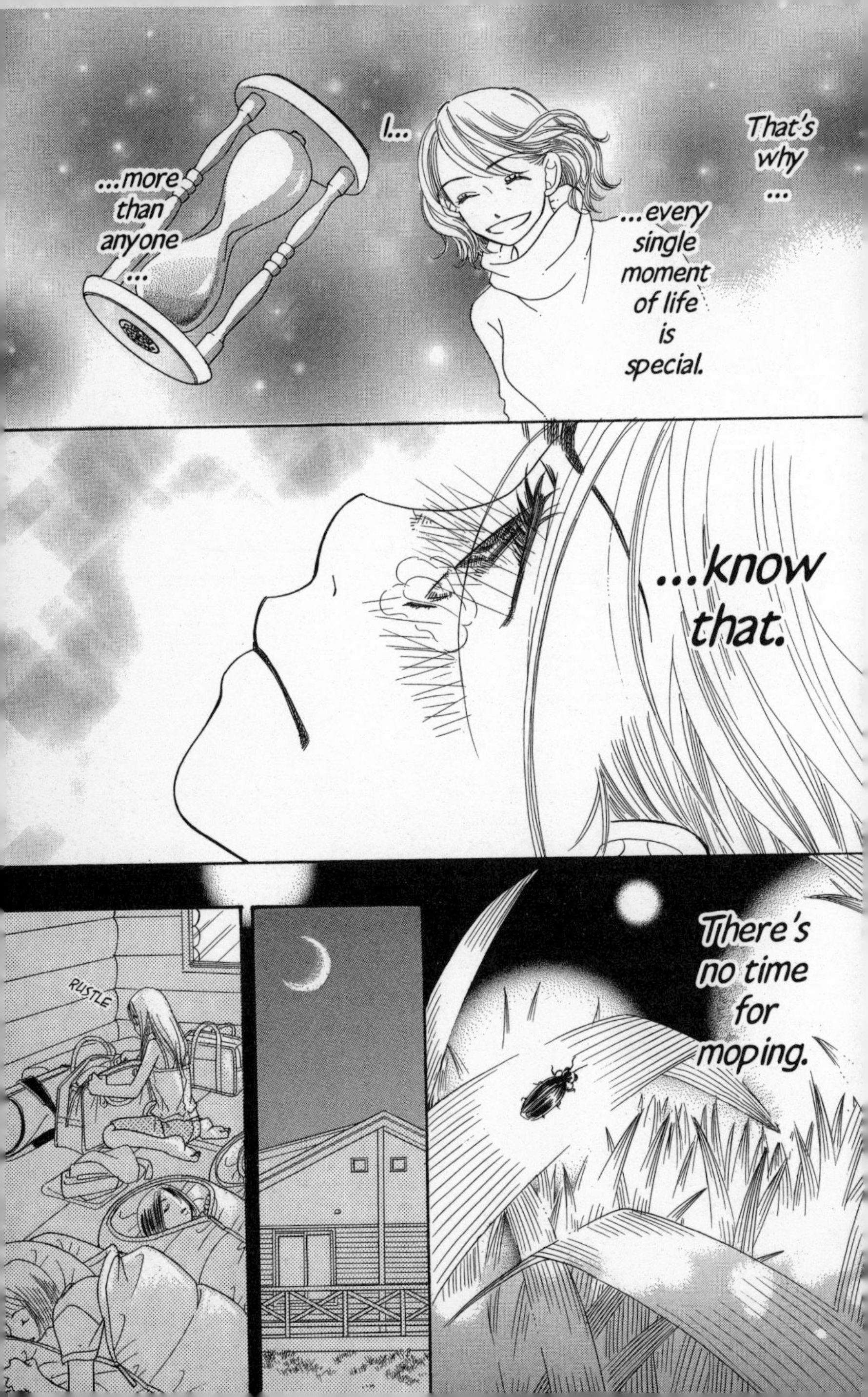
That's why ...
...every single moment of life is special.
I...
...more than anyone ...
...know that.
There's no time for moping.
RUSTLE

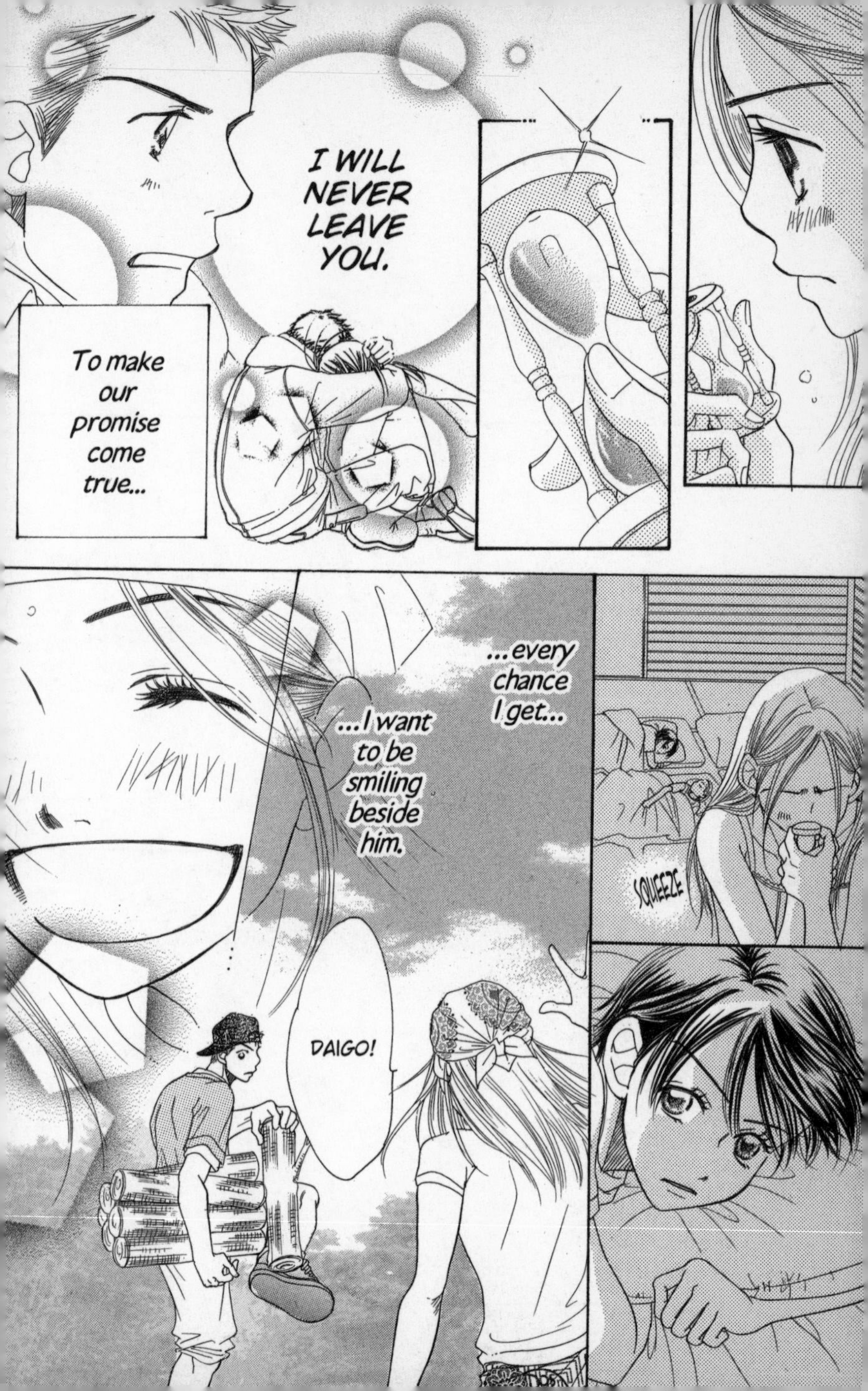
...
...
I WILL NEVER LEAVE YOU.
To make our promise come true...
SQUEEZE
...every chance I get...
...I want to be smiling beside him.
DAIGO!

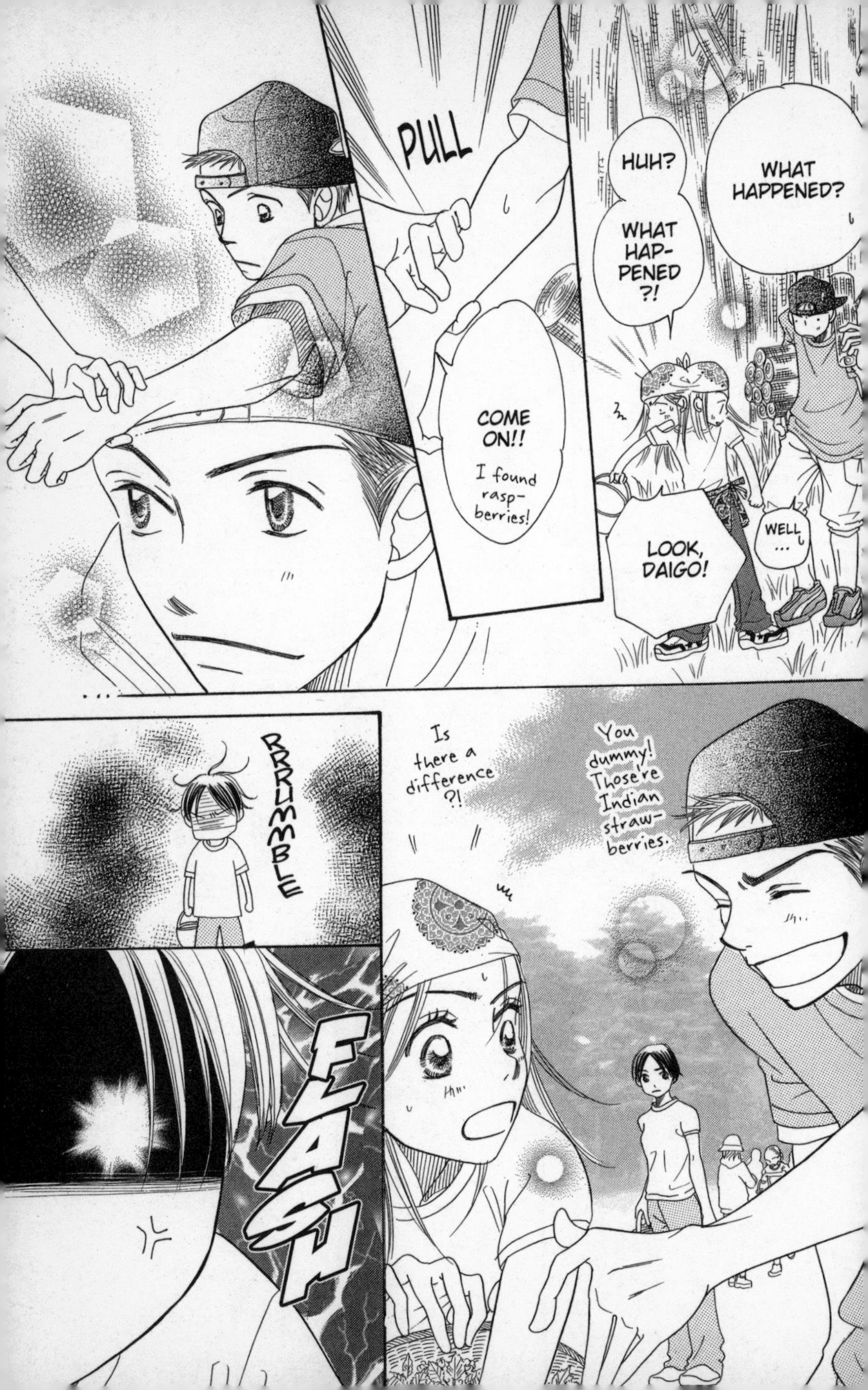

WHAT HAPPENED?
HUH? WHAT HAP-PENED?!
WELL...
LOOK, DAIGO!
PULL
COME ON!! I found rasp-berries!
...
You dummy! Those're Indian straw-berries.
Is there a difference?!
RRRUMMBLE
FLASH

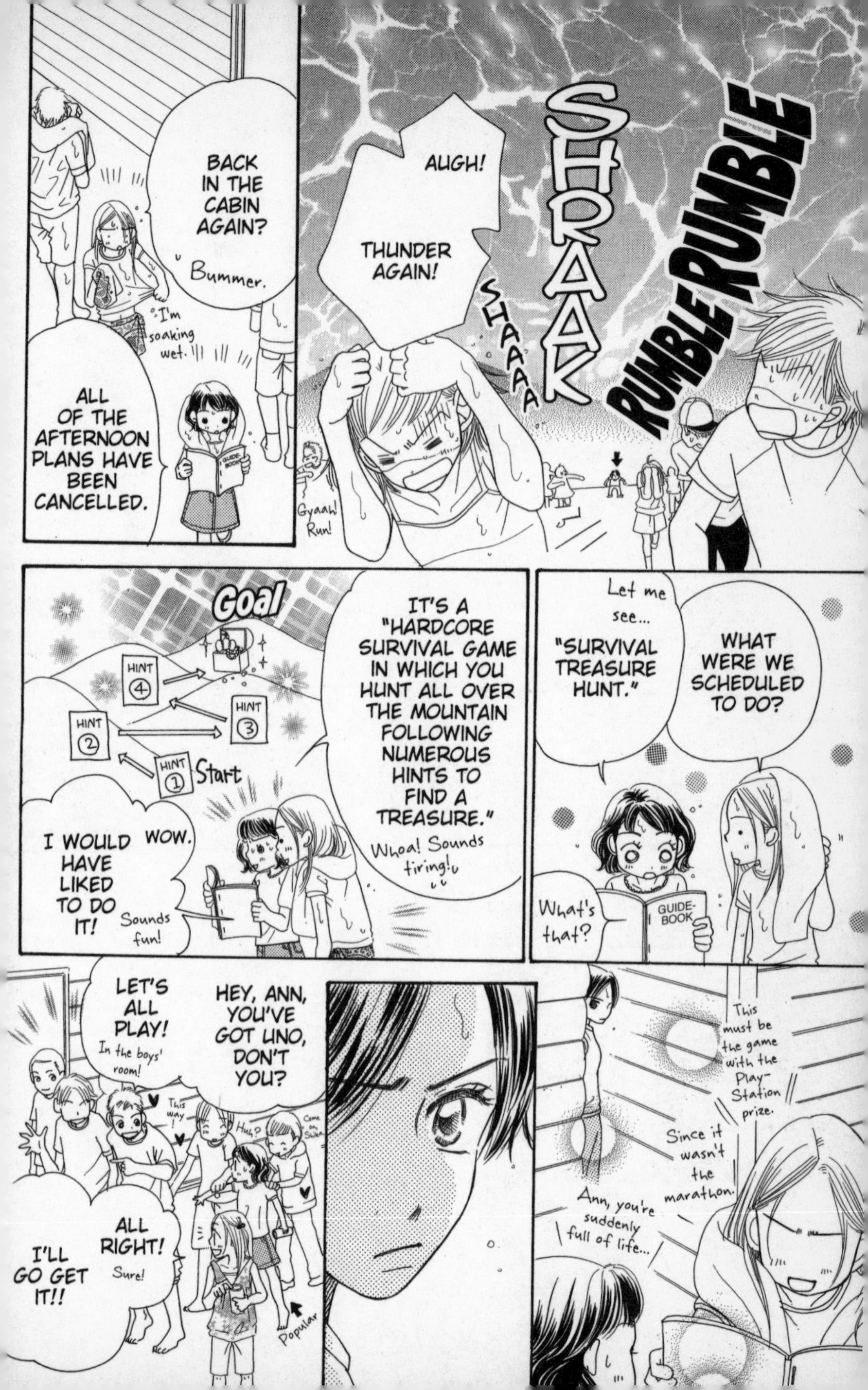

SHRAAK
RUMBLE RUMBLE
AUGH!
THUNDER AGAIN!
SHAAAA
Gyaah! Run!
BACK IN THE CABIN AGAIN?
Bummer.
I'm soaking wet.
ALL OF THE AFTERNOON PLANS HAVE BEEN CANCELLED.
GUIDE-BOOK
WHAT WERE WE SCHEDULED TO DO?
Let me see...
"SURVIVAL TREASURE HUNT."
What's that?
GUIDE-BOOK
IT'S A "HARDCORE SURVIVAL GAME IN WHICH YOU HUNT ALL OVER THE MOUNTAIN FOLLOWING NUMEROUS HINTS TO FIND A TREASURE."
Whoa! Sounds tiring!
Goal
HINT 4
HINT 3
HINT 2
HINT 1
Start
WOW.
I WOULD HAVE LIKED TO DO IT!
Sounds fun!
This must be the game with the Play-Station prize.
Since it wasn't the marathon.
Ann, you're suddenly full of life...
HEY, ANN, YOU'VE GOT UNO, DON'T YOU?
LET'S ALL PLAY!
In the boys' room!
This way!
Huh?
ALL RIGHT!
Sure!
I'LL GO GET IT!!
Popular

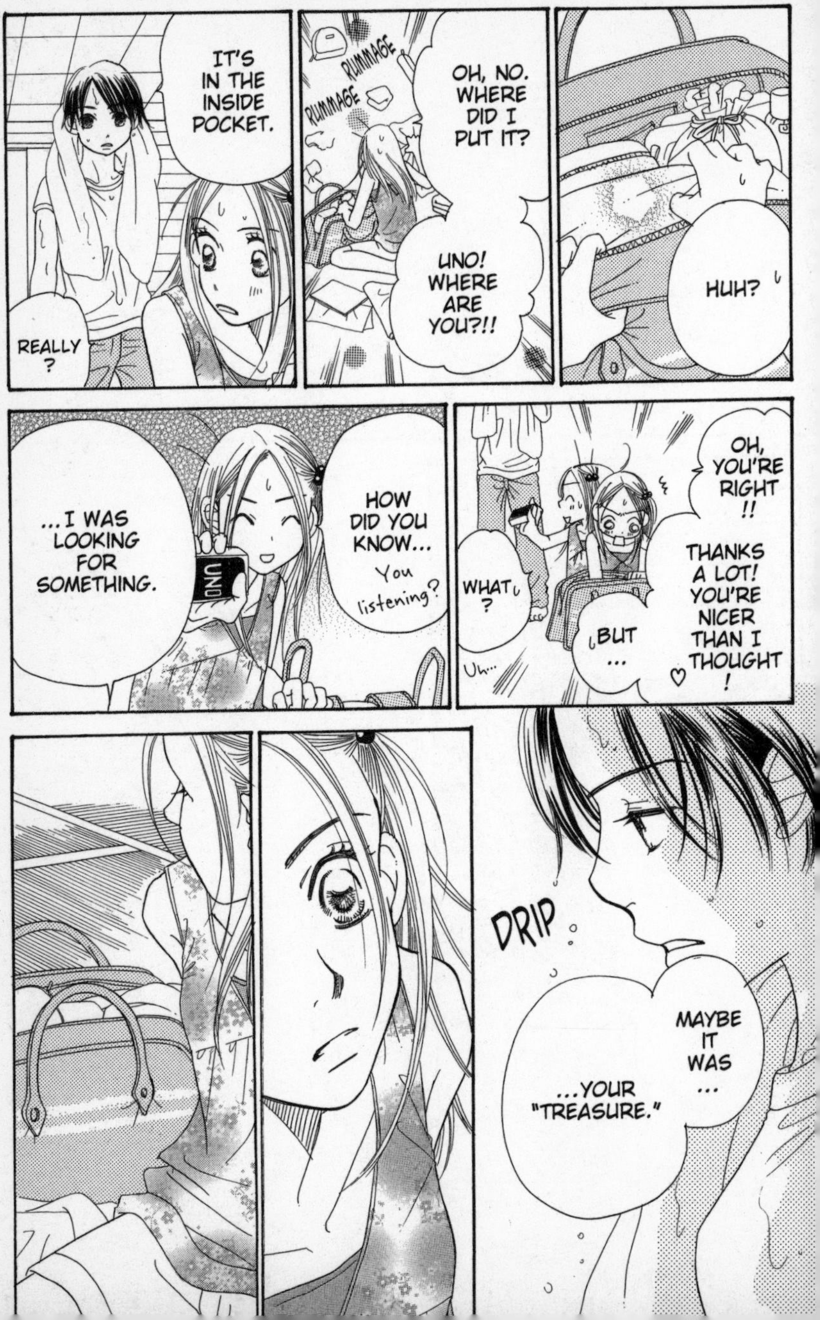
HUH?
RUMMAGE
RUMMAGE
OH, NO. WHERE DID I PUT IT?
UNO! WHERE ARE YOU?!!
IT'S IN THE INSIDE POCKET.
REALLY?
OH, YOU'RE RIGHT!!
THANKS A LOT! YOU'RE NICER THAN I THOUGHT! ♡
WHAT?
BUT...
Uh...
HOW DID YOU KNOW...
You listening?
...I WAS LOOKING FOR SOMETHING.
UNO
DRIP
MAYBE IT WAS...
...YOUR "TREASURE."

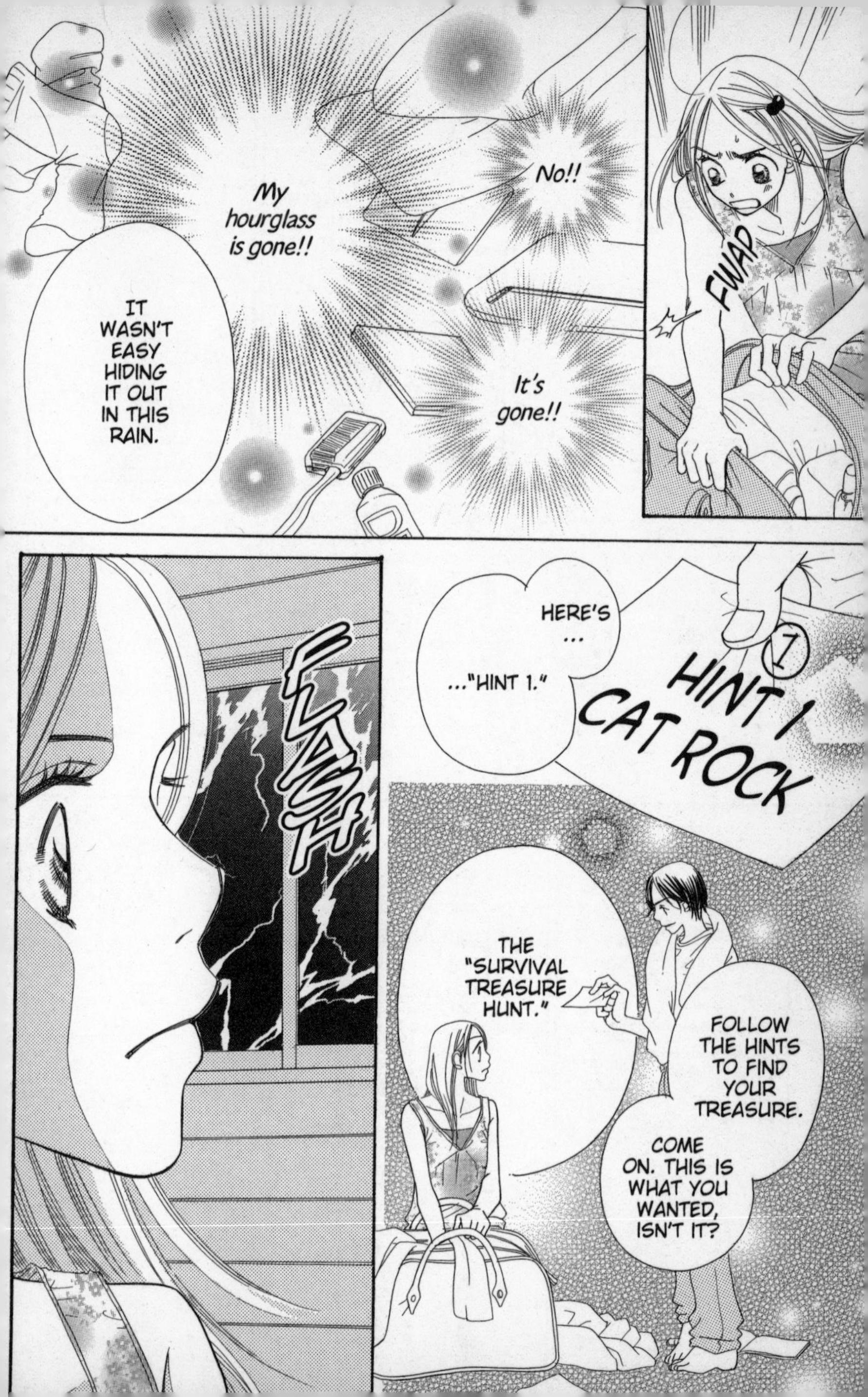
FWAP
No!!
My hourglass is gone!!
It's gone!!
IT WASN'T EASY HIDING IT OUT IN THIS RAIN.
HERE'S ...
..."HINT 1."
1
HINT 1 CAT ROCK
THE "SURVIVAL TREASURE HUNT."
FOLLOW THE HINTS TO FIND YOUR TREASURE.
COME ON. THIS IS WHAT YOU WANTED, ISN'T IT?
FLASH

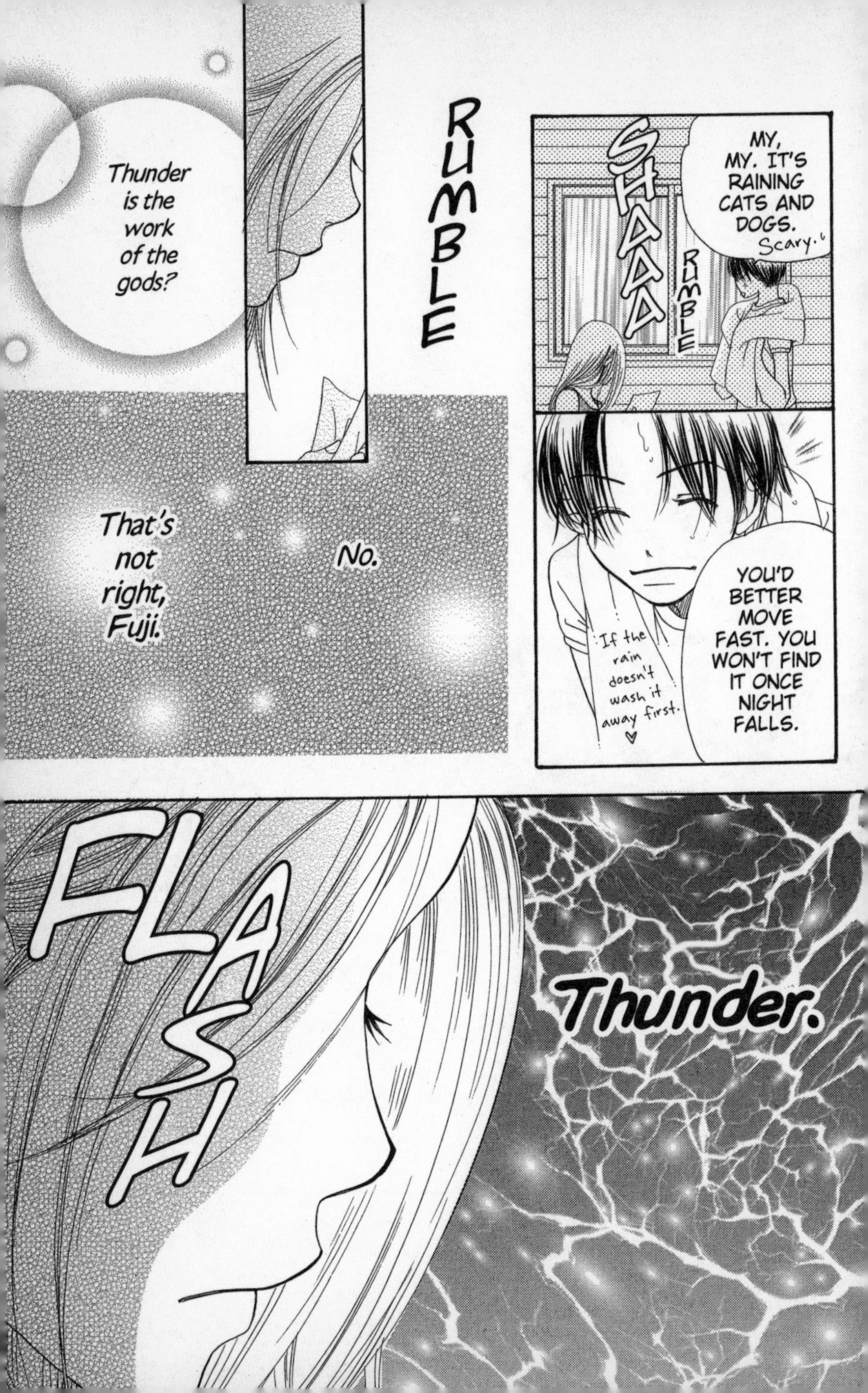
SHAAA
RUMBLE
MY, MY. IT'S RAINING CATS AND DOGS.
Scary.
YOU'D BETTER MOVE FAST. YOU WON'T FIND IT ONCE NIGHT FALLS.
If the rain doesn't wash it away first.
RUMBLE
Thunder is the work of the gods?
No.
That's not right, Fuji.
Thunder.
FLASH

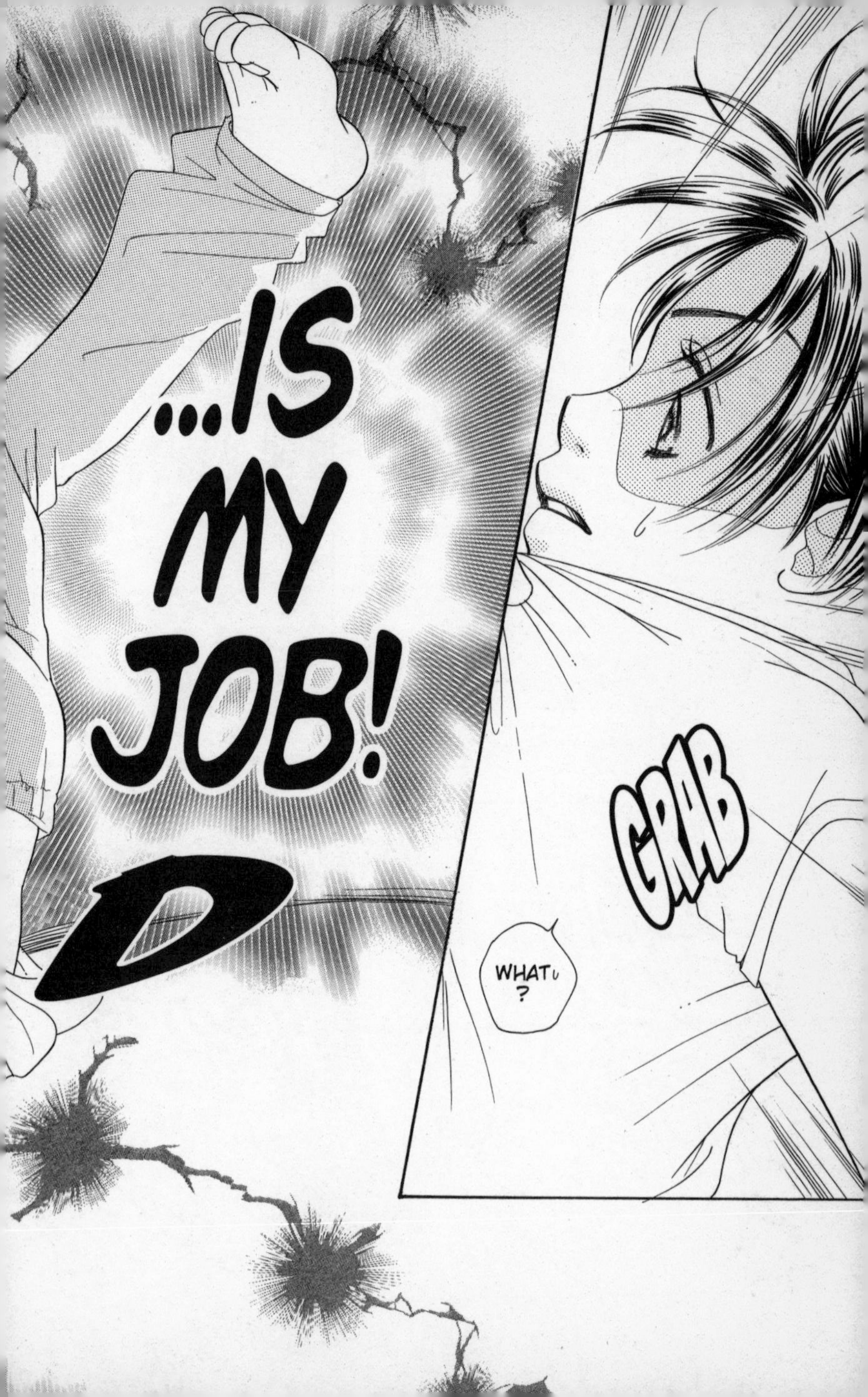
GRAB
WHAT ?
...IS MY JOB!
D

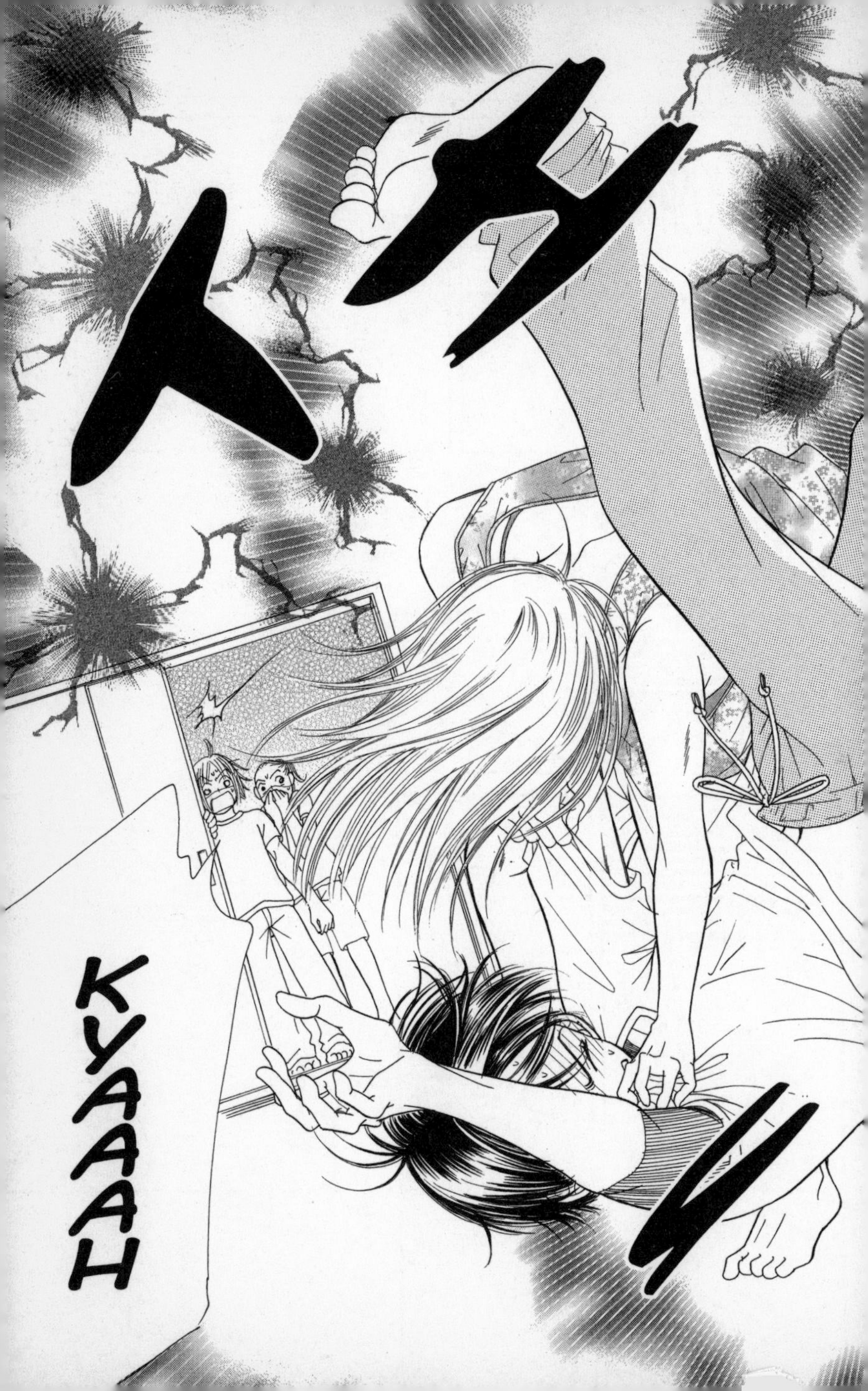
KYAAAH

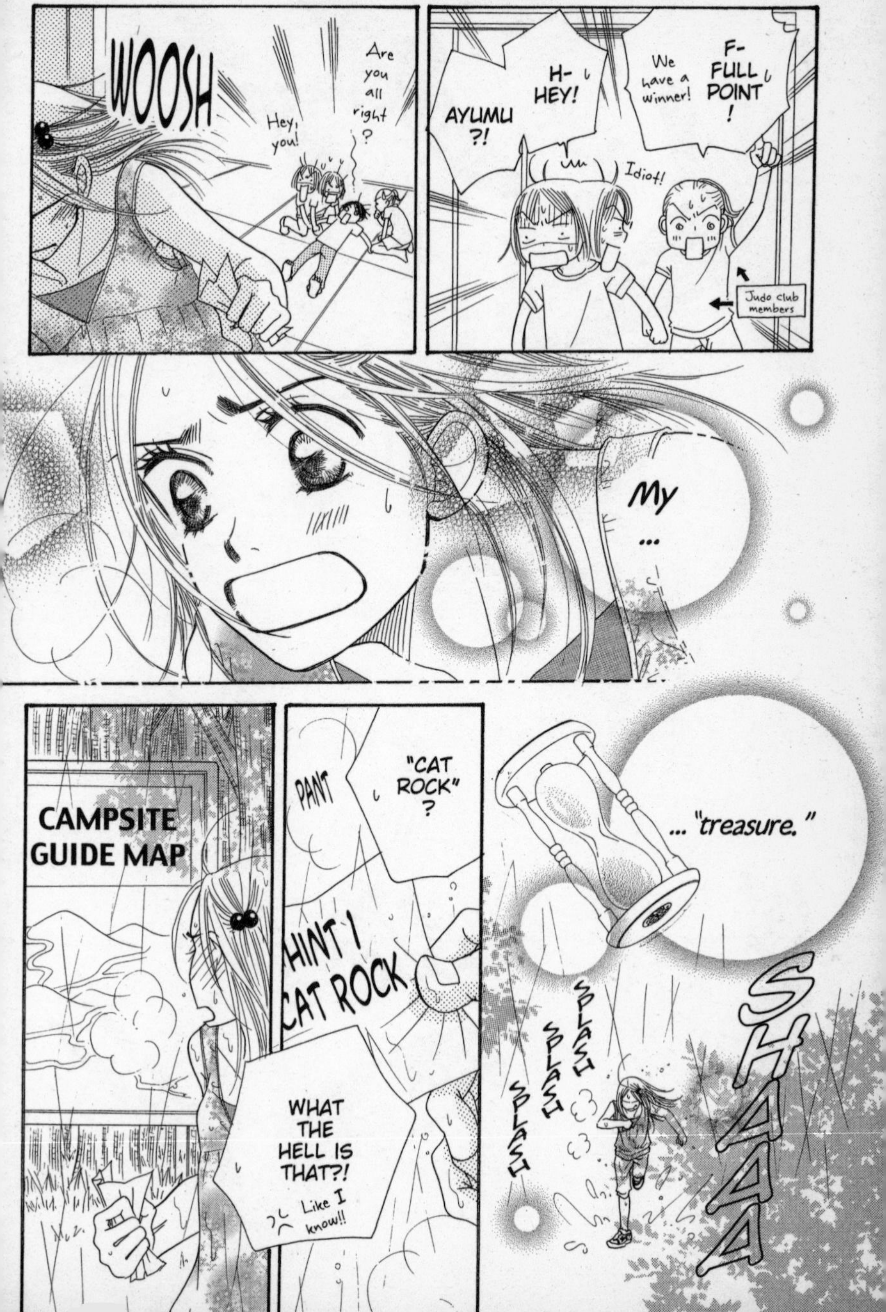
F-FULL POINT!
We have a winner!
H-HEY!
AYUMU?!
Idiot!
Judo club members
Are you all right?
Hey, you!
WOOSH
My ...
... "treasure."
SHAAAA
SPLASH SPLASH SPLASH
"CAT ROCK"?
PANT
HINT 1 CAT ROCK
WHAT THE HELL IS THAT?!
Like I know!!
CAMPSITE GUIDE MAP

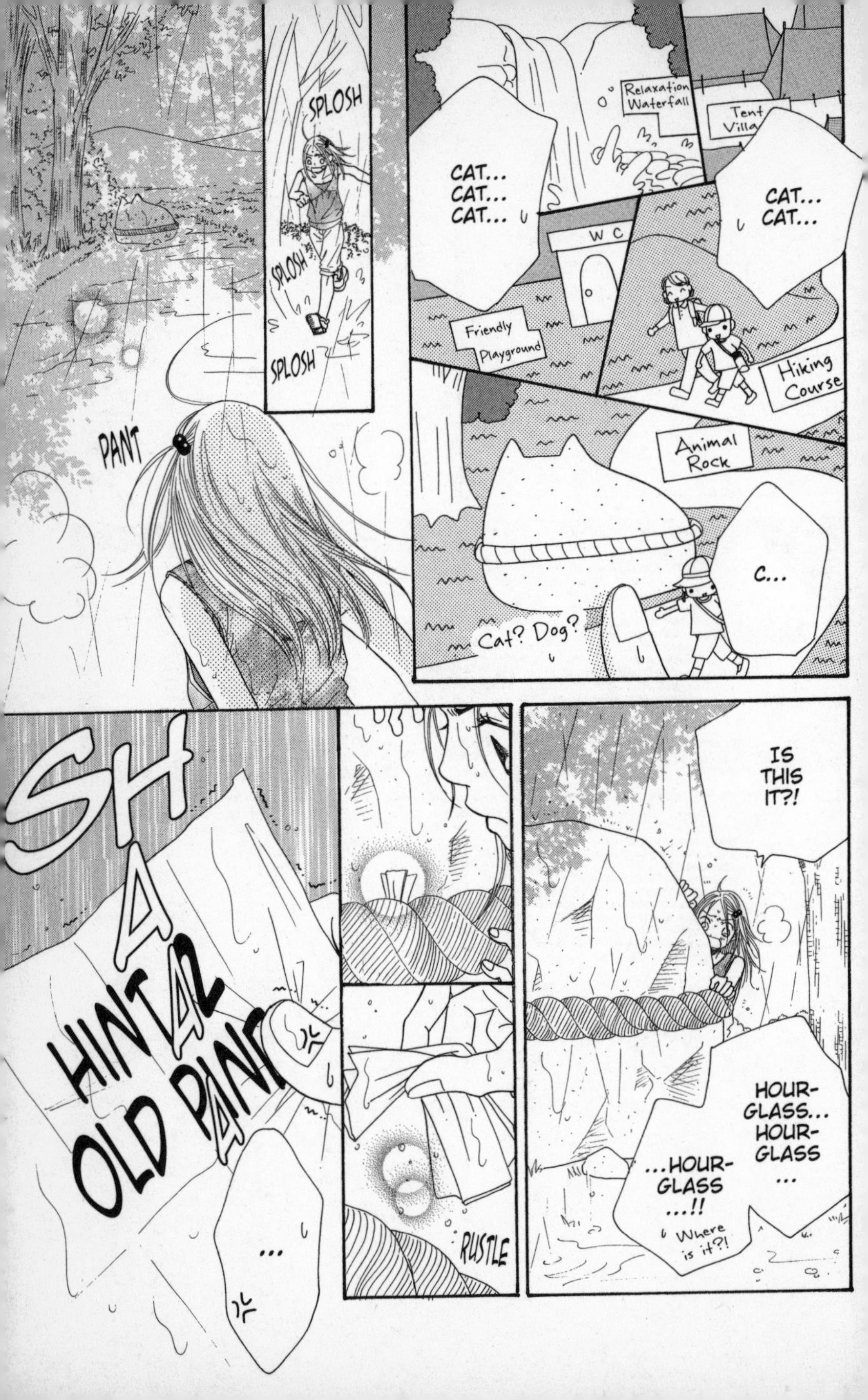
CAT... CAT...
Tent Villa
Relaxation Waterfall
CAT... CAT... CAT...
W C
Friendly Playground
Hiking Course
Animal Rock
C...
Cat? Dog?
SPLOSH
SPLOSH
SPLOSH
PANT
IS THIS IT?!
HOUR-GLASS... HOUR-GLASS...
...HOUR-GLASS...!!
Where is it?!
RUSTLE
SHA
HINT 12
OLD PAN
...

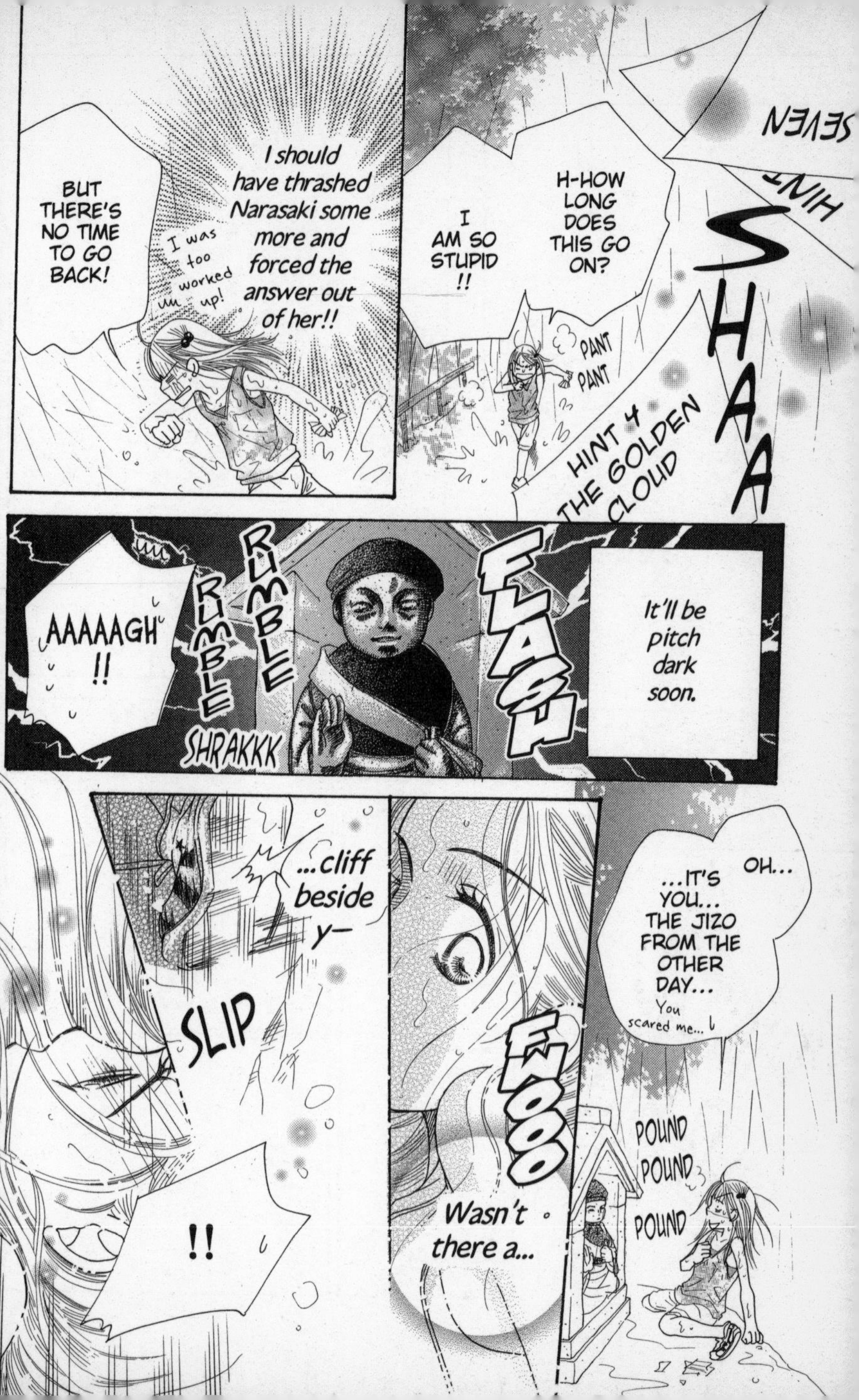
HINT SEVEN
SHAAA
HINT 4 THE GOLDEN CLOUD
H-HOW LONG DOES THIS GO ON?
I AM SO STUPID!!
PANT PANT
I should have thrashed Narasaki some more and forced the answer out of her!!
I was too worked up!
BUT THERE'S NO TIME TO GO BACK!
It'll be pitch dark soon.
FLASH
RUMBLE RUMBLE
SHRAKKK
AAAAAGH!!
OH...
...IT'S YOU... THE JIZO FROM THE OTHER DAY...
You scared me...
POUND POUND POUND
FWOOO
Wasn't there a...
...cliff beside y—
SLIP
!!

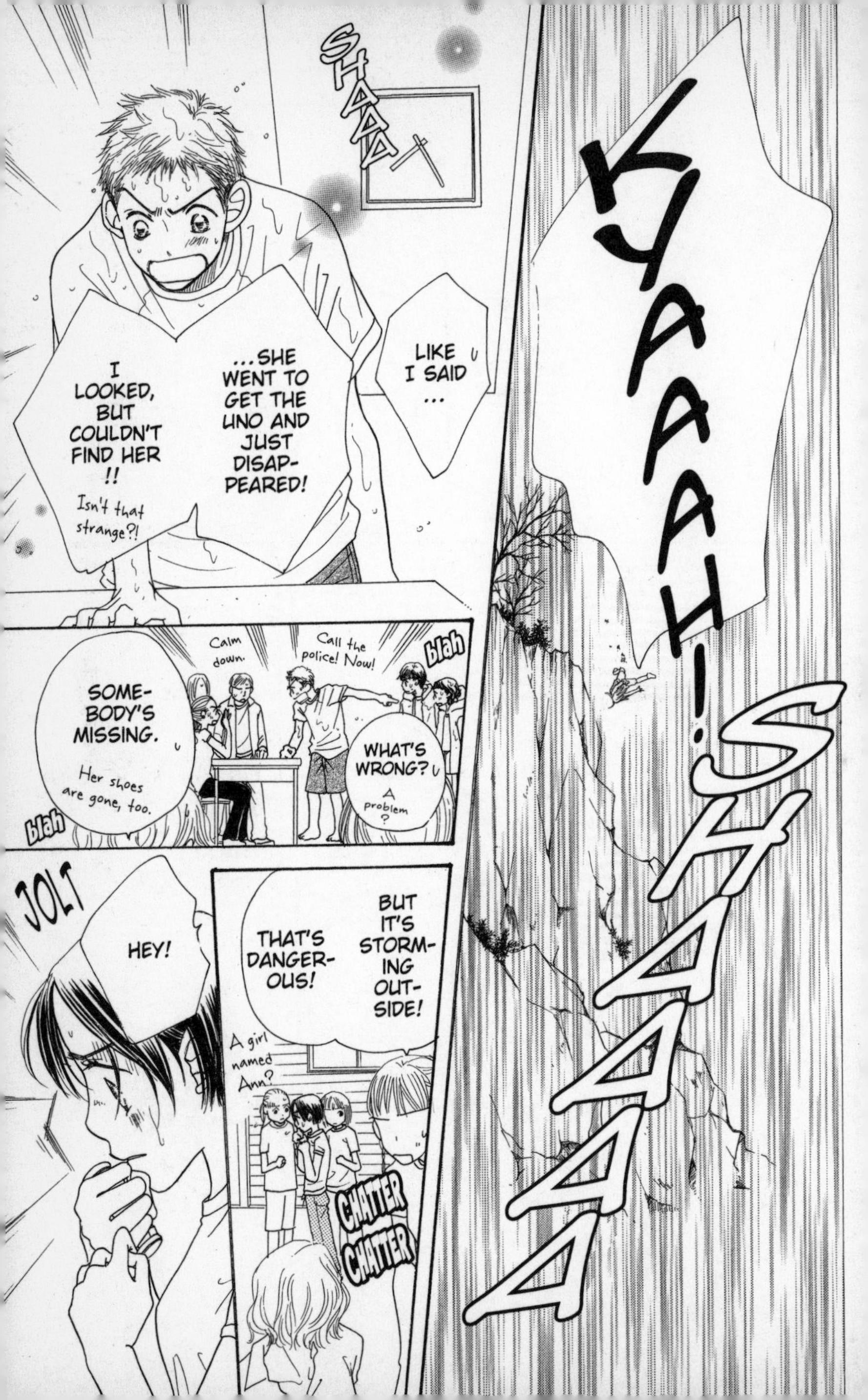
KYAAAH!!
SHAAAAA
SHAAA
LIKE I SAID...
...SHE WENT TO GET THE UNO AND JUST DISAPPEARED!
I LOOKED, BUT COULDN'T FIND HER!!
Isn't that strange?!
blah
Call the police! Now!
WHAT'S WRONG?
A problem?
Calm down.
SOMEBODY'S MISSING.
Her shoes are gone, too.
blah
BUT IT'S STORMING OUTSIDE!
THAT'S DANGEROUS!
A girl named Ann?
CHATTER CHATTER
JOLT
HEY!

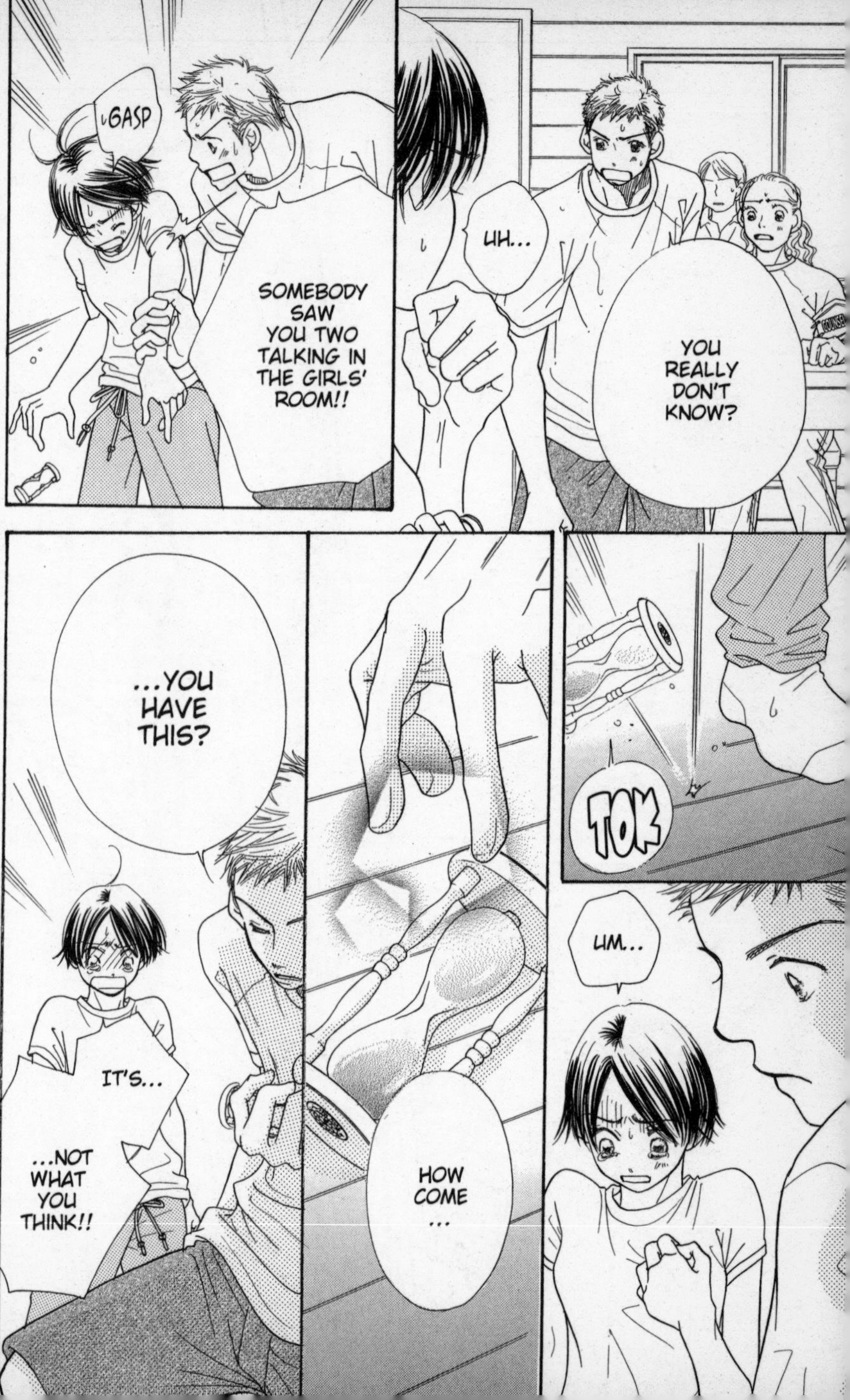
UH...
YOU REALLY DON'T KNOW?
GASP
SOMEBODY SAW YOU TWO TALKING IN THE GIRLS' ROOM!!
TOK
UM...
HOW COME ...
...YOU HAVE THIS?
IT'S...
...NOT WHAT YOU THINK!!

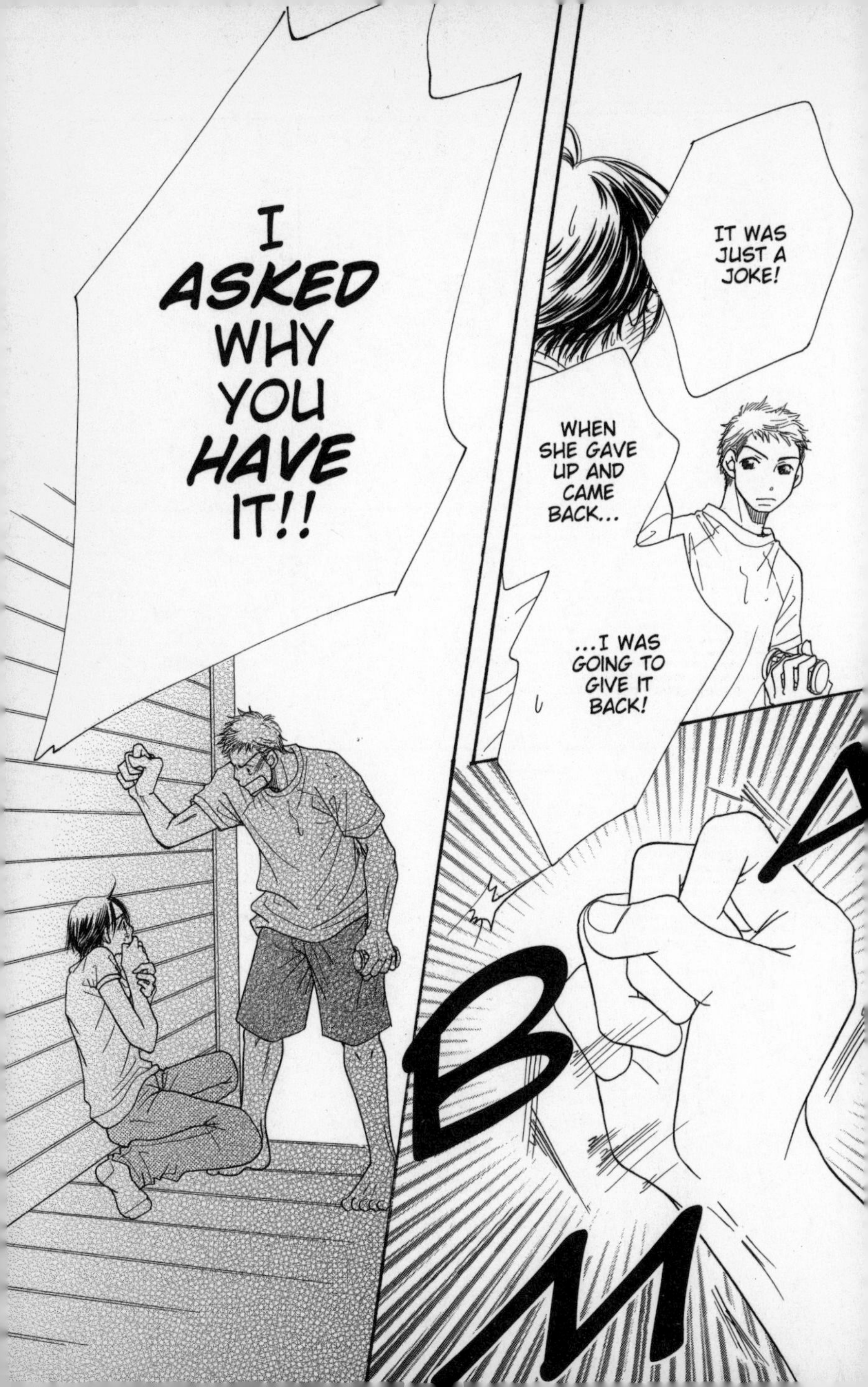
IT WAS JUST A JOKE!
WHEN SHE GAVE UP AND CAME BACK...
...I WAS GOING TO GIVE IT BACK!
BAM
I ASKED WHY YOU HAVE IT!!

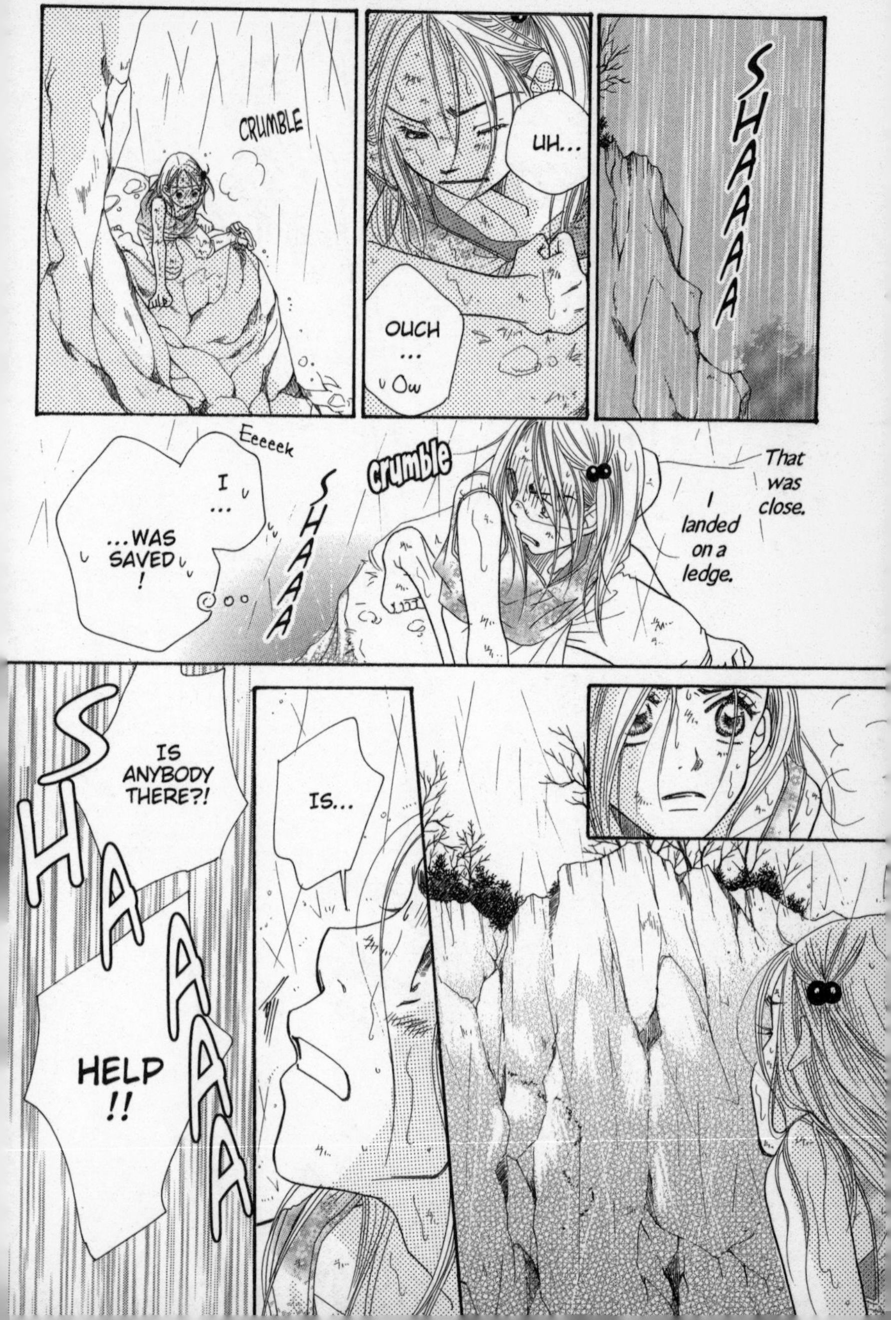
SHAAAAA
UH...
OUCH ... Ow
CRUMBLE
That was close.
I landed on a ledge.
crumble
SHAAAA
Eeeeek
I ... ...WAS SAVED!
IS...
IS ANYBODY THERE?!
SHAAAAAAA
HELP!!

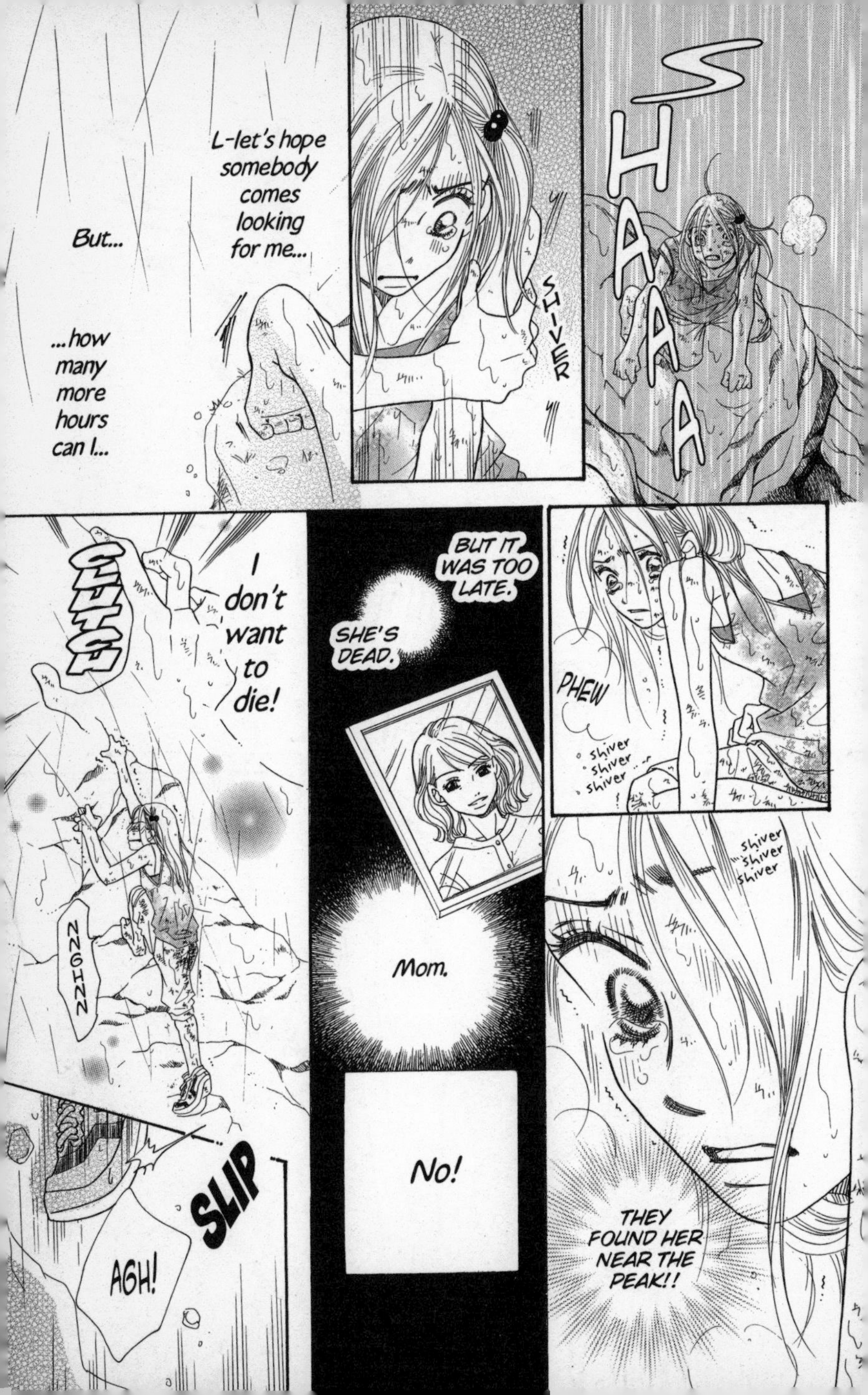
SHAAAA
SHIVER
L-let's hope somebody comes looking for me...
But...
...how many more hours can I...
PHEW
shiver shiver shiver
shiver shiver shiver
THEY FOUND HER NEAR THE PEAK!!
BUT IT WAS TOO LATE.
SHE'S DEAD.
Mom.
No!
CLUTCH
I don't want to die!
NNGHNN
SLIP
AGH!

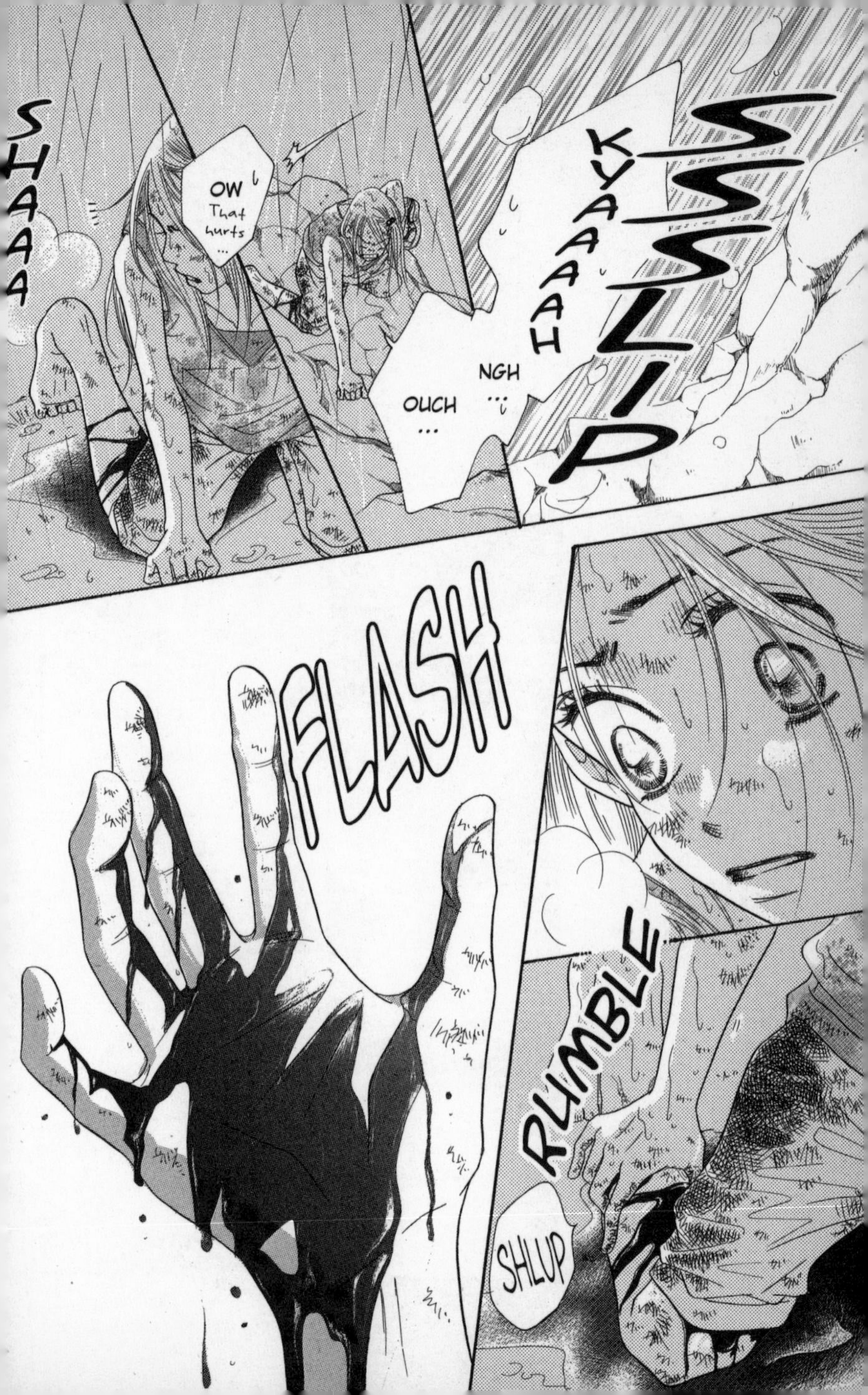
SSLIP
KYAAAAH
NGH...
OUCH...
SHAAAA
OW That hurts...
RUMBLE...
SHLUP
FLASH

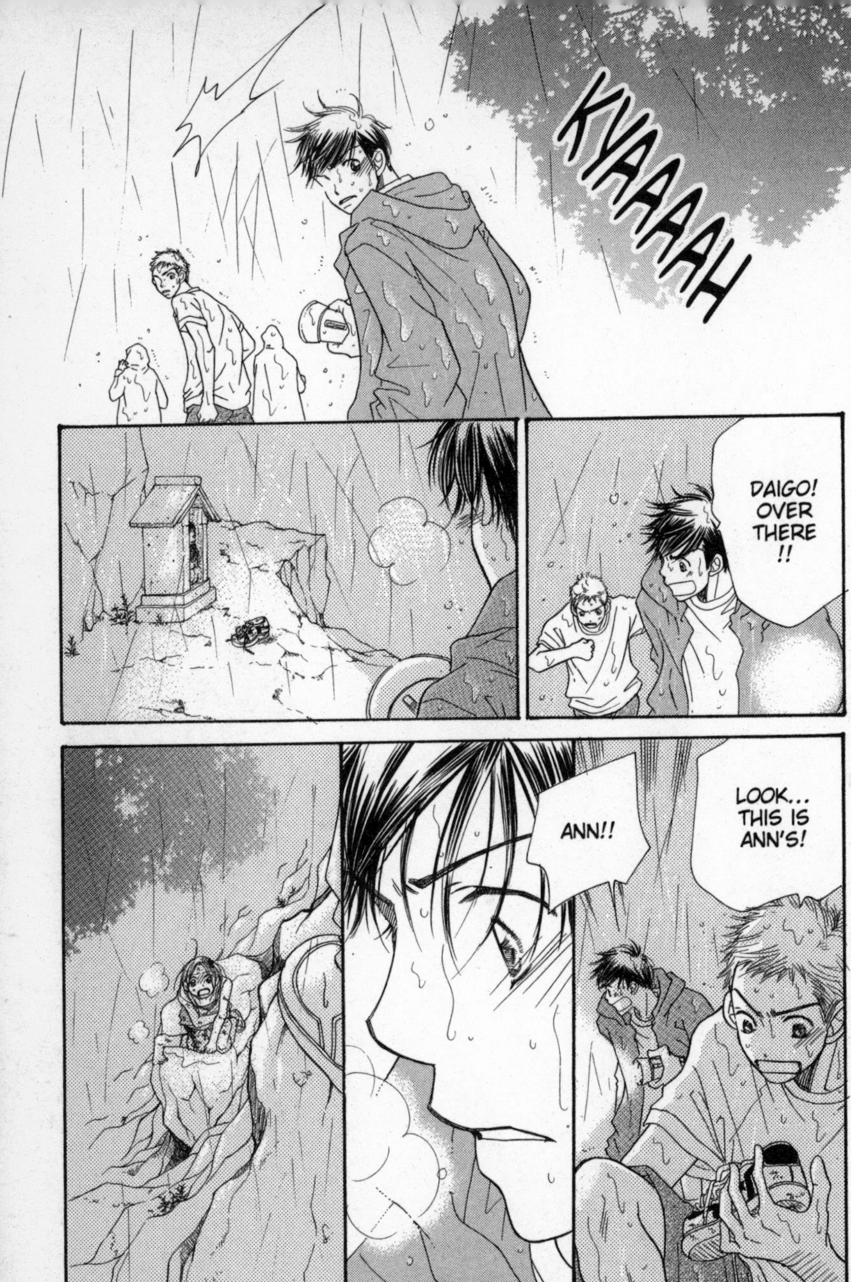
KYAAAAH
DAIGO! OVER THERE !!
LOOK... THIS IS ANN'S!
ANN!!

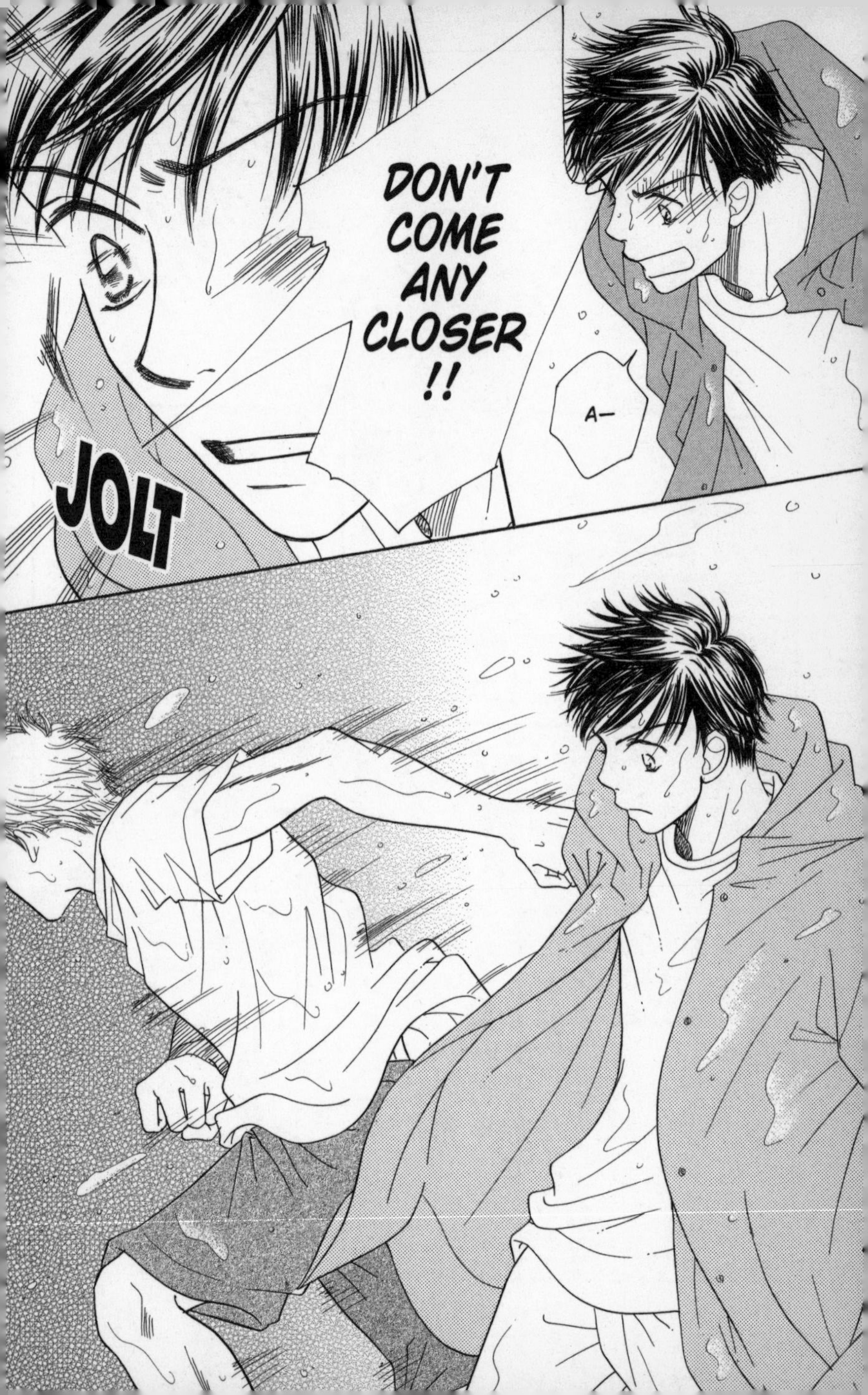
A—
DON'T COME ANY CLOSER!!
JOLT

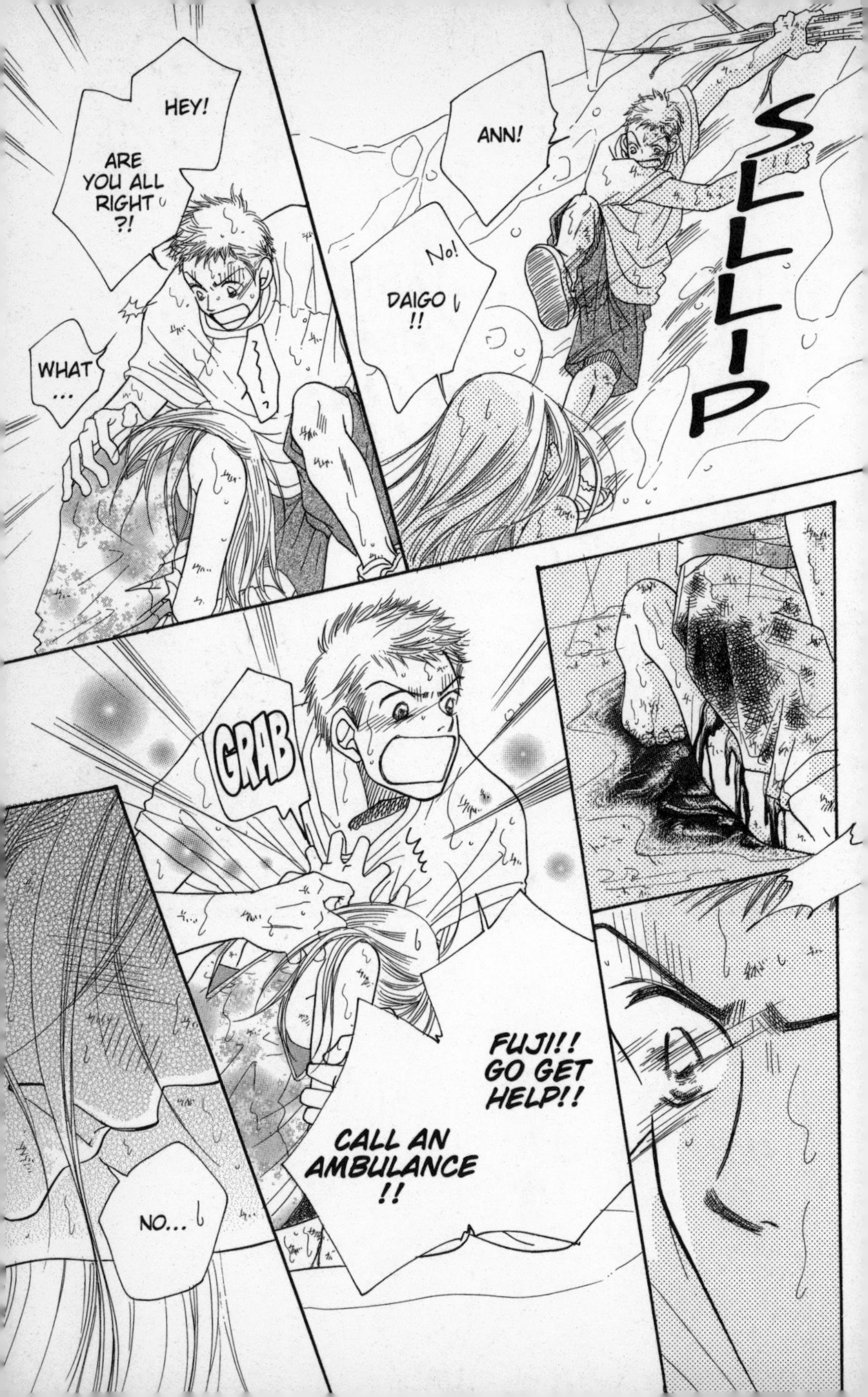
SLLIP
ANN!
No!
DAIGO!!
HEY!
ARE YOU ALL RIGHT?!
WHAT...
GRAB
FUJI!! GO GET HELP!!
CALL AN AMBULANCE!!
NO...

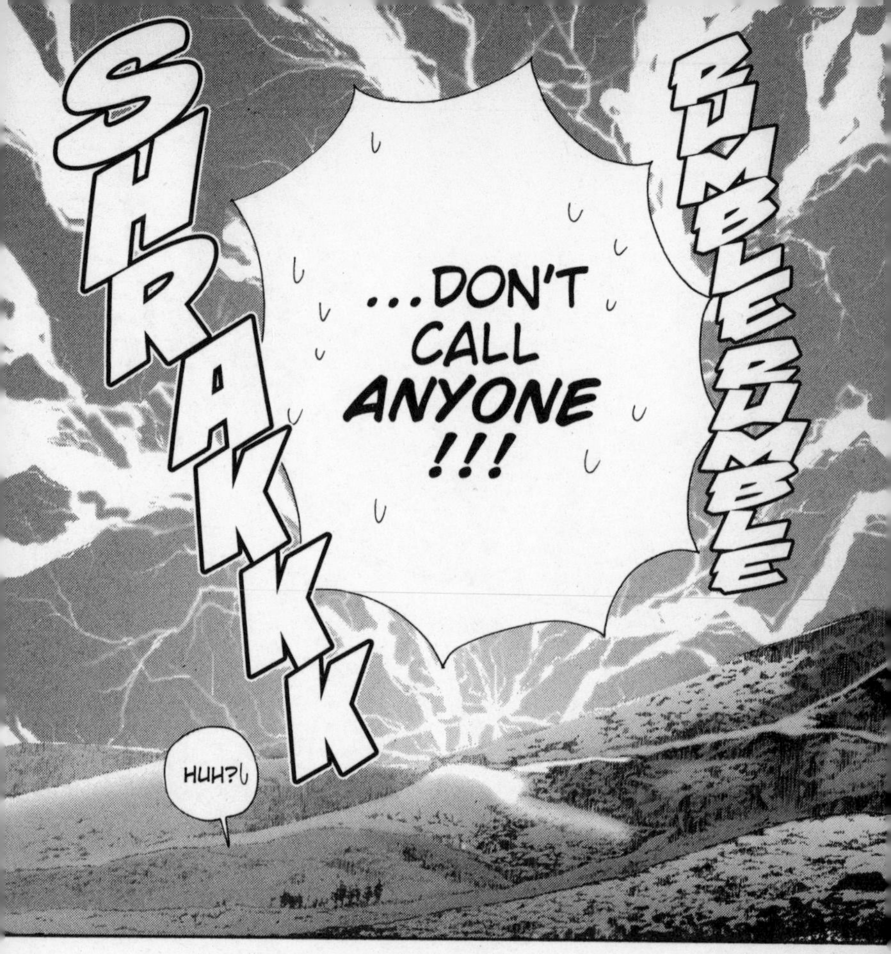
RUMBLE RUMBLE
...DON'T CALL ANYONE!!!
SHRAKKK
HUH?
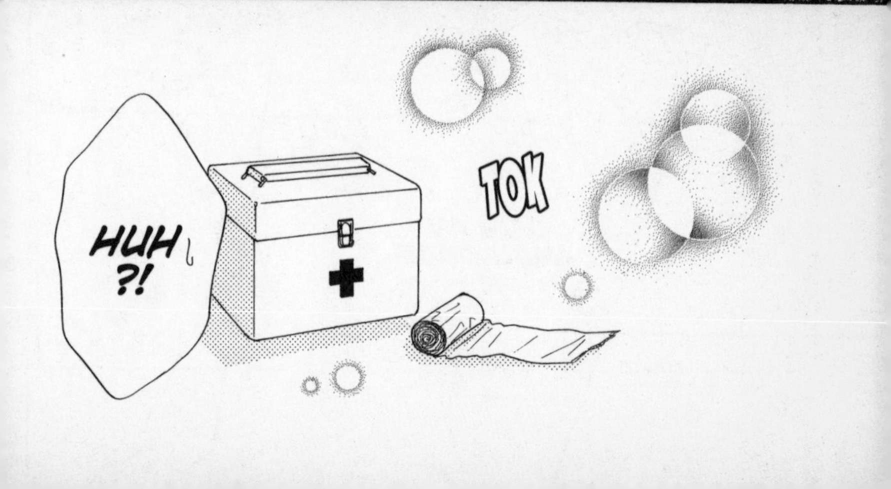
TOK
HUH?!

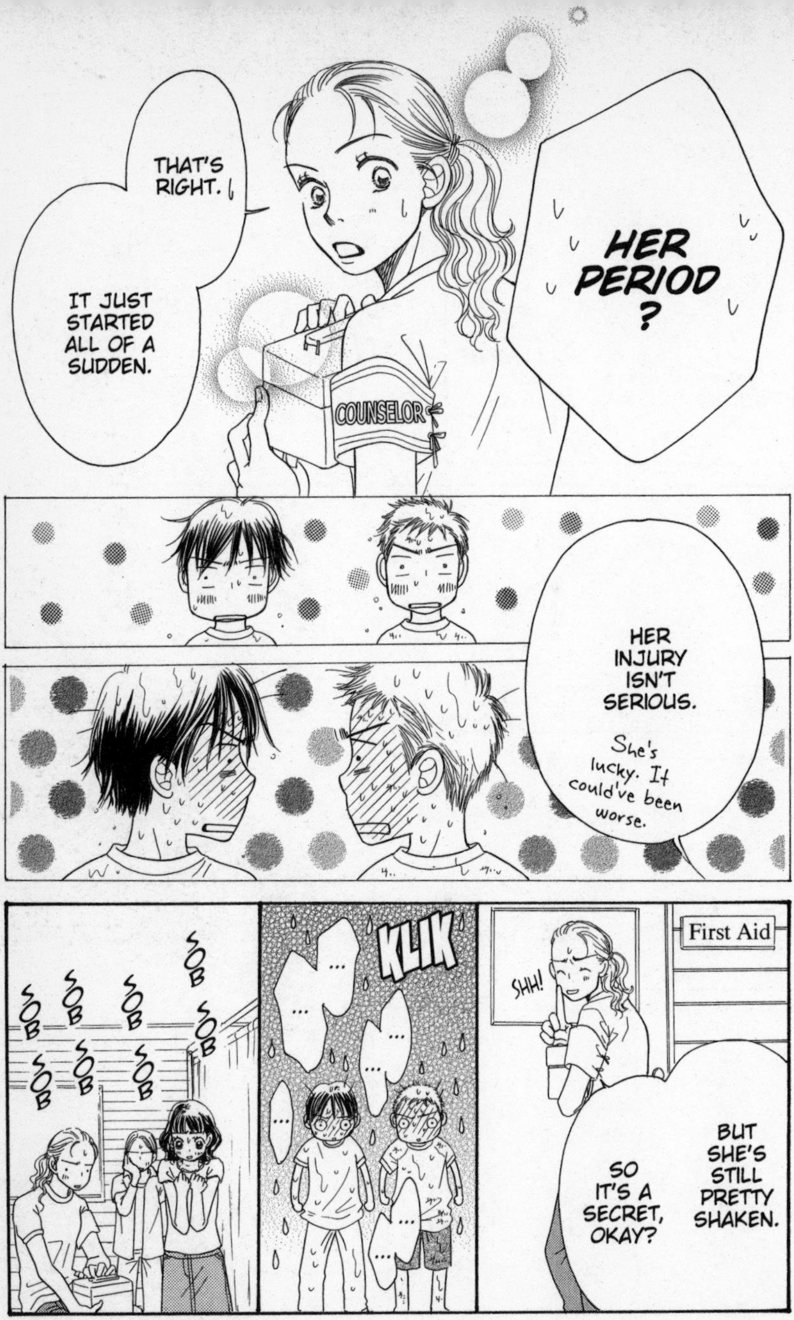
HER PERIOD?
THAT'S RIGHT.
IT JUST STARTED ALL OF A SUDDEN.
HER INJURY ISN'T SERIOUS.
She's lucky. It could've been worse.
First Aid
SHH!
BUT SHE'S STILL PRETTY SHAKEN.
SO IT'S A SECRET, OKAY?
KLIK
...
...
...
...
...
...
...
SOB SOB SOB SOB SOB SOB SOB SOB

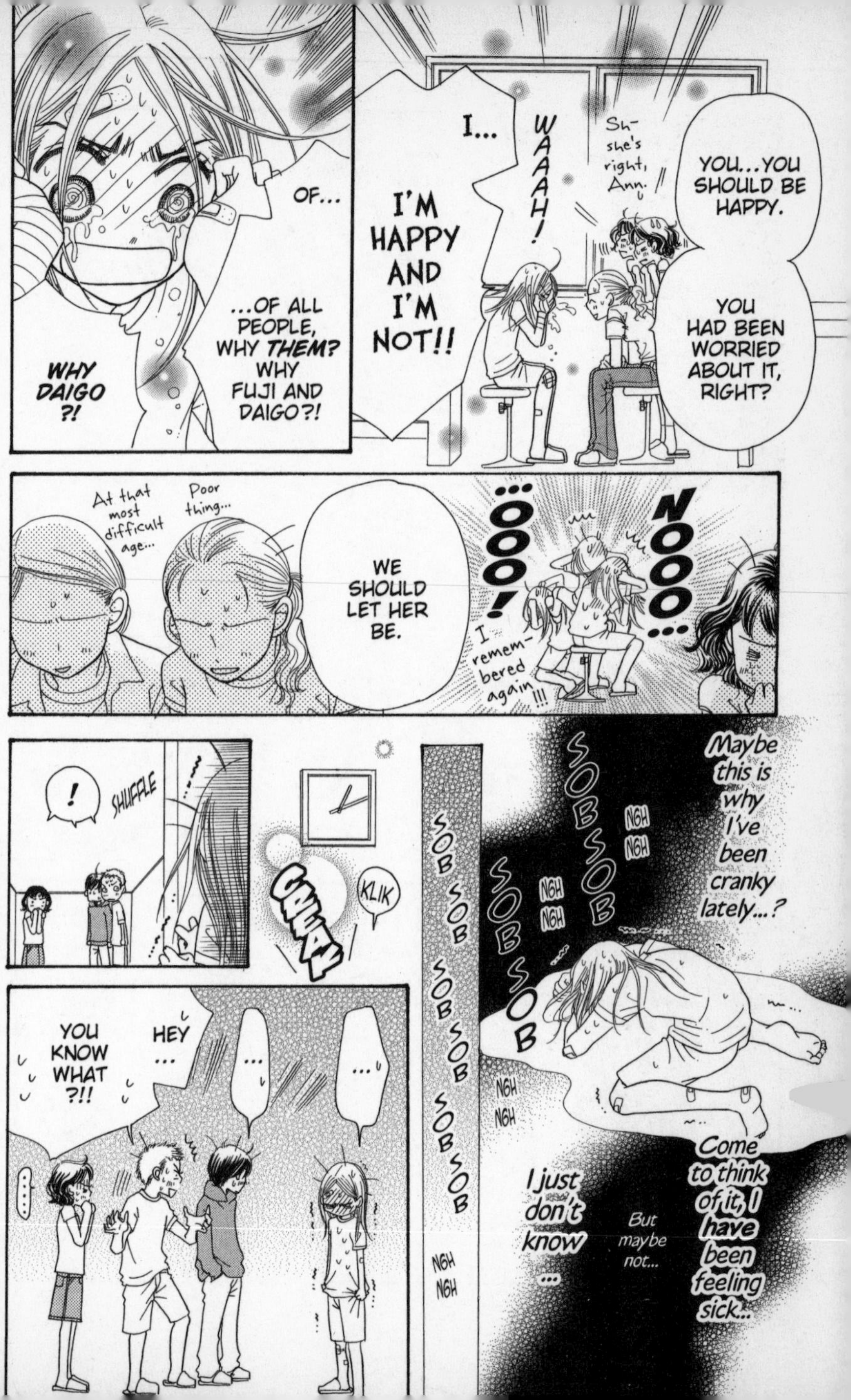
YOU...YOU SHOULD BE HAPPY.
YOU HAD BEEN WORRIED ABOUT IT, RIGHT?
Sh-she's right, Ann.
WAAAAH!
I...
I'M HAPPY AND I'M NOT!!
OF...
...OF ALL PEOPLE, WHY THEM? WHY FUJI AND DAIGO?!
WHY DAIGO?!
NOOOO...
...OOOO!
I remembered again!!!
WE SHOULD LET HER BE.
Poor thing...
At that most difficult age...
Maybe this is why I've been cranky lately...?
SOB SOB
NGH NGH
SOB SOB
NGH NGH
NGH NGH
Come to think of it, I have been feeling sick...
But maybe not...
I just don't know...
SOB SOB SOB SOB SOB SOB SOB
NGH NGH
KLIK
CREAK
!
SHUFFLE
...!
...
...
HEY...
YOU KNOW WHAT?!!
....

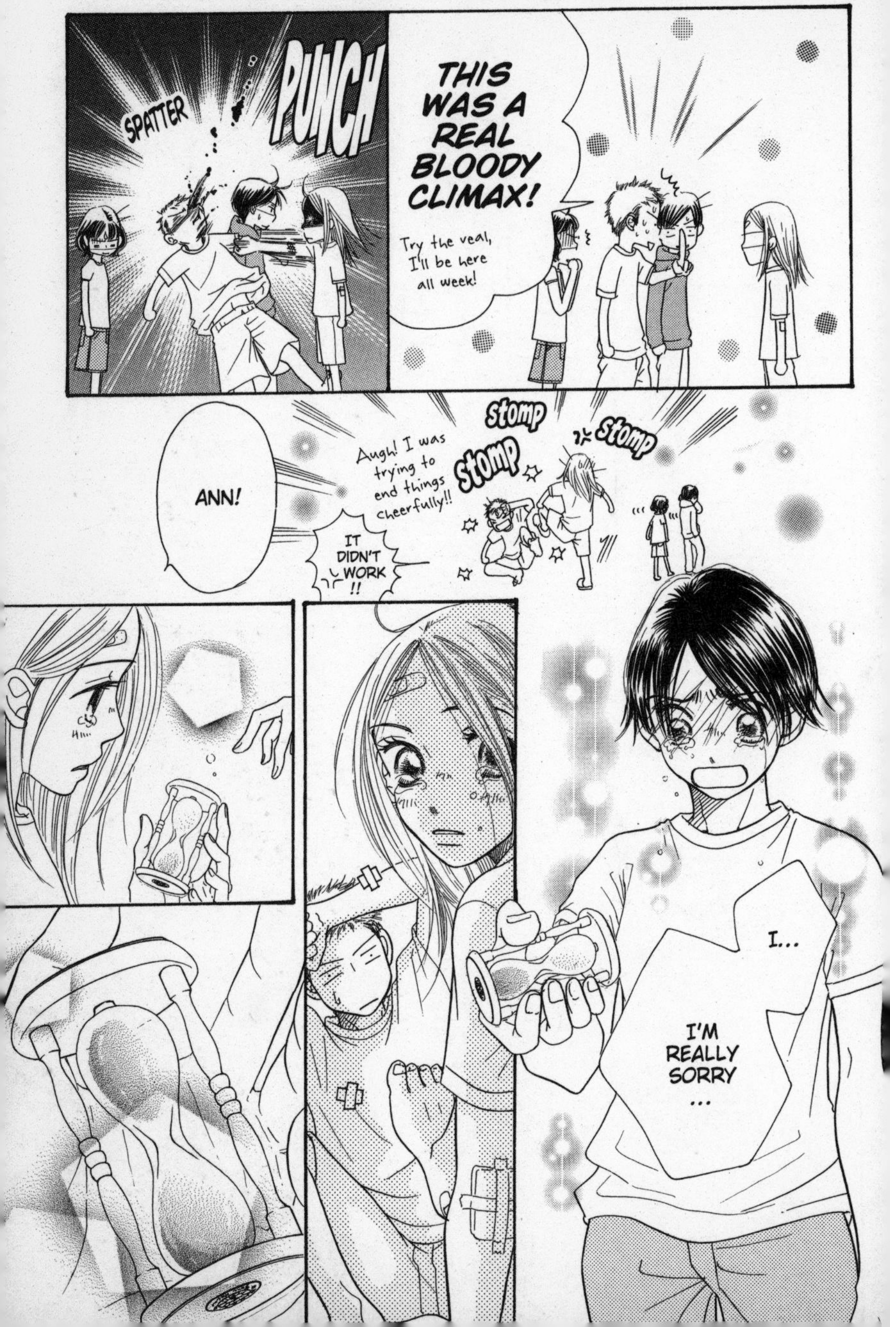
THIS WAS A REAL BLOODY CLIMAX!
Try the veal, I'll be here all week!
PUNCH
SPATTER
Stomp
Stomp
Stomp
Augh! I was trying to end things cheerfully!!
IT DIDN'T WORK!!
ANN!
I...
I'M REALLY SORRY...

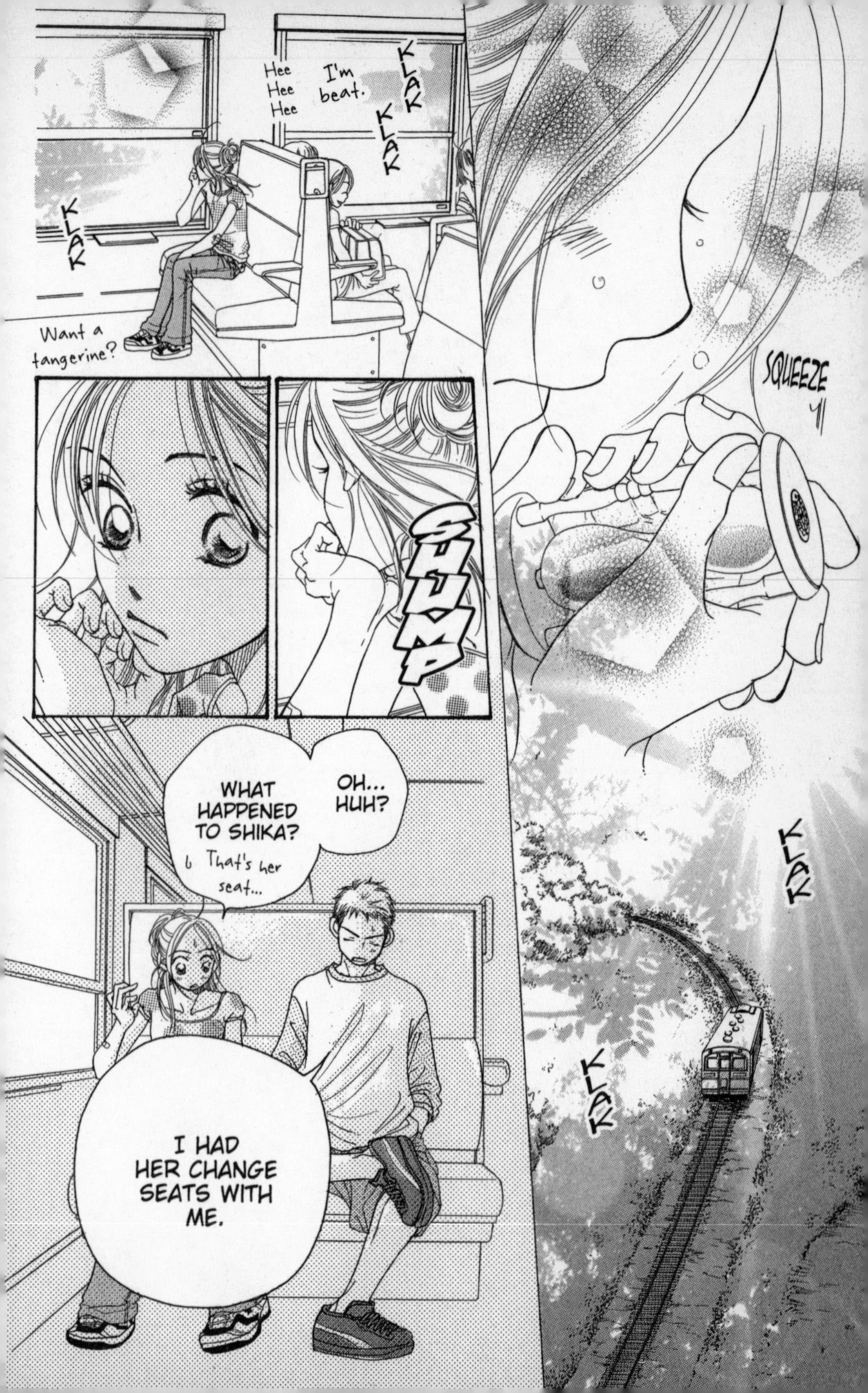
SQUEEZE
KLAK
KLAK
KLAK
KLAK
I'm beat.
Hee Hee Hee
KLAK
Want a tangerine?
SLUMP
OH... HUH?
WHAT HAPPENED TO SHIKA?
That's her seat...
I HAD HER CHANGE SEATS WITH ME.

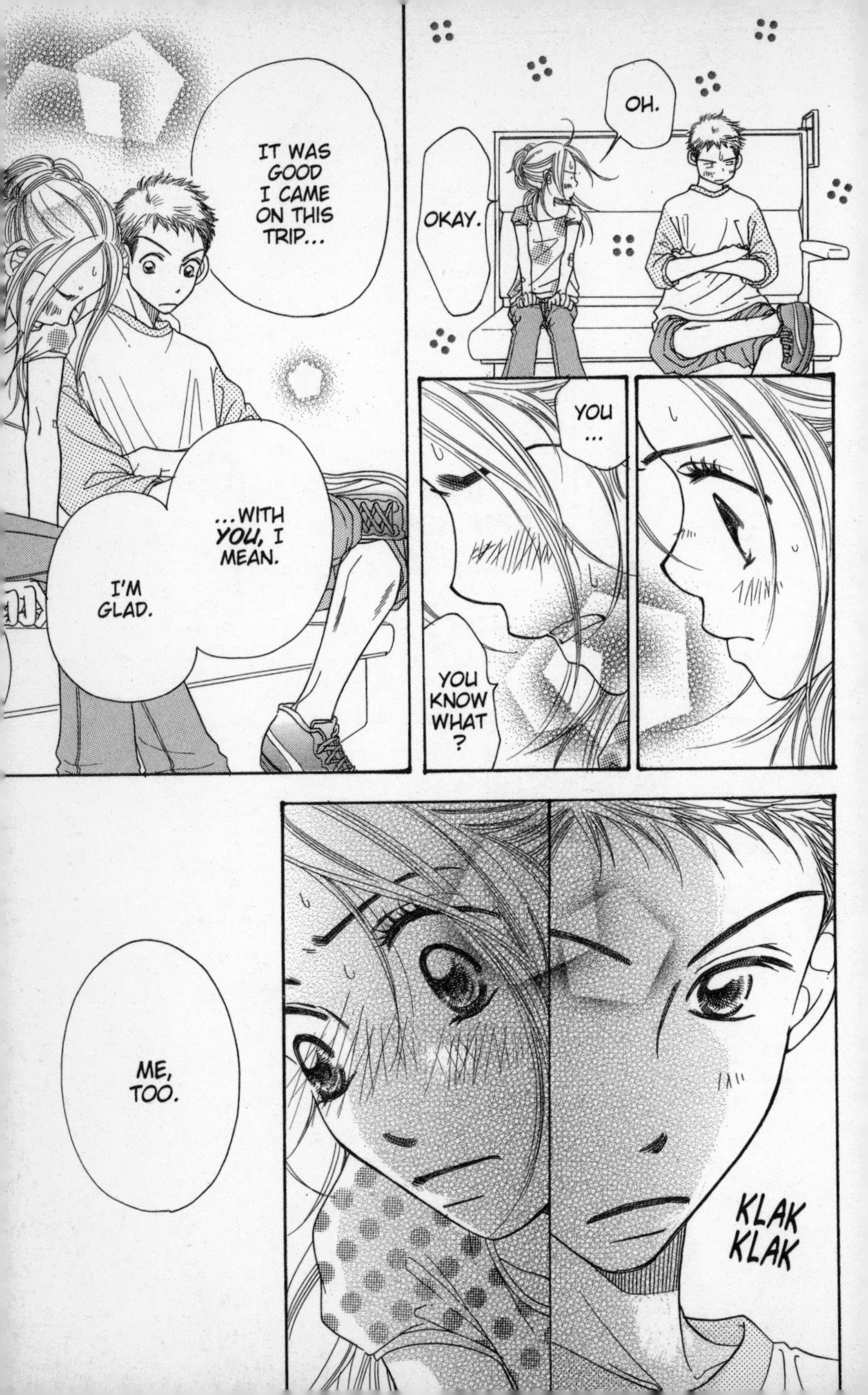
OH.
OKAY.
YOU ...
YOU KNOW WHAT?
IT WAS GOOD I CAME ON THIS TRIP...
...WITH *YOU*, I MEAN.
I'M GLAD.
ME, TOO.
KLAK KLAK

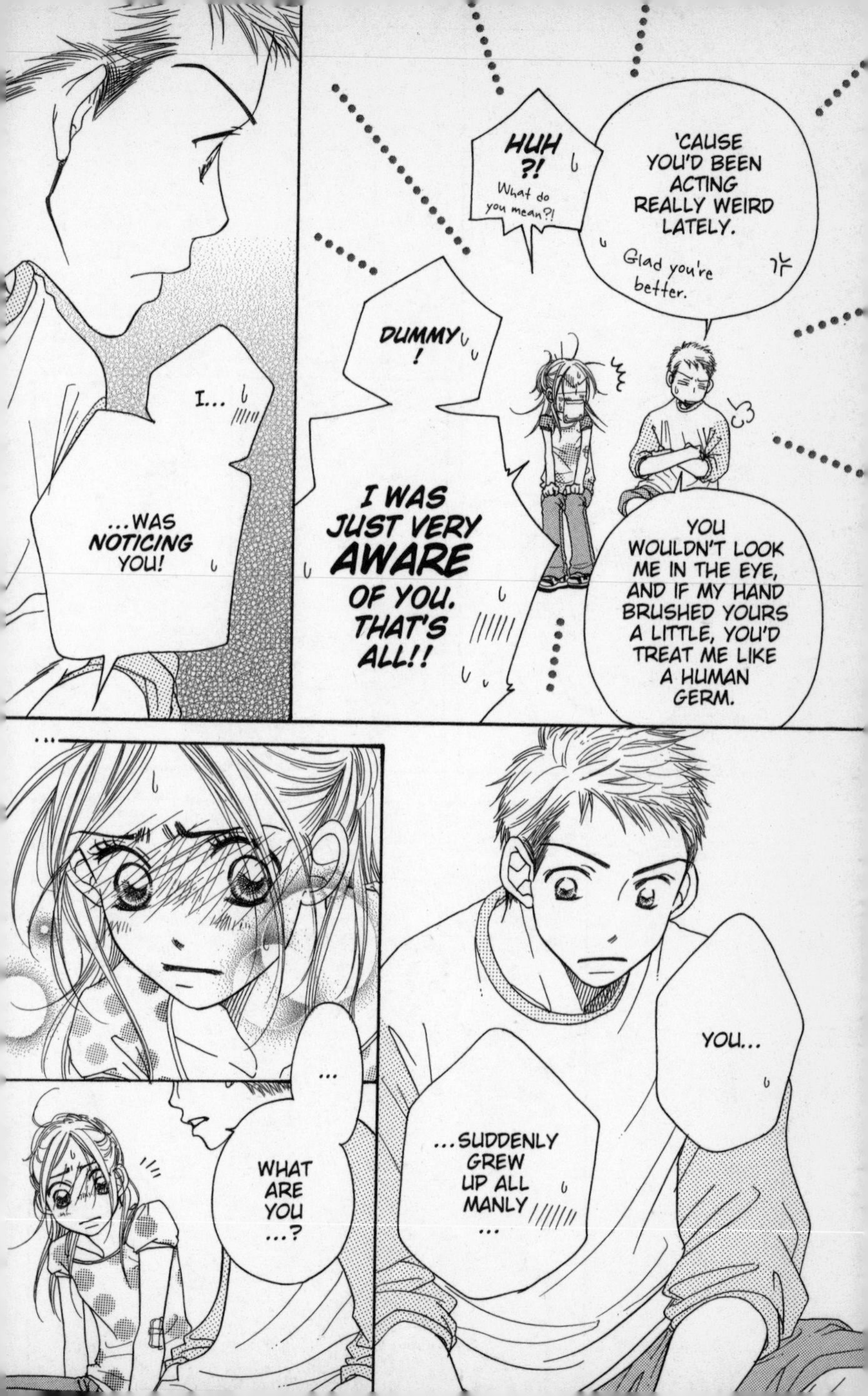
'CAUSE YOU'D BEEN ACTING REALLY WEIRD LATELY.
Glad you're better.
HUH ?! What do you mean?!
YOU WOULDN'T LOOK ME IN THE EYE, AND IF MY HAND BRUSHED YOURS A LITTLE, YOU'D TREAT ME LIKE A HUMAN GERM.
DUMMY!
I WAS JUST VERY AWARE OF YOU. THAT'S ALL!!
I...
...WAS NOTICING YOU!
YOU...
...SUDDENLY GREW UP ALL MANLY...
...
...
WHAT ARE YOU ...?

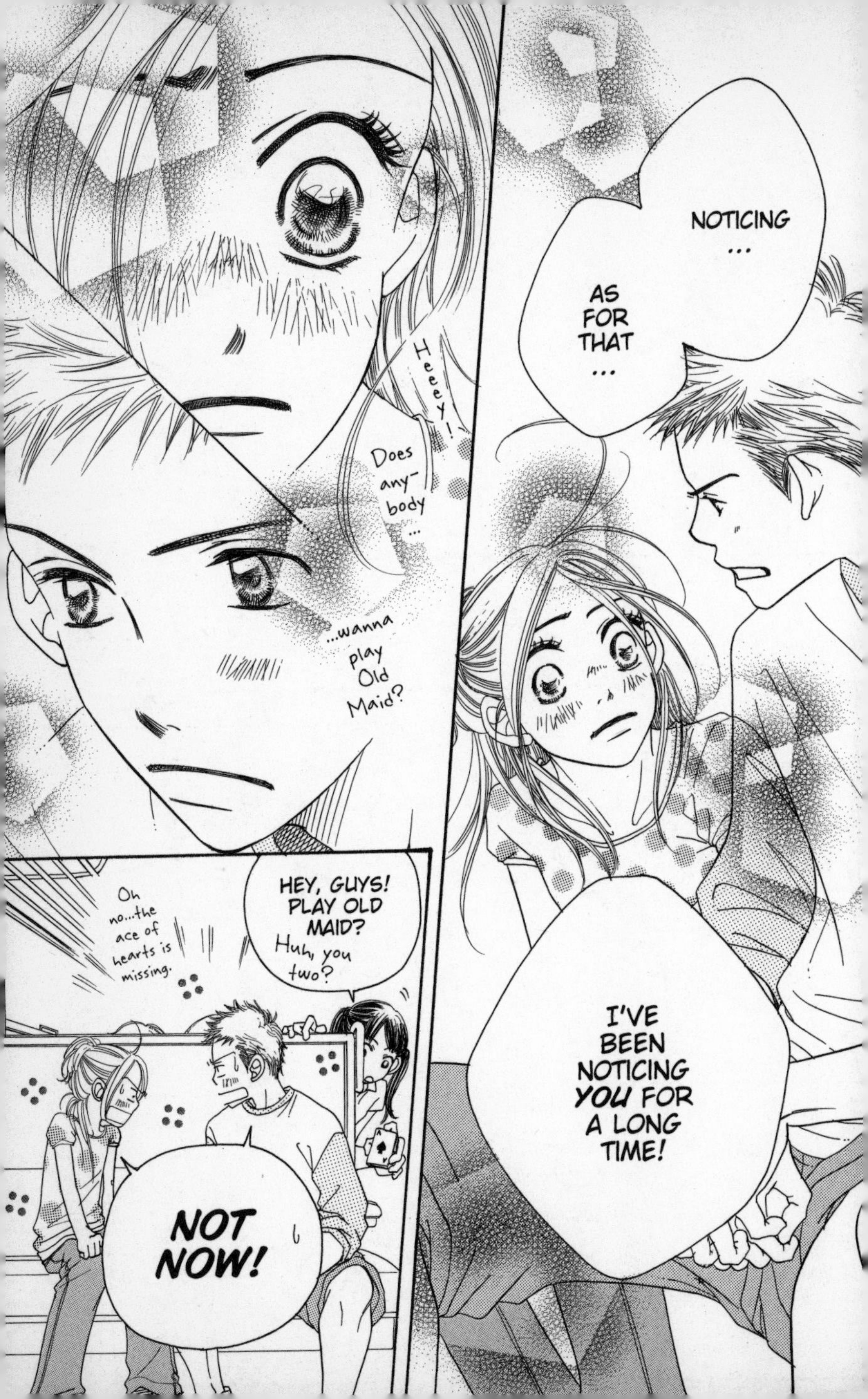
NOTICING ...
AS FOR THAT ...
I'VE BEEN NOTICING *YOU* FOR A LONG TIME!
Heeey!
Does anybody ...
...wanna play Old Maid?
HEY, GUYS! PLAY OLD MAID?
Huh, you two?
Oh no...the ace of hearts is missing.
NOT NOW!

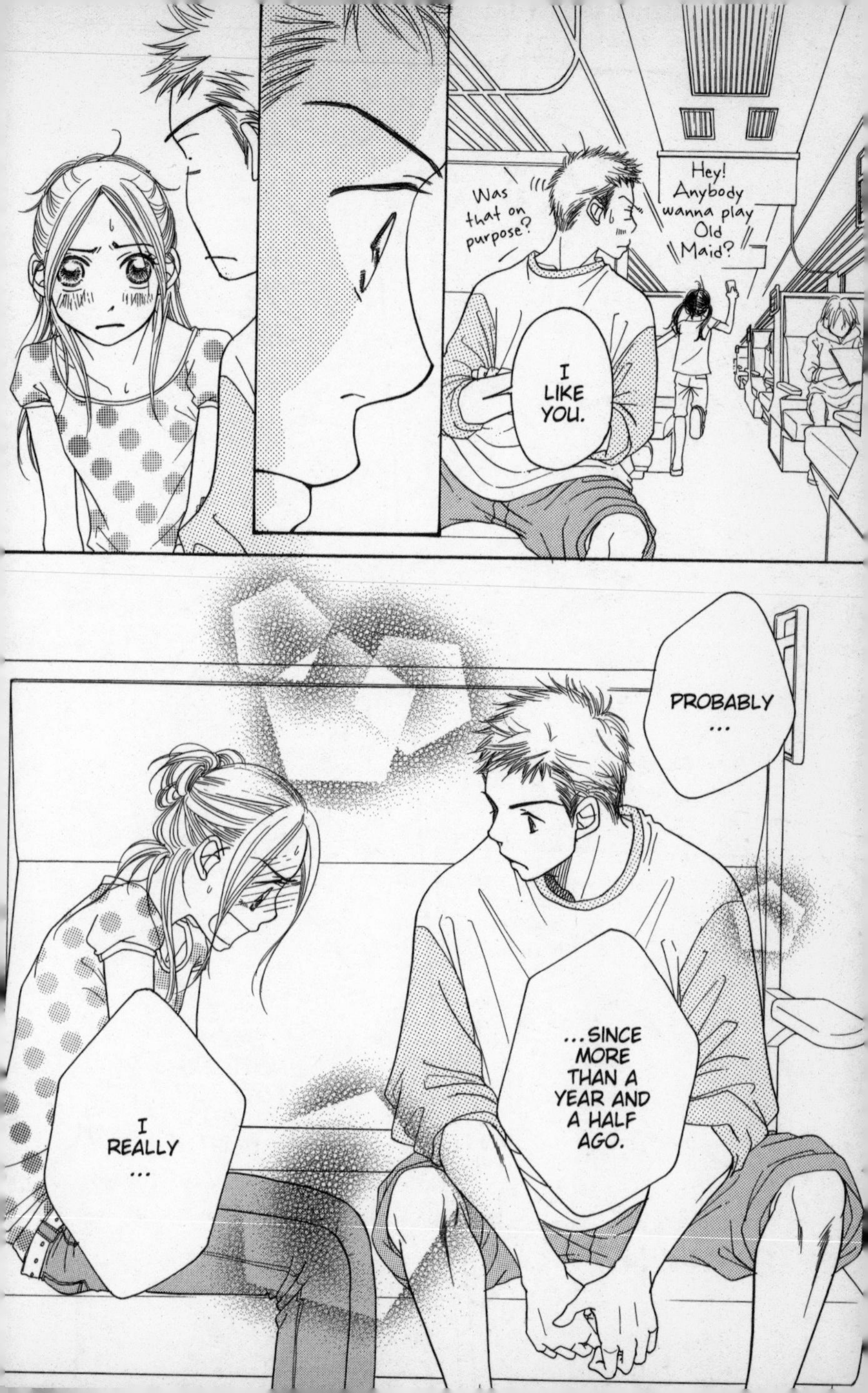
Hey! Anybody wanna play Old Maid?
Was that on purpose?
I LIKE YOU.
PROBABLY ...
...SINCE MORE THAN A YEAR AND A HALF AGO.
I REALLY ...

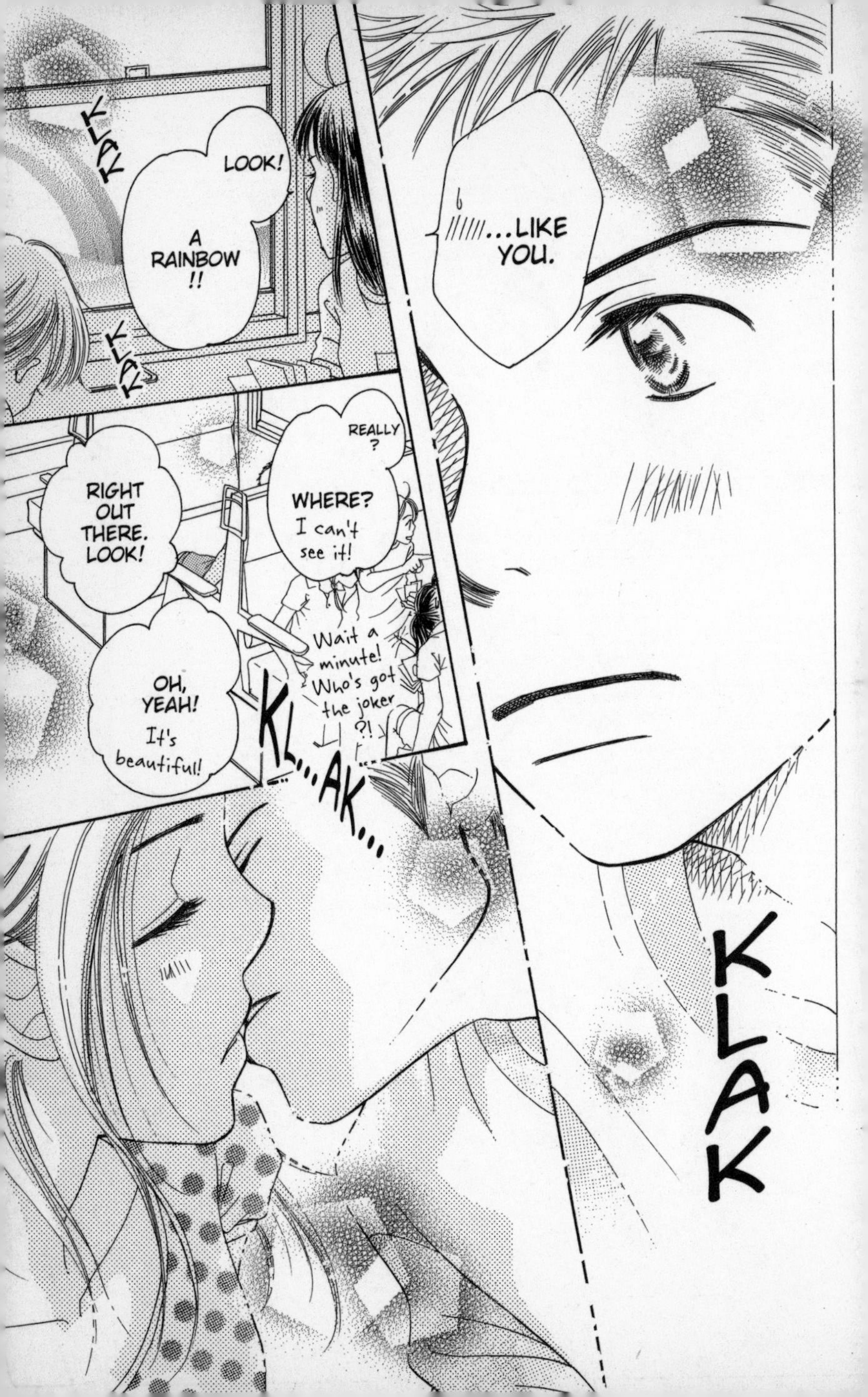
...LIKE YOU.
KLAK
LOOK! A RAINBOW!!
KLAK
KLAK
REALLY? WHERE? I can't see it!
Wait a minute! Who's got the joker?!
RIGHT OUT THERE. LOOK!
OH, YEAH! It's beautiful!
KL...AK...

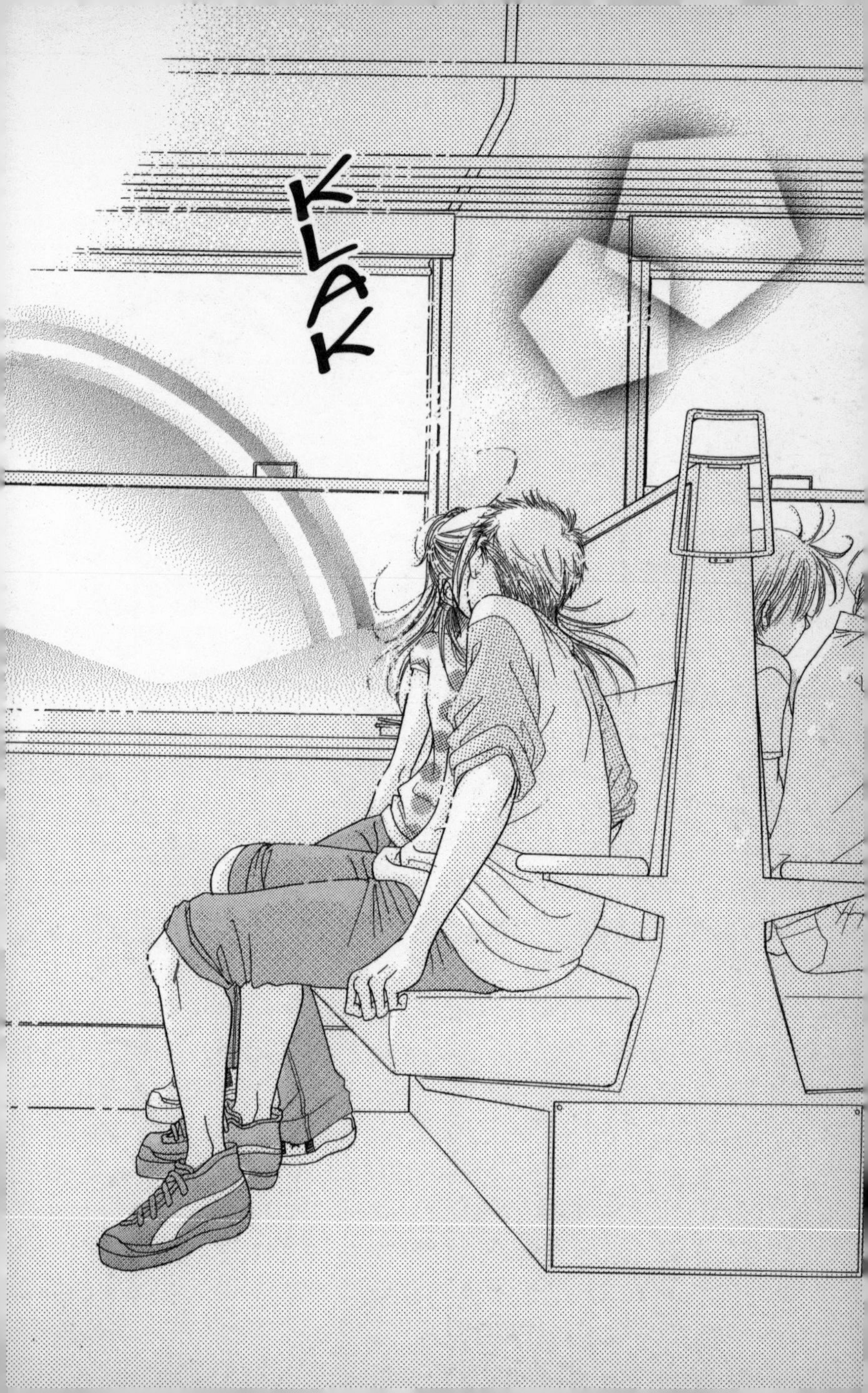
KLAK

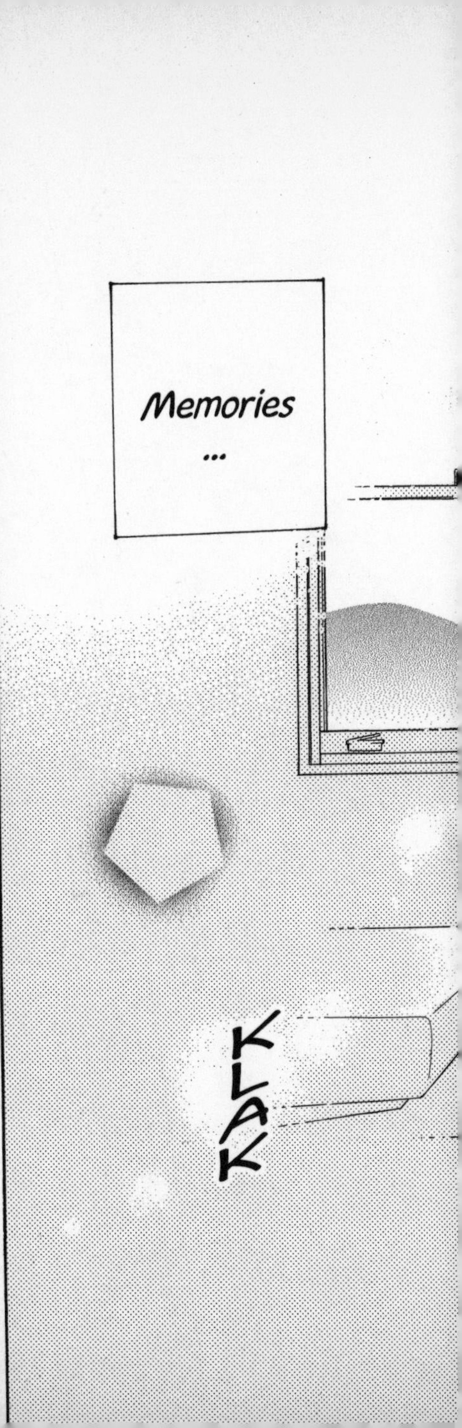
Memories ...
KLAK
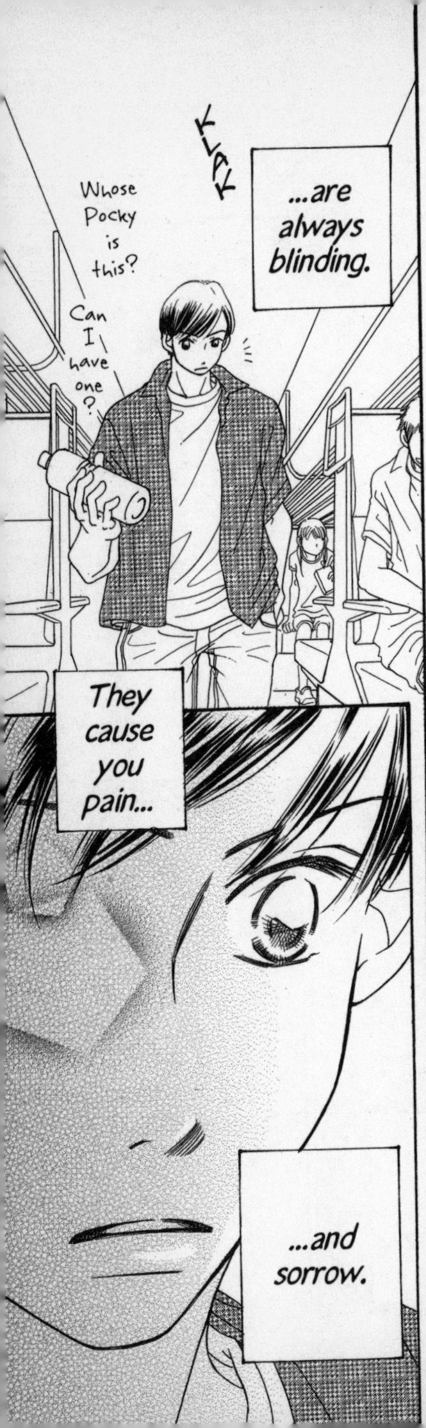
...are always blinding.
KLAK
Whose Pocky is this?
Can I have one?
They cause you pain...
...and sorrow.

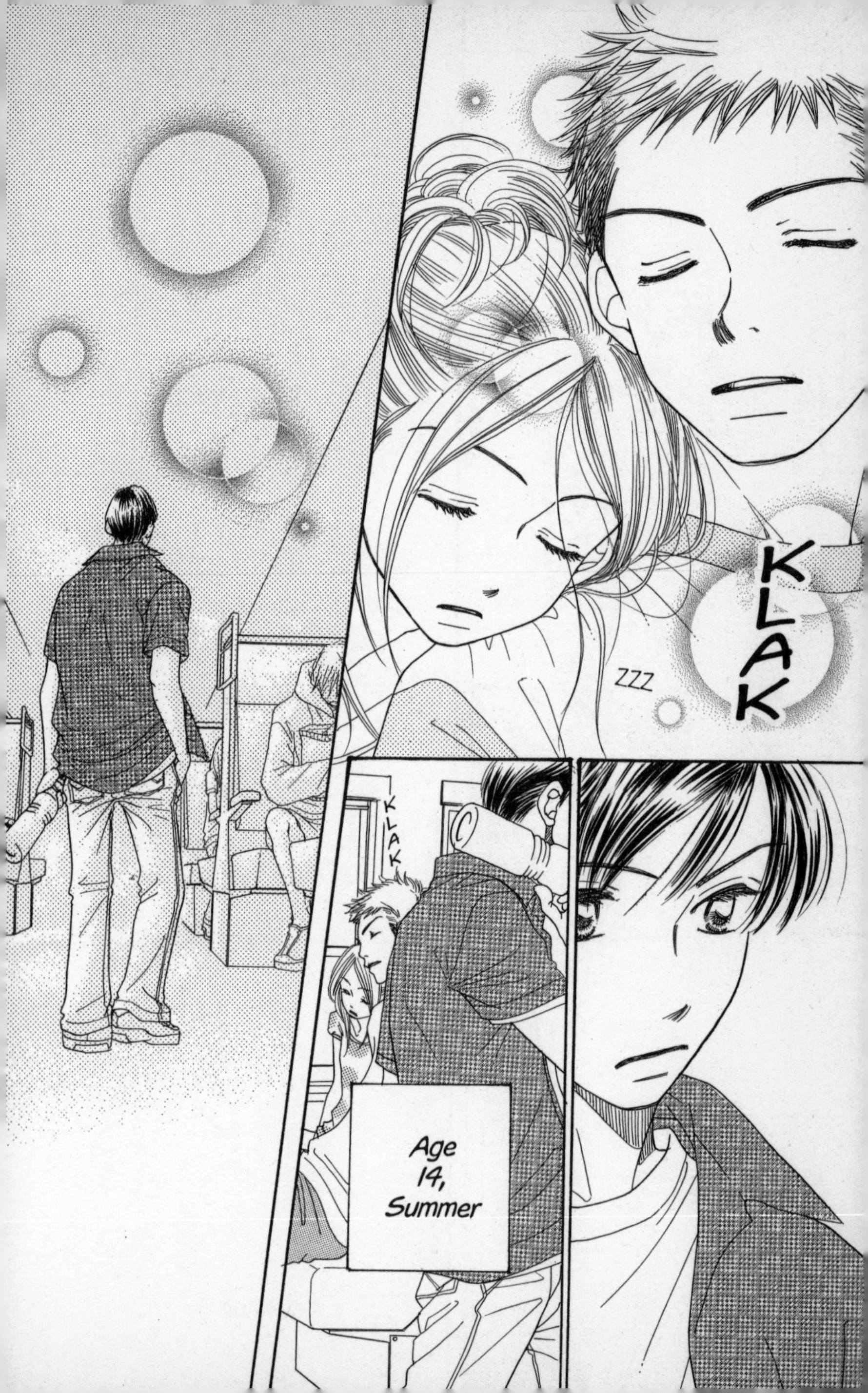
KLAK
ZZZ
KLAK
Age 14, Summer

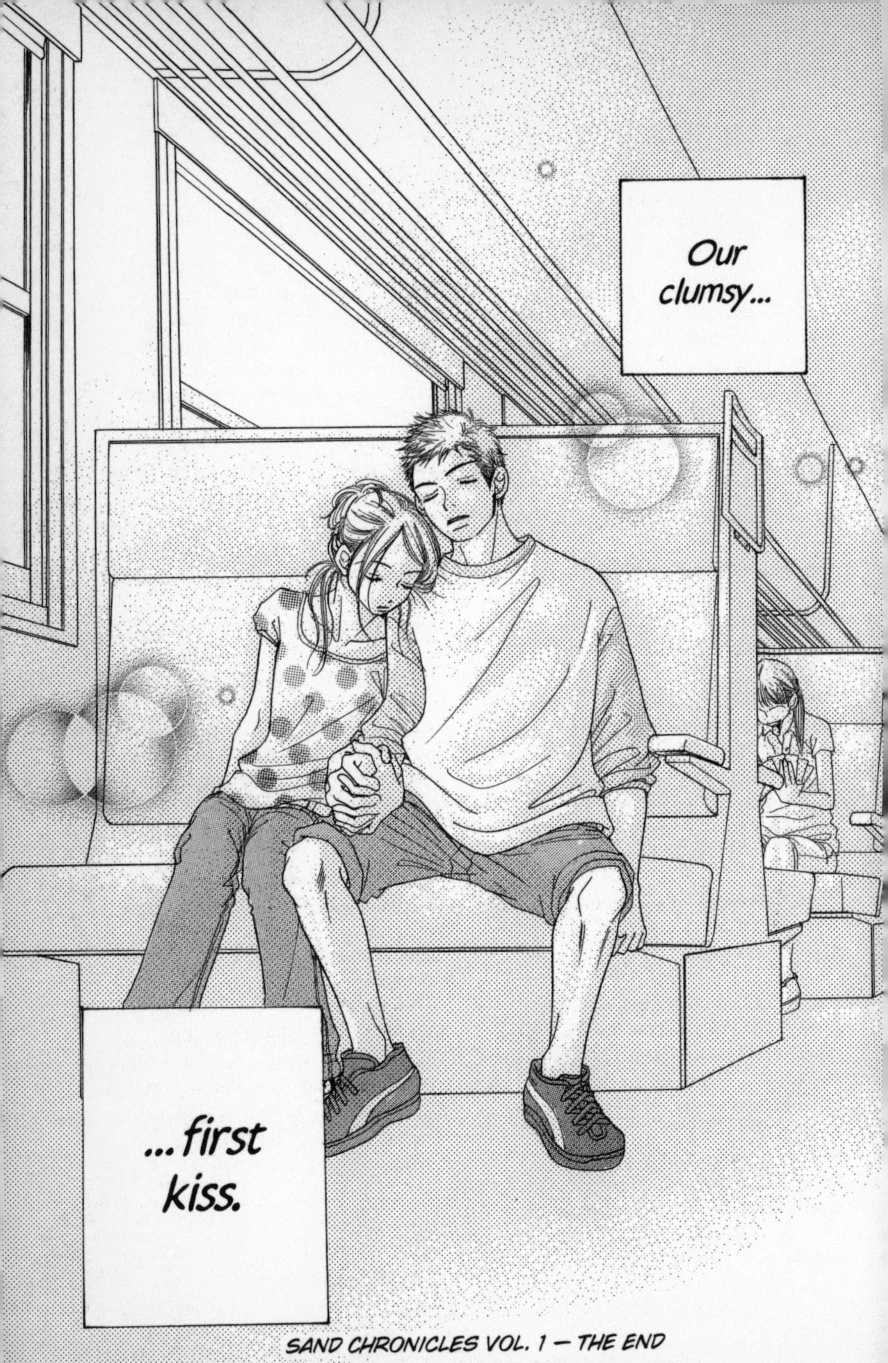
Our clumsy...
...first kiss.

SAND CHRONICLES VOL. 1 — THE END

Glossary

If only adolescence came with an instruction manual.
We can't give you that, but this glossary of terms might
prove useful for this volume.

Page 32, panel 6: Kotatsu
A kotatsu is a table with a blanket and heater underneath. In the colder months people sit or lay with their legs under the blanket.

Page 33, panel 4: Chestnut head
Daigo's haircut resembles a chestnut burr. The original Japanese *igaguri* literally means "head like a chestnut."

Page 39, panel 3: Hotpot
Called *nabe* in Japanese. A gas or electric burner is placed on the table and a variety of things are cooked in a big pot over it.

Page 39, panel 7: Nara Park
Most Japanese living in cities have only encountered deer in Nara, where they can be found wandering freely at certain popular tourist areas. As a Tokyo kid Ann probably went to Nara as part of a school trip or family vacation.

Page 39, panel 7: Deer Biscuits
Tourists can buy rice crackers to feed the deer in Nara Park.

Page 41, panel 1: Nanmaidabu
Ann is trying to recite the Buddhist sutra Namu Amida Butsu, which calls upon the Buddha Amida for aid, but she doesn't know the proper way to say it.

Page 41, panel 1: TING
The saying of Buddhist prayers is often accompanied by the ringing of a small metal bowl. The bowl can be seen in this picture, as can the little rod Ann used to strike its rim.

Page 43, panel 1: Getting therapy
In Japanese it's specified that she started visiting a doctor of psychosomatic medicine, probably in a hospital. In Japan, this is the kind of place where anyone might go if they are feeling overly lethargic, depressed, etc. The doctor would likely give her some practical advice—such as cut back on stress—and then prescribe medication. It does not imply that she was diagnosed with something serious, like clinical depression, nor imply that she was having regular sessions with a psychologist or psychiatrist. However, it's likely she was suffering from a psychiatric disorder and would have benefited from such treatment.

Page 48, panel 5: New Year's preparations
The New Year is the most festive holiday in Japan. With family coming to visit and the preparation of *osechi ryori* (special New Year's foods), it is a very busy time of year.

Page 57, panel 4: Standard Japanese
The characters usually speak in Izumo-ben, a regional dialect with a different vocabulary and intonation than the textbook Japanese spoken in big cities like Tokyo.

Page 58, panel 2: Mochi pounding
Mochi are sticky Japanese rice cakes. It is traditional to pound the rice into the proper mochi consistency with a large wooden mallet during the New Year's season.

Page 59, panel 4: Osechi Ryori
Traditional Japanese New Year's cuisine. *Osechi ryori* consists of various traditional foods, delicately arranged in one box to look beautiful. The fact that Ann's grandmother cooks *osechi ryori* from scratch suggests that she values Japanese traditional culture.

Page 60, panel 4: Weeds never die
A Japanese proverb, literally "Ill weeds never die."

Page 61, panel 3: Ohagi
Japanese rice dumpling covered in sweet bean jam.

Page 67, panel 4: Go to the shrine
Going to the shrine on New Year's to pray for luck in the coming year is called *hatsu-mode*. Many people dress for the occasion in traditional kimono.

Page 68, panel 5: Votive tablets
People write their New Year's wishes on wooden tablets called *ema* and leave them at the shrine.

Page 70, panel 3: Sir
In Japanese, she calls him *Kannushi-san*, which translates as something like "Mr. Priest," and is similar to the way a pastor might be addressed as just "Reverend."

Page 71, panel 1: Burn them
The proper way to dispose of holy items in the Shinto religion is to burn them at a shrine.

Page 75, panel 3: Ozenzai
Sweet red bean soup with pieces of *mochi* (rice cake) in it.

Page 77, panel 3: Coming of Age Day
Japanese are considered adults when they turn twenty. A special ceremony is held to commemorate their coming of age on the second Monday in January. Women usually wear beautiful kimono and men wear suits or *hakama* (kimono).

Page 89, panel 3: Okayu
Rice porridge.

Page 146, panel 3: Gods' voices
The Japanese is *kaminari*, and more literally means something like "the sounds that gods make." *Nari* means "sound" or "cry", like the cry of an animal.

Page 146, panel 4: Done something wrong
The phrase "lightning strikes" in Japanese (*kaminari ga ochiru*) can be used to express punishment by the gods for misdeeds.

Page 150, panel 5: Fireflies
Fireflies are rare in Japan, and are a nostalgic symbol of nature.

Page 164, panel 4: Jizo
The guardian of travelers and children.

Profile of Hinako Ashihara

★Date of birth: 1/25 (Fri.)
  Sign: Aquarius
  Blood type: O

★Debut work: *Sono Hanashi Okotowari
  Shimasu* (*Betsucomi*, Oct. 1994)

★My current personal obsession is my baby
  nephew. He's so cute! His head's a little big,
  but he's still cute!

★Presently contributing to *Betsucomi*

Hinako Ashihara won the 50th Shogakukan
Manga Award for *Sunadokei*. She debuted
with *Sono Hanashi Okotowari Shimasu* in
Bessatsu Shojo Comics in 1994. Her other
works include *SOS, Forbidden Dance,* and
Tennen Bitter Chocolate.

SAND CHRONICLES

Vol. 1

The Shojo Beat Manga Edition

This manga volume contains material that was originally published in English in Shojo Beat magazine #26 through #29. Artwork in the magazine may have been slightly altered from that presented here.

STORY AND ART BY HINAKO ASHIHARA

English Adaptation/John Werry, HC Language Solutions
Translation/Kinami Watabe, HC Language Solutions
Touch-up Art & Lettering/Rina Mapa
Additional Touch-up/Kam Li
Design/Yukiko Whitley
Editors/Pancha Diaz & Annette Roman

Editor in Chief, Books/Alvin Lu
Editor in Chief, Magazines/Marc Weidenbaum
VP of Publishing Licensing/Rika Inouye
VP of Sales/Gonzalo Ferreyra
Sr. VP of Marketing/Liza Coppola
Publisher/Hyoe Narita

Printed in Canada

Published by VIZ Media, LLC
P.O. Box 77010
San Francisco, CA 94107

Shojo Beat Manga Edition
10 9 8 7 6 5 4 3 2 1
First printing, January 2008

store.viz.com

Tell us what you think about Shojo Beat Manga!

Our survey is now available online. Go to:

shojobeat.com/mangasurvey

Help us make our product offerings better!

Find the Beat online!
Check us out at
www.shojobeat.com!